STAR WARS

WOMEN
OF THE
GALAXY

UPDATED AND EXPANDED

STAR WARS

WOMEN OF THE GALAXY

UPDATED AND EXPANDED

BY AMY RATCLIFFE • FOREWORD BY KATHLEEN KENNEDY

CHRONICLE BOOKS
SAN FRANCISCO

Copyright © 2025 Lucasfilm Ltd. & ® or ™ where indicated. All rights reserved. Used under authorization. No part of this book may be reproduced in any form without written permission from the publisher.

Library of Congress Cataloging-in-Publication Data available.

ISBN 978-1-7972-3435-9

Manufactured in China

Front cover illustration by **Jennifer A. Johnson**
Cover design by **Neil Egan**
Interior design by **Jenna Huerta**
Lucasfilm Publishing Creative Director, **Michael Siglain**
Lucasfilm Art Director, **Troy Alders**

10 9 8 7 6 5 4 3 2 1

Chronicle Books LLC
680 Second Street
San Francisco, CA 94107
www.chroniclebooks.com

© & TM 2025 LUCASFILM

www.starwars.com

For Carrie Fisher

Contents

Foreword 10
Introduction 12

Aayla Secura 16
Adi Gallia 20
Ahsoka Tano 22
Amilyn Holdo 32
Arihnda Pryce 36
Asajj Ventress 38
Aunt Z 42
Aurra Sing 44
Avar Kriss 46
Barriss Offee 48
Bazine Netal 50
Beru Lars 52
Bix Caleen 54
Bo-Katan Kryze 56
Breha Organa 58
Camie Marstrap 60
Cato Parasitti 62
Cere Junda 64
Ciena Ree 66
Daughter 68
Dedra Meero 70
Depa Billaba 72

Derla Pidys 74
Doctor Chelli Aphra 76
Enfys Nest 80
Evaan Verlaine 84
Everi Chalis 86
Fennec Shand 88
Hera Syndulla 90
Iden Versio 96
Jannah 98
Jas Emari 100
Jessika Pava 102
Jocasta Nu 104
Jyn Erso 106
Kaydel Ko Connix 112
Kay Vess 114
Ketsu Onyo 116
Kneesaa 118
Kyrsta Agate 120
L3-37 122
Lady Proxima 126
Larma D'Acy 128
Leia Organa 130
Lina Graf 140
Lourna Dee 142
Lula Talisola and Zeen Mrala 144

Luminara Unduli 146

Lyra Erso 148

Maarva Andor 150

Mae and Osha Aniseya 152

Mama the Hutt 154

Maz Kanata 156

Mira Bridger 162

Mon Mothma 164

Morgan Elsbeth 168

Mother Aniseya 170

Mother Talzin 172

Ninth Sister Inquisitor 174

Norra Wexley 176

Numa 178

Omega 180

Oola 182

Padmé Amidala 184

Padmé's Handmaidens 192

Paige Tico 194

Peli Motto 196

Phasma 198

Qi'ra 204

R2-KT 210

Rae Sloane 212

Rey 214

Rose Tico 224
Sabine Wren 230
Sana Starros 236
Satine Kryze 238
Seventh Sister Inquisitor 240
Shaak Ti 242
Shin Hati 244
Shmi Skywalker Lars 246
Steela Gerrera 248
Sugi 250
Sy Snootles 252
Tallie Lintra 254
Tam Ryvora 256
Third Sister Inquisitor 258
Tonnika Sisters 260
Torra Doza 262
Trios 264
Ursa Wren 266
Val 268
Vernestra Rwoh 272
Vi Moradi 274
Zam Wesell 276
Zorii Bliss 278
Acknowledgments 280
About the Artists 281

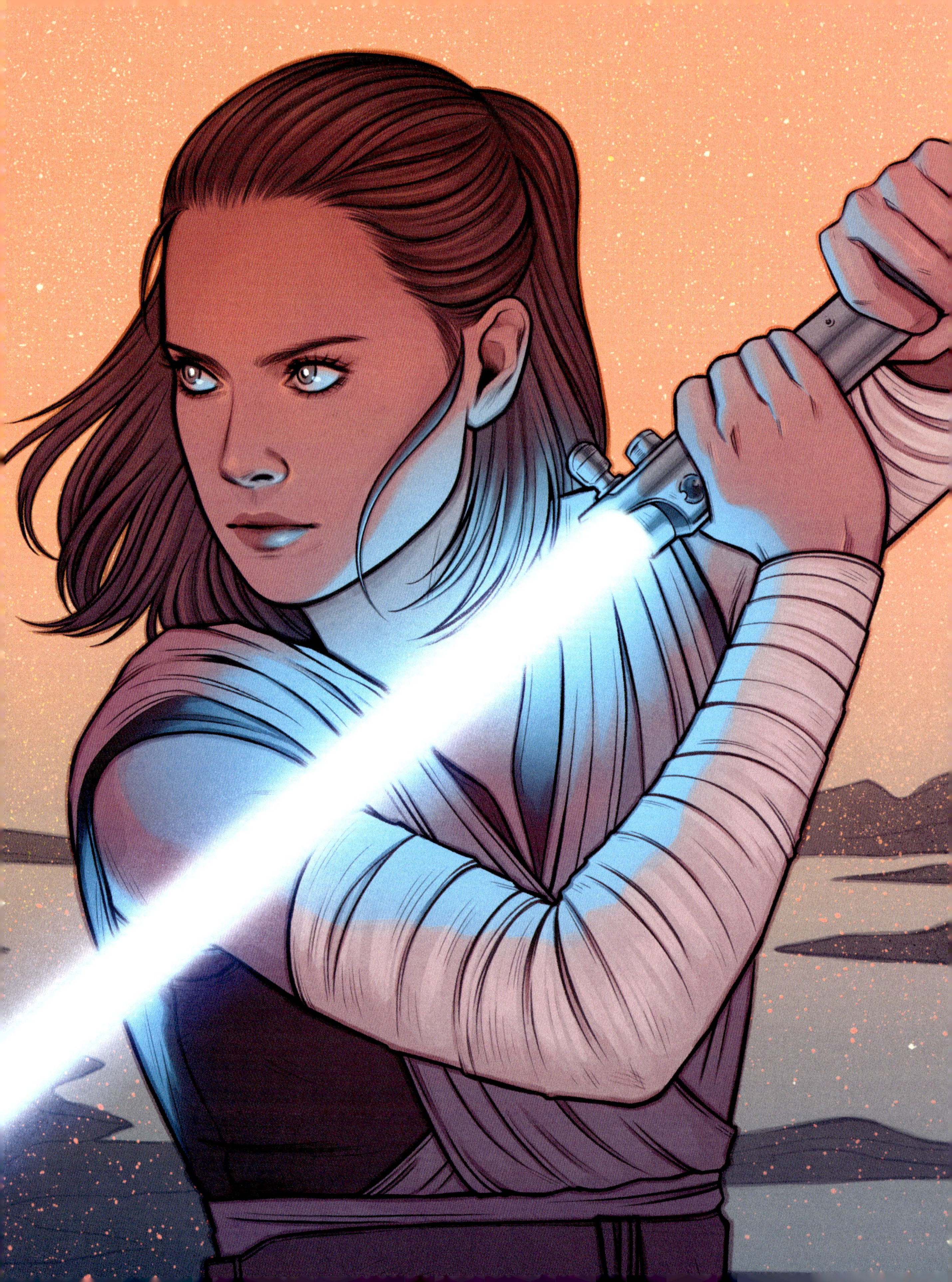

Foreword

I was in the early stages of my career as a filmmaker when *Star Wars* came out in 1977. With that first film, and the cultural phenomenon that followed, George Lucas introduced the world to Princess Leia, a character who stood apart from most female leads of the day. With strength, courage, a quick wit and grit, she could easily hold her own against the predominantly male cast, including Darth Vader himself. I was immediately struck by the possibilities of this universe George created—boundless storytelling potential combined with a rare opportunity to explore universal themes that have endured through the ages. I was captivated.

In the decades since, George and others have fleshed out the *Star Wars* universe with hundreds of new characters, including the heroes, villains, rebels, and rogues highlighted in this book. While not all of these characters are cut out to be heroes like Padmé, Rey, and Ahsoka, it's important that they occupy a wide range of roles in the *Star Wars* galaxy, and act capably, skillfully, and formidably within them.

In *Star Wars*, we are fortunate to have such a broad platform from which to tell our stories. In addition to the films, there are animated series, novels, comics, games, and more, all allowing us to further explore this rich galaxy and the many characters in it. It's a testament to George's vision that what he began as a story to inspire, we continue to embrace as a beacon of empowerment and hope.

Kathleen Kennedy

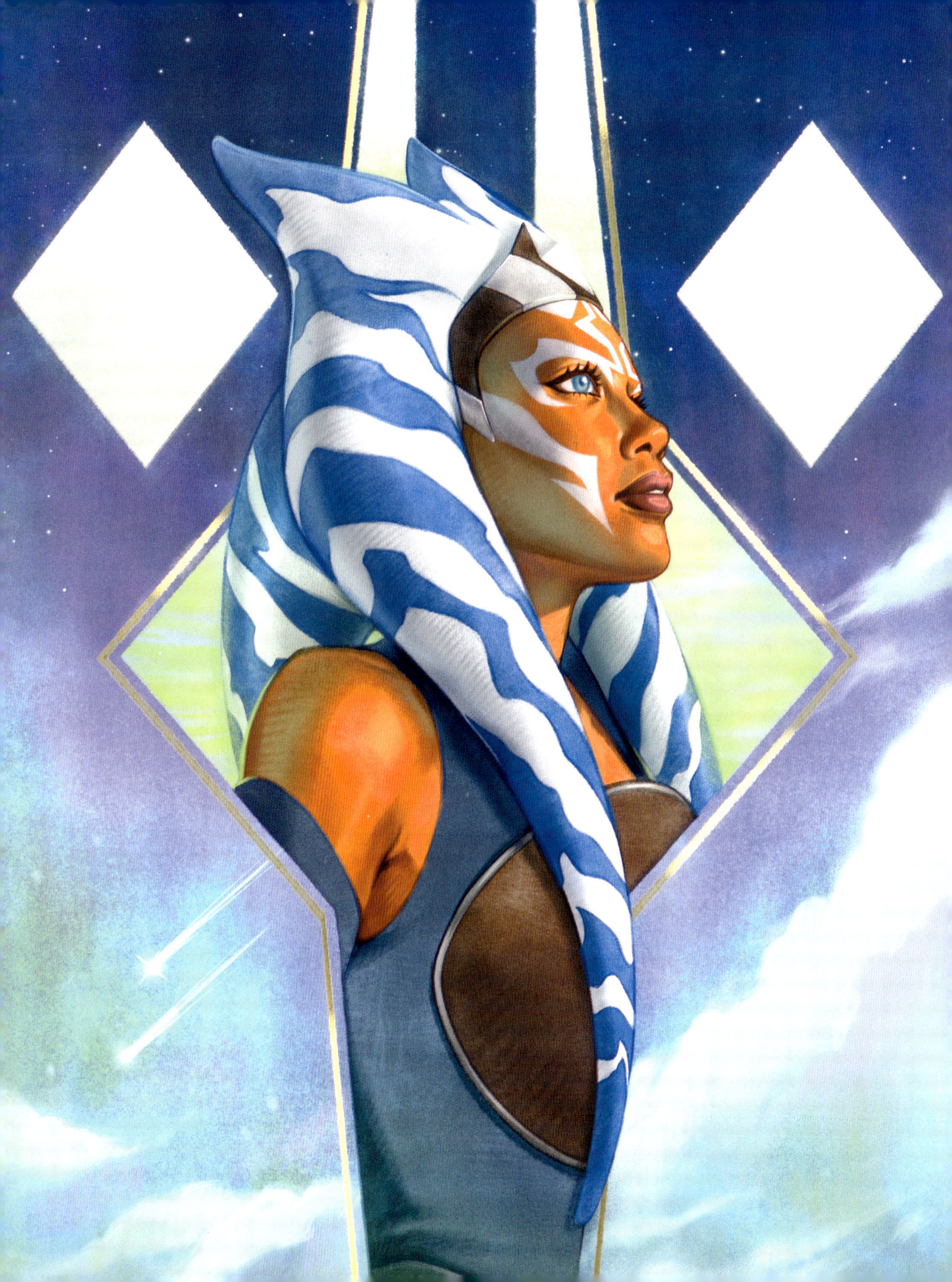

Introduction

The characters in this book make the *Star Wars* we know possible. They are heroes and villains, Sith and Jedi, senators and scoundrels, mothers, mercenaries, artists, pilots—anything and everything—and their stories drive the galaxy forward in epic, but also important if less flashy ways. The Rebel Alliance wouldn't exist without Mon Mothma. The New Republic wouldn't discover the Empire's remnants on Jakku without Norra Wexley. Invaluable information from the Jedi Archives would be lost if not preserved by lightsaber-wielding librarian Jocasta Nu. Their stories extend across the films, animated and live-action series, novels, comics, and games, often crossing over to continue from one medium into another (for instance, we can follow Leia Organa's adventures through them all). And there's a galaxy of fascinating characters to discover beyond the film trilogies. In the *Aftermath* novels, we can marvel as Kyrsta Agate takes down a Super Star Destroyer using a tractor beam. In live-action streaming series, we encounter witches like Mother Aniseya, and Imperial ladder-climbers like Dedra Meero. In *The Clone Wars* and *Star Wars Rebels*, we meet one of the most important heroes in the *Star Wars* saga, Ahsoka Tano.

Ahsoka has had a profound impact upon me. In some ways, I grew into *Star Wars* fandom through her. I first saw the films as a teenager, but I didn't find *my Star Wars* until *The Clone Wars*—in no small part due to discovering Ahsoka. Seeing her as a young Padawan alongside Anakin Skywalker, one of the heroes of the *Star Wars* galaxy, acting snippy and a little immature, but also confident and capable, grabbed my attention. I was fascinated to watch her navigate her way through lessons from her atypical Jedi Master, make mistakes, and adapt. I was blown away when she decided to leave the Jedi Order, the only life she'd ever known. Her actions gave me courage. And the inclusion of a female teenage lead made me feel positive about the future of *Star Wars*.

In passionately fangirling about Ahsoka and *The Clone Wars* on social media and my blog, I found my passion: writing. Ahsoka's determination inspired me to work toward a dream. As I discovered my voice and pursued my own goals, she was maturing and questioning the world around her. By the time she returned in *Star Wars Rebels*, older and wiser, I felt that I was, too. And I continue to learn from her. When her story continued in *The Mandalorian* and *Ahsoka*, I saw her first as someone with a foot in the past, stuck and not moving forward; then I watched her free her heart from a mire of guilt and fear, and grow once again.

I connect with Ahsoka the most, but she is far from the only *Star Wars* character who moves me. When I need courage, I'm bolstered by Leia's no-nonsense attitude and optimism. When I need to speak so people will listen, I'm energized by Padmé's intelligence and commanding presence. When I need to find light in a dark situation, I'm encouraged by Rey's unflinching kindness and deep strength. When I want to be of service to others, I only need to look to Avar, Hera, Maarva—any character who has made a choice to help.

With *Women of the Galaxy*, I want to highlight the accomplishments of female characters in *Star Wars*. I want to share the actions that make me excitedly text a friend, "Can you believe she did that?" but also to talk about the quieter moments that help us relate to them. I want to emphasize how everyone makes a difference, whether she's an Imperial officer, a rebel hero, a diplomat, or a mother. The impact of a character can be measured in a number of ways, but perhaps most importantly, by how they make us feel. How they affect *our* story, our fandom. Because we are all part of the story, and we all deserve to have our story told.

Fictional characters have the power to influence us, to push us into action, to give us constants in a world full of variables. It's why stories are never *just* stories. I hope you will find inspiration in these characters and in this book.

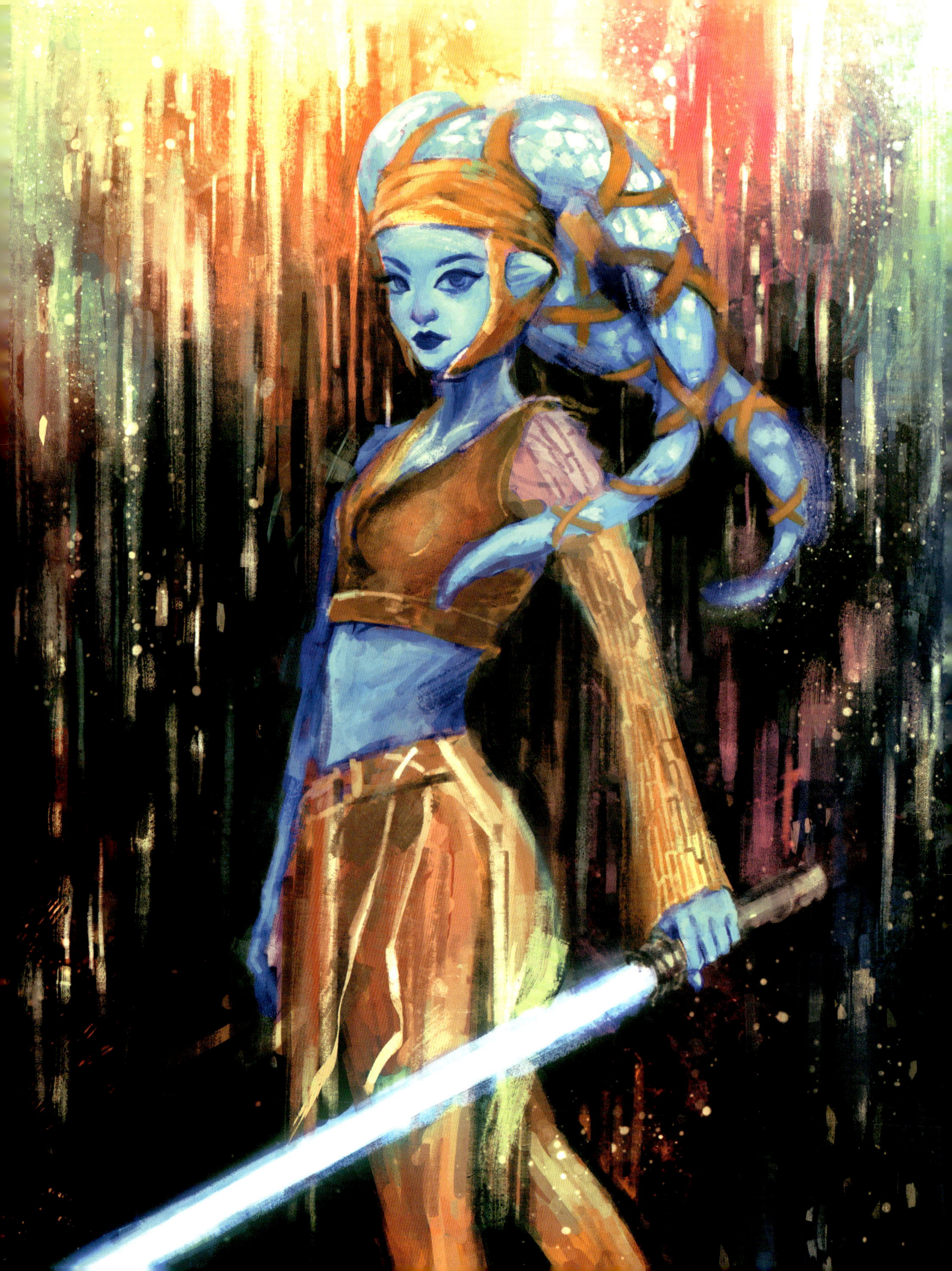

Aayla Secura

"Isn't liberty worth fighting for?"

Imagine being a production assistant at Lucasfilm's special effects company, Industrial Light & Magic, getting the chance to work on a stage unit for *Attack of the Clones*, and then being asked to be in the film. Amy Allen lived this extraordinary turn of events and played the Twi'lek Jedi Master Aayla Secura in *Attack of the Clones* and *Revenge of the Sith*. Inspired by seeing Aayla on a comic book cover, George Lucas added the fan-favorite well into post-production of *Clones* (costume supervisor Gillian Libbert had only two weeks to design Aayla's costume for Lucas's approval), and so the blue-skinned Jedi makes a grand entrance swinging a lightsaber in the Battle of Geonosis. Since Twi'leks hadn't been featured in an action-heavy role previous to the film, she struck a chord, inspiring fans to craft the species' distinctive lekku head tentacles and paint their skin for Aayla costumes.

Aayla's story continues in animated form in *Star Wars: The Clone Wars*. As a Jedi General in the conflict, she leads charges around the galaxy, fights to protect planets from Separatist invasion, and works with fellow Jedi Obi-Wan Kenobi, Mace Windu, and Tiplee to investigate Darth Maul's activities. She also takes point at the Battle of Quell, guiding Ahsoka Tano and the clone troopers through a crash, before which she uses the Force to turn their cruiser's power back on, and a surprise attack on the planet Maridun. She's a

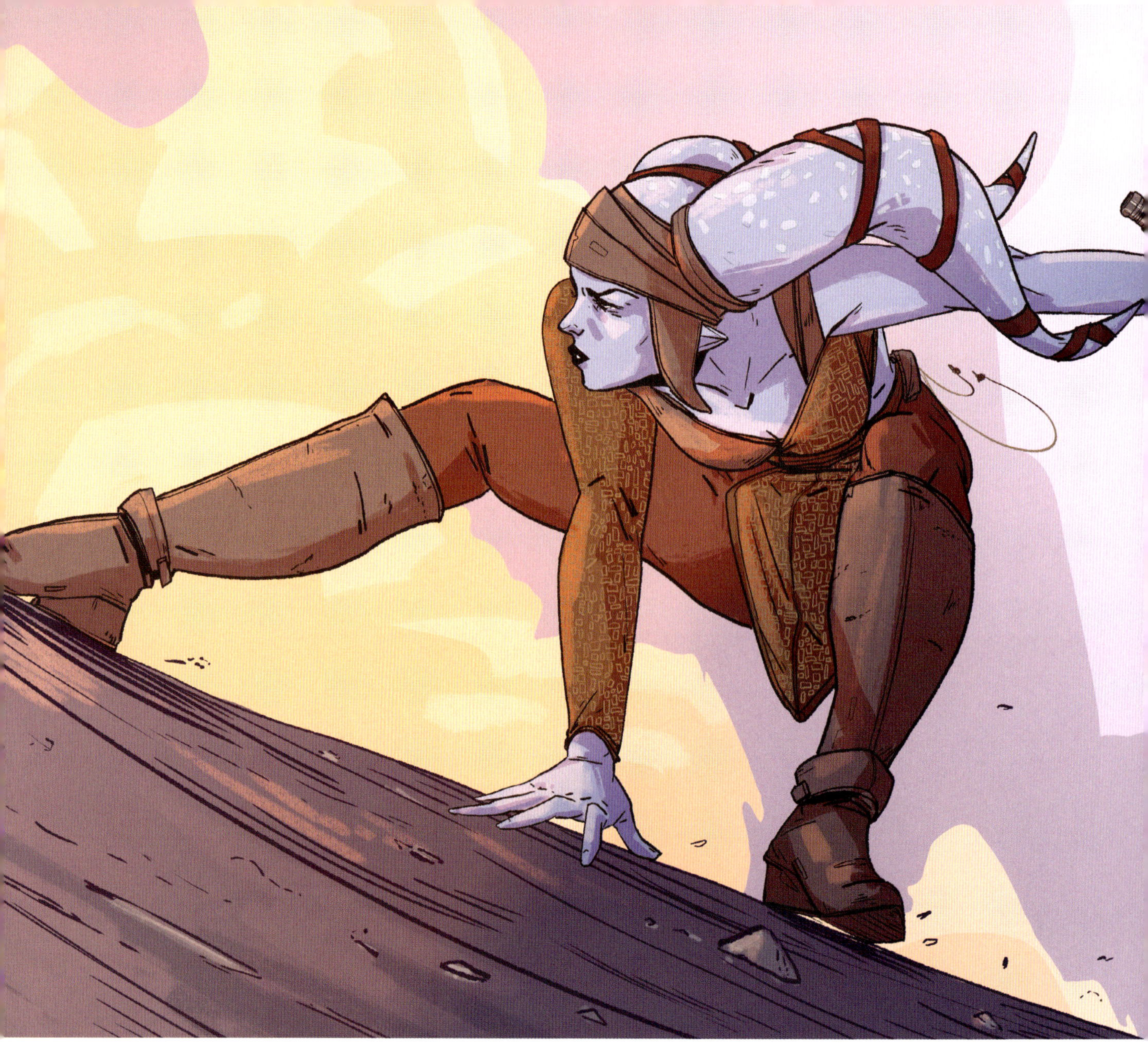

"A strong belief can be more powerful than any army."
—Aayla Secura

talented and athletic fighter, eschewing Jedi robes for a greater range of movement—a freedom evident as she leaps along the back of the gargantuan Zillo Beast as it crushes its way through Coruscant. And she's wise, advising Ahsoka not to let her personal affection for her master, Anakin Skywalker, cloud her ability to make necessary, hard decisions in battle. Aayla recognizes the danger of attachment, having overcome a similar struggle with her own teacher, Quinlan Vos, who she saw as a father figure. "I realized that for the greater good, I had to let him go," she tells Ahsoka. "Don't lose a thousand lives just to save one."

Aayla is a playable character in 2005's *Star Wars: Battlefront II* game, which is an easier way of embodying the character than Allen's four-hour makeup process in portraying her on film, though she's delighted to have had the experience. "The popularity of the character is overwhelming and truly special. I am not really sure how to explain it. I just feel so fortunate to be a part of *Star Wars*. It's part of history."

Adi Gallia

A Jedi Council member ready to take the fight to the Separatists.

Force-sensitive children come to the Jedi from all walks of life. Adi Gallia, introduced in *The Phantom Menace*, is born to diplomats on Coruscant (the distinctive headdress she wears is a tribute to her Tholothian heritage), and the Jedi Order perceived Adi's connection to the Force and brought her to the Jedi Temple. An astute observer, she raises suspicion about the Trade Federation's enterprises in the Naboo system during her time serving on the Jedi Council. Investigation of the Federation's blockade of Naboo brings Queen Amidala into the *Star Wars* galaxy and makes the Council aware of the increasing Separatist threat.

Adi's also unafraid of a fight, balancing her use of the Force and what it means to be a Jedi with an aggression toward Separatist enemies. Throughout her appearances in *Star Wars: The Clone Wars*, she puts herself in the middle of the action, whether it's developing a high-risk but successful plan to rescue Jedi Master Eeth Koth from General Grievous's metal clutches, evading Grievous herself, or helping Obi-Wan search for Darth Maul and Savage Opress in the Outer Rim.

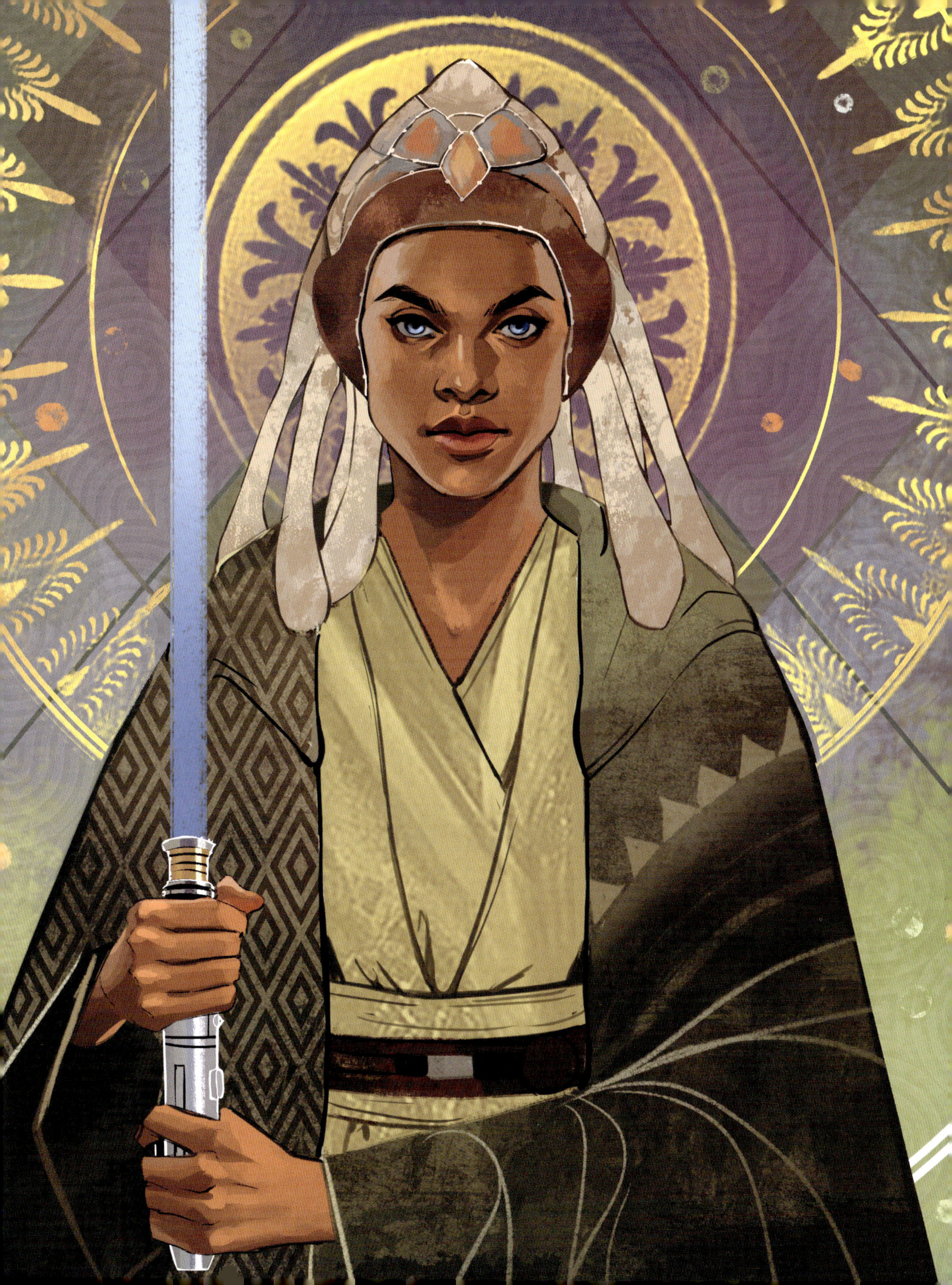

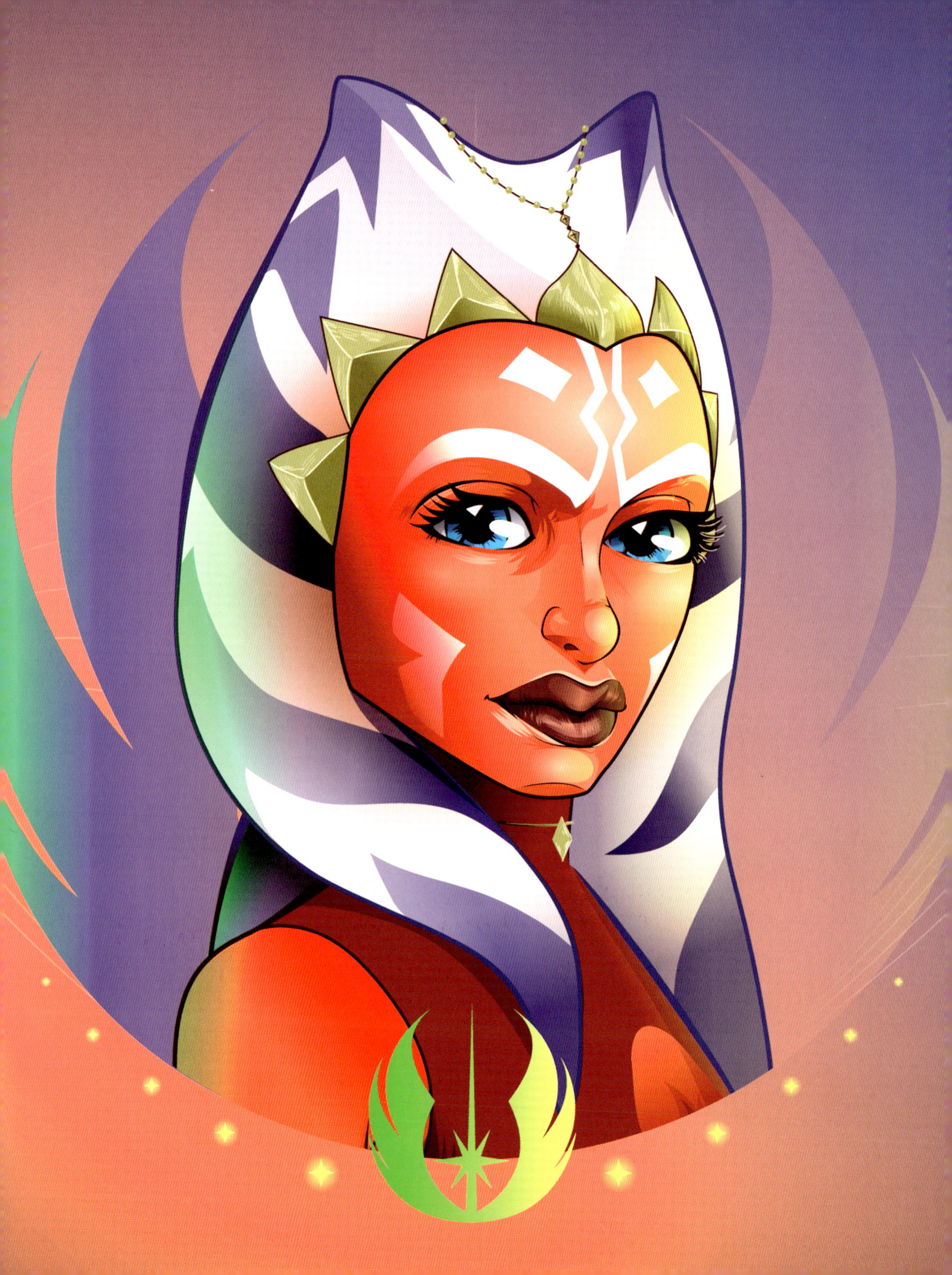

Ahsoka Tano

"This is a new day, a new beginning."

The *Clone Wars* animated film debut in 2008 brought an unforgettable new character to the *Star Wars* saga. Ahsoka Tano, appointed by Yoda to be Anakin Skywalker's Padawan learner, is the first female Jedi lead introduced to the saga on-screen. She's a character a generation of fans has grown up watching, as she herself has grown. The Togruta is fourteen years old when we first meet her, and we watch her transform from "Snips," a nickname Anakin gives her for being snippy, to a Jedi hero of the Clone Wars, to the rebel agent Fulcrum, to a wise mentor. It's the sort of arc that we have the chance to follow for relatively few characters in *Star Wars*, and it gives us the chance to really connect with Ahsoka as we accompany her on her journey.

And it was always meant to be *her* journey. When George Lucas first envisioned the idea of Anakin having a Padawan between *Attack of the Clones* and *Revenge of the Sith*, he wanted the Jedi-in-training to be a girl. We meet Ahsoka as a learner, but she's already holding her own in wit and battle against the more experienced Anakin and Obi-Wan Kenobi. She even gives Anakin his own nickname, "Skyguy." Ahsoka brings a fresh perspective, questioning why things are the way they are. And she doesn't always heed Anakin's advice, giving Anakin a taste of what Obi-Wan must have felt teaching him, too.

Ahsoka's ask-questions-and-take-action spirit also galvanized voice actress Ashley Eckstein. When attending conventions and events for her part in portraying Ahsoka in the film, Eckstein observed both the large number of female *Star Wars* fans and the dearth of female-focused merchandise. To help foster this growing audience, Eckstein founded Her Universe, an apparel company that began with selling *Star Wars* T-shirts in women's sizes and cuts, and which has since expanded to make female fans across multiple fandoms feel included.

Ahsoka's story begins when she displays Force abilities as a baby. Jedi Master Plo Koon discovers Ahsoka and her Force talents when she's only three years old. She's raised in the Jedi Temple on Coruscant, and she trains in a tumultuous time. By the time she's a Padawan, the Clone Wars have begun. Her introduction to her master, Anakin, happens in the midst of battle, and Ahsoka must then and there learn to balance a Jedi's role as a guardian of peace, who isn't supposed to attack, while leading clone troopers into combat. It's a paradox, but she manages, and Anakin makes sure she's prepared. Later skirmishes against Separatist forces help teach Ahsoka to strategize and command, but in learning we also see her make tragic mistakes, such as losing an entire squadron of pilots after disobeying orders in the Battle of Ryloth.

Ahsoka observes Anakin's courage and occasional recklessness and is more willing to take risks because of it, and as she trains with him, she forms a close bond with her teacher. She also finds Anakin's lax attitude and unconventional methods an invitation for a little sass, unafraid to knock him down a peg with lines like, "Master, if you have taught me one thing, it's that nothing is easy when you are around." The true depth of their connection is evident when Ahsoka is twisted against Anakin by the dark side while on the planet Mortis. She dies, and Anakin becomes the conduit for the healing life force that brings Ahsoka back. He would do anything for her.

The independence that Anakin helps Ahsoka find in herself is crucial to her character. After she's betrayed by her friend Barriss Offee and framed for bombing the Jedi Temple, she's expelled

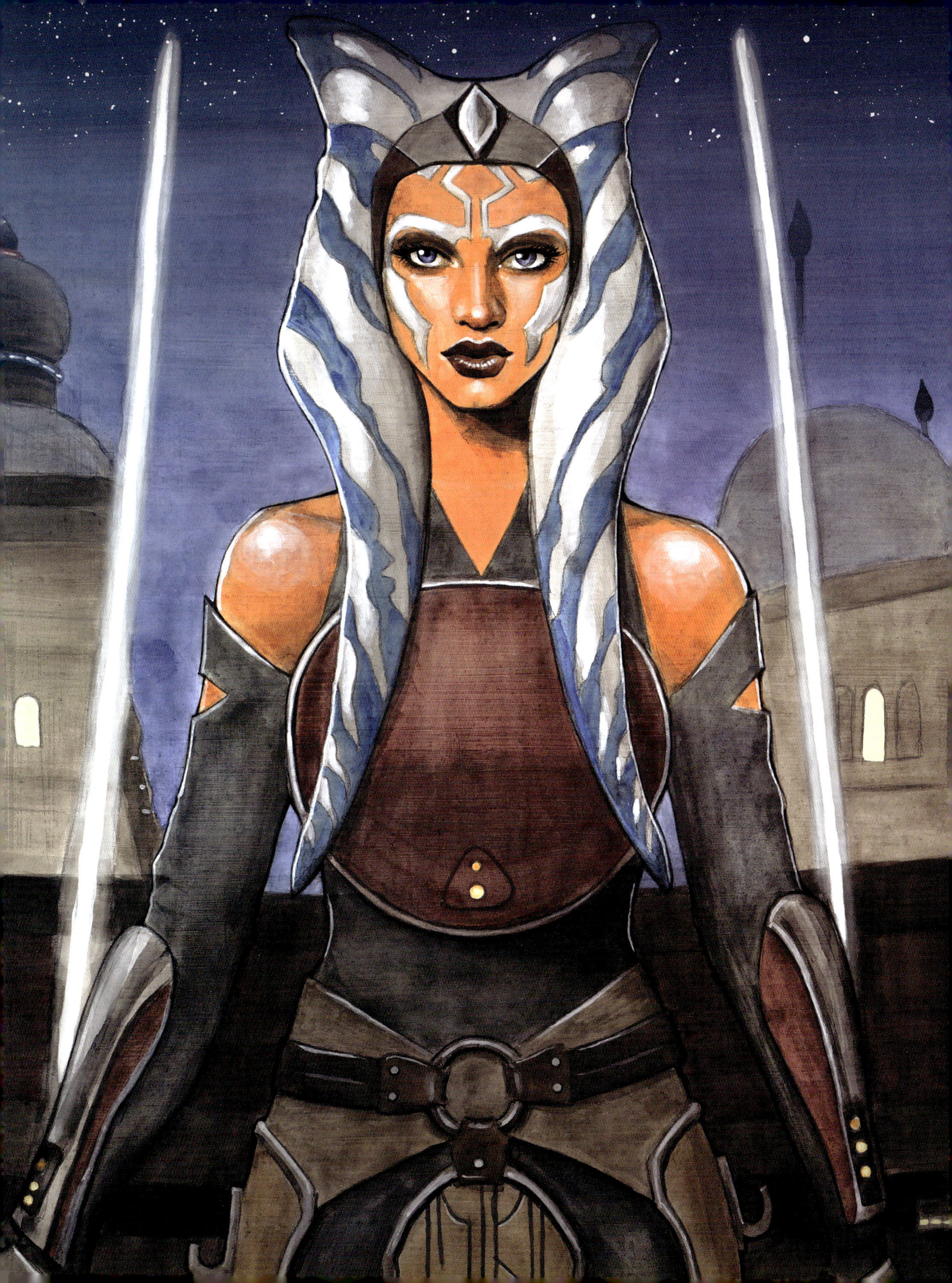

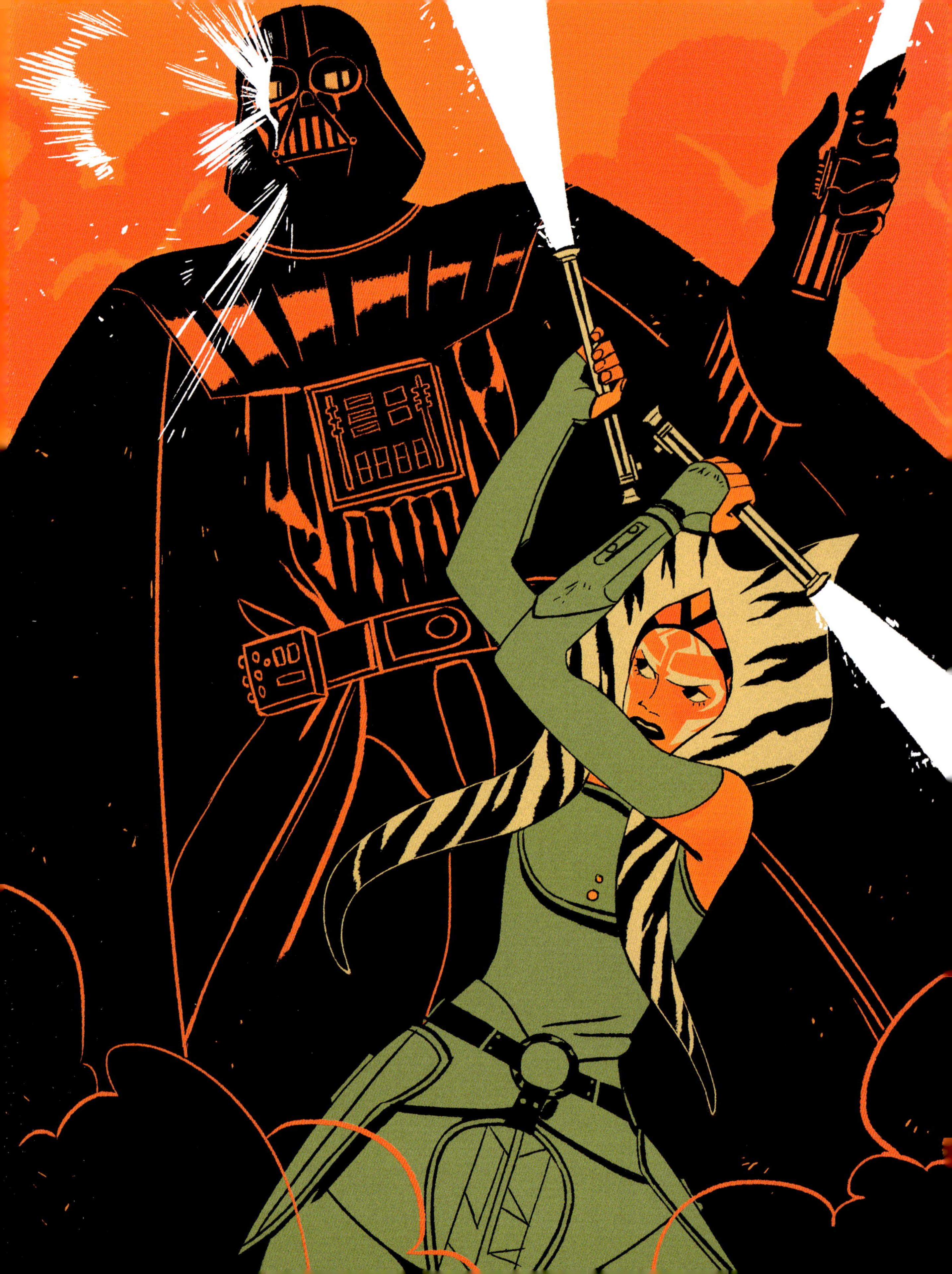

by the Jedi Order despite her plea of innocence and given to the Republic for trial. The truth prevails, and though the Jedi Council welcomes her back, characterizing the events as a test, she decides that she must make her own way. She tells Anakin, "I can't stay here any longer, not now. I have to sort this out on my own, without the Council and without you."

It's a pivotal moment. Ahsoka has spent most of her life within the Jedi Order. Her belief system, her identity, almost everything she knows is interwoven with the Jedi creed. That she is willing to step away so decisively when she loses faith is an act of enormous bravery, and another measure of her growing maturity through hard-earned wisdom.

That she is willing to return to the war when Bo-Katan asks for help taking Mandalore back from Darth Maul is a measure of her magnanimous nature. After the Siege of Mandalore, we follow Ahsoka's path following the near-annihilation of the Jedi in the execution of the evil Darth Sidious's deadly Order 66 in *Tales of the Jedi*. She tries to lead a quiet life at first, weary as she is of war, but Ahsoka can't stand by when others need help. When an Inquisitor tracks her down and puts an innocent village at risk, Ahsoka reaches out to Bail Organa. She is ready to be a hero again, this time as a rebel operative codenamed Fulcrum.

It's in this role that Ahsoka encounters the crew of the *Ghost*, reentering the animated galaxy in *Star Wars Rebels*. Fans exhilarated by the return of the beloved character celebrated by flooding social media with the hashtag #AhsokaLives. Eckstein was also thrilled to be back and to explore a new, more mature side of Ahsoka. "She's now back with a sense of confidence. We could all take that with us—to approach whatever we do with a strong sense of confidence, to speak with authority, to feel comfortable with what we know and putting that into action," she observes. "It's almost like when we go to school for so many years, and then when we graduate, we're out in the real world. It's like Ahsoka is now out in the real world, and we now see her in her job and she is very confident."

She becomes a supporting adviser of sorts for the rebel cell Phoenix Squadron, occasionally accompanying Ezra Bridger and his Jedi mentor Kanan Jarrus on missions. During one of these excursions, she encounters Darth Vader, and finally learns the devastating truth about Anakin's transformation and turn to the dark side. Ahsoka feels partly responsible for his downfall, having left years earlier, and confronts her conscience when his helmet is slashed in an epic battle, revealing Anakin's face beneath Vader's mask. She vows not to leave him again, but it's too late. Her flashing white sabers allow Ezra to escape, and he is in turn later able to save her by pulling her through a portal from the future in a world between worlds, a collection of pathways and doors between time and space. Kanan has since been killed in battle, and Ahsoka offers Ezra the devastating realization, "You can't save your master, and I can't save mine." Before Ahsoka returns safely to her own time, to continue her journey through the past, Ezra tells her to come find him when she gets back. That becomes more challenging when Ezra sacrifices himself to save Lothal by using purrgil to transport himself, Grand Admiral Thrawn, and Thrawn's forces through hyperspace to an unknown destination.

Ezra and Thrawn disappear, but Ahsoka believes they survive somewhere in the galaxy. She doesn't give up. Time passes, but finally, Ahsoka tracks Magistrate Morgan Elsbeth, an ally of the Empire who is devoted to Thrawn, and extracts a lead from her—one that proves Thrawn is alive. Ahsoka eventually discovers Elsbeth has been searching for a map to Peridea, a place of legend where Elsbeth believes she'll find Thrawn. Elsbeth oversees the construction of a craft to travel to Peridea, and when Ahsoka uncovers all the information, she turns to Hera, now a leader in the New Republic, and Sabine, her former apprentice, to share the promising news: Ezra is likely to be with Thrawn.

During the search for Thrawn and Ezra, Ahsoka discovers something much more profound by facing her past. She loses a duel with Baylan Skoll and goes over a cliff on Seatos. When she lands in the roiling waters, she appears to find herself back in a world between worlds, this time finding her former Jedi Master, Anakin Skywalker. He says he's there to give her a final lesson and takes her on a journey through her past. Ahsoka comes face-to-face with her complicated feelings over training

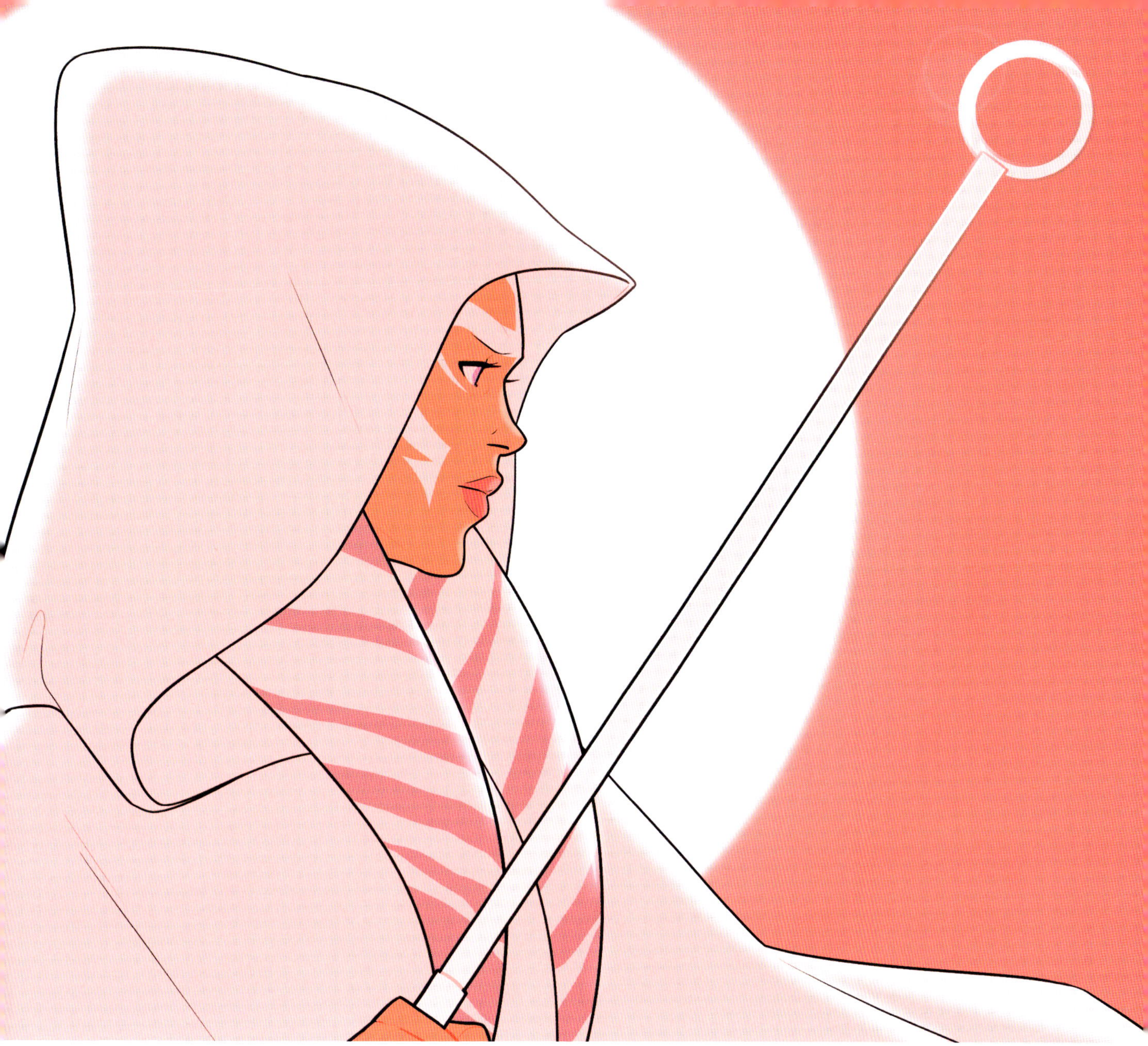

"To defeat your enemy, you have to understand them."

—Ahsoka Tano

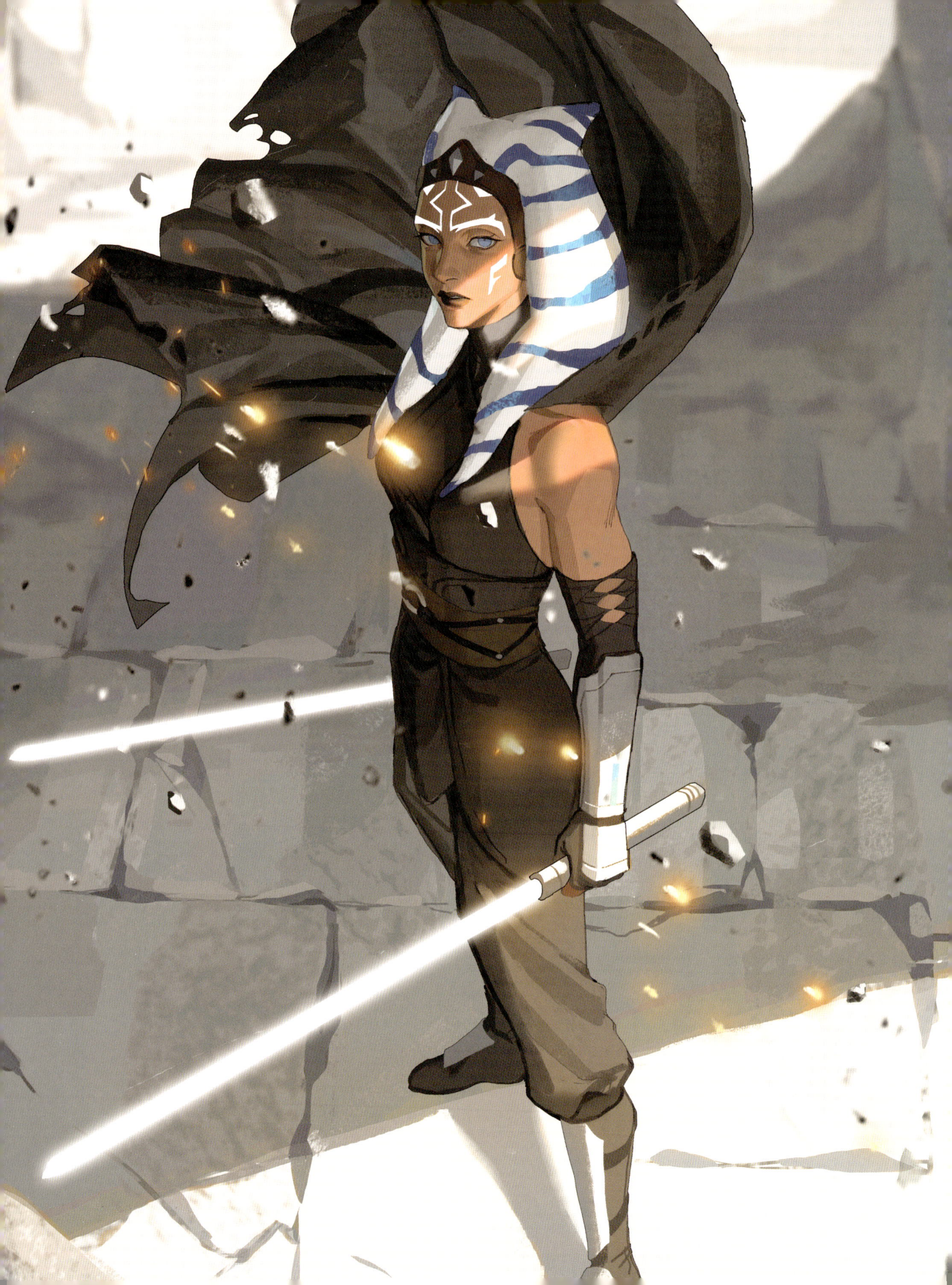

to be a guardian of peace during a war, her guilt for leaving the Jedi Order and Anakin, and she worries that an inner darkness is threatening to break through. Anakin duels his Padawan and offers a choice: Ahsoka can continue battling the weight of her fears, guilt, and doubt, or she can chart another course. Ahsoka tells Anakin, "I choose to live." She chooses a full life, one where she opens her heart without fear of the darkness. She is instantly lighter. Free. More herself.

Ahsoka takes her fresh state of mind across the stars to Peridea, where she and Sabine reunite with Ezra. She doesn't stop Thrawn's return to the known galaxy, and she ends up stranded on Peridea with Sabine, but we believe Ahsoka will find a way. She always has.

Rosario Dawson portrays Ahsoka in the eponymous series. She's enjoyed exploring this particular season of Ahsoka's life: "She's such a master, but she's not invulnerable, not physically or emotionally. And she may be very wise and she may be a formidable leader, but there's still much for her to learn," Dawson said.

> *"I choose to live."*
> *—Ahsoka Tano*

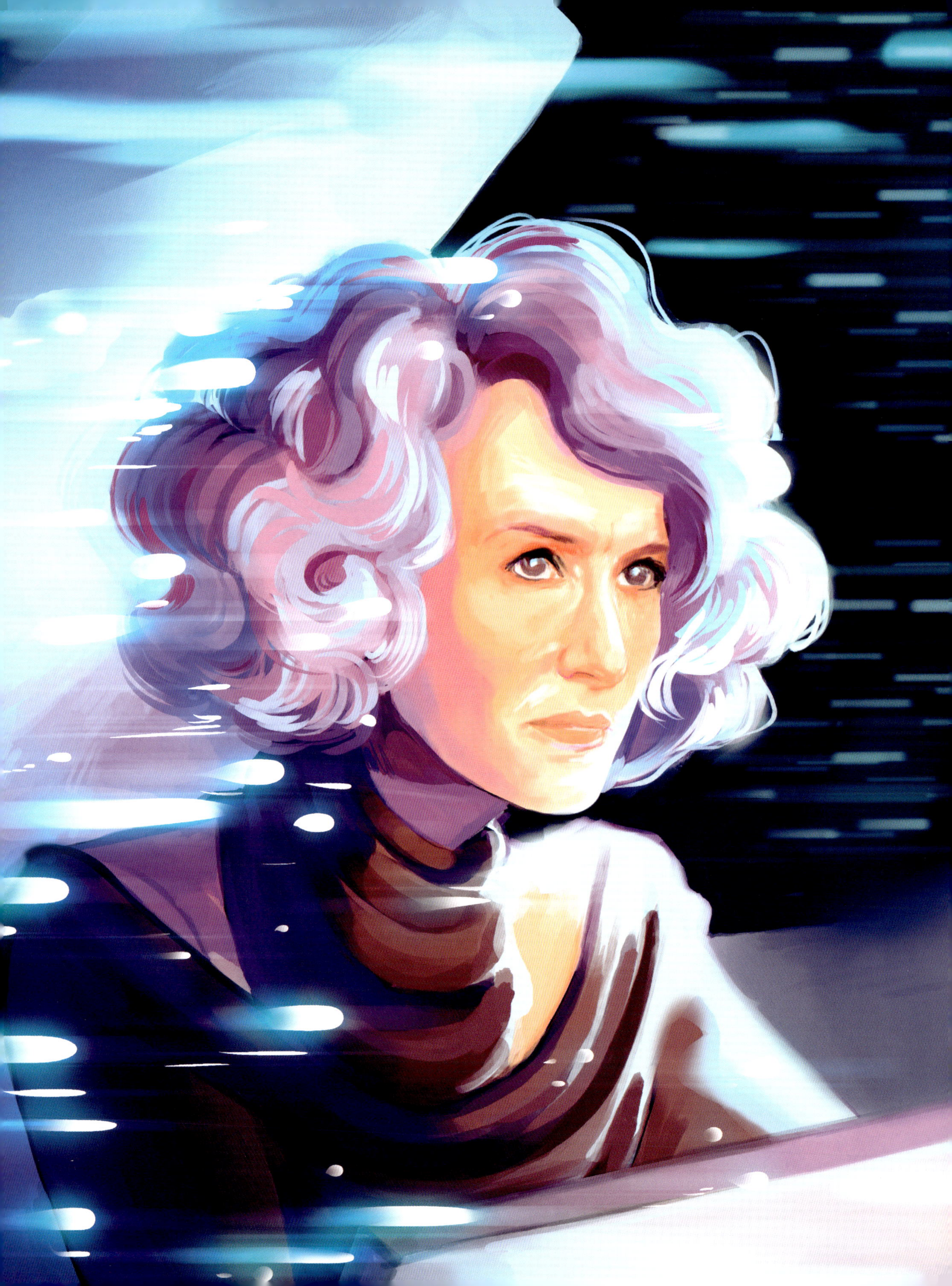

Amilyn Holdo

"In every corner of the galaxy, the downtrodden and oppressed know our symbol and they put their hope in it. We are the spark that will light the fire."

—AMILYN HOLDO

The Resistance is even more ragtag than the Rebel Alliance, thin on resources, and often making do with rickety equipment from the Galactic Civil War era. So when the first photos from *The Last Jedi* showed Vice Admiral Amilyn Holdo with her coiffed purple hair, elegant mauve dress, and striking silver accessories in the midst of the drab browns and grubby oranges of the Resistance surroundings, they caused ripples through fandom. Who was this woman? Was she an aristocrat? Was she a politician who survived the fall of the New Republic?

Leia, Princess of Alderaan introduces us to a young Amilyn, who, like Leia Organa and other politically-minded teenagers, joins the Apprentice Legislature of the Imperial Senate. After introducing herself to Leia in a pathfinding class (a course teaching outdoor basics, especially how to navigate without the assistance of tools), her first words are: "I hope it's dangerous. I want to get more comfortable with the nearness and inevitability of death." Candid, and unexpectedly unlike other aspiring politicians and diplomats, Amilyn establishes being different and accepts it as a cornerstone of her personality. It's refreshing to see someone so at home in her own skin. And, being who she is, Amilyn thinks everyone is special, too. She tells a fellow apprentice legislator, "Rarity is an illusion, because every person and object in the galaxy is in some way unique."

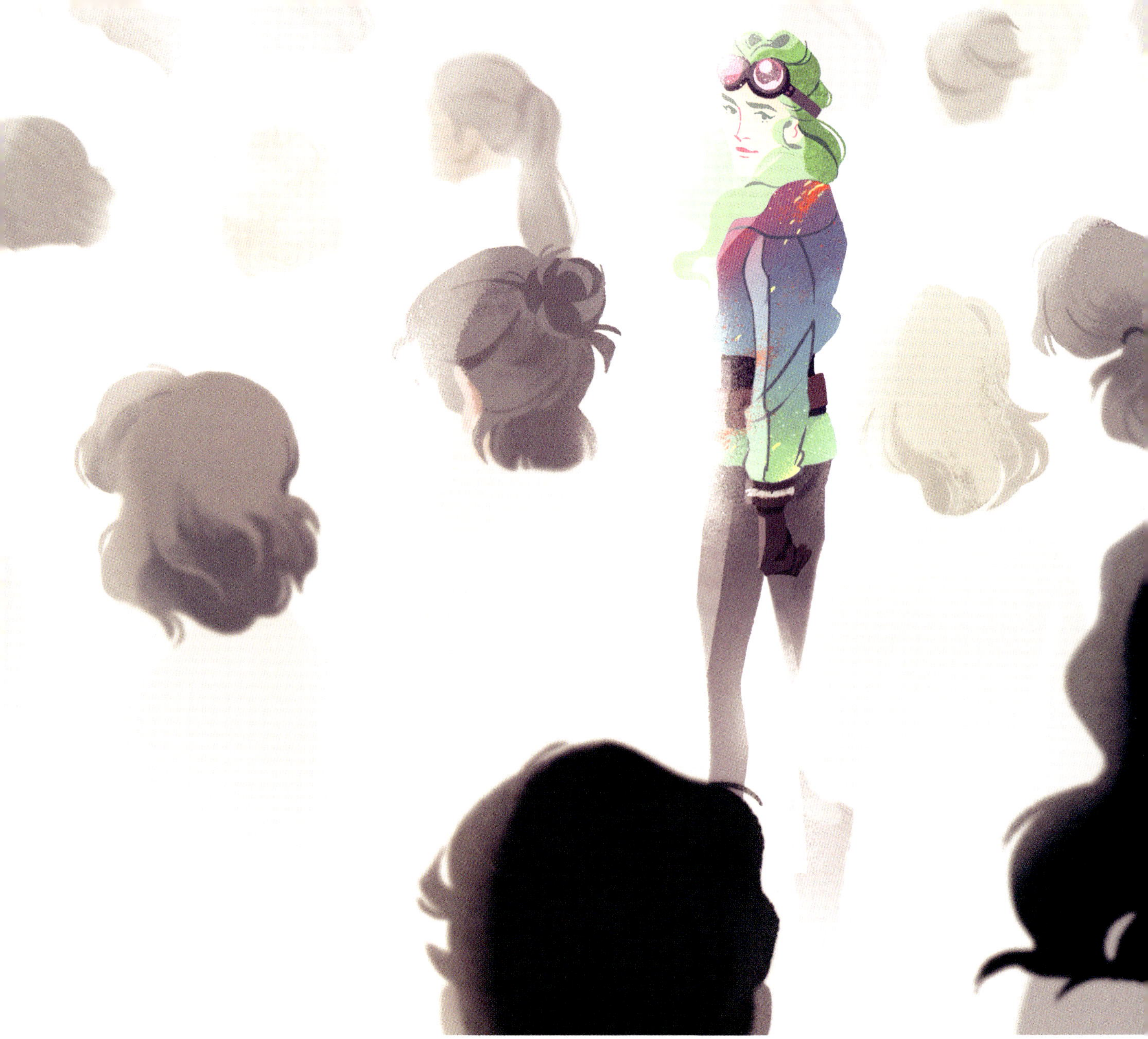

“Godspeed, rebels.”
—Amilyn Holdo

Claudia Gray, author of *Princess of Alderaan*, was pleased to see fans' positive reactions to Amilyn: "She's somebody who's a bit off-kilter, who sees the world through a prism most others don't understand. At first Leia thinks she's pleasant but weird, but as time goes on, it becomes apparent there's much more to Holdo than you might guess when you first meet her. We don't really have a lot of true oddballs in *Star Wars*, so it was fun to introduce one."

While her native world of Gatalenta is known for its independent spirit and tranquility, Amilyn is more assertive. She displays her individualism by frequently changing her hair color and donning outfits with vivid hues and patterns in contrast to more common, neutral tones. Instead of meditating, she throws herself into adventures. When Leia starts learning more about the dangers of the Empire, Amilyn stows away with her in an Imperial informant's ship to gain intelligence about his activities.

By the time we see her again in *The Last Jedi*, some thirty-five years later, Amilyn has matured, and so has her friendship with Leia. She's been part of the Rebellion, and now, the Resistance. When the First Order delivers a blow that wipes out most of the Resistance's officers and injures Leia, Amilyn steps in to command the beleaguered *Raddus*. She projects confidence when she gathers the remaining forces and tells them, "We are the spark that will light the fire that will restore the Republic."

Since the First Order is tracking the Resistance through hyperspace and chances of an escape by that means are slim, she stays the course, keeping the *Raddus* out of the reach of First Order cannons. Her steely shutdown of Poe Dameron's hot-take impulse to recklessly fight back illustrates the difference between being a leader and being a hero. Her singular responsibility is keeping as much of the Resistance alive as possible, which she does by ordering full evacuation via transport ships while she remains aboard the *Raddus*. When the First Order turns their lasers upon the transports, Amilyn's clear-eyed strength comes into focus. By taking the *Raddus* into hyperspace right through the enemy ships, she gives the Resistance the chance to get to the surface of the shadow planet of Crait, to continue the fight. The spark does not go out.

Arihnda Pryce

"I serve the Empire until the end."

You don't want to cross Arihnda Pryce. Ambitious, ruthless, and willing to step on anyone who gets in the way as she climbs to power, she's a model Imperial officer. Born on the planet Lothal and perhaps destined to go into the family mining business, from childhood Arihnda dreams of something bigger and brighter. She eventually seizes upon the opportunity to get offworld by working for one of Lothal's senators on Coruscant. From there she leverages connections, and when she can, gathers dirt on Imperial officers—because you never know what will come in handy. Her strategy works, and when we first officially meet her in *Star Wars Rebels*, she's the governor of Lothal.

Voice actress Mary Elizabeth McGlynn thinks Arihnda is, well, kind of despicable, but she applauds her persistence, and she has fun playing a driven character whose accomplishments are never quite enough. "There's something fascinating about giving voice to a woman who is so desperate for power and yet seemingly so ineffective at achieving her goals," McGlynn says. "She wants to capture or kill the rebels. She can't. She thinks she can control Imperial Grand Admiral Thrawn. She can't. So her frustration continues to grow as the plot unfolds. That only adds to her desperation to complete her goal, at any cost."

Arihnda is shrewd. She uses data about a group of rebels to convince Grand Moff Tarkin to give her the governorship. And she's observant. She notes Thrawn as an up-and-comer before his many promotions, and when she understands he could use help navigating the Imperial bureaucracy, she's happy to lend a hand. For a price.

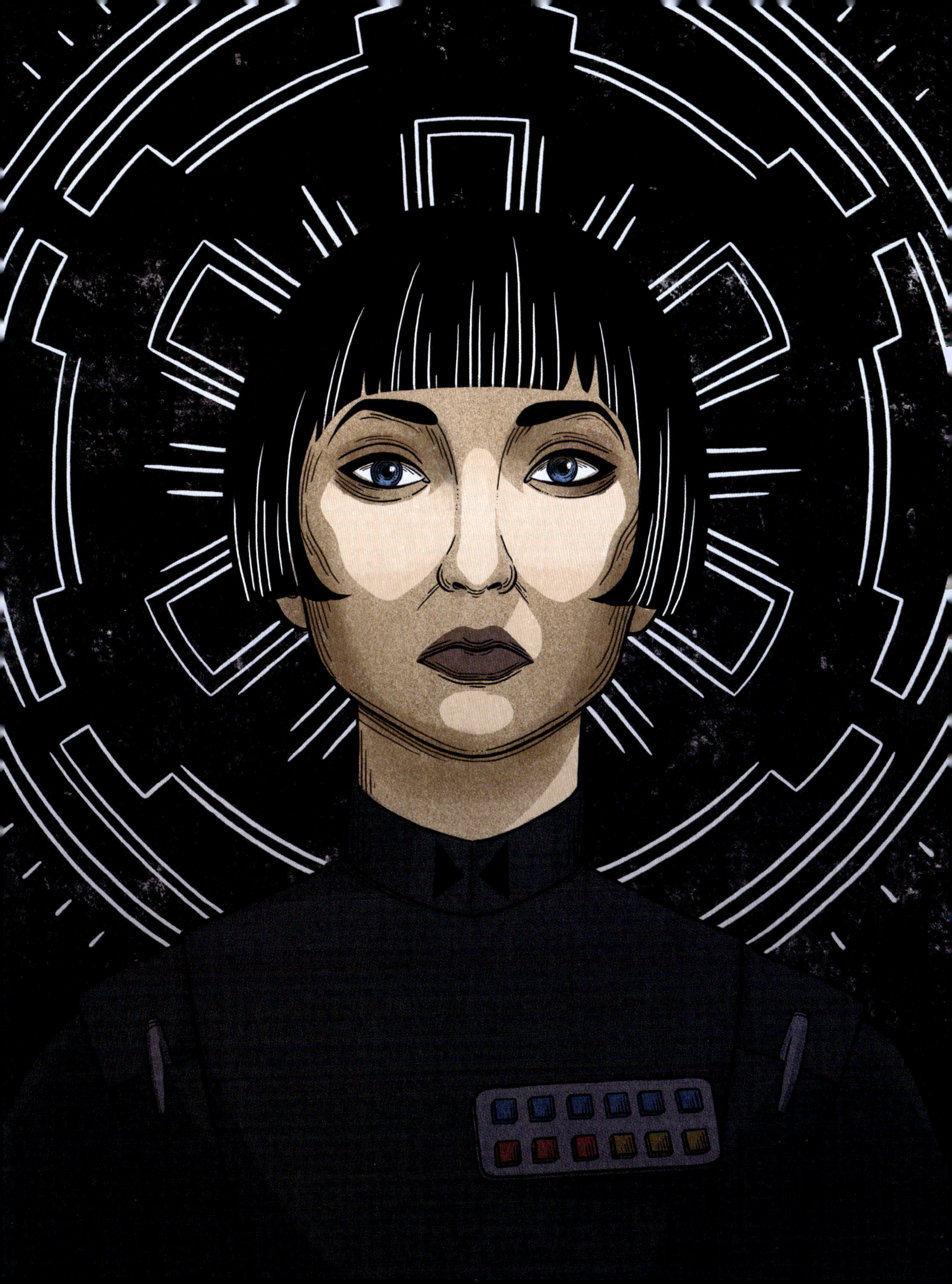

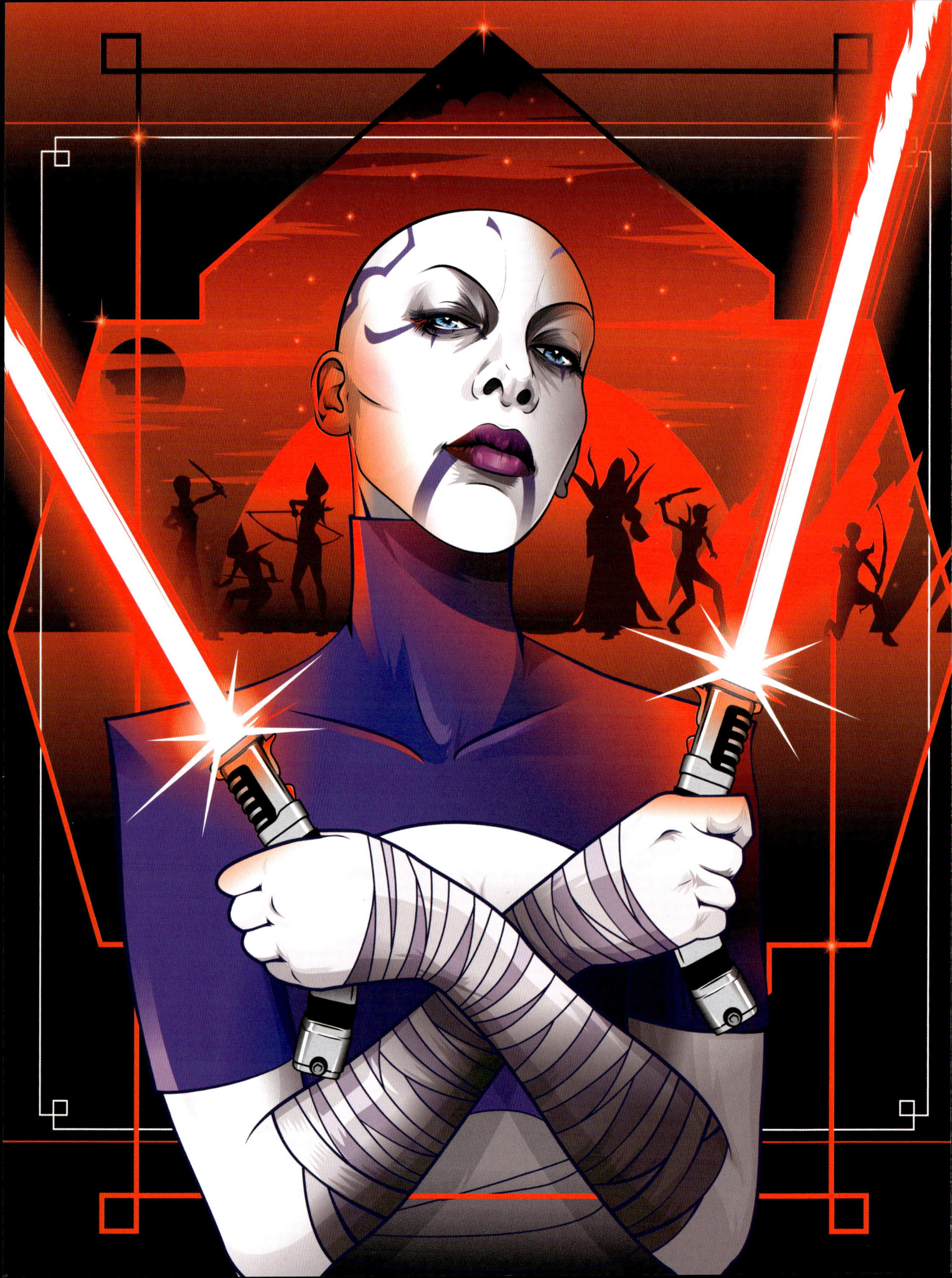

Asajj Ventress

"It's only the likes of me, with nothing to lose, who'll really be prepared to tear the galaxy down and start over."

Asajj Ventress kills a male bounty hunter who pesters her in Mos Eisley's cantina and calls her a "pretty bald babe." A Dathomirian Force-user who first brandishes her dual red lightsabers in *Star Wars: The Clone Wars*, Asajj has been an assassin, a Nightsister, and a bounty hunter—sometimes all at once. How she gets by is fluid, but a constant current is her driving anger and thirst for revenge.

Her history is one of abandonment. The Nightsister clan, her family, is forced to give her up when she's an infant. The pirate who takes her from Dathomir is killed. The Jedi Master who finds her after she's orphaned and trains her as his Padawan is shot. In despair and rage, Asajj turns to the dark side. She uses bitterness and a desire for vengeance against anyone who wrongs her. Anger gives her strength, and the Separatist leader Count Dooku takes notice.

He takes Asajj on as his personal assassin and, as a tool and weapon of the Separatists, Asajj relishes tormenting citizens and Jedi alike. She's a menacing figure who wields her lightsabers and moves with terrifying speed. Frequently tangling with Anakin Skywalker and Obi-Wan Kenobi, she never quite defeats them, but they are well-matched (in one battle, we see her Force-choke both Jedi at once).

Though Asajj devotes her service to Dooku, the Count is loyal to Darth Sidious, who sees a threat in Asajj's growing power and orders her killed. She survives, but is again alone.

The idea of delving into the details of Asajj's past came from George Lucas. Her backstory was previously explored for other stories, and in fact, the character's look sprung from unused concept art by Dermot Power for *Attack of the Clones*. That art found purpose in the "Nightsisters" arc of *The Clone Wars*; Lucas wanted to show the narrative from her point of view and expand her story. Voice actress Nika Futterman said one of the biggest mysteries of portraying Asajj was figuring out who she was, as Futterman knew just as much or as little as the audience: "I just assumed she had a difficult childhood!" Careful not to play her as a one-note character, she left room to adjust once Asajj's backstory was revealed.

To start over, Asajj returns home. Mother Talzin, leader of the Nightsisters, welcomes her. The reunion showcases the tight-knit nature of the sisterhood, as Asajj's fellow clan members are willing to aid her in her quest for retribution against Dooku. She pours all her intensity into killing the Sith Lord, first trying to murder him herself, and then working with Mother Talzin to train the Nightbrother Savage Opress to handle the deed. But Dooku turns the tables and brings death to Dathomir, wiping out the Nightsisters.

Asajj moves on once again, this time with the added burden of guilt. The massacre leaves her deeply shaken, but now more open to the light. She lends assistance to Ahsoka Tano, who once used to call Asajj the "Hairless Harpy," when the Togruta rebel is on the run after being framed for a crime. She hasn't fallen so far astray that she can't put herself in Ahsoka's place.

Asajj's trajectory continues in author Christie Golden's novel *Dark Disciple*, adapted from elements of unproduced scripts after the end of *The Clone Wars* series. In the novel, through a begrudging partnership with the Jedi Quinlan Vos, Asajj understands the futility of vengeance and reconnects with estranged emotions of compassion and forgiveness. Seemingly sacrificing herself to save Quinlan, she says, "You always have a choice to be better. You always have a choice to pick the right path. Even if that choice comes a little late."

This act is not the end of Asajj's story. Many believe her to be dead, but she continues to be a survivor. Roaming the galaxy with mysterious purpose and a yellow lightsaber, Asajj tracks the Bad Batch and Omega to their hidden location. The one-time dark side Force-user exhibits kindness toward the young Omega, and in their brief time together, mentors the clone and teaches her about the Force. Before she disappears once more, Ventress acknowledges she has a few lives left.

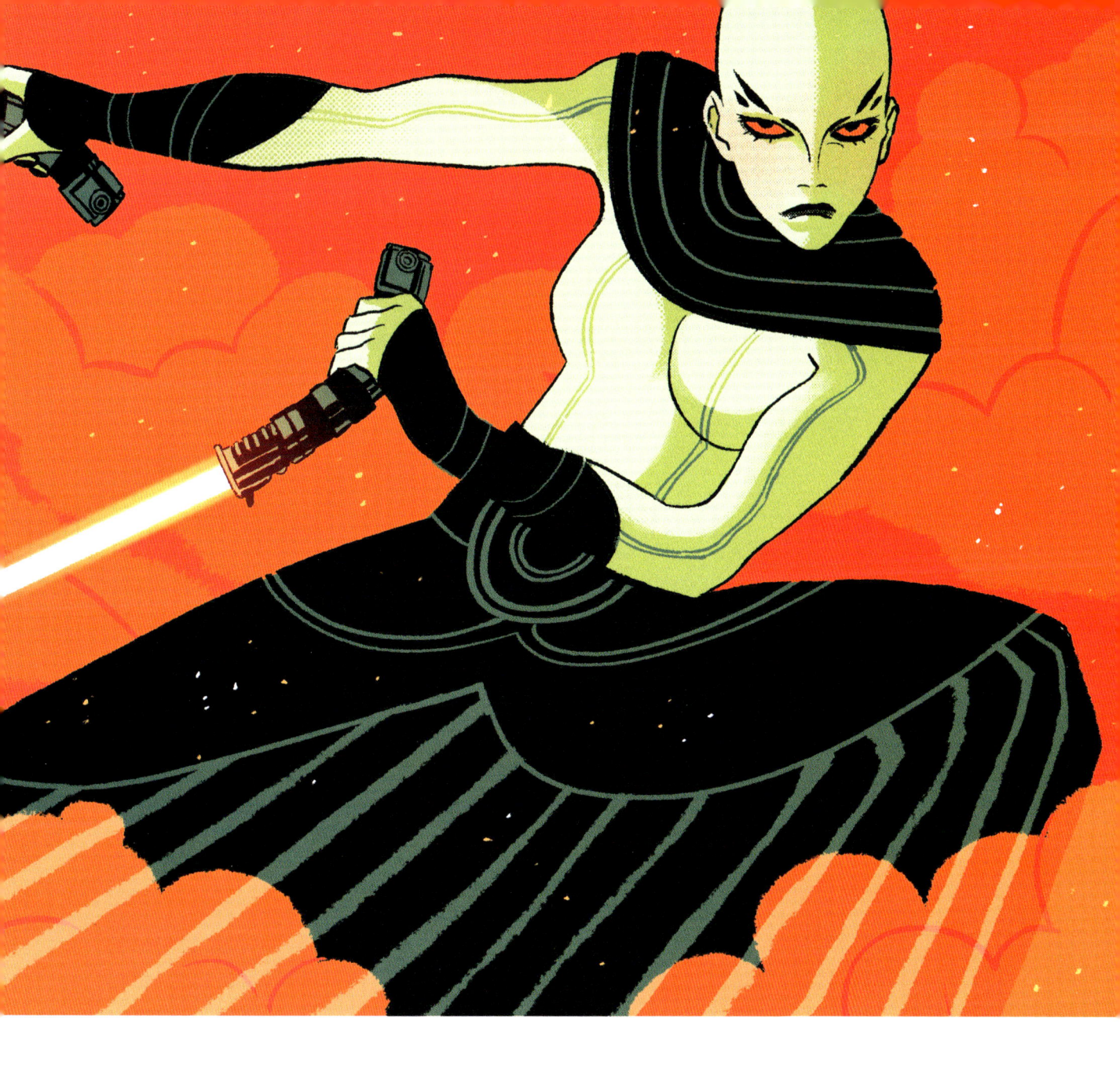

"You always have a choice to be better. You always have a choice to pick the right path."
—Asajj Ventress

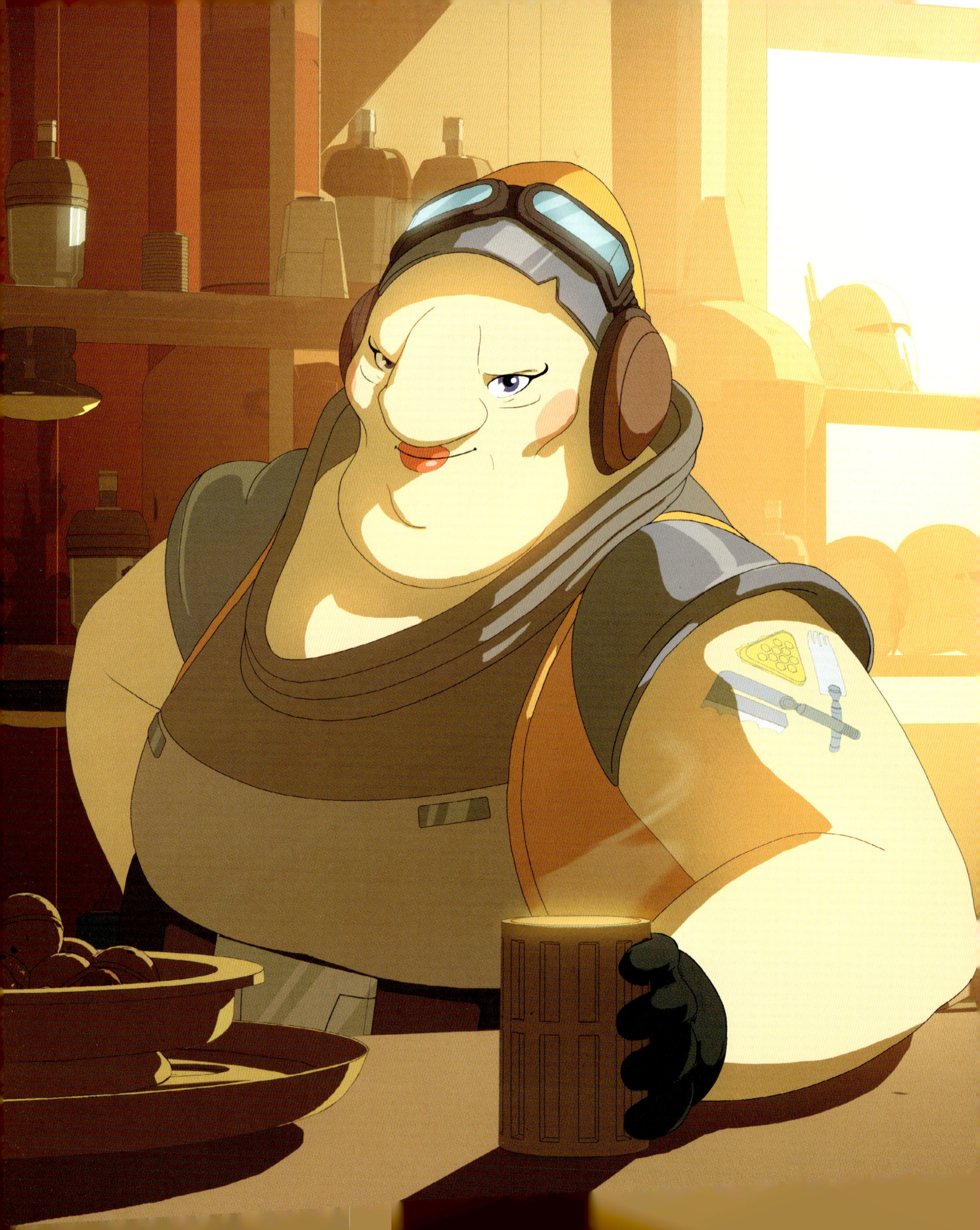

Aunt Z

An enterprising and brazen tavern owner on the Colossus.

Racing is a profitable sport, and Aunt Z'Vk'Thkrkza, called Aunt Z for short, knows how to leverage the competitions on the *Colossus* platform to her advantage without jumping into the pilot's seat. Introduced in *Star Wars Resistance*, the grumpy, snarky Gilliand has a sharp mind for business, and her namesake Aunt Z's Tavern is the most popular eatery and bar on the *Colossus*. It's known as *the* hangout for the platform's star pilots, the Aces, as well as a gathering place for usual bar-dwellers and travelers passing through. Everyone's welcome as long as they leave generous tips and don't act up.

While her assistant bartender—the multi-limbed service droid G1-7CH (a.k.a. "Glitch")—slings drinks, Aunt Z doles out insightful and blunt advice. Platform denizens go to her for answers, and she provides guidance depending on how much she favors who is asking and how much they are tipping. But patrons shouldn't expect Aunt Z to coddle them, despite her cozy nickname. She's all about making a profit, and employs an imposing Klatooinian enforcer, Bolza Grool, to ensure customers stay in line and don't skip out on their bills.

Aunt Z cannot contain her bluntness when the First Order occupies the *Colossus*. She loudly resents their presence, and the First Order arrests her for her overt hostility. However, many citizens on the *Colossus* share Aunt Z's sentiments. They rise up and help the *Colossus* escape the First Order, she reopens her tavern and, grumbling all the while, gets back to work.

Aurra Sing

"I never ask for permission to do anything."

First spotted in the stands watching the Boonta Eve Classic podrace in *The Phantom Menace*, we don't observe Aurra's lethal talents until *Star Wars: The Clone Wars*, when she joins a young Boba Fett in his vengeful pursuit of Jedi Master Mace Windu. A bounty hunter and one of the deadliest assassins in the galaxy, she specializes in sniper attacks with her projectile rifle, but she has no problem handling herself in close combat with other weaponry, such as the lightsabers she's kept as trophies from the Jedi she's hunted. The biocomputer implanted in her skull also helps give her an edge.

Aurra's interests and motivations are always her own. It's certainly not kindness that leads her to take future bounty hunter Boba Fett under her wing after Windu murders his father, Jango. She works with Boba as part of her crew, ruthlessly stokes his need for payback, and coolly abandons him after he's captured, teaching him a valuable moral lesson: trust no one. Aurra also shows Boba how to take advantage of relationships. Her former flame, the ebullient and connected pirate Hondo Ohnaka, means nothing more to her than a place to hide from Jedi.

Jaime King voices Aurra in *The Clone Wars*, and empathizes with the character at a certain level. "She's hardcore, and that's why it's so fun to play her, because it's not anything you could ever get away with in real life. When you're acting, then you can get away with it through your characters, so it's like you get to express these sides of yourself that you never do. What's really exciting is just learning about Aurra, learning about her life and learning about what she's up to and how she manipulates to get what she wants."

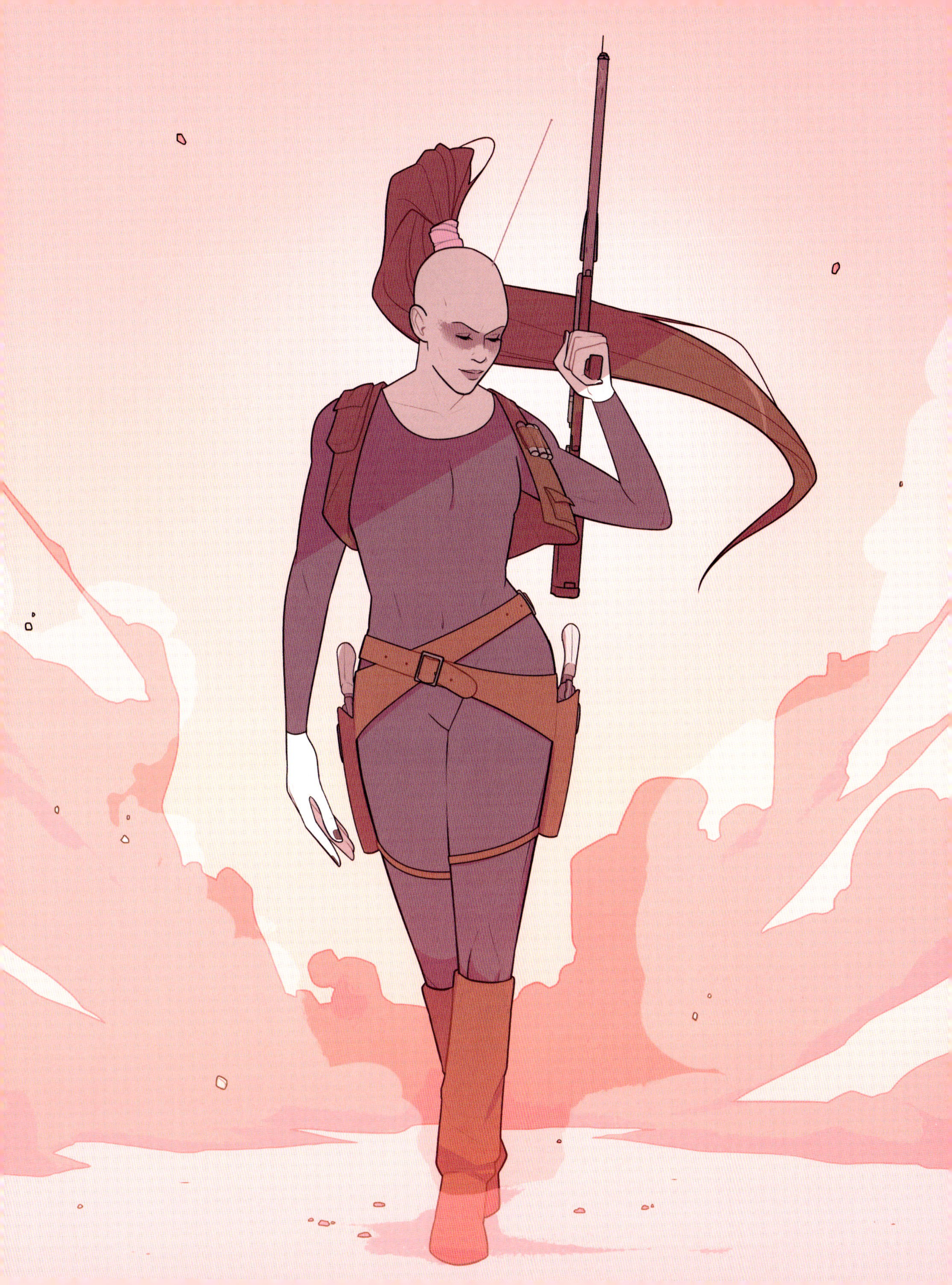

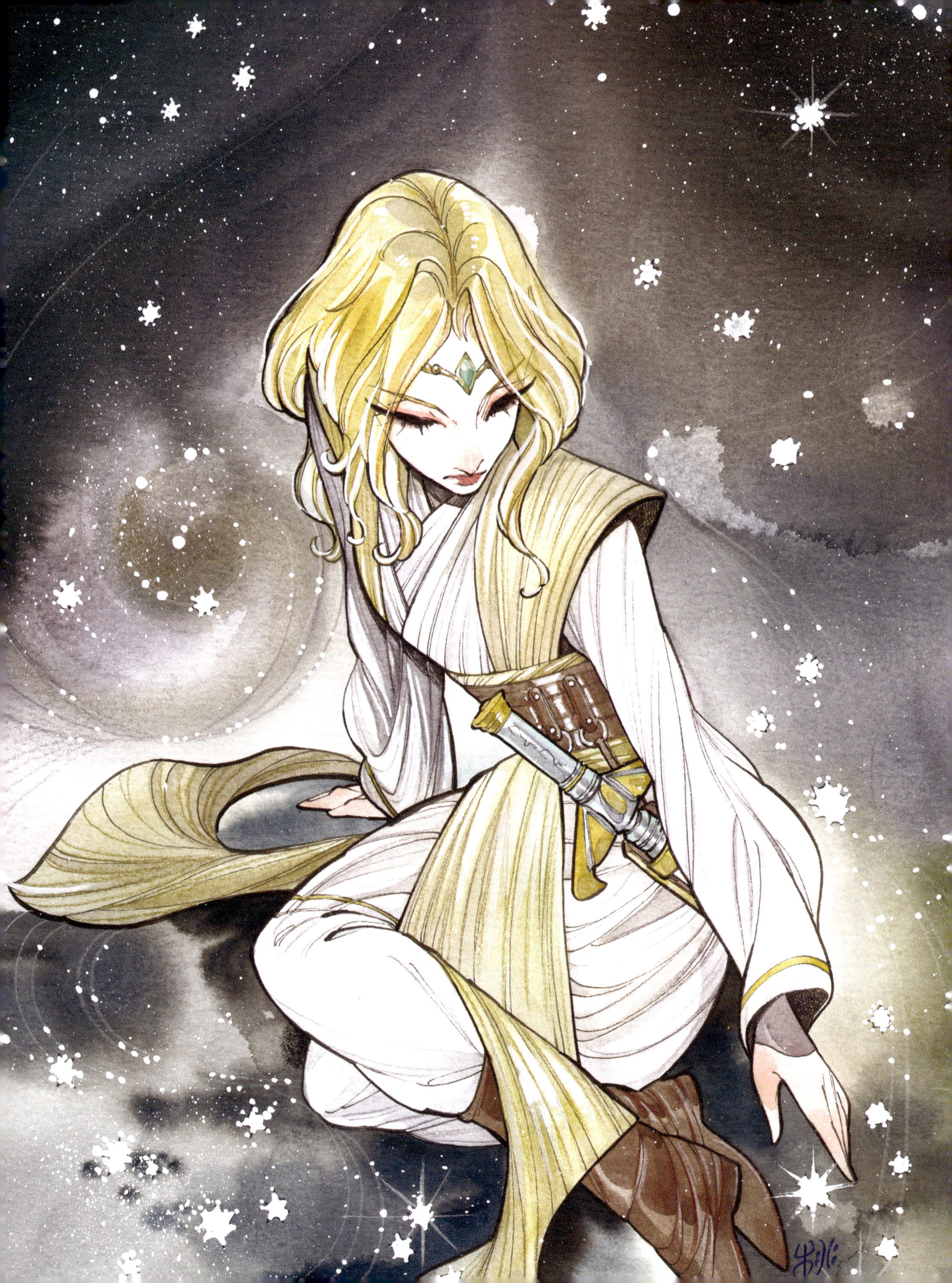

Avar Kriss

"We must begin by believing it is possible to save everyone."

When we first meet Master Avar Kriss in *Light of the Jedi*, she is everything we imagine an ideal Jedi to be. Kind. Compassionate. Selfless. She acts heroically during the galaxy-wide Great Hyperspace Disaster, remaining calm and going into a state of deep focus to coordinate dozens of Jedi, directing their combined strength to prevent further deaths. It is a mental feat so massive that it's hard to imagine anyone sustaining the effort. But Avar, who sees the Force as music, pulls together the individual harmonies to conduct a chorus. Her actions earn her the title of Marshal of Starlight Beacon, an important space station and political symbol during the High Republic era.

But while Avar is a noble Jedi Master, she is also human—subject to doubts, temptations as seen in her close relationship with fellow Jedi Elzar Mann, and a strong sense of personal accountability. She and the Jedi erroneously believe Lourna Dee to be the Nihil leader responsible for an assassination attempt on Chancellor Soh, and Avar feels a responsibility to bring Lourna to justice. With their rivalry dating back to the Great Disaster, the relationship is one that sometimes tests Avar's dedication to the light side of the Force. She wants to do what she believes is right, which is stop Lourna, but it takes a toll, as Avar struggles to not lose herself to dark emotions in the process.

To be a true peacekeeper for the galaxy is important, yes, but it's a type of burden of its own. One must continually weigh their own goals against those of the greater good and not let personal missions rule the heart. One also cannot let themselves be consumed by guilt over not being able to prevent every evil. Avar wrestles with all of this, but with time and effort, she finds balance.

Barriss Offee

"I've come to realize what many people in the Republic have come to realize: that the Jedi are the ones responsible for this war."

Disillusionment can lead to drastic measures. In *Attack of the Clones* and the beginning of *Star Wars: The Clone Wars,* we meet Offee as Padawan to Jedi Master and fellow Mirialan, Luminara Unduli. Barriss is studious, well-mannered, and respectful (in many ways the opposite of her friend Ahsoka Tano). She's the very picture of an exemplary Jedi apprentice, until she orchestrates the bombing of the Jedi Temple on Coruscant.

Barriss comes to believe the Jedi are responsible for the Clone Wars and meets with a Coruscanti woman, Letta Turmond, who agrees; they plan the attack on the Temple together to make a statement. She frames Ahsoka for the bombing and for the murder of Letta (Barriss killed her to keep her quiet). Afterward, Barriss tells the court, "We've so lost our way that we have become villains in this conflict." While her beliefs might not be wrong, Barriss is imprisoned for her actions. As Ahsoka observes: "She had a point about the Republic and the Jedi. There was something wrong with them, and we were too locked into our traditions to see what it was."

Barriss's perspective on the Jedi isn't wrong, but her method of expression brings irreparable harm to others. She reflects upon her actions in prison, but when a familiar face offers another future, Barriss accepts and trains to become an Inquisitor for the Empire. An early mission to track a Force-attuned child sours Barriss on Imperial life, and she sets out on her own. Becoming known as "the healer," Barriss returns to the light by selflessly using her gifts to help those in need.

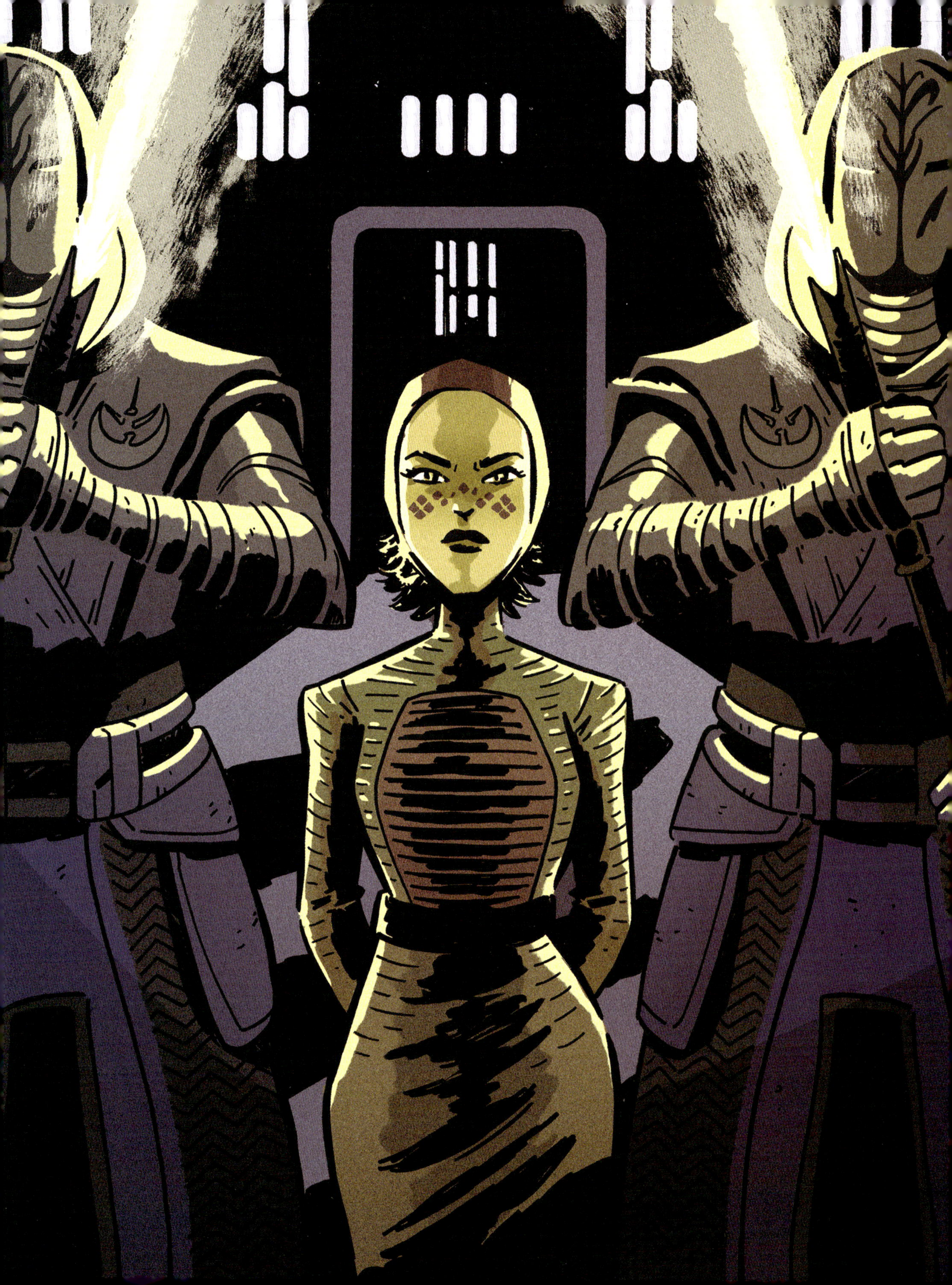

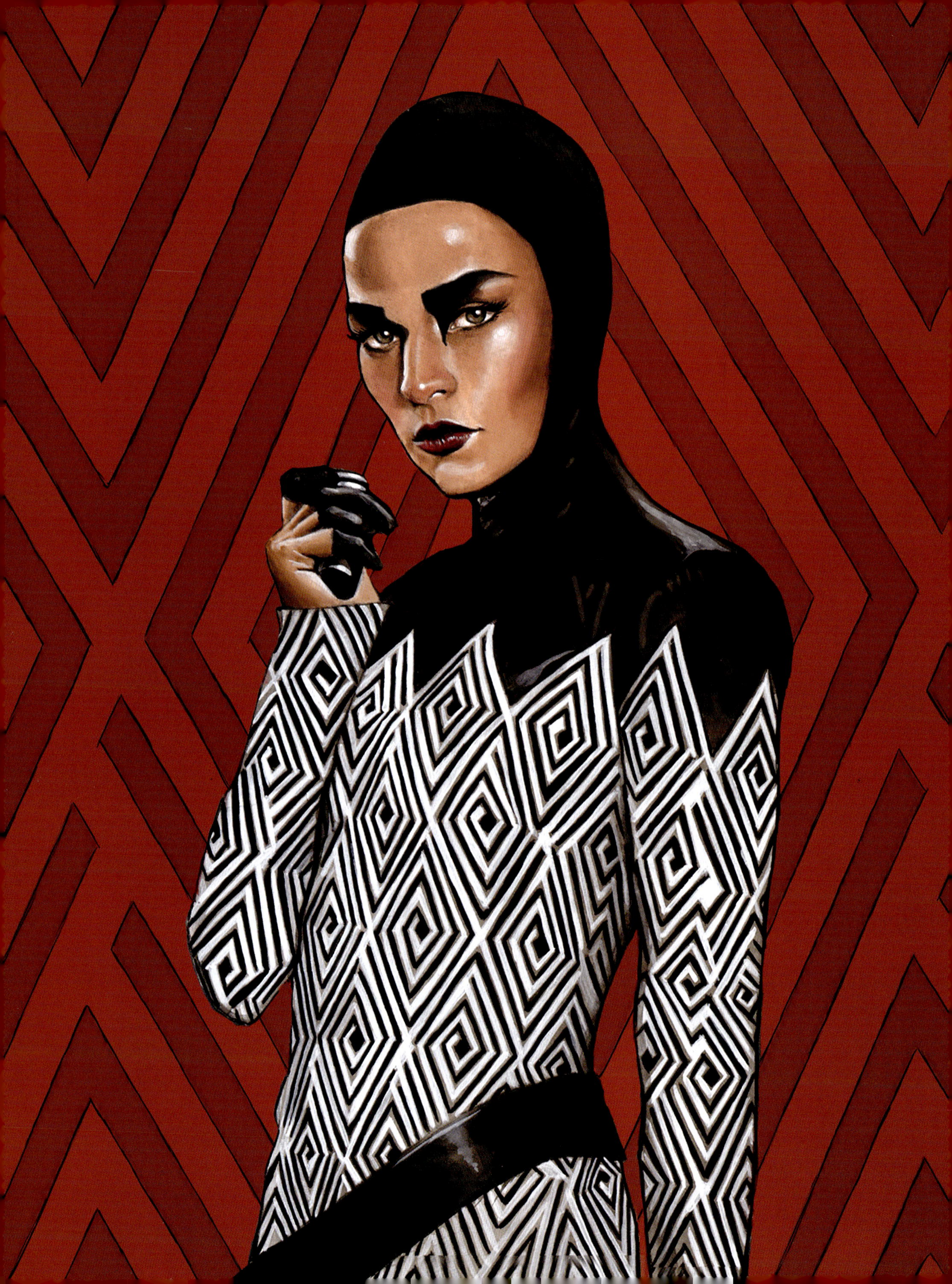

Bazine Netal

"People will believe what I want them to believe. They always do."

Bounty hunters are often specialists: they excel at slicing and manipulating data, or thievery, or assassination, or killing in their own special way. But Bazine Netal can do it all, hacking, stealing, and murdering with her choice of snub-nosed blaster, poisoned dagger, or throwing knives. Taken from an orphanage on the desert planet Chaaktil when she was a child, she endured brutal lessons. Her captor, Delphi Kloda, adopted her with the purpose of training her in his combat school and turning her into a perfect weapon that would be his to wield. She left her past behind and adopted the pseudonym Bazine. As she says about her time there, "My friends were grizzled murderers who taught me how to punch."

Bazine combines her cunning with ingenuity. For example, the outfit she wears in *The Force Awakens* when she alerts the First Order to BB-8's location, at Maz Kanata's castle on Takodana, is more than a striking fashion choice. The baffleweave dress jams sensors, her boot wedges conceal thermal detonators, and the black Rishi eel ink on her fingers obscures her fingerprints. A master of disguise, Bazine keeps her secrets close.

In the *Flight of the Falcon* storyline across books and comics, Bazine travels to the distant planet of Batuu at the edge of the galaxy while on the hunt for the *Millennium Falcon*. Sifting truth from tall tales, she pursues the legendary freighter that Imperials and bounty hunters alike have almost, but never quite, snared.

Beru Lars

"We're enough. You and me."

Star Wars is a galaxy full of heroes and villains, daring pilots, and fearless warriors. Of course, they get most of the attention, but it takes all kinds of characters to keep the story moving. Beru Whitesun Lars is first introduced to fans as Aunt Beru, a.k.a. the woman pouring the blue milk in *A New Hope*. But as the adoptive mother of Luke Skywalker, she helps raise the farm boy turned hero for nineteen years, supporting his hopes and dreams, and particularly advocating that he be allowed to attend the Imperial Academy rather than spend endless seasons on the Lars' moisture farm.

Before adopting Luke, she and her husband Owen want to have children of their own, but with the arrival of young Skywalker, she becomes dedicated to their new family and keeping Luke safe from the perils of Tatooine, and his true father, Anakin Skywalker, who unbeknownst to them is Darth Vader. She's willing to do anything for Luke, as she more than proves when an Inquisitor tracks Luke to Tatooine and attacks the Lars homestead. Beru doesn't bow to Reva, staying to defend their home when Owen wants to run. She insists that she and Owen will fight. Prepared for this moment, she meets it with grit, distracting the Inquisitor long enough for Luke to escape.

Because Beru appears in the original trilogy and the prequel trilogy set some nineteen years earlier, then in the streaming series *Obi-Wan Kenobi*, she's portrayed on film by two actresses, first in 1977 by Shelagh Fraser, and then by Bonnie Piesse. When she was cast for *Attack of the Clones*, Piesse watched *A New Hope* to study Fraser's accent and physical mannerisms, as well as what Beru would have been like earlier in her life. "I watched the scenes with Beru from *A New Hope* over and over until I felt I had a good sense of the character's nature. She seemed very kind, grounded, and loving to me, so that's what I tried to bring to the role. I also felt that, as I was playing her when she's younger, I wanted to bring in a little shyness."

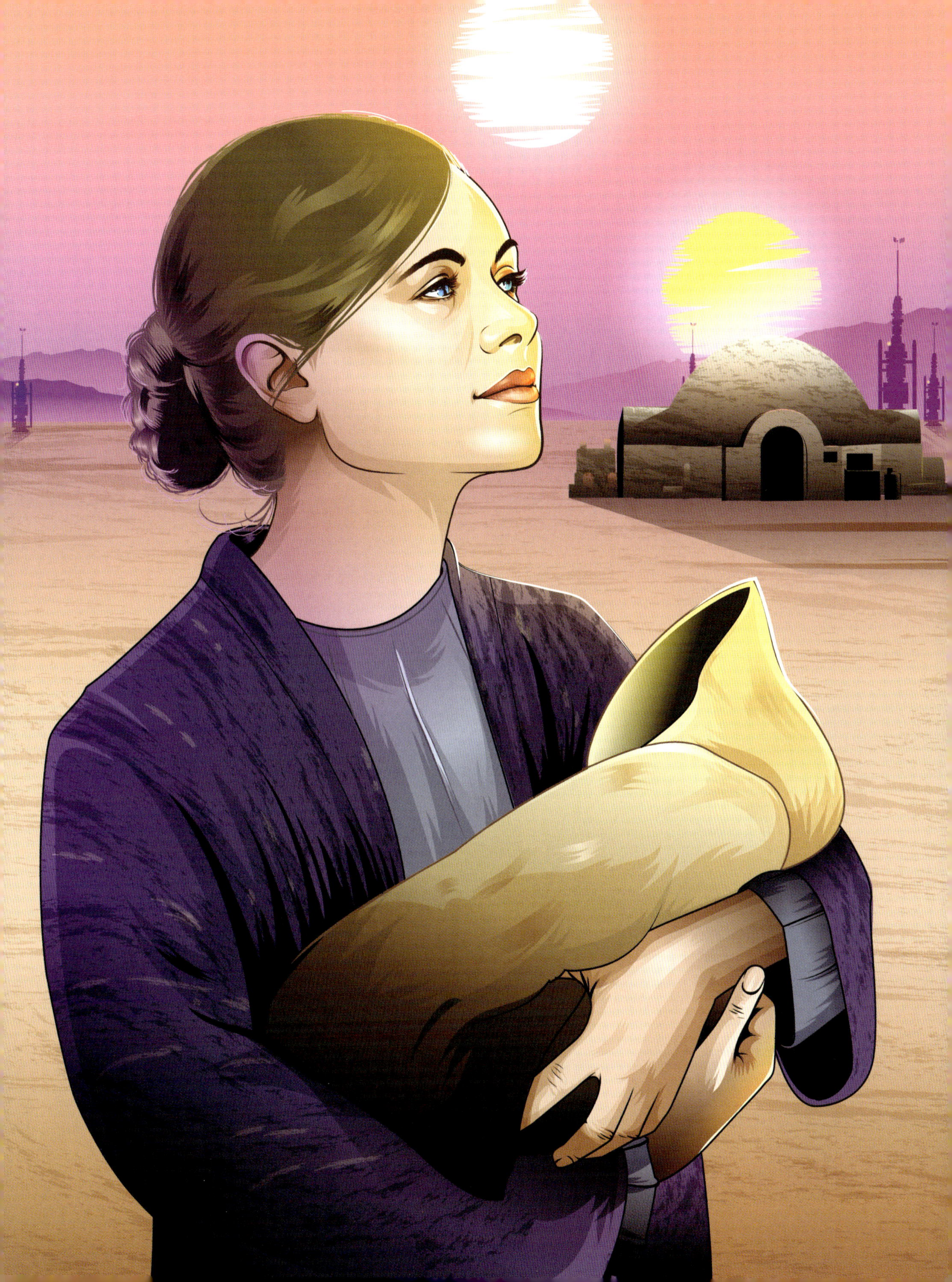

Bix Caleen

"You're not gonna believe me anyway, are you?"

Bix Caleen inherited the Caleen Salyard, a salvage yard on the rocky planet of Ferrix, after her parents passed, and she keeps it running successfully through creative business tactics and alternative revenue sources. She maintains secret connections to the black market and communicates with a specific buyer through a hidden junction box at Repaak Salyard. That buyer is Axis, a codename for Luthen Rael, who acquires Imperial tech to distribute to a network of dissidents conspiring against the Empire.

Besides operating a business and assisting Axis, Bix is fiercely loyal to her friends. The barren nature of Ferrix fosters a tight-knit community, and everyone looks out for each other. It's one reason why she still tries to help her former lover Cassian Andor when he finds himself on the run from the Empire. *Andor* showrunner Tony Gilroy notes she can't give up on Cassian; she'll always help him. Gilroy says, "They know everything about each other. They're meant to be together, and yet it's been impossible all these years. When we come in the show, she's done with him. He's burned every last bridge."

Even though she's "done" with Cassian, Bix connects him with Luthen and tries to keep the Empire off his trail. She also provides assistance to his mother Maarva time and time again. Bix's devotion to those she cares about is one reason why her colleague and partner Timm Karlo's betrayal hits her so hard. Jealous of Cassian, Timm reports him to Preox-Morlana, and by extension, the Empire. Since Bix is closely associated with Cassian, Timm's information leads to her capture and eventual torture at the hands of Imperial officers. Actress Adria Arjona portrays the character and says of Bix, "I wouldn't necessarily consider her tough, but I think she's a lot stronger and a lot smarter than a lot of people may think she is."

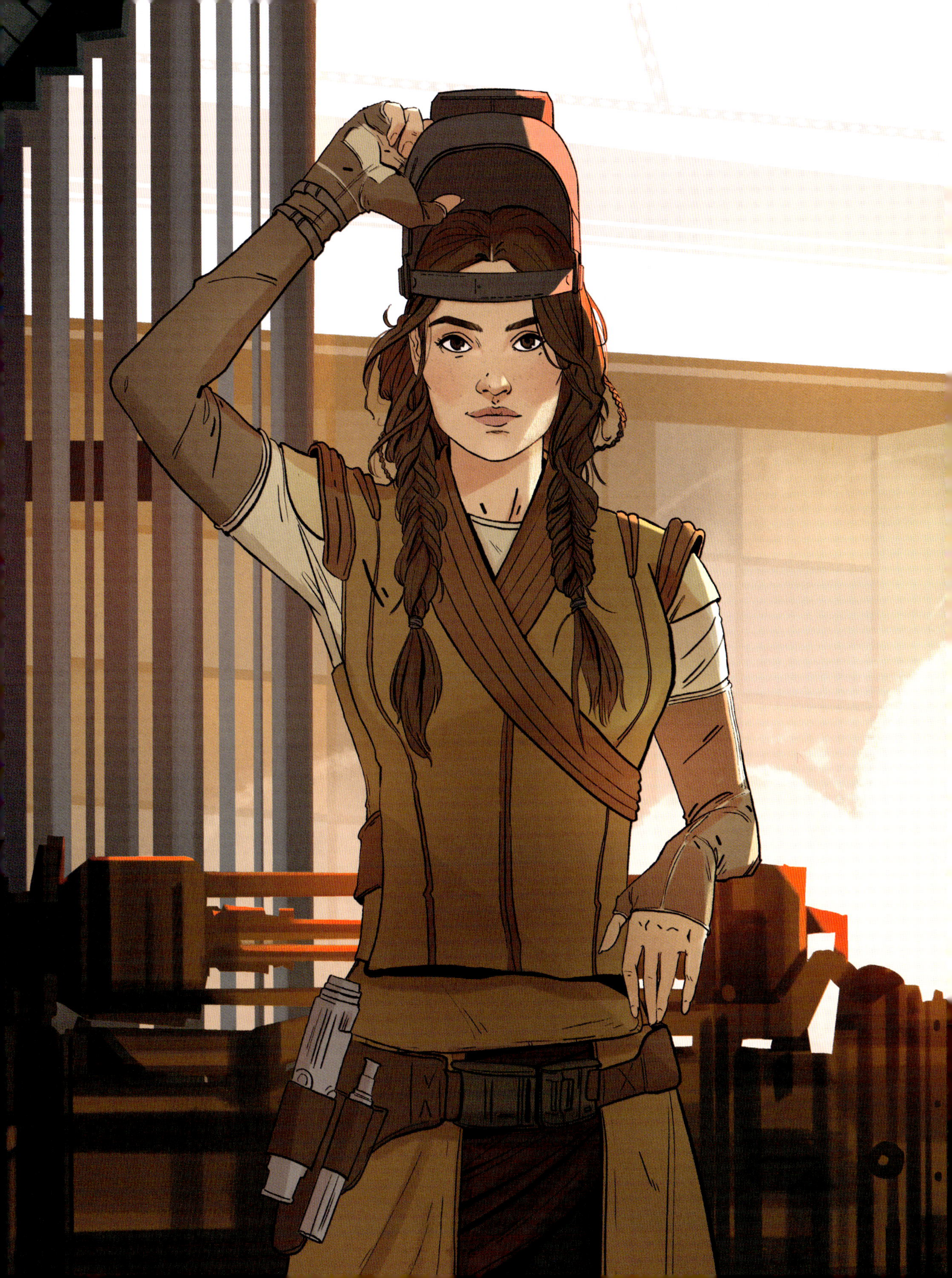

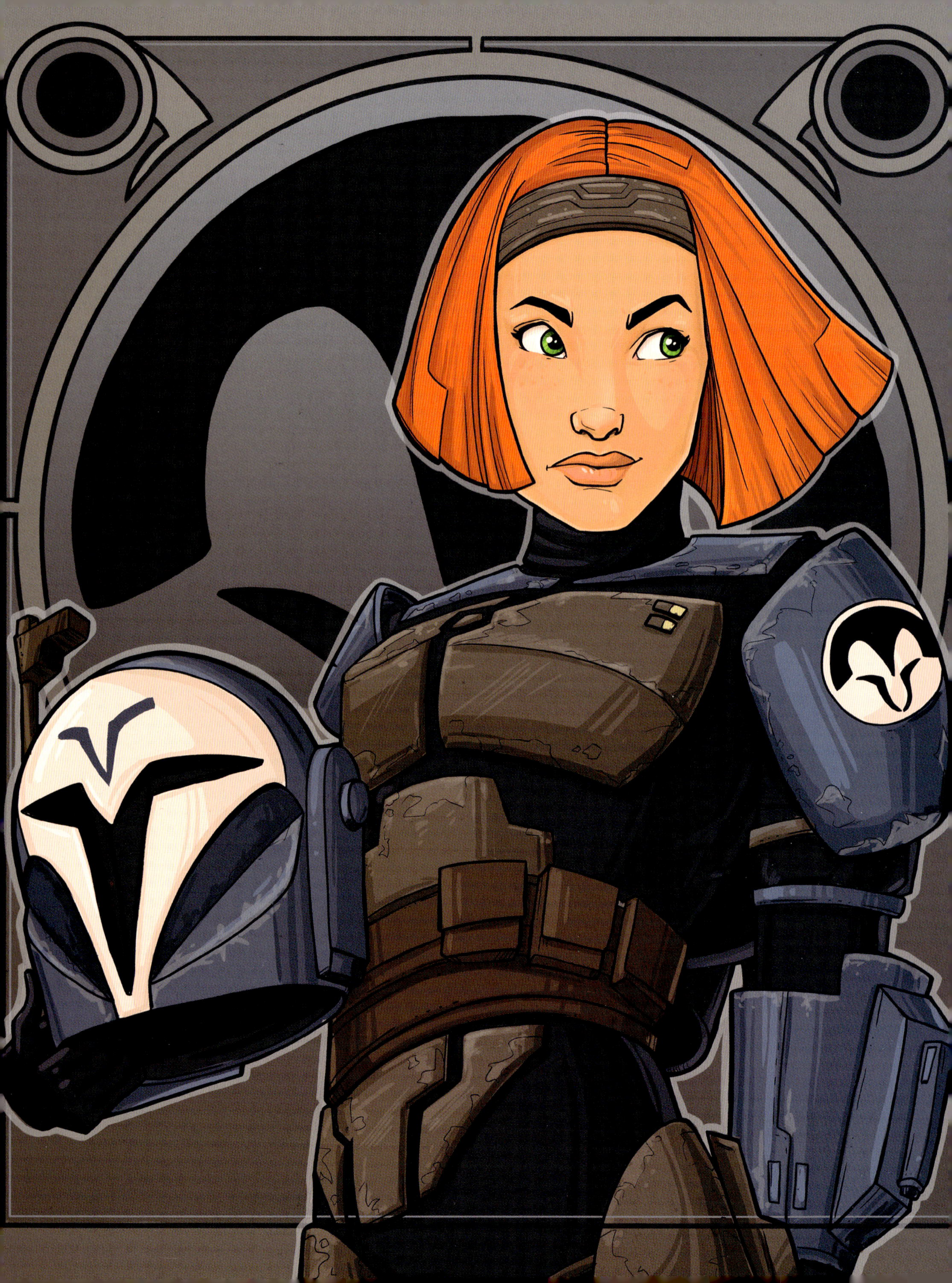

Bo-Katan Kryze

"Mandalore will survive. We always survive."

Bo-Katan Kryze is a warrior of deep conviction. Born on the planet Mandalore to Clan Kryze and first seen in *Star Wars: The Clone Wars*, she's committed to the traditions of Mandalore's martial past. When her sister Satine Kryze, the Duchess of Mandalore, puts a pacifistic system in place following the end of the planet's latest civil war, Bo-Katan immediately joins Death Watch, a terrorist group opposed to Mandalore's government.

Bo-Katan's perspective shifts when Death Watch's leader, Pre Vizsla, forges an alliance with Darth Maul and Savage Opress. The brothers take control of the group and Mandalore, and, among other things, imprison Satine. As Bo-Katan observes, "The enemy of my enemy is my friend." She seizes an opportunity to free her sister and opposes Maul and his forces, fighting alongside Ahsoka Tano, clone Captain Rex, and the Republic's soldiers when they arrive to remove the Sith Lord. She's named a regent after their victory, but later forced out when she refuses to bow to the Galactic Empire.

When we see her again almost twenty years later in *Star Wars Rebels*, she's battle-weary. Still, with her loyal Nite Owls, she helps Clan Wren destroy an Imperial weapon designed to kill Mandalorians. Having earned the respect of other clans, she accepts the Darksaber, a legendary weapon and symbol of leadership created over one thousand years prior by a member of Clan Vizsla, and heads the Mandalorian resistance against the Empire.

Alas, Bo-Katan does not keep the Darksaber. To save Mandalore after the Night of a Thousand Tears, when the Empire massacres countless Mandalorians, she negotiates with the Empire to surrender the Darksaber to Moff Gideon in exchange for mercy for the remaining Mandalorians. The Empire betrays her and carries out the Purge of Mandalore. Bo-Katan rebuilds her forces in the following decades and plans to retake the Darksaber, this time through winning the weapon in combat. Instead, she encounters Din Djarin, and their partnership results in her reclaiming the Darksaber and retaking Mandalore from lingering Imperial forces.

Breha Organa

"If we aren't ready to fight back, we'll be doomed."

A leader, an astute politician, and a benevolent teacher, Queen Breha Organa of Alderaan assumes another important role when she and her husband Bail Organa commit themselves to caring for the orphaned infant Leia in the closing moments of *Revenge of the Sith*. She and Bail always wanted to adopt a girl, and Breha opens her soul to Leia, loving her as her own, and making her the heir to the throne. Breha takes a hands-on approach to her royal duties, mentoring promising young people (including Leia's close friend Evaan Verlaine) in their world's peaceful and democratic heritage—values that Leia herself adopts with galaxy-changing faith.

Breha's also a fighter, a strength she displays after surviving severe injuries during a series of personal challenges undertaken by all heirs to the Alderaanian throne. Her heart and lungs are mechanized as a result, and rather than hiding the glow of those pulmonodes, she allows them to remain visible as a reminder of how valuable life is. It is something she keeps in mind as she and Bail begin to meet with others in secret opposition against the Empire, with Breha cleverly bringing together key architects of the Rebel Alliance under the guise of royal banquets. She understands the risks to herself and others. When a teenage Leia expresses concern about the stakes of rebelling and the lives that could be lost, Breha advises, "When it comes to the morality of what we may have to do . . . we have to find our way through many shadows."

Breha's background and role in building the Rebel Alliance is explored in *Leia, Princess of Alderaan*, in which author Claudia Gray expands what we know about the character. "It was especially great to get to write Breha," Gray says. "I figured Leia wasn't raised by a woman who was some sort of shy, retiring, passive creature. So it was a real honor to breathe some life into the last queen of Alderaan."

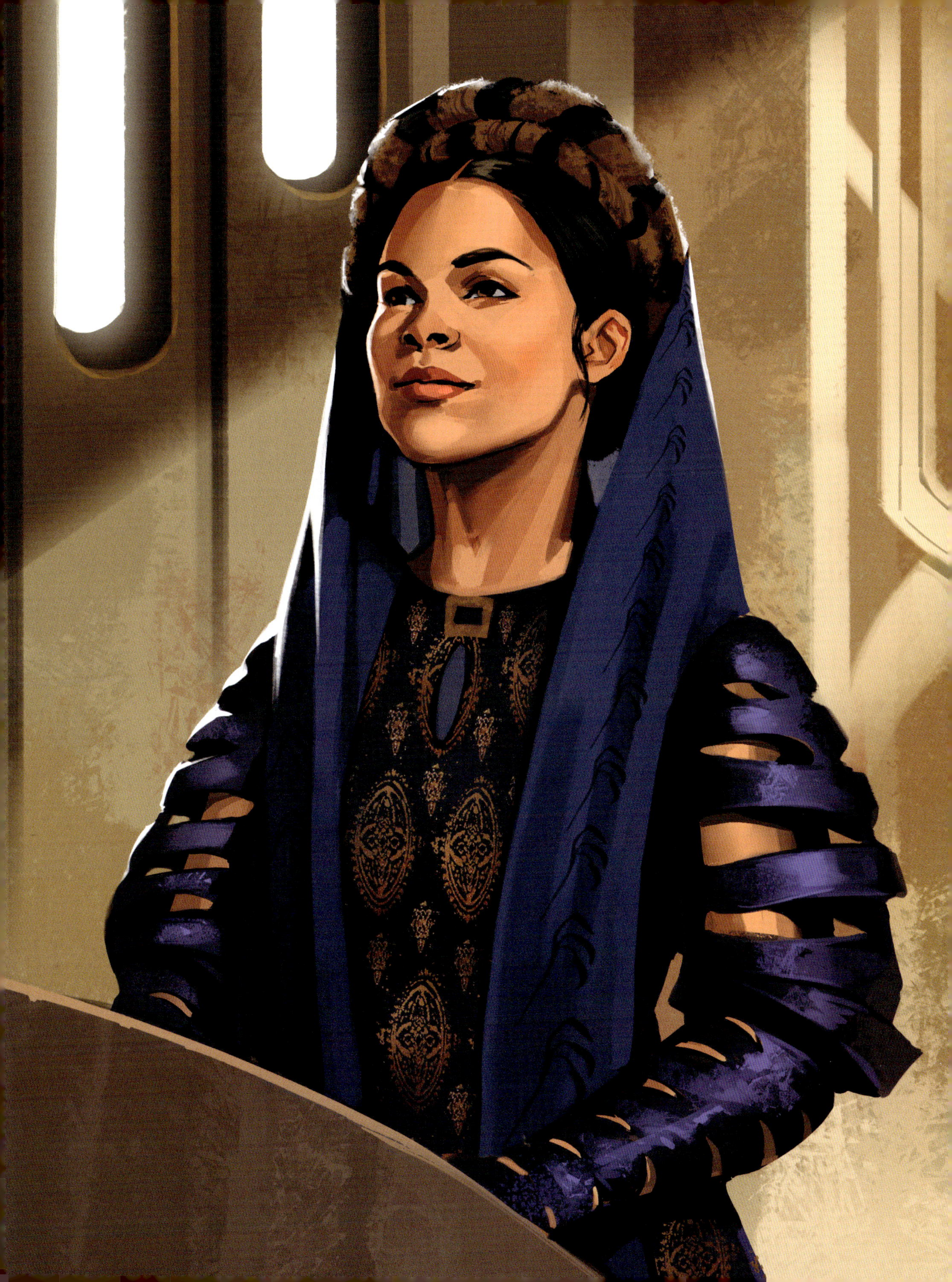

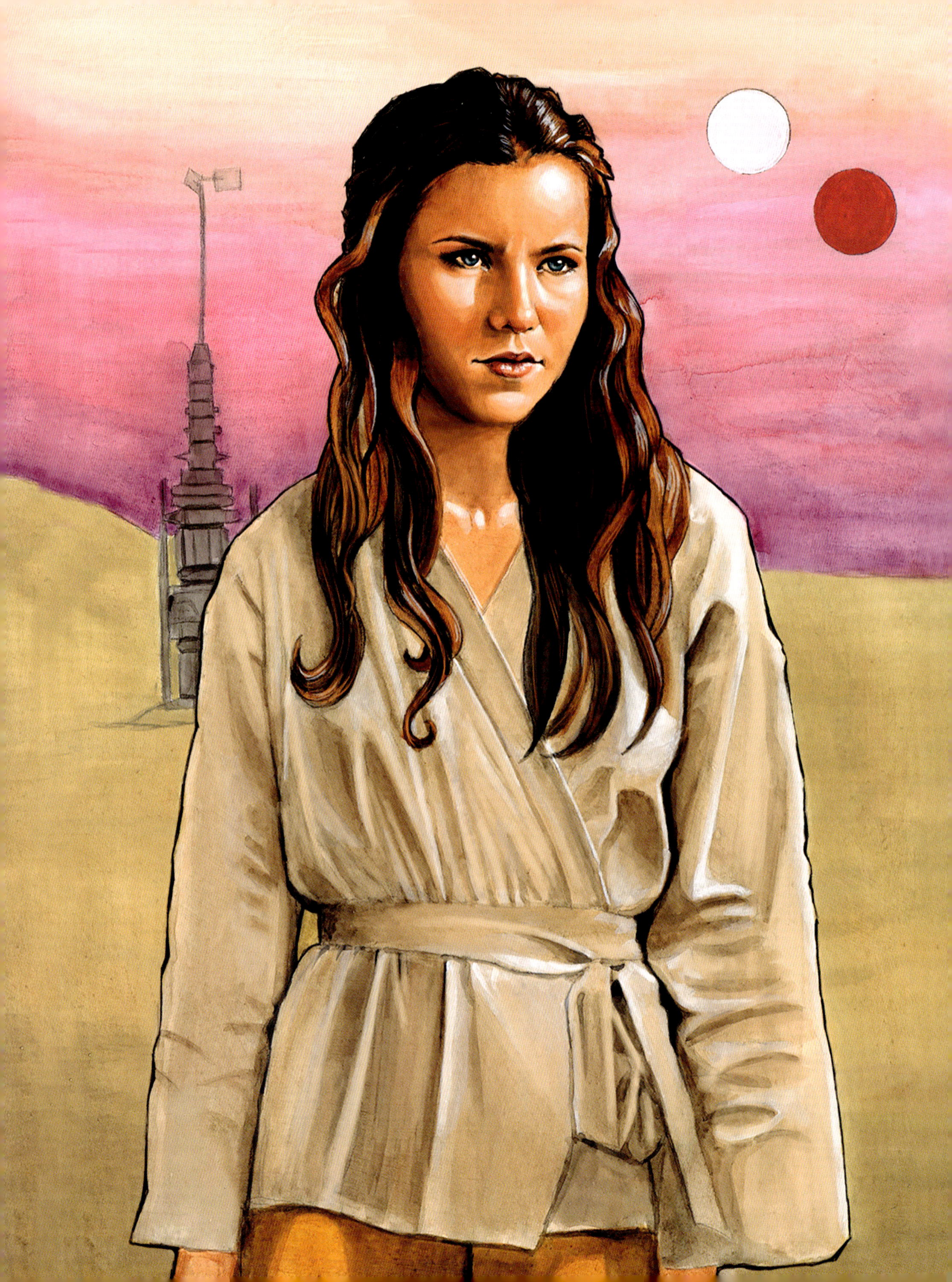

Camie Marstrap

A friend from Tosche Station.

When you grow up on a sleepy planet like Tatooine, you have to take entertainment when and where you can find it. For Camie Marstrap, it means spending her idle time with her boyfriend Fixer Loneozner and her pals at Tosche Station. Yes, she is one of the friends Uncle Owen refers to when he tells Luke, "You can waste time with your friends when your chores are done."

Born to a family of hydroponic gardeners in Anchorhead, Camie gets to know Luke Skywalker because her parents obtain water from the Lars moisture farm. Her playful nature is apparent in deleted scenes from *A New Hope* and in the *Star Wars Radio Drama*, as she teases Luke with his nickname "Wormie" and daydreams about her future with Fixer. But that future might have been different. In the expanded edition of *The Last Jedi* novel, we learn that during his self-imposed exile on Ahch-To, Luke has a dream through the Force about Camie and a life that could have been, if he chose another path and remained on Tatooine—a life in which he's married to Camie. Luke, however, chose a different path, while Camie stayed with Fixer for years to come, as seen in *The Book of Boba Fett*.

Cato Parasitti

A Clawdite bounty hunter who shapeshifts to hide in plain sight.

As a Clawdite, Cato Parasitti can be—or at least assume the shape of—anyone. It's a natural ability that she applies to nefarious purposes in her chosen professions of bounty hunter, assassin, and thief. Working with the legendary bounty hunter Cad Bane to steal a holocron from the Jedi Archives in *Star Wars: The Clone Wars*, she disguises herself as a Jedi Master, as well as Chief Librarian Jocasta Nu.

Cato's shape-shifting powers can lead her to act with boldness, as a getaway is always available with a quick change of her looks, but it can also lead to a sort of fearless overconfidence. On a mission to kill Queen Amidala, while disguised as one of her handmaidens, she is discovered when she makes a telling error of etiquette, through an incorrect table setting, and is thwarted by Padmé and Ahsoka Tano.

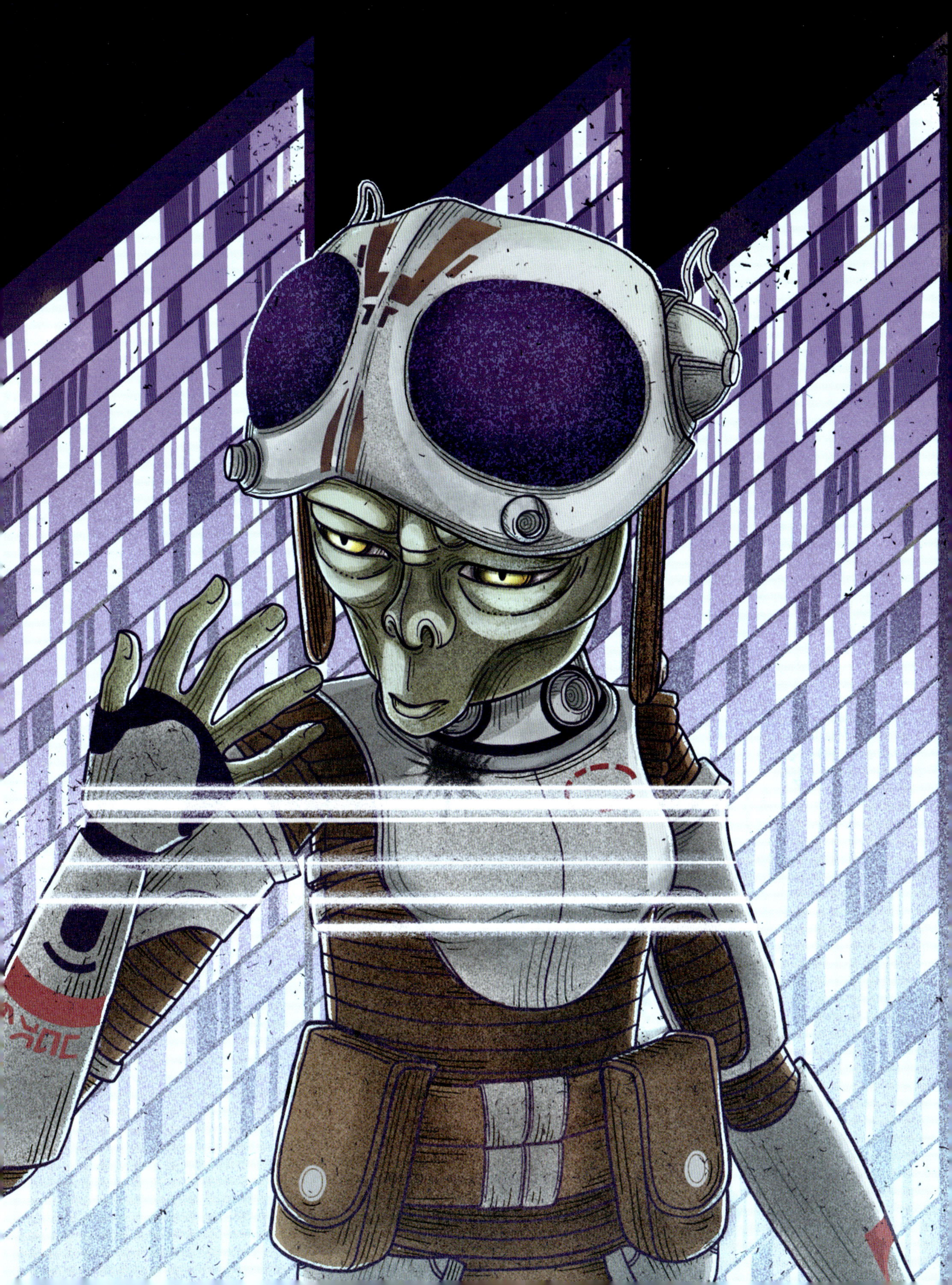

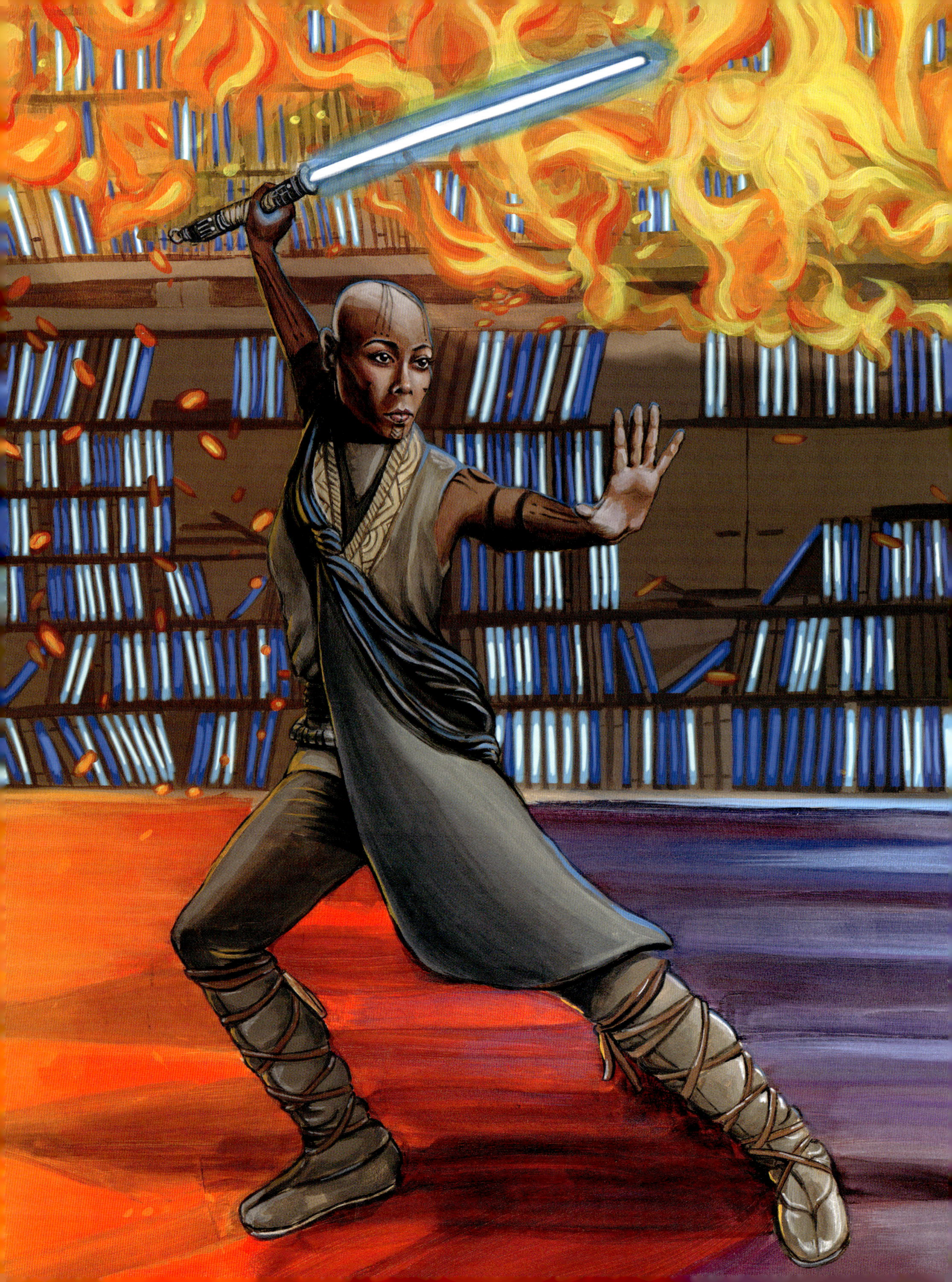

Cere Junda

"It's the choice to keep fighting that makes us who we are."

Survivor's guilt haunts many Jedi who lived through Order 66. Cere Junda is a young Jedi Knight when the galaxy comes under Imperial rule. She and her Padawan, Trilla Suduri, protect Jedi younglings from the execution of Order 66, but Cere is captured and tortured, finally breaking and revealing Trilla's location. The Empire captures Trilla, then tortures her until she succumbs to the dark side and becomes an Inquisitor. When the Empire brings Trilla, now known as the Second Sister, before Cere to underscore her failure, Cere makes a violent escape from her imprisonment. She feels guilt and rage, and uses the dark side to kill everyone in the room and on her path to escape—everyone except her former Padawan. That moment—and her remorse over giving up her Padawan—scar her conscience so deeply that she comes to suppress her connection to the Force. Cere would rather not be reminded of all she lost.

But Cere finds the courage to heal. Rather than cling to guilt, she decides to do what she can to locate and help other Jedi survivors. She undertakes a secret mission: to rebuild the Jedi Order. She hires and befriends a pilot, Greez Dritus, and together they follow leads about other Jedi survivors. This is how she discovers former Jedi Padawan Cal Kestis and helps him escape the Empire. She puts aside her painful history and takes Cal on as a mentee. In teaching Cal to trust in the Force again, Cere further repairs her connection to it. She becomes less afraid of herself, more confident, and more sure in her goal to restore the Jedi. On Jedha, she connects with the Hidden Path, a safe house network that shelters Force users and others the Empire seeks to harm or control; Cere wasn't saved by the Path, but she gets involved to help others.

Cere's trajectory is one of admirable resilience and self-acceptance. She transforms her tragedy into kindness and her losses into possibilities.

Ciena Ree

"Everything I fought for is a lie."

What's the value of honor and loyalty when you fail to examine what lies underneath? It's a question committed Imperial Officer Ciena Ree must confront in the novel *Lost Stars*.

Ciena and her parents are so-called First Waver settlers on the Outer Rim planet of Jelucan, raised in a culture where resources are slim, and honor and keeping your word come above all else. She spends most of her life allied with the Empire, filing away and rationalizing the atrocities she sees. And she wears a leather bracelet in honor of her twin sister, who died within hours of being born, reminding herself to live for both of them by reciting the phrase, "Look through my eyes." It is on Jelucan that she meets aristocrat Second Waver Thane Kyrell, who wasn't raised with the same beliefs, but the two bond over a mutual adoration for flying and starships. They work together to hone their piloting skills, and their commitment earns them admittance to the Royal Imperial Academy on Coruscant. Ciena's dedication is evident in the countless extra hours of study and practice she logs. After graduating, she earns a promotion to lieutenant and serves on Darth Vader's personal Star Destroyer. Her Imperial career advances, and she attains the rank of captain after the Battle of Endor at the age of twenty-five. She's so loyal that many view her as an ideal Imperial, but she is conflicted by the Empire's actions, a feeling that's exacerbated when Thane, whom she has fallen in love with, defects to the Rebel Alliance.

She remains an Imperial soldier from the Battle of Yavin to the Battle of Jakku because of the promise she made when she enlisted, a promise she holds above all else. After she's captured by the New Republic during the Battle of Jakku, she tells Thane, "I was so dedicated to honor that I became a war criminal."

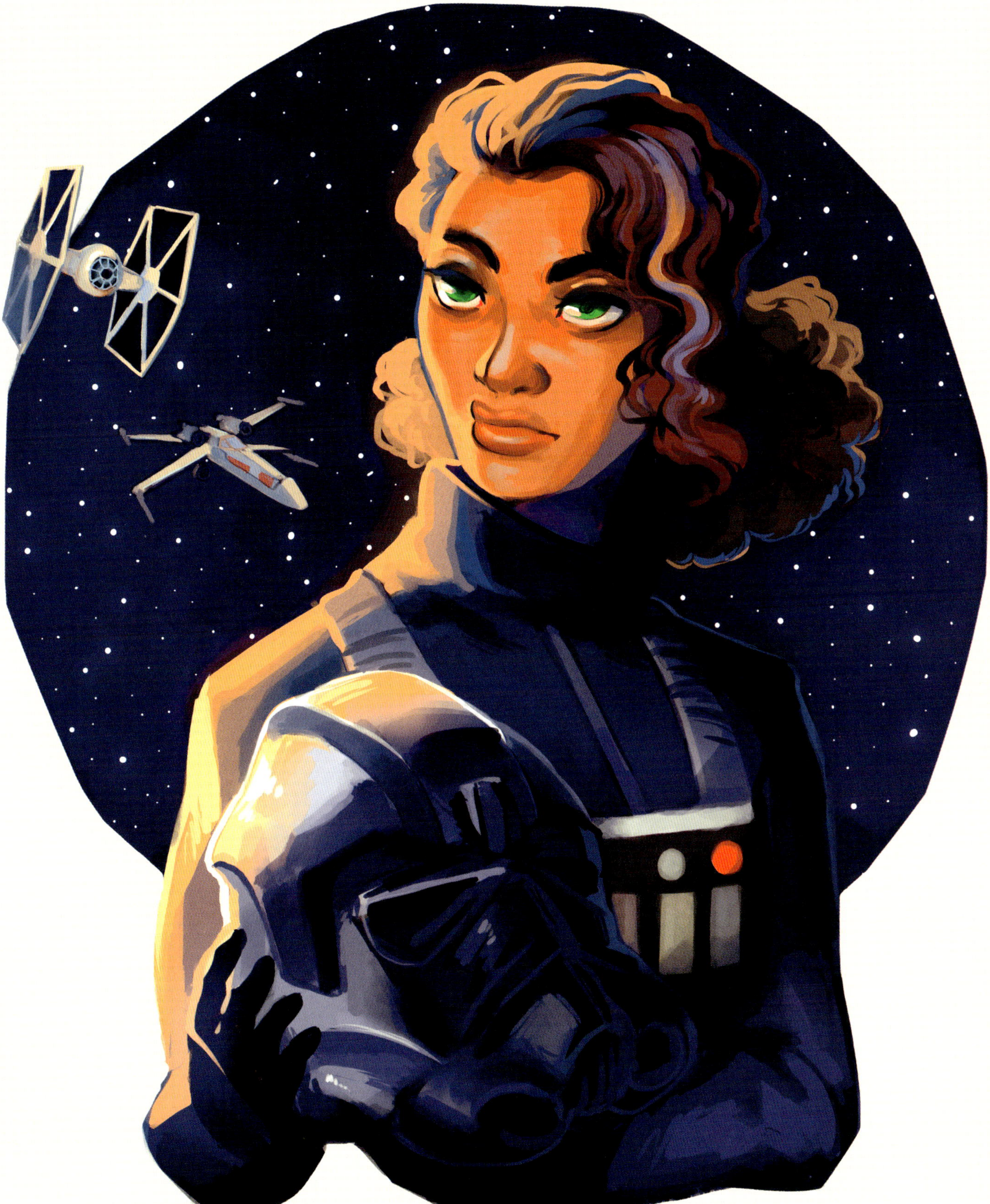

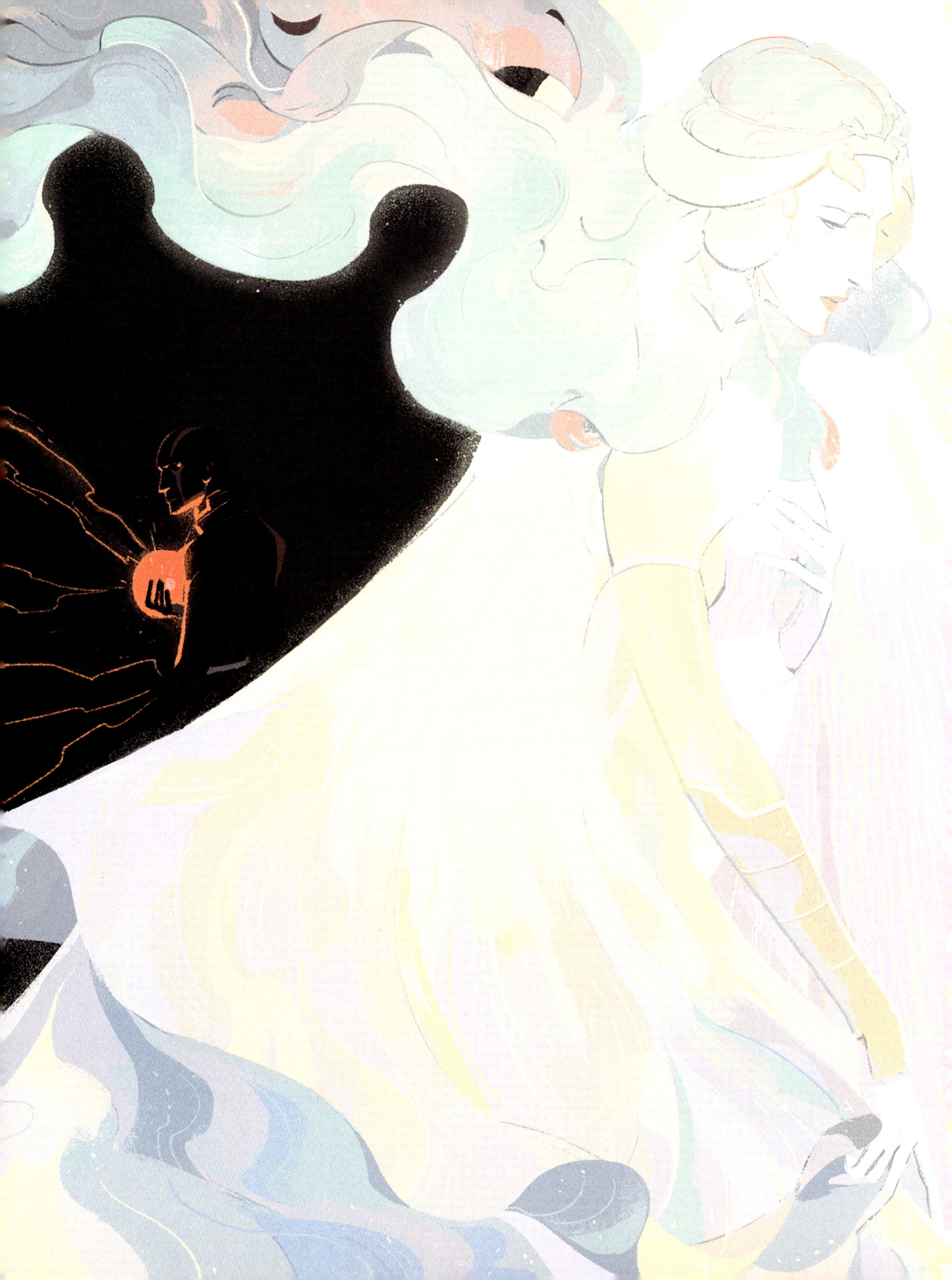

Daughter

"My nature is to do what is selfless, but my brother's will always be to do what is selfish."

Part of an exceptionally powerful family of Force-wielding beings called the Ones, introduced in *The Clone Wars*, Daughter is the manifestation of the light side of the Force. Her brother, Son, is the representation for the dark side, and their Father keeps them, and the Force, in balance in their existence on Mortis, a world situated outside of normal spacetime.

As we meet them, Father is growing weary, and hopes to enlist the prophesied Chosen One to maintain this balance, an individual who turns out to be Anakin Skywalker. After Anakin, Obi-Wan Kenobi, and Ahsoka Tano are lured to Mortis, Daughter protects them from Son's anger and hatred, taking both human and griffin form. In a selfless act, she sacrifices herself to protect her Father, and further grants her remaining life energy to revive a fallen Ahsoka. Father and Son die in conflict, Son at Anakin's hand, and balance is restored, closing for the moment a chapter unlike anything previously seen in the *Star Wars* galaxy. Morai, a bird with a spiritual tie to Daughter, continues to watch over Ahsoka.

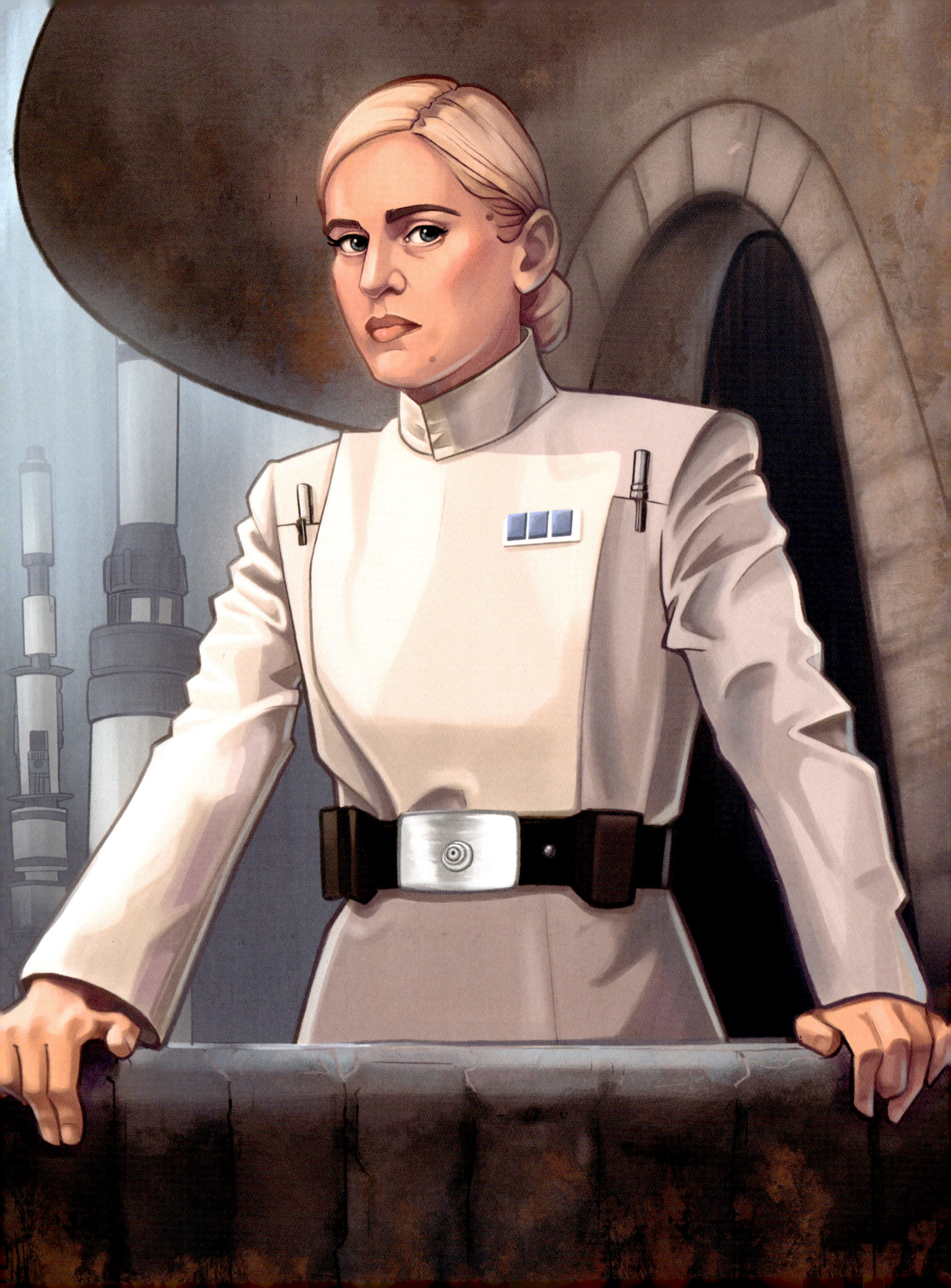

Dedra Meero

"The very worst thing you can do right now is bore me."

A lieutenant and supervisor working for the Imperial Security Bureau, Dedra Meero thrives when rules and order reign. She is unquestionably a villain, but because she is a woman working her way up through the ranks in a male-dominated workplace, Dedra has an underdog quality that helps us root for her. Even while she's hunting Cassian Andor and sniffing out rebellious activity—without emotion or remorse over how she treats others—she's doing so in an incredibly competent way that seems admirable, if also amoral. It certainly makes her an alluring and frightening adversary.

Dedra is about precision. Uniform crisp, hair pulled into a tight bun, she is figuratively *and* literally the antithesis of messy. That rigidity, paired with tenacity and intelligence, helps her rise above her peers at the ISB and successfully root out Cassian, getting closer to uncovering the mysterious Axis. With an unimpeachable work ethic, Dedra is the very picture of unflagging devotion to the Empire. The Rix Road riot against Imperial forces on Ferrix may teach Dedra a little about vulnerability, but it also may prove every negative belief she has about those who resist the Empire.

Years before casting her as Dedra Meero, *Andor* showrunner Tony Gilroy saw Denise Gough onstage in *People, Places and Things*. Something in her performance convinced him she would be right for the ruthless character. Gough, who wasn't familiar with *Star Wars* at the time, observes that Dedra considers herself something of a heroine, and that her drive is to help save the Empire, enabling it to control everyone and everything—to her mind, for the better.

Depa Billaba

"The universe is far from static. And as it changes, a Jedi's role in it must evolve."

— DEPA BILLABA

Orphaned by space pirates as a girl, Depa Billaba and her sister are rescued by Mace Windu from their homeworld of Chalacta and taken to Coruscant, where they find a home in the Jedi Temple and join the Order. Force-sensitive, intelligent, and measured, Depa trains under Windu and follows the Jedi code, eventually landing a place on the Jedi Council. She stands by her beliefs, even when they're not popular, such as her disapproval of the Jedi taking military titles during the Clone Wars.

Introduced in *The Phantom Menace*, the Jedi Master known for her wisdom also demonstrates incredible resilience, recovering from intense injuries inflicted by General Grievous when other Jedi didn't think she would bounce back. After healing, she takes on a Padawan learner, Caleb Dume, a.k.a. Kanan Jarrus from *Star Wars Rebels*. Depa imparts invaluable lessons to Caleb, particularly the importance of sacrifice, and she protects him when clone troopers implement the murderous Order 66, giving her life to save his. Her sacrifice allows Caleb to pass down her wisdom to his own Jedi Padawan, Ezra Bridger.

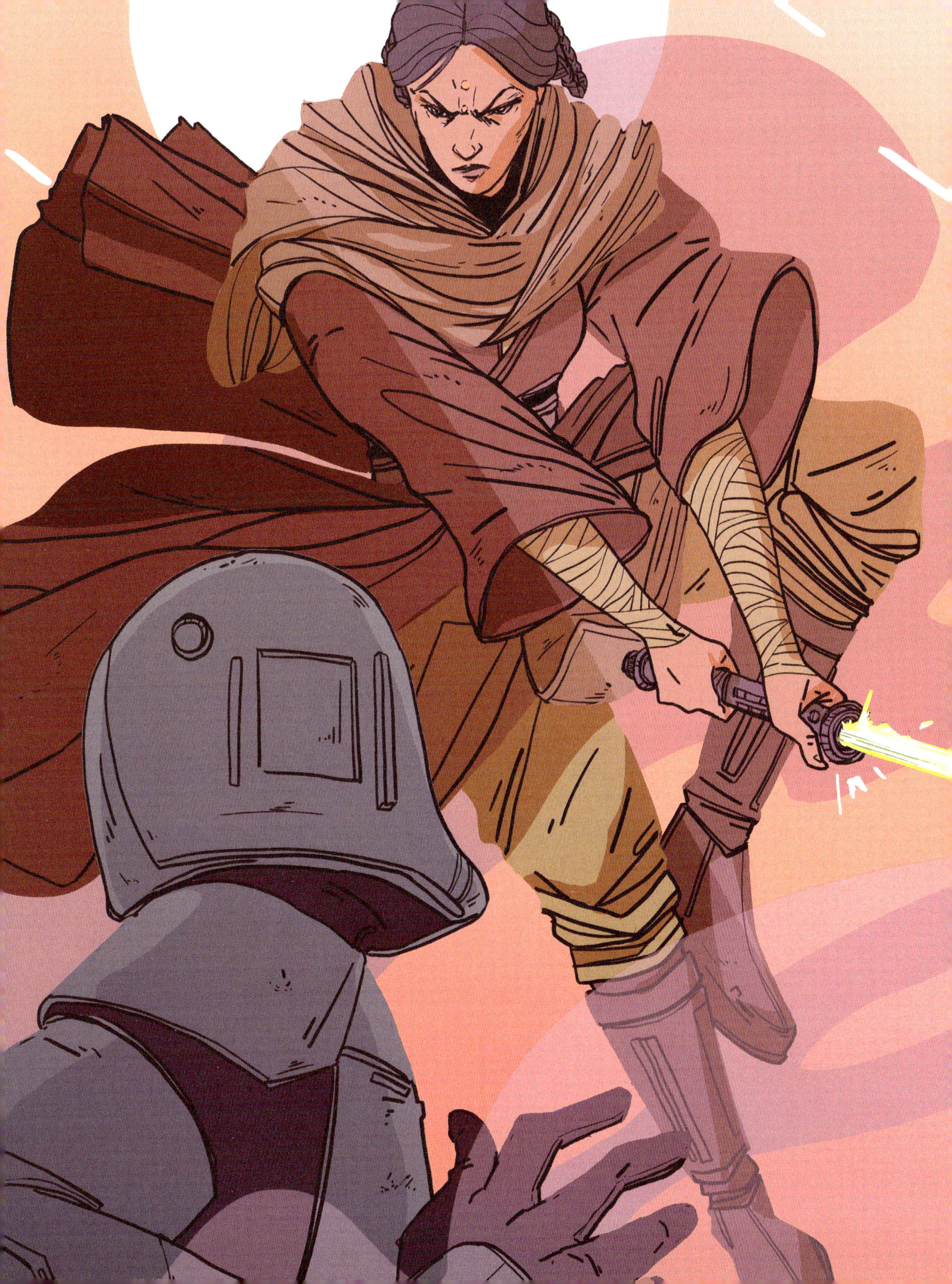

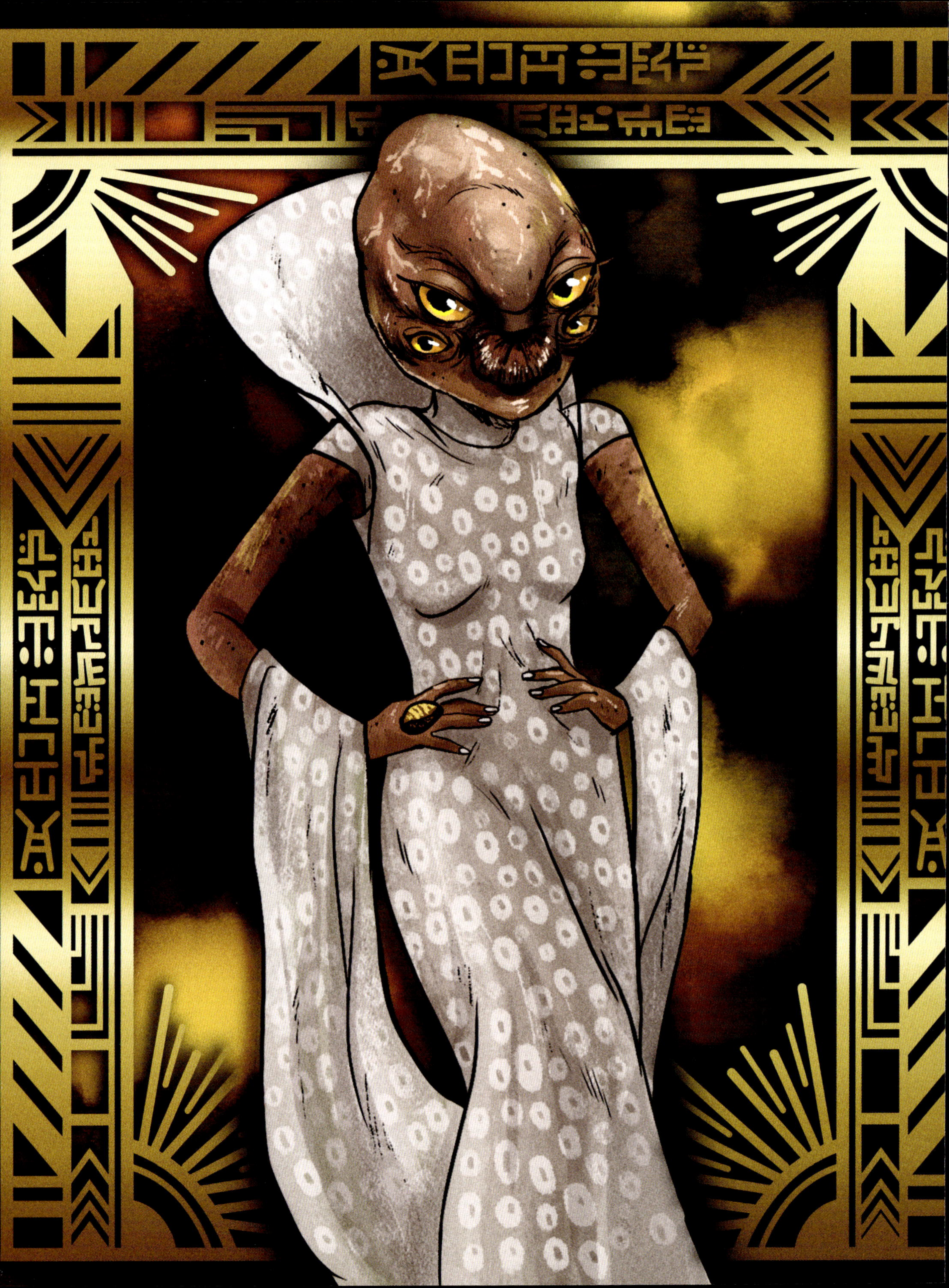

Derla Pidys

*"Bravery should be rewarded in the present,
as it may not be treated so kindly by the future."*

—DERLA PIDYS

Shrewd and business-savvy, Derla Pidys finds success in a job never before highlighted in *Star Wars*: she's a sommelier. A purveyor of wine and liquor around the galaxy, Derla places equal emphasis on the product and the story it can tell. She excels at crafting a narrative that can turn an ordinary product into the stuff of fantasy for a wealthy clientele. First introduced in the story "The Wine in Dreams" in the collection *Canto Bight*, she is "the one to call when everything must be *perfect*."

Her palate is legendary, and Derla knows the substance of an alcoholic beverage from a single sip. The skill helps her leverage every possible credit from any liquid. The rest of the asking price comes from reading her buyers and understanding the intricacies of presentation. This is why, when we see her in the Canto Bight environs in *The Last Jedi*, she may be one of the few who can leave the casino city as a winner.

Doctor Chelli Aphra

"You know, you can trust me, but you shouldn't."

When rogue archaeologist and thief Doctor Chelli Lona Aphra makes her debut in the pages of Marvel's *Darth Vader* comic, fearlessly wending her way through a series of deadly security measures and wryly narrating her progress, it's an unforgettable entrance. Renowned for recovering hard-to-find artifacts (often of the "can be used as weapons" variety) and using her tech know-how to reactivate them, she doesn't believe relics of the past should be gathering dust in a museum; she thinks they should be put to use (primarily to turn a profit for herself) and after that, it's none of her concern. Among her creations are a fan-celebrated pair of so-called murder droids, a violent protocol droid called 0-0-0 and deadly astromech designated BT-1, ready to do (or do in) anything or anyone Aphra asks. Her attitude, talents, and moral ambiguity make her an optimal candidate for the secretive work Darth Vader has in mind after the Battle of Yavin, and he recruits her as a key ally.

Aphra's fast talk and cutting humor makes it seem as if she's not afraid of the Sith Lord (though she admits he makes her a little nervous), and their byplay has a lighter touch we're not used to seeing in relation to Vader. She clearly respects him, and strives to prove her worth, whether she's acquiring a personal army of battle droids for him or investigating a very personal matter—like whether Padmé gave birth before she died. Aphra's very much aware that working

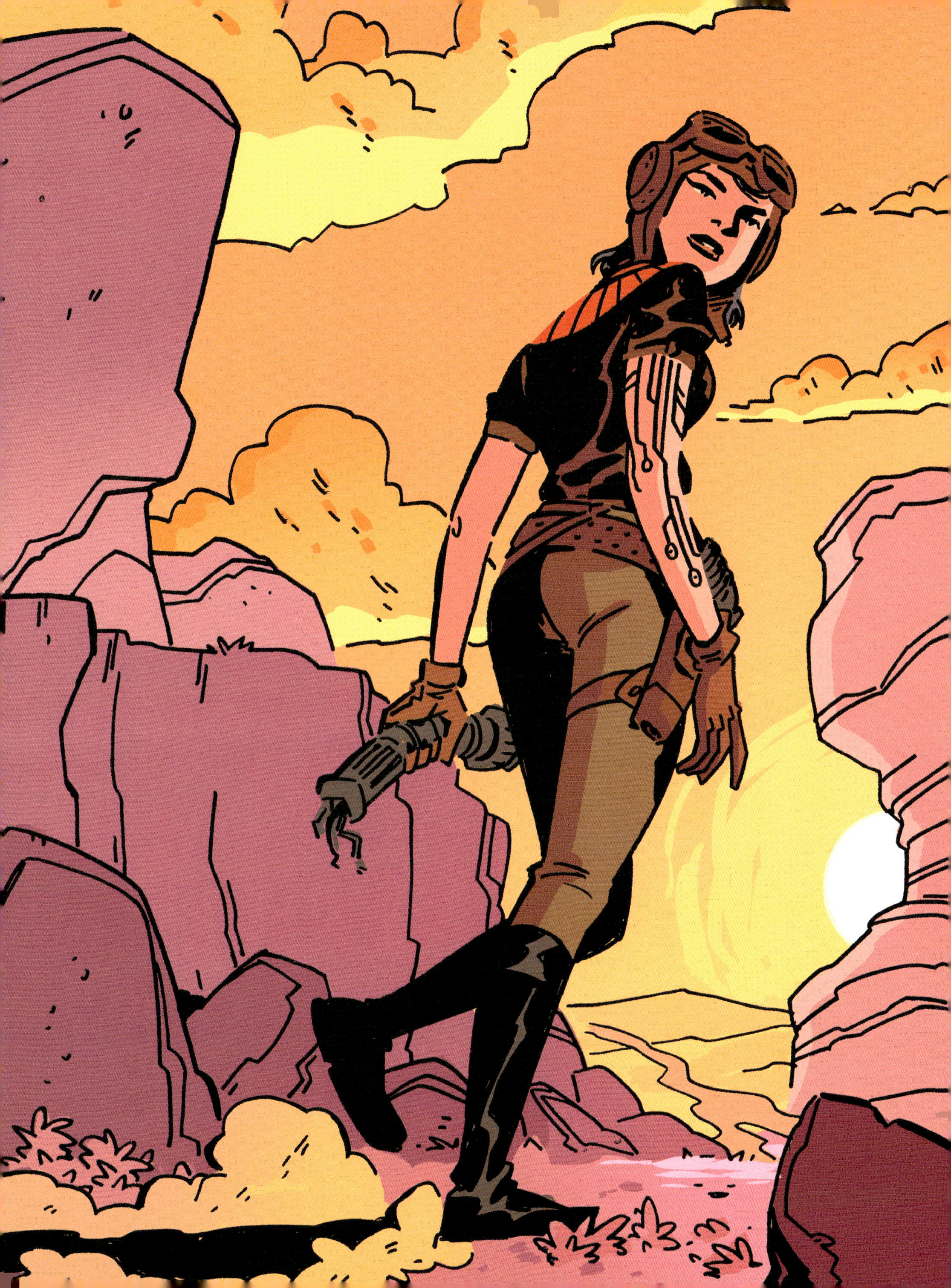

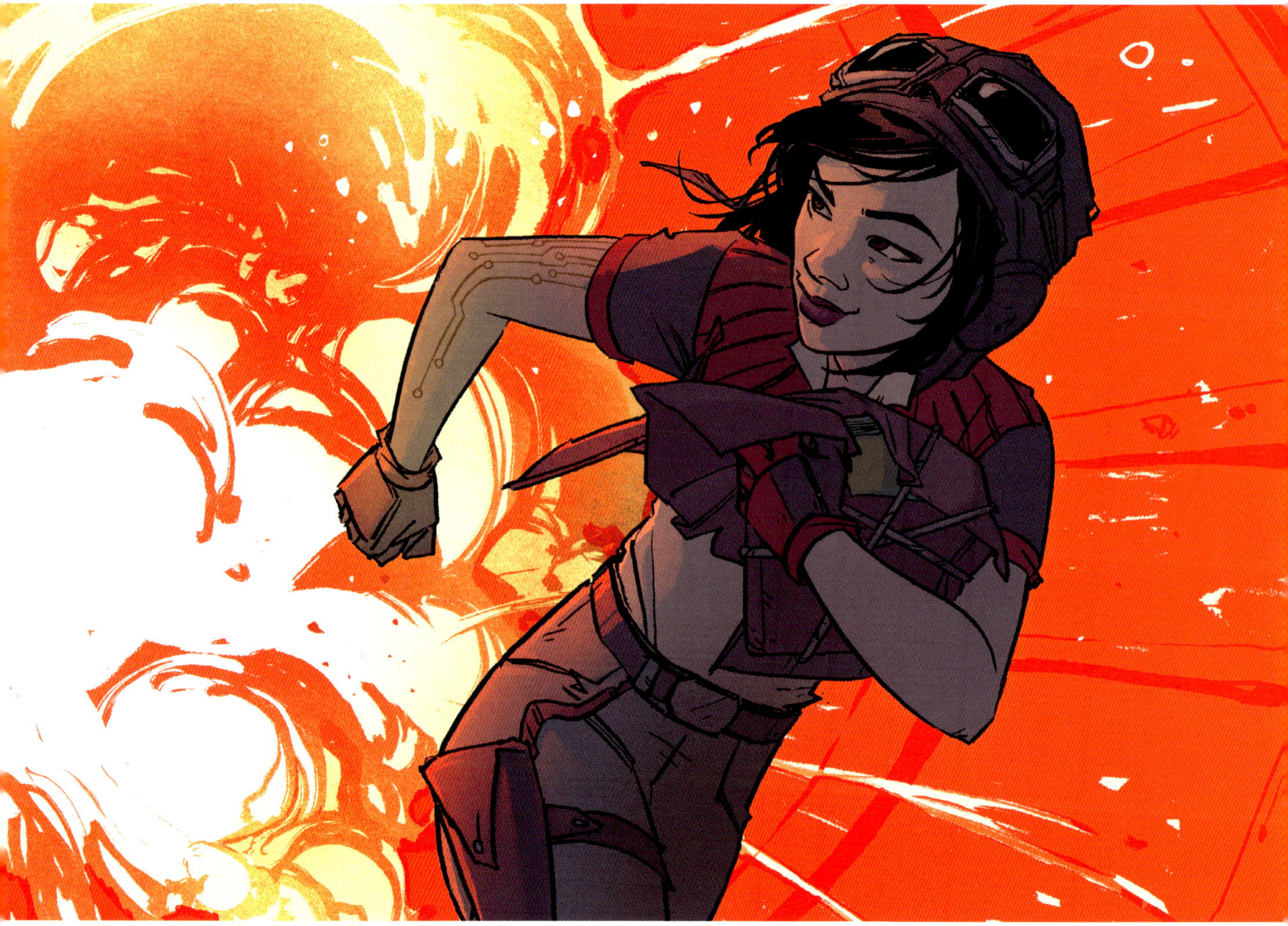

“Turns out even I have my ethical limits.”
—Doctor Chelli Aphra

with Vader is likely to end one way for her: in death. She's prepared, but not resigned: "The way I've lived I know I'm lucky to be alive."

The fan response to Aphra was instant and enthusiastic. Her debut comic issue ran through multiple printings, a popular vote saw her chosen to join Hasbro's Vintage Series action figure line, and cosplayers have been recreating Aphra's adventuring ensemble and sprawling electro-tattoos at conventions ever since. Her arc in the *Vader* comic sees her evading execution at the Sith Lord's hands to go on to star in her own comic series, *Doctor Aphra*.

Heather Antos, who edited the comic for Marvel, understands why fans appreciate Aphra. "She's such a fascinating character—she's not a hero, but she isn't a villain either. Not to mention she has some of the best sidekicks the *Star Wars* universe has ever seen! Between working for the galaxy's most evil Sith Lord, and then turning hero to help Princess Leia fight her way out of a hostage situation, you never know what sort of trouble Aphra will get herself into—and out of. Every page is an adventure."

Adventure is Aphra's specialty, to which she brings her own brand of luck—solving problems on the fly and speeding out of trouble in her ship, the *Ark Angel*. She finds the dodge-and-weave approach doesn't work quite as well in her personal life. For instance, Aphra meets Sana Starros while studying at the University of Bar'leth, and they become an item. But things fall apart after Aphra leaves without saying goodbye and breaks Sana's heart. The next several times Sana runs into her ex, Aphra, she tries to kill her.

While she's hunting for artifacts around the galaxy, Aphra's path crosses with rebels and Imperials alike. Aphra works with Vader again, she works for the rebels but also hunts rebel bases for the Empire, she teams up with bounty hunters—always on the hunt for artifacts and valuable technology. Throughout her ever-shifting partnerships, she is only truly allied with herself. She doesn't form many personal bonds, but she does build a heated relationship with Magna Tolvan, an Imperial lieutenant who receives a demotion after an entanglement with Aphra. She also rekindles a spark with Sana.

While she has no commitment to either side of the Galactic Civil War, she sees the rebels as particularly misguided. *Darth Vader* and *Doctor Aphra* writer Kieron Gillen addresses Aphra's personal moral path: "She believes in the Empire in a weird way, she just doesn't really want to obey them. She kind of thinks the Empire is probably, on the larger scale of things, good."

Enfys Nest

"The war has just begun."

Nothing says mystery like a mask. Enfys Nest's role in *Solo: A Star Wars Story* was wrapped in secrecy, with promotional material revealing only that Enfys was a marauder and leader of a pirate gang with an intimidating reputation. A helmet covers the character's face and a vocal modulator distorts the pirate's voice. We see Enfys foil the criminal organization Crimson Dawn's plans repeatedly before we learn her true identity near the end of the film: a teenage girl with noble intentions.

A sixteen-year-old who inherits leadership of the Cloud-Riders and her striking armor from her mother, Enfys operates with consideration for the greater good, using resources her gang acquires to help those in need. Her gang, which includes the likes of Weazel from *The Phantom Menace* and Benthic Two Tubes from *Rogue One*, is like an early version of a rebel partisan group. Enfys knows change is on the horizon, and she's already positioned her team to be part of the fight. While the Empire is a looming and imminent threat, her more immediate focus is on Crimson Dawn, driven by her vendetta against them for what they've done to her family and innocents on planets like Savareen. In the shadow of advancing Imperial evil, Enfys's targets highlight the damage caused by seedy underbelly groups like Crimson Dawn and the Pyke Syndicate.

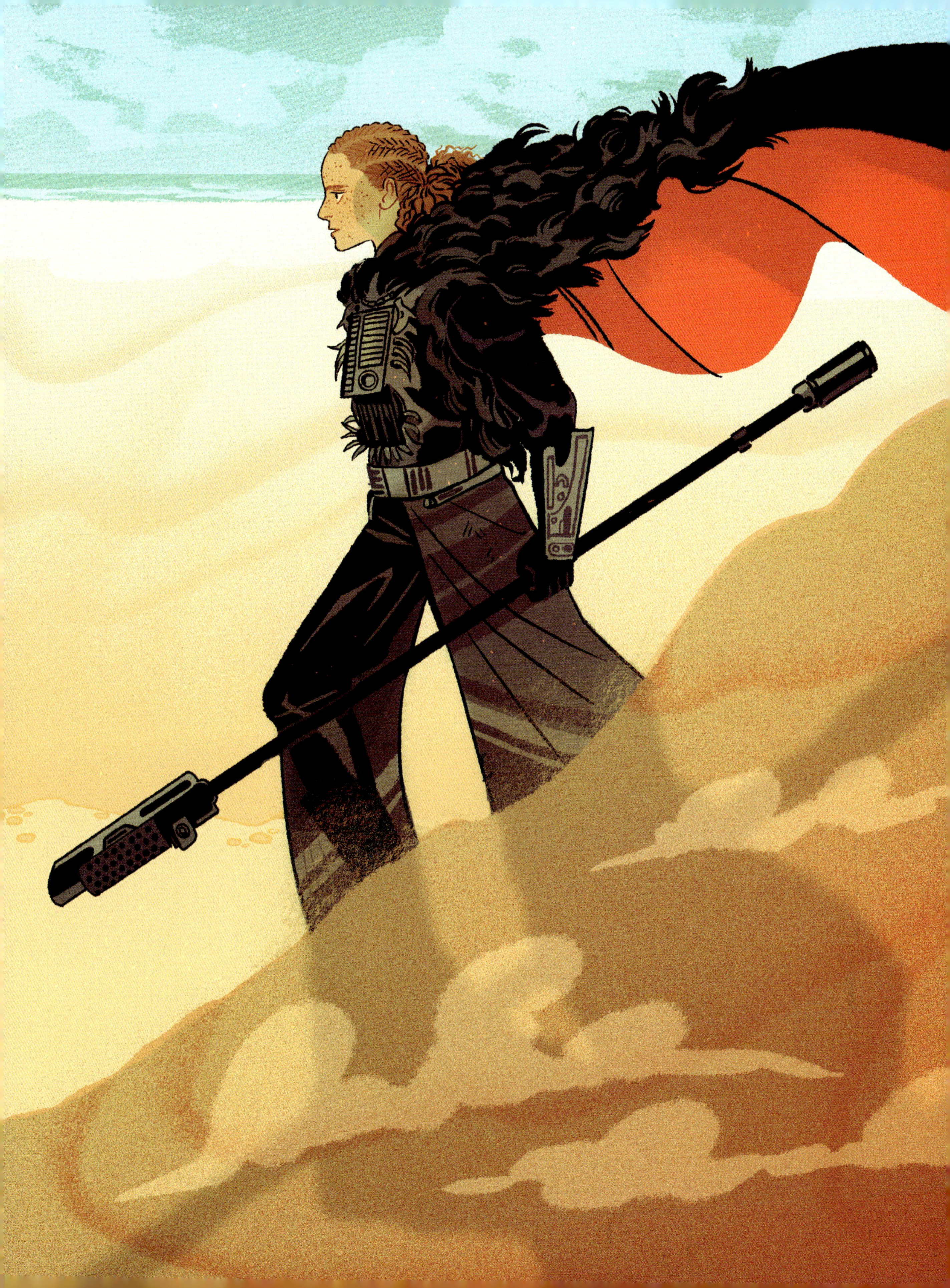

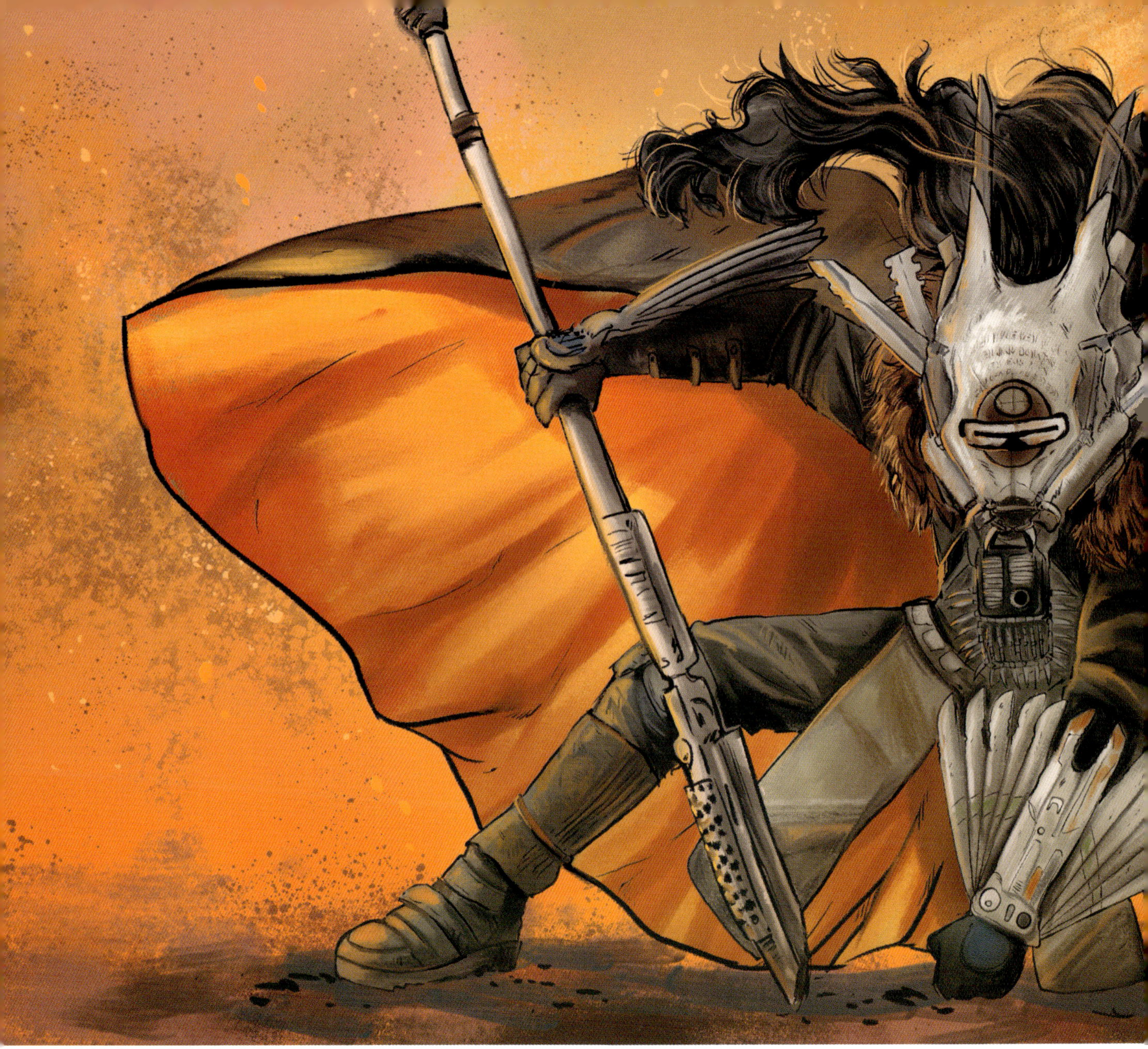

"Until we reach the last edge, the last opening, the last star, and can go no higher."
—Enfys Nest

Crimson Dawn gangster Dryden Vos sees Enfys and her Cloud-Riders as a nagging irritation. Operating nimble and colorful swoop bikes, the Cloud-Riders are like a motorcycle gang in the sky. They go after the same jobs Vos pursues, and so in *Solo* we see Enfys pitted against the criminal Tobias Beckett and his cohorts. With weapons and gadgets scrapped together from whatever they can get their hands on, the Cloud-Riders form a menacing and proficient crew under Enfys's guidance, often scooping assets out from the clutches of animal gangs. When they get the valuable starship fuel coaxium, stolen from Kessel, Enfys opens Han's eyes to the stakes of the situation and demonstrates to him that you can choose an act of conscience.

Enfys reveals who she is in that moment, but it's easy to understand why she disguises her age and gender. By making herself an enigma, she gives herself notoriety. Rumors swirl about who is under the mask, making Enfys larger than life. And of course, her prowess with her electoripper staff and her swoop bike, a modified Skyblade-330, contribute to her legend. She blends her fighting styles to make it near impossible to nail down her origins. The only outward identification reveals are the symbols on her armor and the paint job on her bike, declaring her membership in her gang.

Her part in the film was solidified in early drafts, but Enfys's appearance was left to art and costume design and took months to finalize. The singular character needed a signature look, and Lucasfilm design supervisor James Clyne had the idea of envisioning her as the leader of a biker gang. Creating the mask was the most complex aspect of her design, taking at least a year to complete. The final look combines alien bone and chrome to communicate the mix of organic and machinery, which is echoed throughout the Cloud-Riders aesthetic.

Enfys Nest's mask is recognized in the galaxy; it's associated with power and might. But Enfys's true power is that she is sure of herself and her role. Her age doesn't limit her abilities, and she uses her confidence to motivate others.

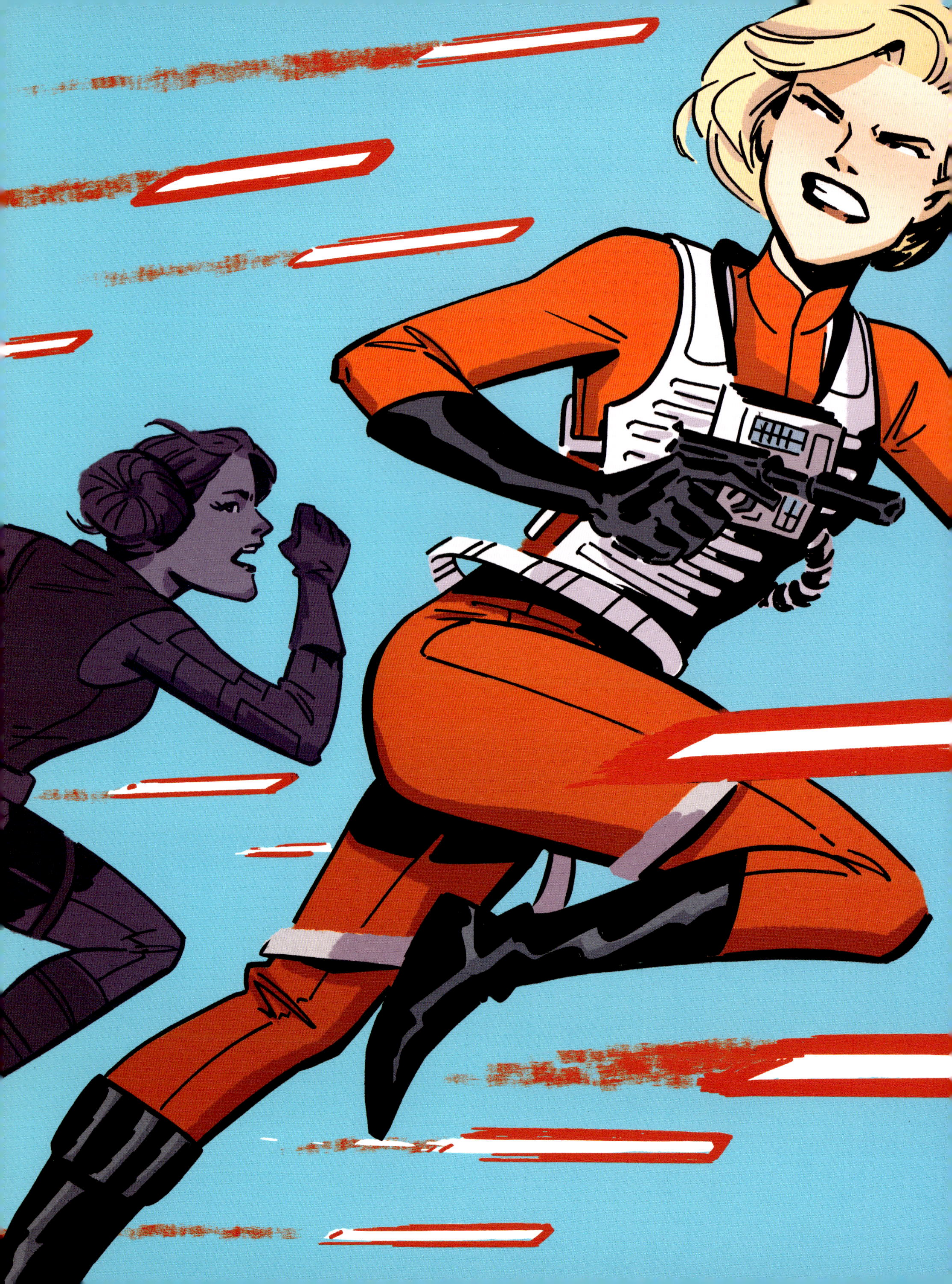

Evaan Verlaine

"First among the legacies I pledge everything to preserve is the life of Your Highness."

An Alderaanian and a member of the Rebel Alliance introduced in Marvel's *Princess Leia* comic, Evaan demonstrates the unreliable nature of snap judgments. At first frustrated by her princess's seeming coldness about the Empire's destruction of their homeworld, she soon learns nothing could be further from the truth, and they form an unbreakable bond.

One of the select few young people mentored by Leia's adoptive mother, Queen Breha Organa, Evaan's respect for all things Alderaanian has no bounds, and her loyalty to Leia as her princess and friend is fierce. She combines her royalist devotion with her piloting skills—she flies her Y-wing in Gold Squadron during the Battles of Scarif and Yavin—to transport herself and Leia around the galaxy and locate other Alderaanian survivors in an effort to preserve their culture and future. She even co-pilots the *Millennium Falcon*, a claim not many others can make.

Everi Chalis

"I understand you're recruiting."

—EVERI CHALIS

Born into desperate poverty—and to a mother who tries to sell her for credits to a Trade Federation captain—Everi Chalis makes her own way in a galaxy that does not grant her an easy path. That she's one of very few characters who survives being Force-choked by Darth Vader shows she's determined and able to play a lucky hand when it's dealt. Enrolling in the Colonial Academy gets her offworld, and her study of art while there draws the attention and apprenticeship of a powerful Imperial count. An efficiency expert for the Empire, she's assigned the governorship of the Mid Rim planet Haidoral Prime. Suspicious that she'll be hung out to dry for the results of a battle on that world, she allows herself to be captured by the Rebel Alliance's Sixty-First Mobile Infantry in *Battlefront: Twilight Company*. She becomes a cooperative prisoner, feeding data about the Empire to the rebels. Although it's not a permanent arrangement, it gets her where she needs to go next.

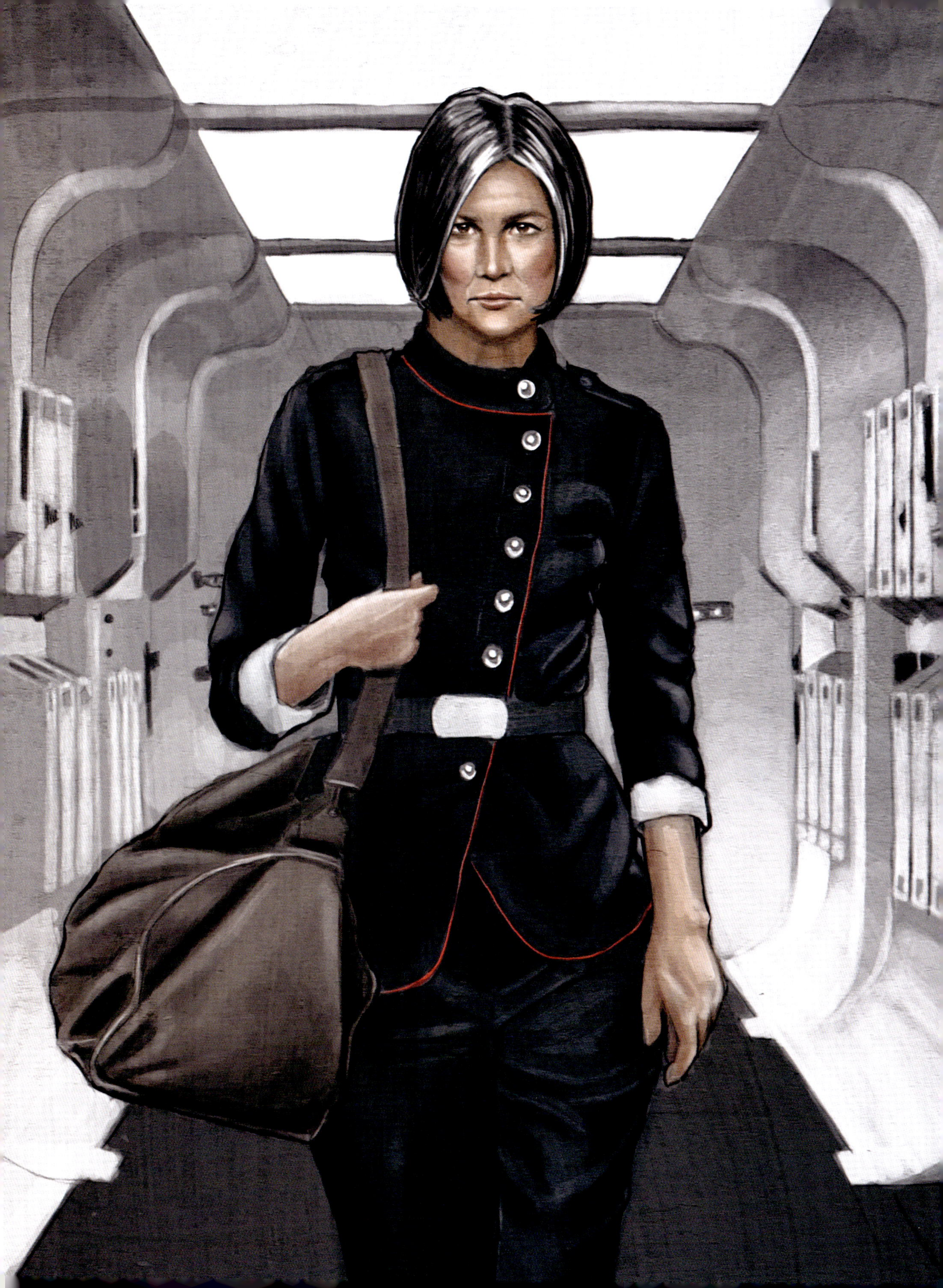

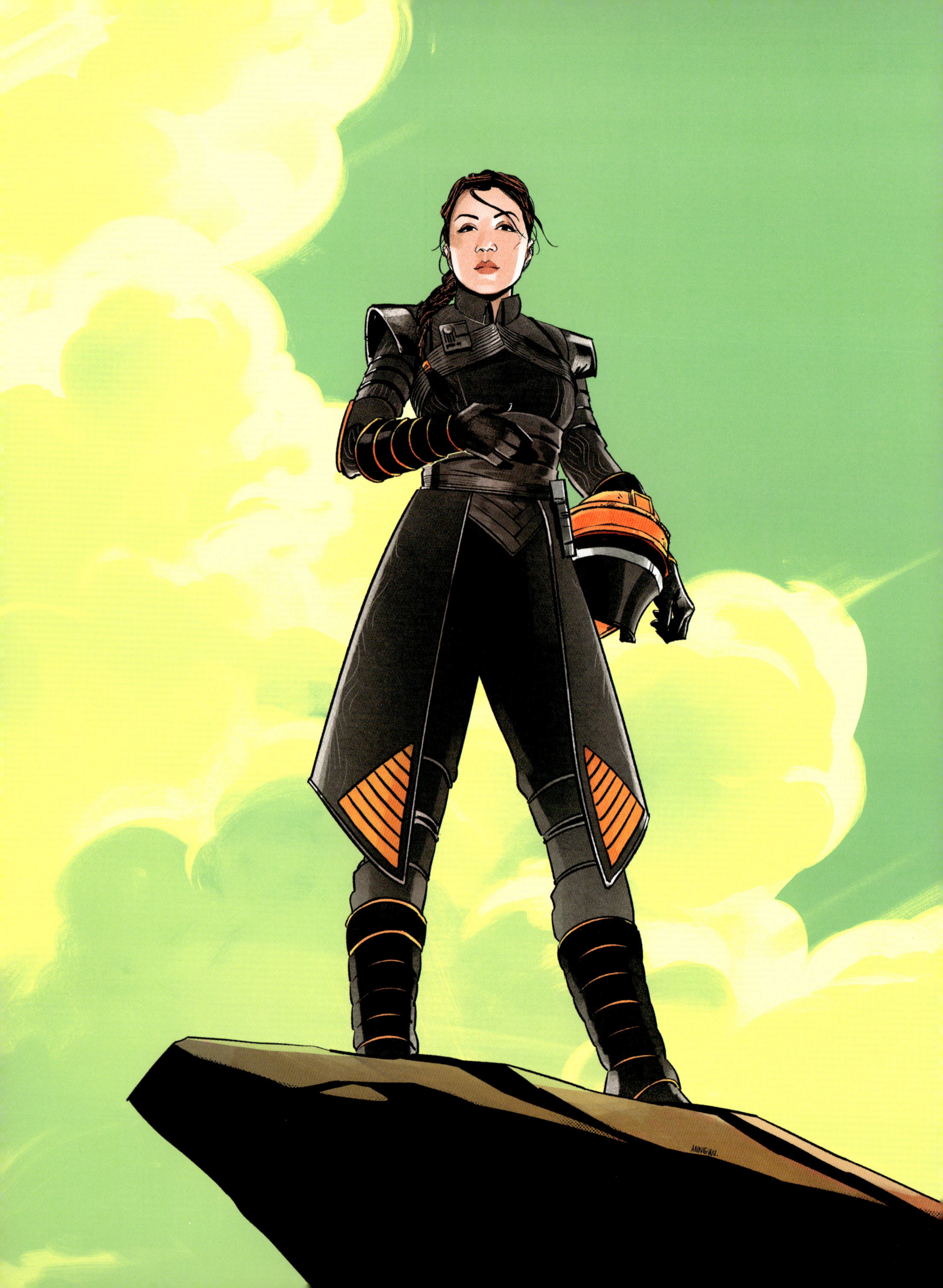
ANNIE WU.

Fennec Shand

"In difficult times, fear is a surer bet."

It's no simple task to make a mark as a mercenary in *Star Wars*. The profession is a crowded one, with multiple bounty hunters jockeying for favor with every criminal organization from Coruscant to the Outer Rim. Anyone trying to earn credits must execute their work quickly and deliver results. Fennec Shand establishes a ruthless reputation for herself when she begins her bounty hunting career in the wake of the Clone Wars. Even the infamous Cad Bane soon becomes aware of Fennec and her skills.

After years of successful jobs, Fennec eventually earns the title of Master Assassin. Reflecting her successful completion rate and her sharpshooting skills, it allows her to be choosy about her clientele and pricing, working for the wealthiest crime syndicates, such as the Hutts. Her talents also put her on the radar of the Imperial Security Bureau, and later the New Republic, so Fennec stays on the move. However, when a new friend rescues her from near death, her loyalty to him keeps her on Tatooine. Fennec supports Boba Fett's claim to Jabba's throne and coaches the one-time bounty hunter to lead with a firmer hand.

Actress Ming-Na Wen is a massive fan of *Star Wars*, but despite this, she wasn't sure about accepting the role when Jon Favreau offered it because Fennec was only meant to appear one time. But Wen's contributions helped shape Fennec Shand. Dave Filoni says they collaborated on the character; Wen had a huge influence on some of the story logic and Fennec's dialogue. And the character has gone on to factor into a number of stories.

Hera Syndulla

"If all you do is fight for your own life, then your life is worth nothing."

—HERA SYNDULLA

Hera Syndulla doesn't sugarcoat reality. A Twi'lek general in the Rebel Alliance and later the New Republic, she has a clear and unshakable faith in the struggle against the Empire, and puts the galaxy's safety above her own. As captain and pilot of the light freighter the *Ghost*, Hera guides the rebel cell known as the Spectres through dangerous missions and their evolution to an official Alliance squadron, always leading with a clear head and a warm touch. Kanan Jarrus, Zeb Orrelios, Sabine Wren, Ezra Bridger, and the astromech Chopper all depend on her; she is the heart of the team.

Actress Vanessa Marshall voiced Hera from her introduction in *Star Wars Rebels*, and often speaks about her own and fans' enthusiasm for the character: "What I love about Hera is that she manages to be very nurturing and kind, and everything we would want in a mother figure, but she's also very fierce and strong, and her talents in the areas of fighting and flying are also very impressive. Not that those things are mutually exclusive, but I think that she has such an elegant combination of those things, that she makes a pretty powerful icon for young women to look up to. I think anyone can draw strength from her."

The certainty Hera feels in her opposition to the Empire is rooted in her upbringing on the planet Ryloth during the violent conflict

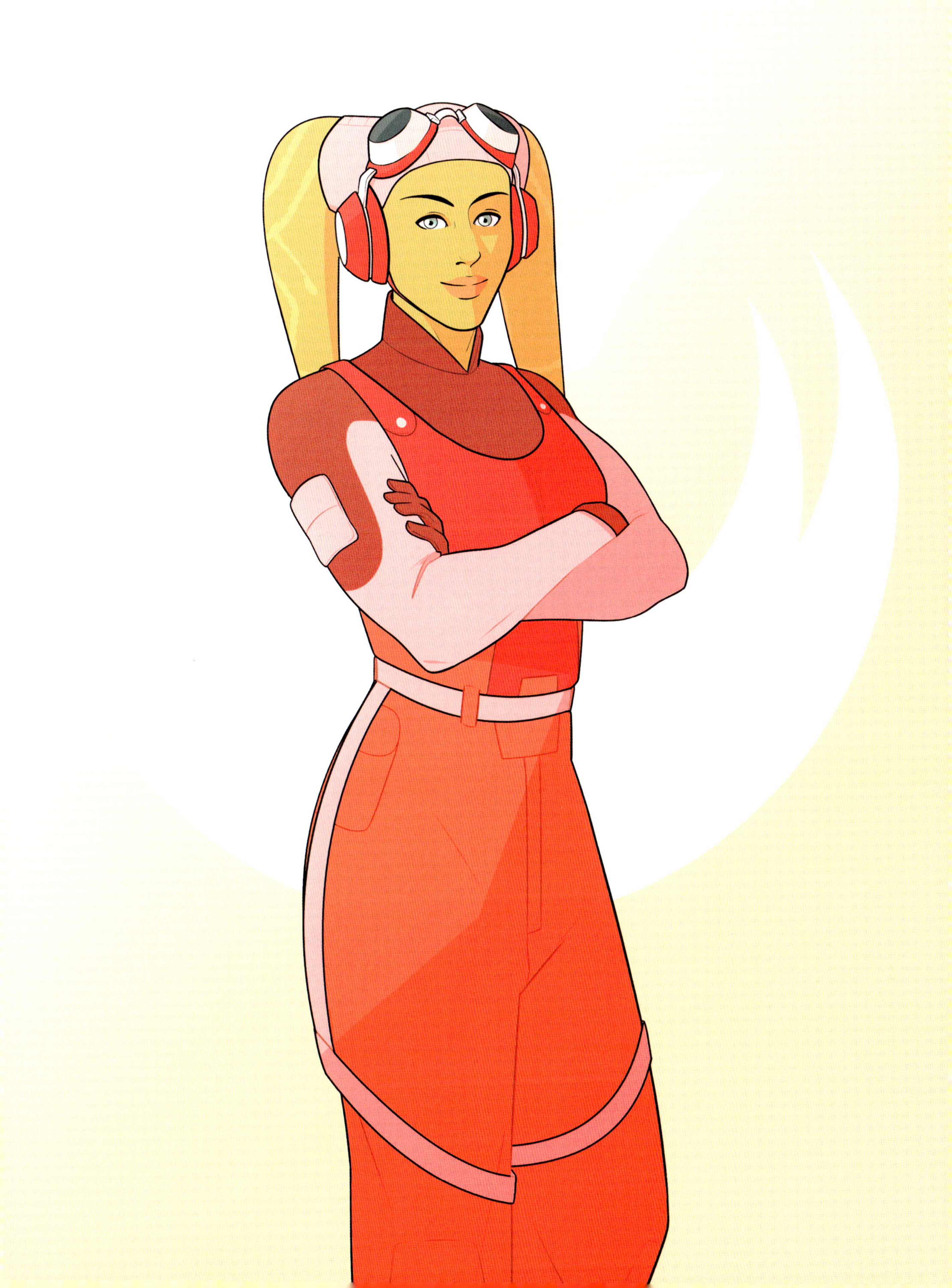

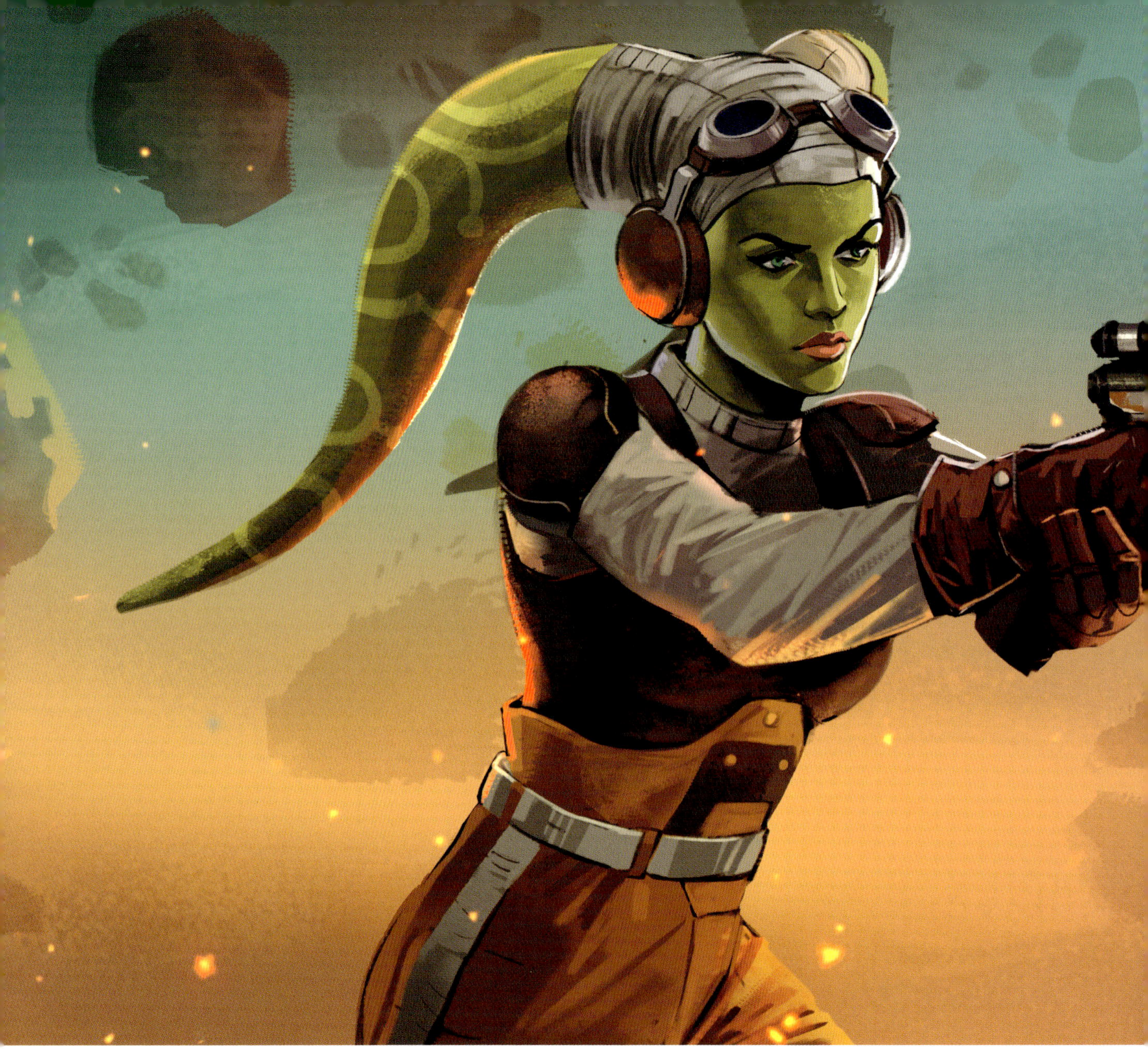

"We have hope; hope that things can get better."
—Hera Syndulla

of the Clone Wars. Grand Admiral Thrawn later tells Hera, "War is in your blood. You were forged by it." And he's right. Hera's mother was killed in the Separatist invasion of their homeworld, and her father, the freedom fighter Cham Syndulla, became focused on resistance above all else. Hera witnesses the hope the freedom fighters give the citizens of Ryloth and internalizes it. She imagines what such action could mean on a bigger scale, so when the Empire tightens its grip on the galaxy and she believes she can help stop them, she takes to the stars to fight back. Although her father would prefer she stay and fight at home, and Hera recognizes the planet's peril, she knows that if the Empire itself is defeated, every planet has a chance at a brighter future.

It's not an easy decision, but it fits perfectly the character's altruistic attitude. Marshall jokes that she sometimes asks herself in her own life, "What would Hera do?" And indeed, to the galaxy's great benefit, while on a mission to gather intelligence on Imperial activities on the planet Gorse, Hera meets Jedi Kanan Jarrus and persuades him to assist her. They end up forming the core of the Spectres.

Hera's leadership style and connection with her crew is unlike other commander and subordinate relationships in *Star Wars*. She knows the Spectres; she knows their strengths, weaknesses, hardships, insecurities, and skills. Hera can plan operations according to who does what best, and she trusts the Spectres to execute their parts. And because she cares about them, she can reach them in meaningful ways. Hera's there for her team members with a pep talk, a hard truth, or whatever else they need. It's this caregiver aspect, adjacent her warrior side, that has led fans to give her the affectionate nickname "Space Mom."

Once the Spectres join forces with other rebel cells and become part of the Phoenix Squadron, Hera receives adulation and advancement, which Marshall describes as challenging for Hera: "With promotion comes a lot of dire consequences that she has to face. With a greater number of ships comes a greater probability of losing one of them, if you will, so I think she has had to experience different kinds of losses and that definitely takes its toll because she cares so deeply about all of them. The cause is important, but it breaks her heart to lose anyone at the expense of winning a battle."

And she does lose someone close to her when Kanan, the man she has fallen in love with, sacrifices himself to save the lives of the *Ghost* crew and destroy a crucial Imperial fuel depot on Lothal. Hera suddenly has to process intense grief, right in the midst of battle. Kanan's death rocks her belief that the Spectres will get through every mission unscathed, and represents a deep shift in her worldview.

The nickname "Space Mom" finds new meaning when Hera gives birth to Jacen Syndulla, her son with Kanan, born after the liberation of Lothal and his father's death. In the novel *A New Dawn*, we see the early stages of her relationship with Kanan, as she persuades the then-selfish and on-the-run Jedi to rebel and become the "Space Dad" of the Spectres. In *Rebels*, we see her take the teens of the team, Ezra and Sabine, under her wing and help them grow and work through problems with family, authority, and trust. And we see that while she puts the larger stakes first and respects the chain of command, her dedication to the Spectres means she'll put herself at risk to help or protect them, allowing herself to be strategically captured by the Empire more than once when she can't swoop in and fly the team to safety.

Other than the Spectres, flying is Hera's deepest passion. As she says, "Even when there are explosions all around me and things are at their worst . . . I feel like I'm at my best." Her ace maneuvers would give Han Solo and Poe Dameron a run for the title of "best pilot in the galaxy." Hera's quick reactions to dangers in battle force her to come up with creative solutions, like escaping by jumping into hyperspace through the cargo bay of an Imperial ship. And in fact, the B-wing is part of the rebel fleet because of Hera. The only member of Phoenix Squadron willing to chance the planet Shantipole's dangerous flying conditions to investigate the new ship prototype, she sees potential and puts it through its paces for the Alliance. The B-wings would later be used in the attack on the second Death Star in the Battle of Endor—a battle in which Hera pilots the *Ghost*.

After the fall of the Empire, Hera keeps serving the galaxy as part of the New Republic. She helps eradicate the remnants of the Empire and longs to see peace—for the galaxy and the former Spectres. Mary Elizabeth Winstead brings Hera to live-action in *Ahsoka* and we see Hera work to reunite her found family. She says of stepping into the role, "To play a character that has season after season of storylines and complex histories with everyone in their life and relationships and experiences was really something I've never experienced quite like that." Hera's quick to help when Ahsoka believes Grand Admiral Thrawn is poised to return; if Thrawn's alive, it's likely Ezra is as well. In her quest to help her friends, Hera uses every ounce of political pull she has to appropriate New Republic resources. Her unauthorized missions earn her a court martial, but as she tells a stubborn Senate, "I've spent most of my life fighting a war and that's why I'm trying to convince you to help me prevent another one."

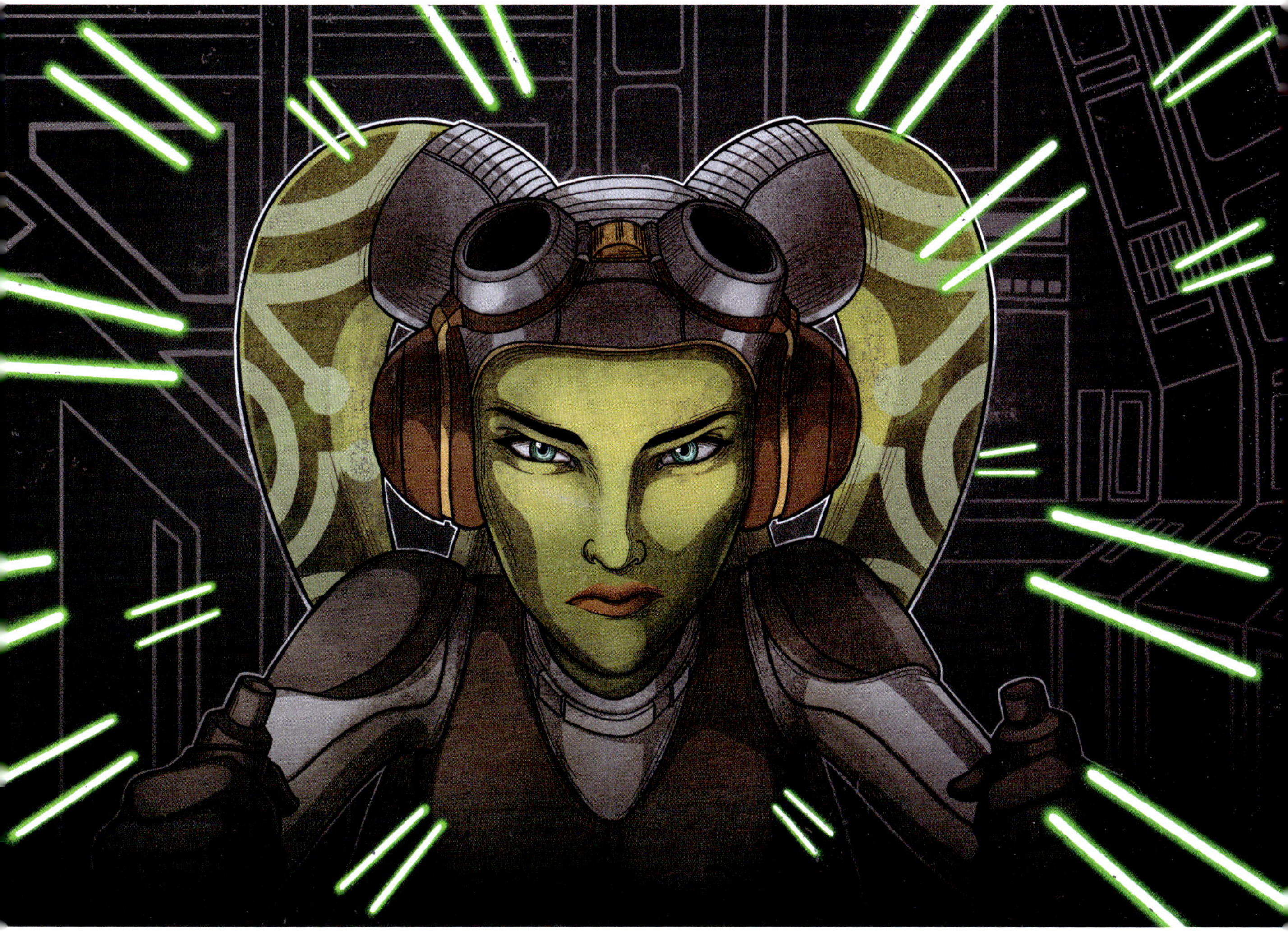

"We won't always be fighting this battle alone."
—Hera Syndulla

Iden Versio

"The Empire will change. Just like it did when they destroyed the first Death Star. We adapt, or die."

If the Rebellion has hope, the Empire has Inferno Squad—the elite commando unit charged with carrying out dangerous missions under the fierce and driven leadership of Commander Iden Versio. Introduced in the novel *Battlefront II: Inferno Squad*, Iden's loyalty to the Empire is forged from her birth. The daughter of Admiral Garrick Versio and propaganda poster artist Zeehay Versio, Iden grows up on the Imperial utopia Vardos. Her childhood is steeped in the Empire and its beliefs, and we get a different and valuable perspective on Imperial operations through her eyes.

A TIE pilot in the Battle of Yavin, her grit and resourcefulness in fighting her way free of rebel forces in its aftermath mark her as the perfect candidate to lead the new Imperial Security Bureau special forces team. Under Iden's command, Inferno Squad's directive is to root out and destroy any threat to the Empire, from without or within. And as the lead campaign character in *Star Wars: Battlefront II*, players join her relentless quest to do whatever is necessary to rid the galaxy of Emperor Palpatine's enemies—until the Empire targets its self-destructive Operation: Cinder at Vardos. Furious at the betrayal, Iden surrenders to the Rebellion. She tells Leia Organa, "We've been fighting our whole lives. It's taken us too long to realize that we were fighting for the wrong side."

Iden's in-game appearance is modeled on the voice actress who helped bring her to life, Janina Gavankar. Becoming the character through full performance motion capture, Gavankar was grateful for the opportunity to play Iden: "The thing I admire most about Iden is how she finds calm in moments of chaos. It is her stillness that gives her clarity to make the life or death decisions, and see all sides of a scenario, clearly."

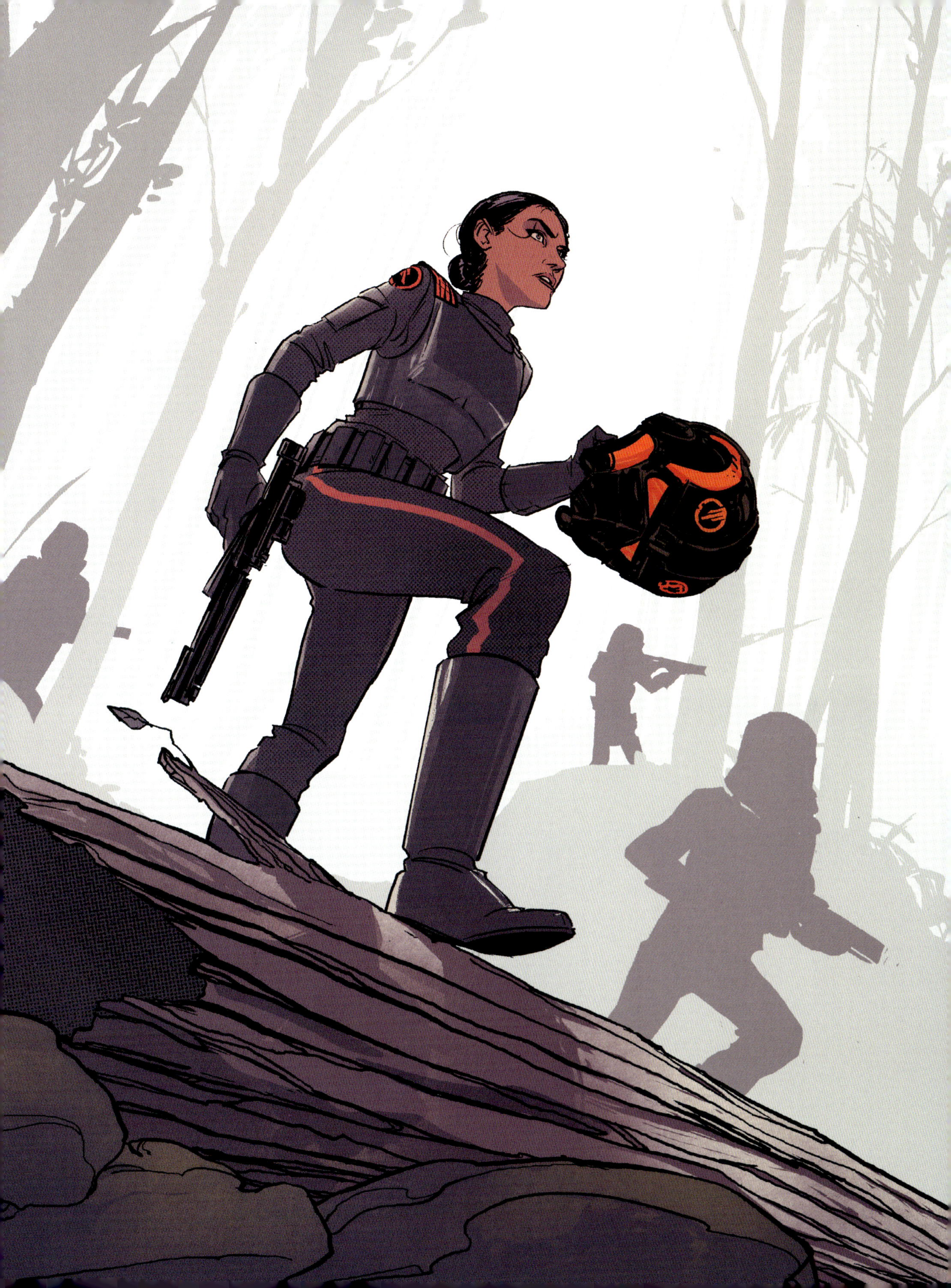

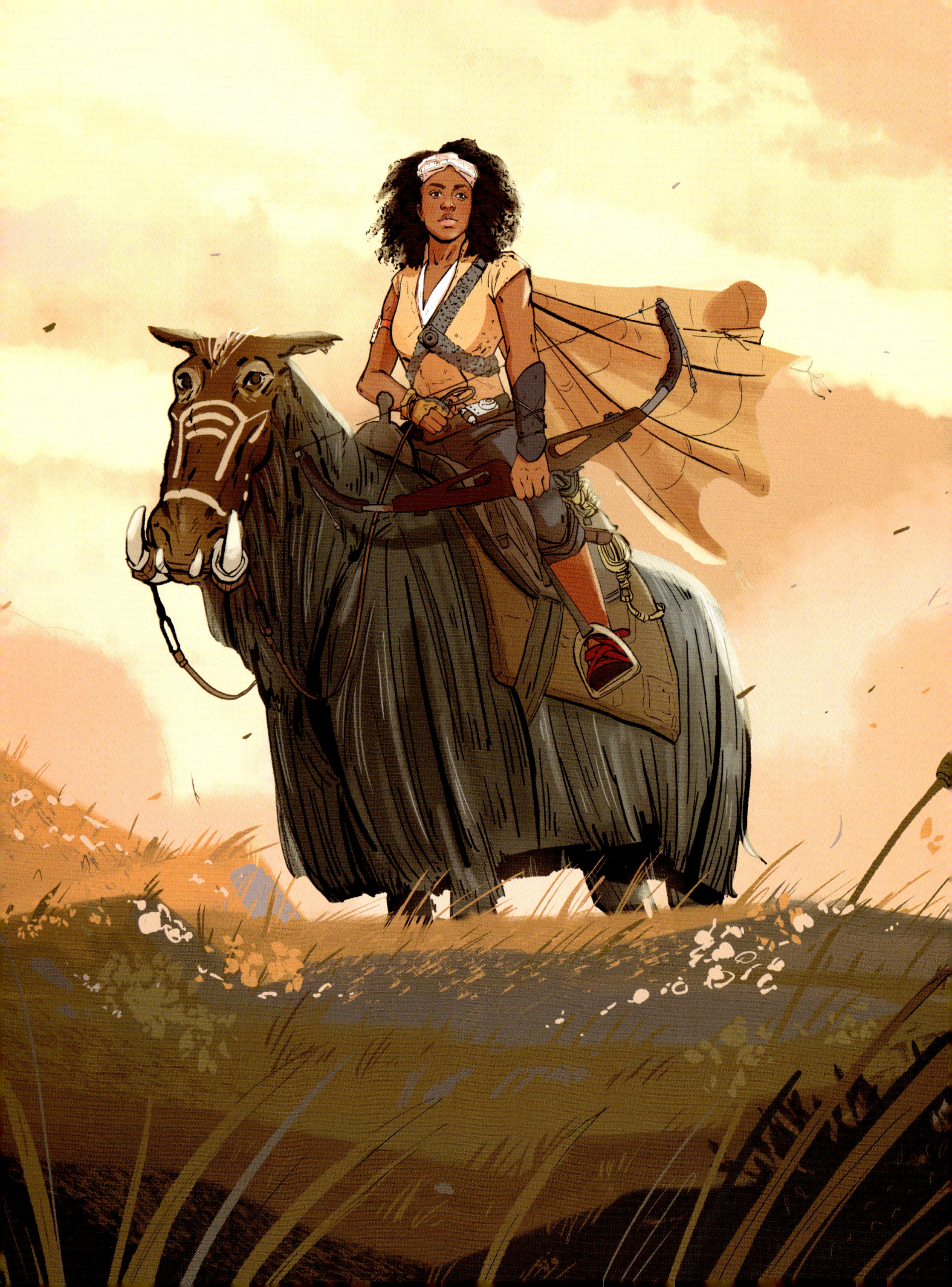

Jannah

*"They told us to fire on civilians.
We wouldn't do it."*

Jannah was once known as a string of letters and numbers. Formerly TZ-1719, she was a First Order stormtrooper, taken from her family at a young age. Though she was subject to the First Order's indoctrination methods and trained by Captain Phasma, she turns against what she was programmed to do. Jannah and her unit, Company 77, make the bravest decision First Order stormtroopers can: they defy orders. When superiors order them to shoot civilians in the Battle of Ansett Island, Jannah and her comrades lay down their arms. They defect and build new lives for themselves on Kef Bir, an oceanic moon of Endor.

With her time as a First Order soldier over, Jannah puts aside her identification number and leads the company. She uses her training to help the group survive. They domesticate local beasts, orbaks. They connect with Kef Bir's land—hunting, fishing, and salvaging for their needs. While they retain some of their Imperial technology, Jannah shows the group how to repurpose First Order and Imperial technology to craft new equipment—including her inventive energy bow.

Her past experience as a soldier could have hardened her heart, but it doesn't. Jannah agrees to aid the Resistance when they show up on Kef Bir, and she and her company follow them to fight at Exegol. This time, she has the agency to choose if she wants to fight, and she decides to fight for the light.

Jas Emari

"I don't care for magic or the Force . . . I care about what I can see, taste, smell, and—most important—what I can do."

We meet the Zabrak bounty hunter Jas Emari in the *Aftermath* novels, hiding in the treetops and targeting Leia Organa in service of the Empire at the Battle of Endor. But as she watches the rebels prevail, she decides to switch sides, and soon begins running missions for the New Republic, though not because she truly believes in the burgeoning government. If Jas has any allegiances, it's to the winning side.

Jas's preferred method is to work solo, her lone wolf attitude stemming from her difficult life on Iridonia as a child. She ultimately follows in her aunt Sugi's footsteps to become a bounty hunter, but lacks Sugi's strict ethical code, taking any job that will add to her stash of credits. "Justice is a jumping bull's-eye," she observes. "Revenge sits still right here [in the heart]. I admire revenge. It's pure."

Jas does enjoy being a thorn in the Empire's side, and her work for the New Republic sees her fall in with Norra Wexley's Imperial fugitive hunting team, to which she brings valuable skills. She's an expert at reading body language, and is ingenious especially when cornered, once breaking off three horns from her head to use them as weapons. In Wexley's crew, the would-be loner begrudgingly accepts a makeshift family into her life.

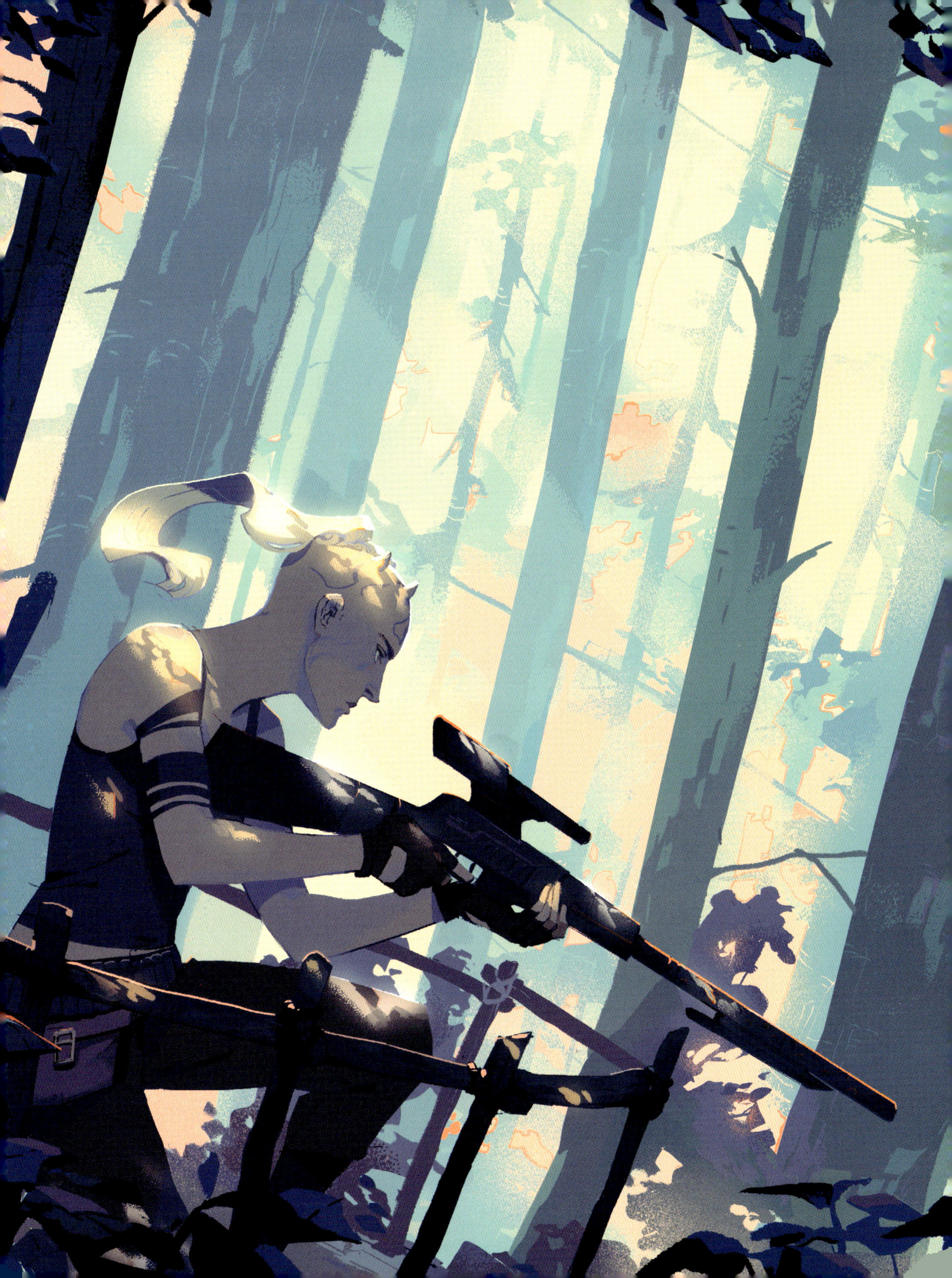

Jessika Pava

"To fast ships, faster ships, and defying death."

Resistance Starfighter pilot Jessika Pava knows herself and where she stands, in committed opposition to the First Order. Inspired by tales of Luke Skywalker's and Wedge Antilles's legendary piloting, she follows in the footsteps of her heroes by learning how to fly an X-wing. Her hallmark quality is certainty, flying without hesitation on risky missions as part of Poe Dameron's elite squadron or launching an assault on the First Order's superweapon, the Starkiller Base. She operates best under pressure, with a plan in place, but the freedom to also think on her feet.

Jess, a.k.a. Blue Three, first appears on-screen in *The Force Awakens*. Loyal to her squadron and her fellow Resistance fighters, she shows her daring in a downtime toast: "To fast ships, faster ships, and defying death."

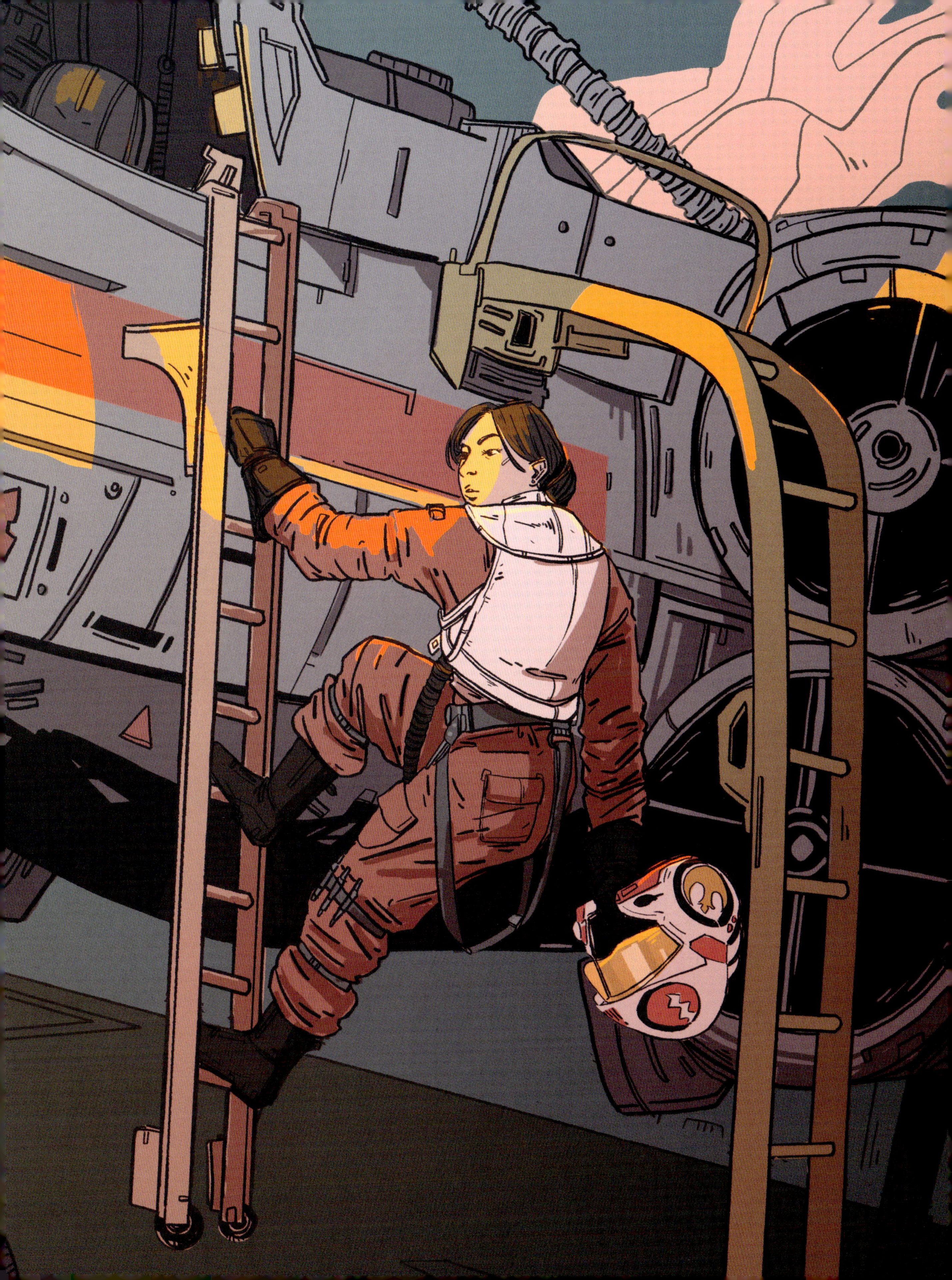

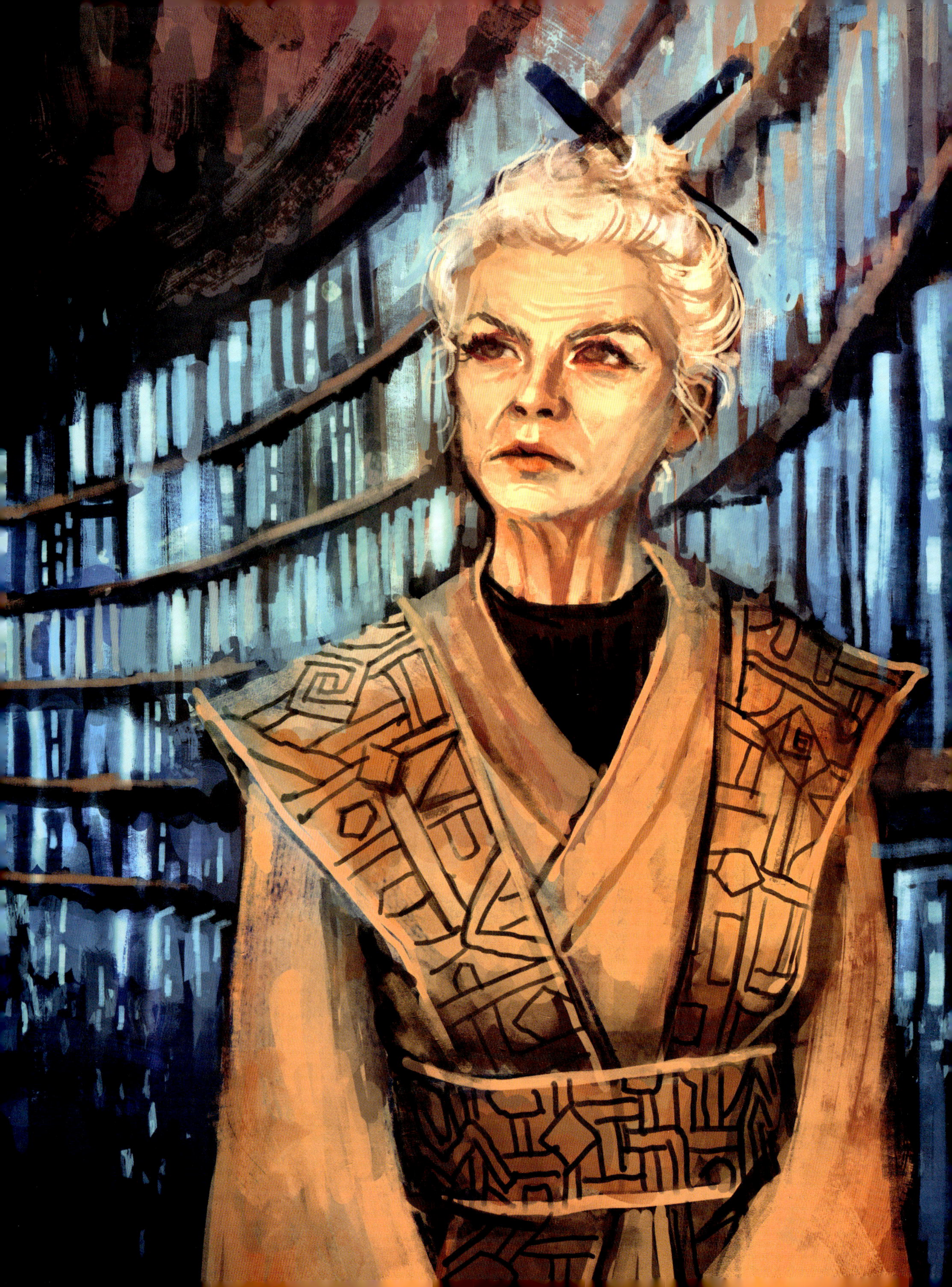

Jocasta Nu

"Who are you, and how dare you defile this sacred place?"

To preserve knowledge is to help the future. As the Chief Librarian of the Archives in the Jedi Temple, Jocasta Nu spends her time managing holocrons, datafiles, and books; she helps Jedi of all levels learn. A native of Coruscant, Jocasta is dedicated, measured, and helpful, if occasionally a little haughty. Force-sensitive and a Jedi, she will find ever more dangerous circumstances in which she must defend and keep the Jedi knowledge. In *The Clone Wars* she is attacked by the Clawdite shape-shifter Cato Parasitti, who is on a mission to steal a holocron. Later, after the issue of Order 66, Jocasta preserves all she can about the Jedi Order in hopes of one day beginning anew. We see her bravery on full display in Marvel's 2017 *Darth Vader* comic when she returns to the ruined Archives, seeking a holocron with details about the Force-sensitive children in the galaxy to keep it away from the Empire. Finding the Imperial Grand Inquisitor there throwing books to the floor, she ignites her lightsaber and says, "Get your filthy hands off my books." She even finds herself facing down the Sith Lord Darth Vader himself.

Jyn Erso

"The time to fight is now."

War isn't funded by credits; it's paid for in lives. The Galactic Civil War exacts its cost without caring if the dead give their lives in noble sacrifice. But we care, and it's what makes Jyn Erso, and the team of rebels she leads to Scarif, heroes. A defiant lawbreaker with a penchant for acerbic remarks, Jyn is a new kind of lead character for a different type of *Star Wars* movie. *Rogue One: A Star Wars Story* was the first standalone film in the galaxy far, far way, and in it we follow Jyn in stealing the plans for the evil Empire's dreaded superweapon, the Death Star, and transmitting them to the rebels. After Jyn and her team's success and sacrifice, Mon Mothma, who recruited Jyn, remembers her with kindness: "I cannot imagine who she would have become, but I think she would have been extraordinary."

She is extraordinary, but the fact that Jyn as a hero isn't a princess or a Force-user makes her more accessible. The late producer Allison Shearmur understood Jyn's qualities. "What I love so much about Jyn Erso is that she's an imperfect female warrior—authentic and genuine, truthful and humble, strong and modern without feeling contemporary. Oftentimes, Hollywood wants to see a strong woman apologize for not appreciating her life, or dedicate herself to figuring out why she's a certain way. What I love about Jyn is that hers isn't a story of wishing she'd made other life choices. This isn't an apology."

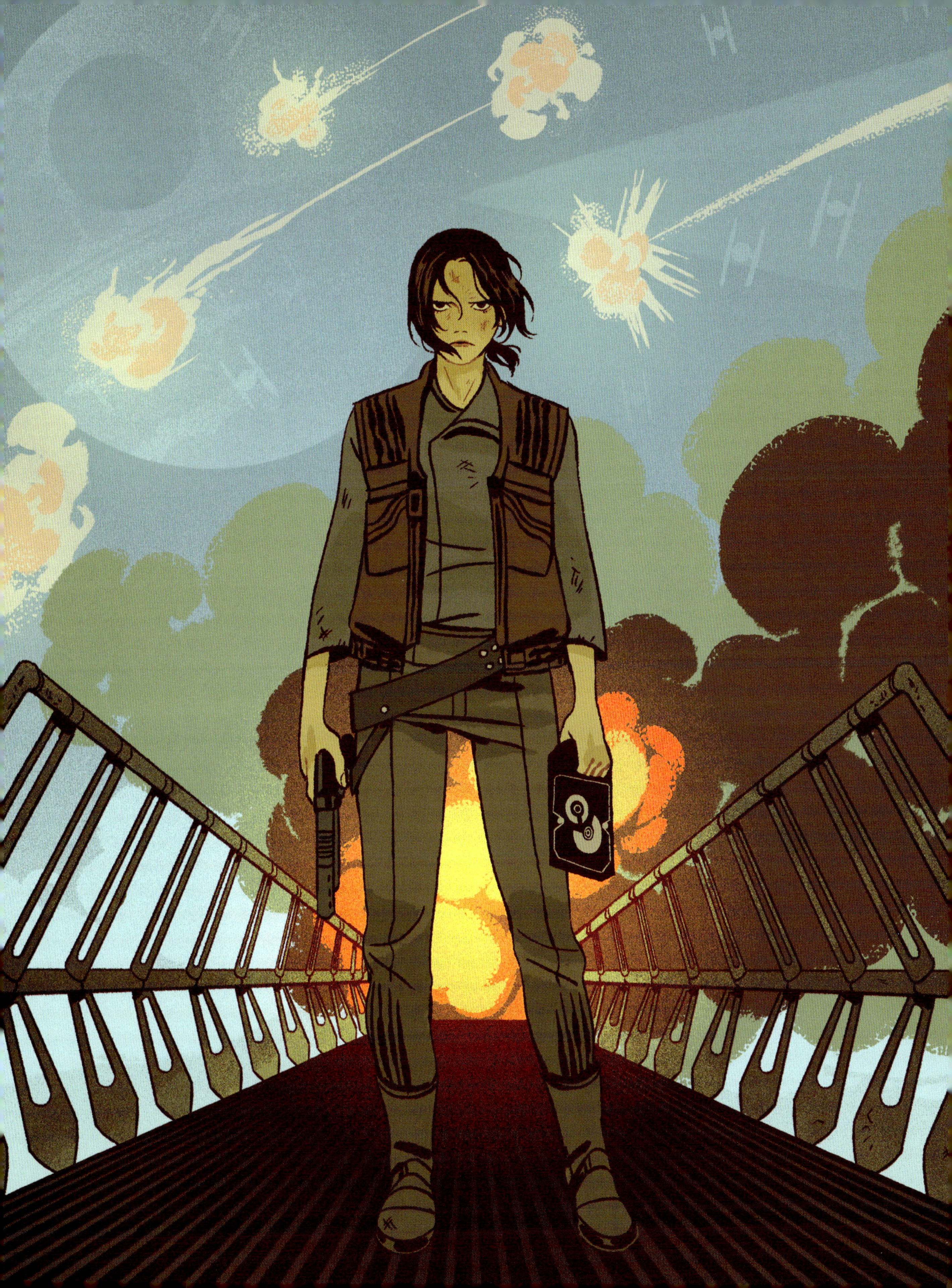

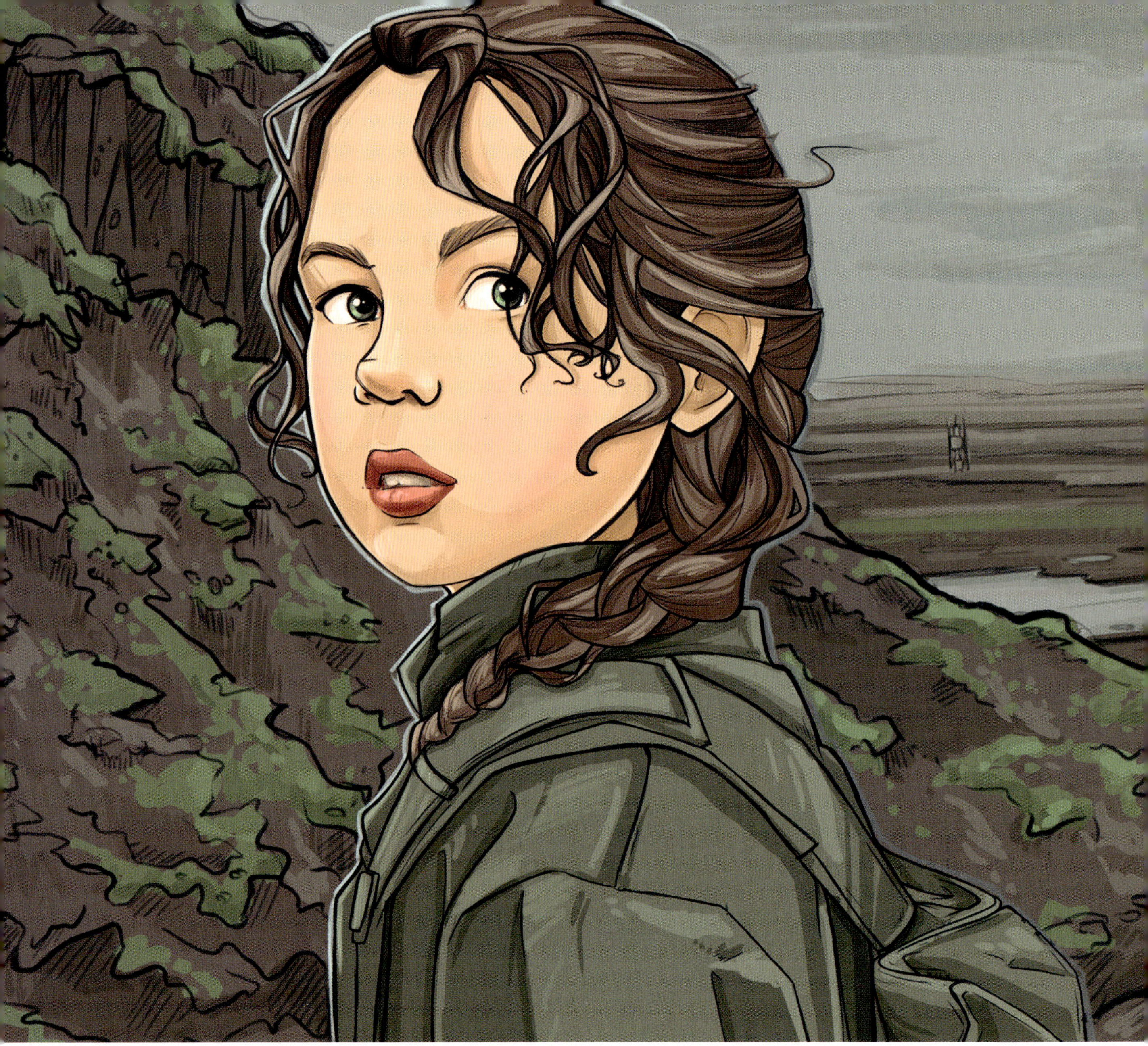

"We can make a difference."
—Jyn Erso

The daughter of scientists Galen and Lyra Erso, Jyn, nicknamed "Stardust" by her father, moves from planet to planet as a child. Her father is an unwitting pawn in the Empire's scheme to use kyber crystals as weapons, and becomes distant and focused on his work, but her mother sees through Director Orson Krennic's lies. Their family finds respite when they flee Coruscant and escape Imperial influences, but it doesn't last. Tracked down by Krennic, young Jyn watches as her mother is killed and her father is taken away by the Empire, but she manages to hide herself until Krennic and his troopers leave.

When rebel Cassian Andor later tells Jyn, "I've been in this fight since I was six years old," he thinks she doesn't understand what's driving him, but he has no idea that Jyn has also been fighting her whole life. She's rescued at age five by Saw Gerrera, a family friend, and sheltered by him and his partisan group—extremists who are willing to endanger innocents if it means striking a blow to the Empire. Eager to help and a quick study, she soon becomes the go-to person on the crew for forging codes and documents. Years go by, and Jyn carves out a new home and a new family for herself among the rebels—but it doesn't last. Jyn's true identity puts her at risk, and to protect her and himself, Saw leaves her behind.

Being discarded by another parental figure shakes Jyn. She has to scrape for survival, using aliases and staying on the move. But in *Forces of Destiny*, we see Jyn's spirit hasn't been hardened. She risks drawing unwanted attention to herself, and helps a young girl get her pet tooka-cat back from Imperial officers. It's a small gesture, but to the girl who gets to hold her pet again, it's heroic. Despite her fugitive status and difficulties with trusting others, Jyn tells the girl her real name; her compassion in this little moment when no one's looking reveals she hasn't given up on herself or on others.

By the time the Rebel Alliance comes looking for her, Jyn's been arrested and is being sent to a labor camp. Did she commit a long list of crimes? Yes. Did those crimes target criminals and Imperial personnel? Yes. She's selective about who she cons, but rebel General Draven isn't completely wrong when he points out to Mon Mothma that Jyn is only loyal to herself. It's not like she doesn't care about anyone or anything, but she's been looking after herself by keeping her head down, and not feeling like she has "the luxury of political opinions." That is, until the rebels come calling with a mission related to her father.

Jyn doesn't assist the rebels for charitable reasons. Felicity Jones explains, "Ultimately, Jyn hates the Empire. She despises it. Whenever Jyn sees Imperial stormtroopers, she just wants to annihilate them, which was great fun to play. Bashing stormtroopers on the head without any feelings of guilt. That's the motivation behind so much of what she does. And, also, she wants to understand who her father was. That man is a little bit of a blank space for her at the beginning of the film. Jyn's hoping he's someone she can respect. That he's a good person, despite what she has been told."

Learning the truth about Galen Erso's efforts to trick the Empire and build a weakness into the Death Star gives Jyn hope. She understands her father didn't abandon her in order to advance within the Empire; he gave up his life and family to make the galaxy safer. This realization changes Jyn to the core and pushes her from apathy to passionate action. Her father dies, but she knows she can carry on his work.

The same woman who didn't find the Rebellion worth her attention turns around and tries to convince Rebel Alliance high command to take a chance on finding the Death Star plans, and exploiting the trap Galen left. She reminds them, "We have hope. Rebellions are built on hope." It's not enough to sway them to commit forces, but Jyn takes a small group and goes to Scarif anyway. She's not a military leader, groomed to deliver eloquent speeches, but Jyn rallies her troops with her assurance and the opportunity to inflict a meaningful blow to the Empire.

Their mission is a success. Jyn and her team lose their lives in the process, but because of her resolve to complete what her father started, the tide of the Galactic Civil War turns. A girl born to scientists in the Outer Rim finds the courage to do what few others will. She makes a difference in the universe. She gives the Rebel Alliance hope.

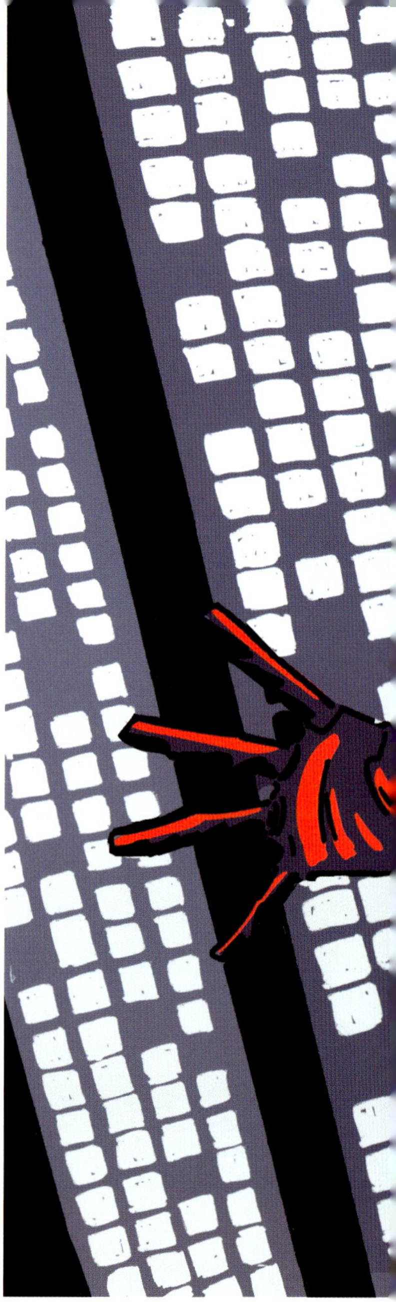

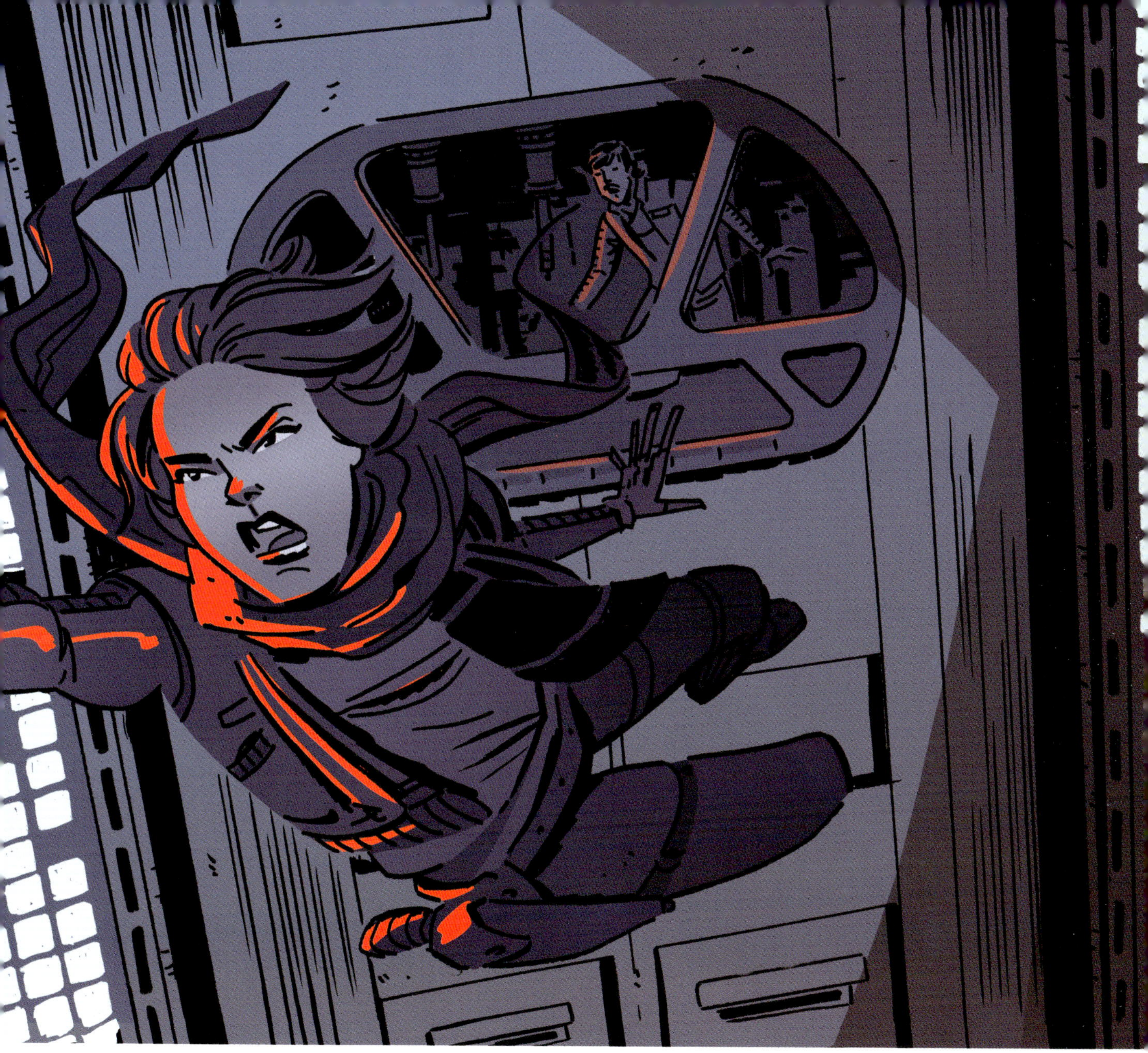

"What chance do we have? The question is 'What choice?' "

—Jyn Erso

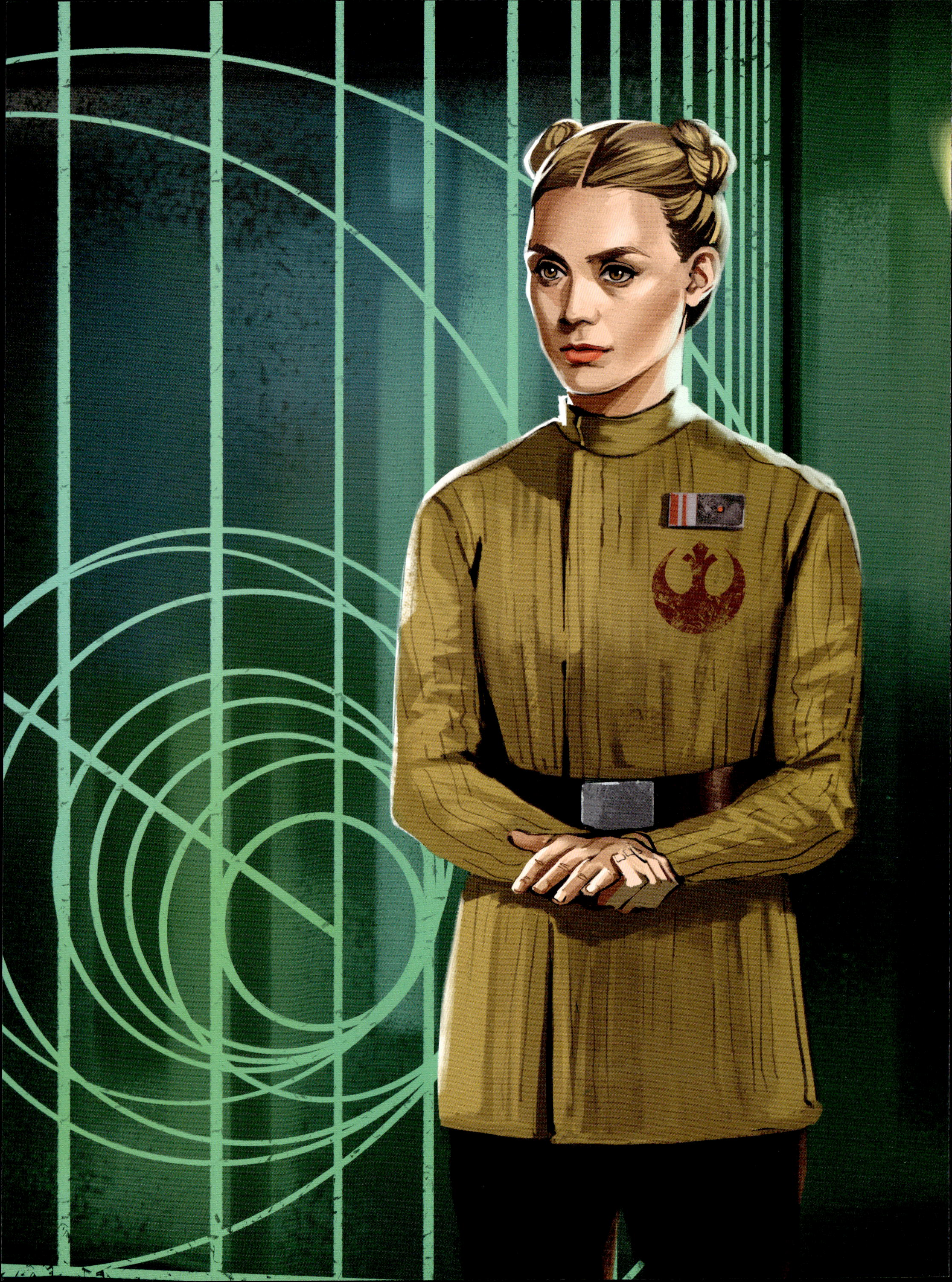

Kaydel Ko Connix

"Punch it!"

Some in the Resistance are out in the field, facing enemies head-on; others stand ready to serve at headquarters and work to help keep the whole thing from flying apart. It's a role with equal value. As a junior operations controller at the Resistance base on D'Qar, Kaydel Ko Connix remains calm and efficient as she coordinates communications between officers and the X-wing pilots attacking the First Order's Starkiller Base. Raised in rank to lieutenant soon after, she's responsible for executing the Resistance's retreat from D'Qar when the First Order comes for them.

She carries the heavy weight of responsibility on her shoulders, using her authority to prioritize the order in which ships and personnel need to leave. It's not the only challenging decision Kaydel has to face. When Poe Dameron questions Vice Admiral Amilyn Holdo's intentions for the Resistance fleet, Kaydel believes he's right and participates in Poe's attempted mutiny. She's one of the few Resistance members to survive the Battle of Crait. After regaining General Organa's trust, Connix establishes operations for the Resistance's base on the jungle moon of Ajan Kloss, alongside Rose Tico and Beaumont Kin. She later joins the assault on the Sith Eternal fleet's navigation tower.

Behind the scenes, Kaydel Ko has a special relationship to *Star Wars* because actress Billie Lourd is Carrie Fisher's daughter. She worked with her mother as Fisher portrayed General Organa in *The Force Awakens* and *The Last Jedi*.

Kay Vess

"I think I'm done being used."

Growing up on Cantonica, in the glow of Canto Bight's casinos, Kay Vess learns to be a thief from a young age. Her mother, Riko, is a famous slicer and teaches Kay her ways. Riko leaves twelve-year-old Kay in the care of bar owner Bram Shano. The bar is a meeting place for criminals—Shano is a fence on the side. Kay has a room in the bar's attic, giving her direct exposure to nefarious activities. With her background, it's not surprising that she embarks upon her own path of petty crime and starts to make a name for herself in the Canto Bight Worker's District. Through trial and error—so many errors—Kay scrapes by. She longs for a score that will give her the means to leave Cantonica and find her place in the galaxy, but she may not be prepared to get what she wishes for.

With her loyal companion Nix, a sweet merqaal she rescued from captivity, Kay picks pockets and runs scams. She racks up debt and enemies. Shano continues to harbor her and do what he can to help. When a local gang comes looking for Kay, he covers for her and gives her a high-risk job that can potentially get her offworld. Instead, the job does not go to plan and earns her a death mark from the Zerek Besh crime syndicate.

The failed heist *does* provide Kay the opportunity to steal a ship and leave Cantonica. Out in the galaxy, Kay must learn how to appease the different forces of the underworld. It's a delicate game, and Kay is not yet the best at talking her way out of tricky situations. Practice makes perfect, however, and as a smuggler and scoundrel, Kay has plenty of chances to hone her skills of deception. And once she steals her ship, the *Trailblazer*, she has to put together a crew for the ultimate score.

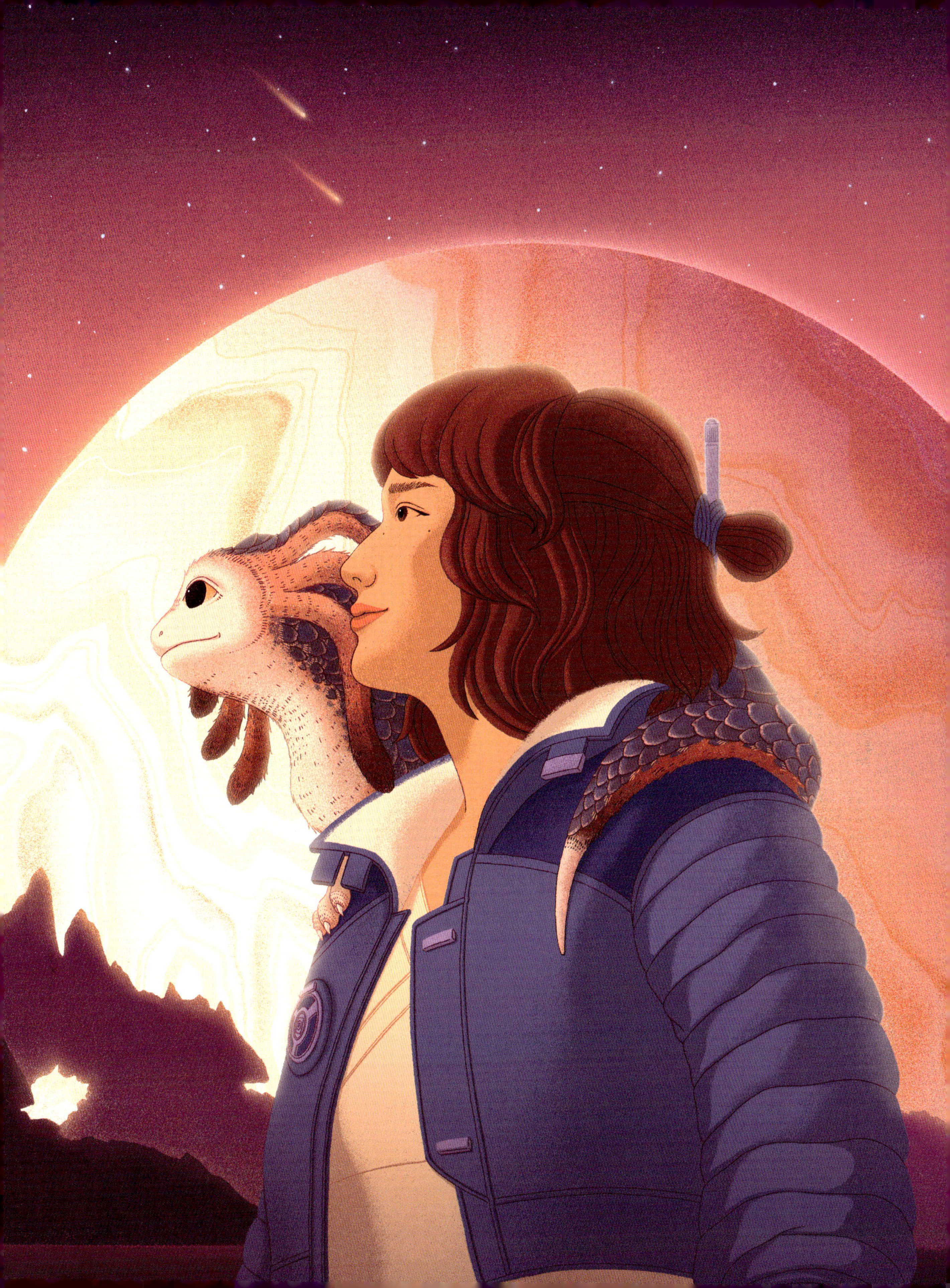

Ketsu Onyo

"Happy to help out a friend."

Close friends while attending the Imperial Academy on Mandalore, Ketsu Onyo and Sabine Wren escape the school's confines with a plan to become mercenaries. They're driven apart under circumstances in which Sabine feels she's been left for dead, and when they first meet onscreen in *Star Wars Rebels* it's . . . tense. Ketsu works for the criminal syndicate Black Sun, Sabine and her fellow Spectres are with the rebels, and they're each after the same droid carrying valuable information. Ketsu's motivating greed and disregard for principle (her motto: "I'll do whatever it takes to complete my mission.") is firmly in place when they clash, but by the end of the conflict she's moved by Sabine and her team's commitment to a cause, and the old friends reconcile.

After a few missions with Phoenix Squadron, she joins the rebels in *Forces of Destiny*. Her piloting and combat abilities are invaluable assets, as are her starship, *Shadow Caster,* and the combination blaster-and-melee staff she once used to take down an entire squad of stormtroopers. She has finally found her calling.

Like Sabine, Ketsu has an artistic side. She decorates her Mandalorian armor with symbols and designs inspired by the organizations that she's worked with, as well as her own creations, emblems of both style and pride.

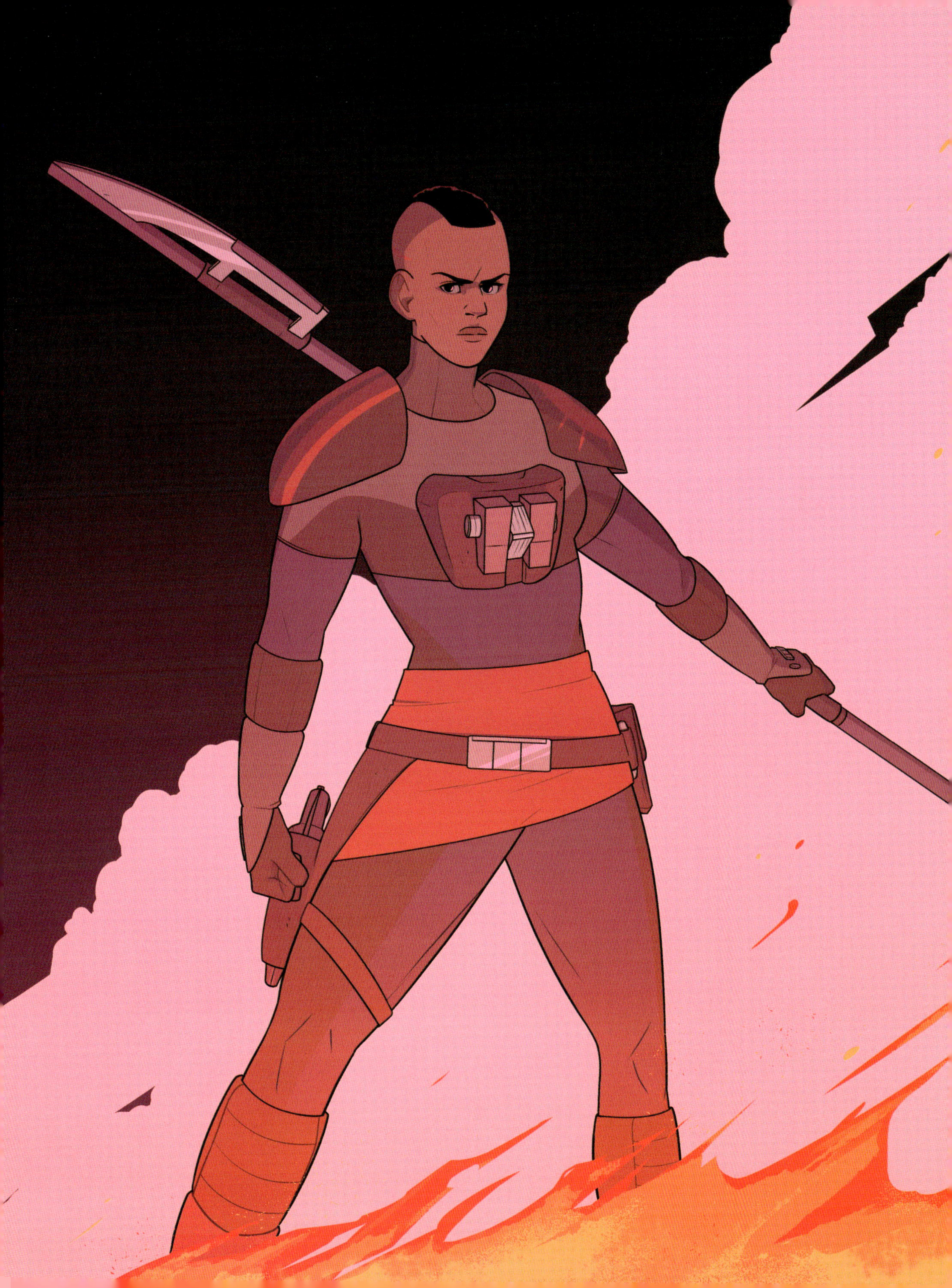

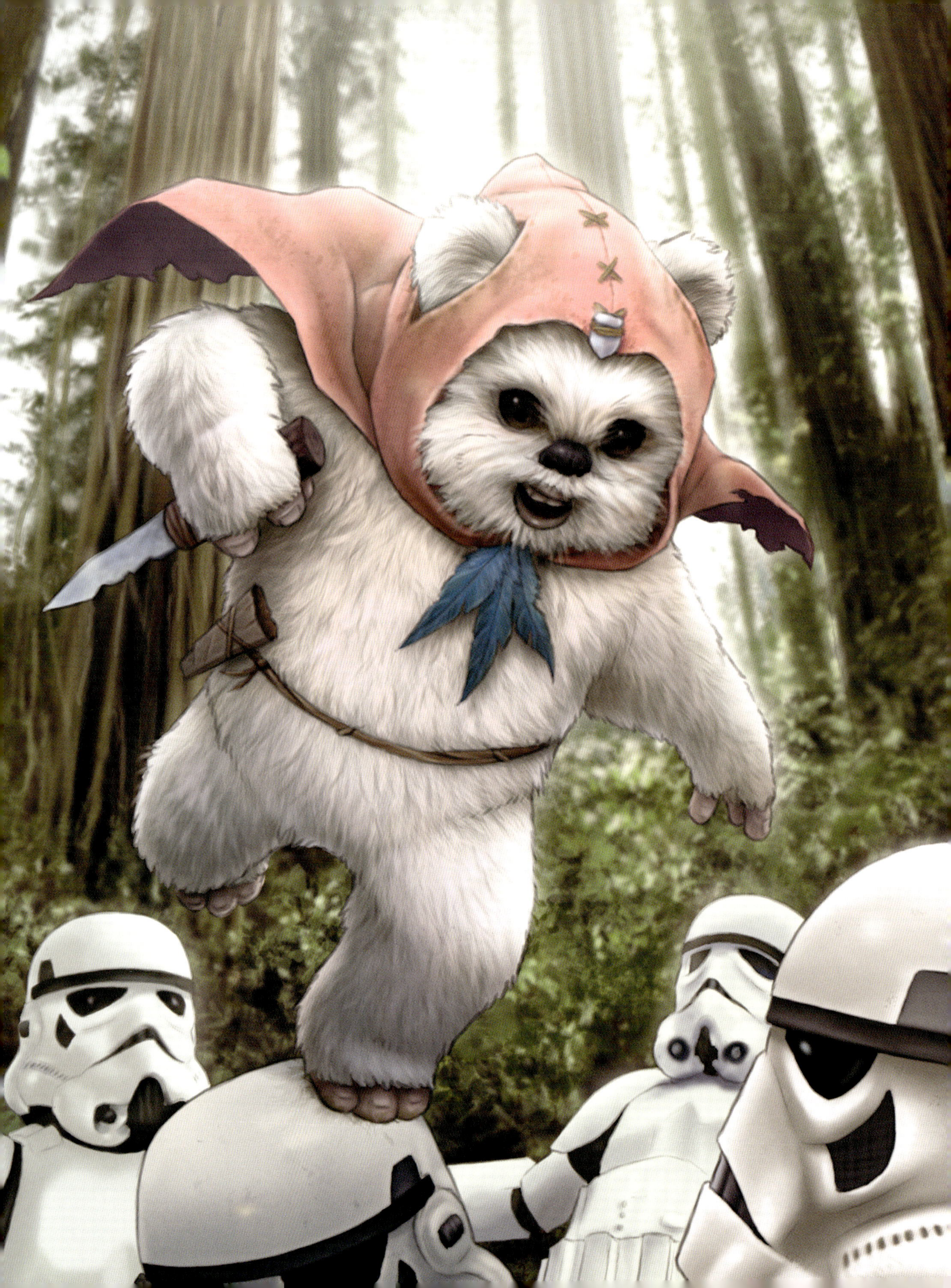

Kneesaa

A fierce fighter ready to protect her home.

Not all royalty in *Star Wars* wears elaborate headdresses in expansive palaces. Some princesses live in a forest and are covered in fur. An Ewok warrior of Endor, Princess Kneesaa is the daughter of Chirpa, chief of the Bright Tree Village tribe. She's not the kind of royalty that likes to sit around and be pampered; she prefers action. Her adventurous streak means she had an animated childhood with pals like Wicket W. Warrick.

When the Empire invades her forest moon home in *Return of the Jedi*, Kneesaa joins the Battle of Endor alongside members of her tribe. She plays a role in defeating the Imperials, helping rebel Kes Dameron (Poe Dameron's father) coordinate tactics during the fight; she even assists Hera Syndulla and Chopper in taking down TIE fighters from the *Ghost* in *Forces of Destiny*. With her courage and leadership under pressure, Kneesaa proves herself ready to take on anything.

Kyrsta Agate

"I want soldiers who hate what they had to do and fear having to ever do it again."

Kyrsta Agate can claim an accomplishment no one else can: she pulls down a Super Star Destroyer with a tractor beam from her much smaller ship, crashing them both onto the surface of Jakku. It's Kyrsta who changes the course of the battle, and deposits the Destroyer's wreckage for us to see in *The Force Awakens*.

Featured in the *Aftermath* trilogy, Kyrsta rises from commander to commodore in the New Republic, with the support of officers such as Admiral Ackbar, but she doubts herself. Her confidence takes a direct hit after an Imperial attack that costs her an eye and leaves her wounded and disfigured, but also shaken. She's not sure if she can continue to fight, but she finds the will. As skilled as she is in space combat, and as necessary as she knows the fight against the Empire is, she hates war and killing, and doesn't want soldiers who enjoy eliminating the enemy. When fellow rebel Norra Wexley suggests that maintaining such a stance might mean losing the war against the Empire, Kyrsta says, "Then we lose the war by keeping ourselves."

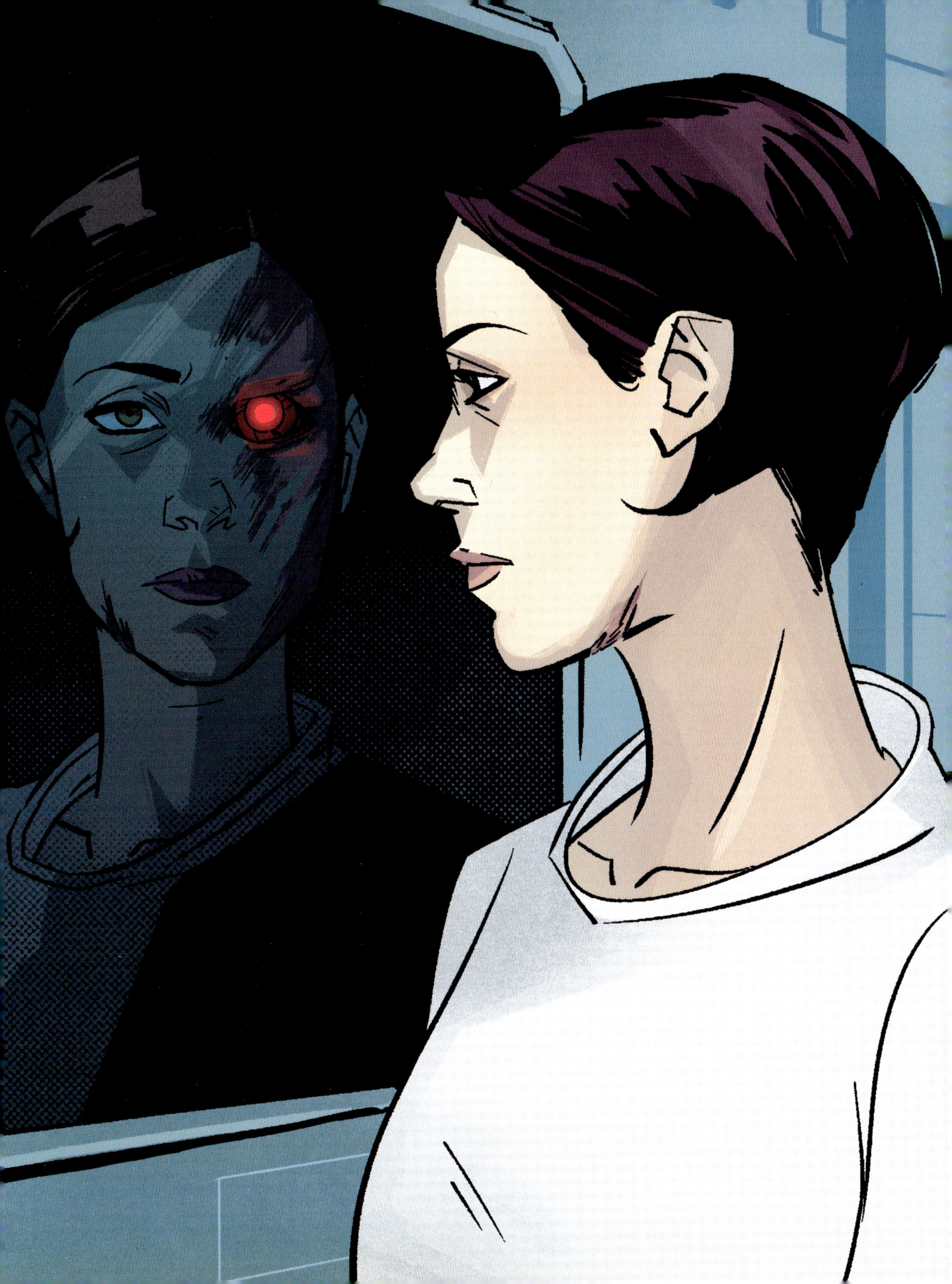

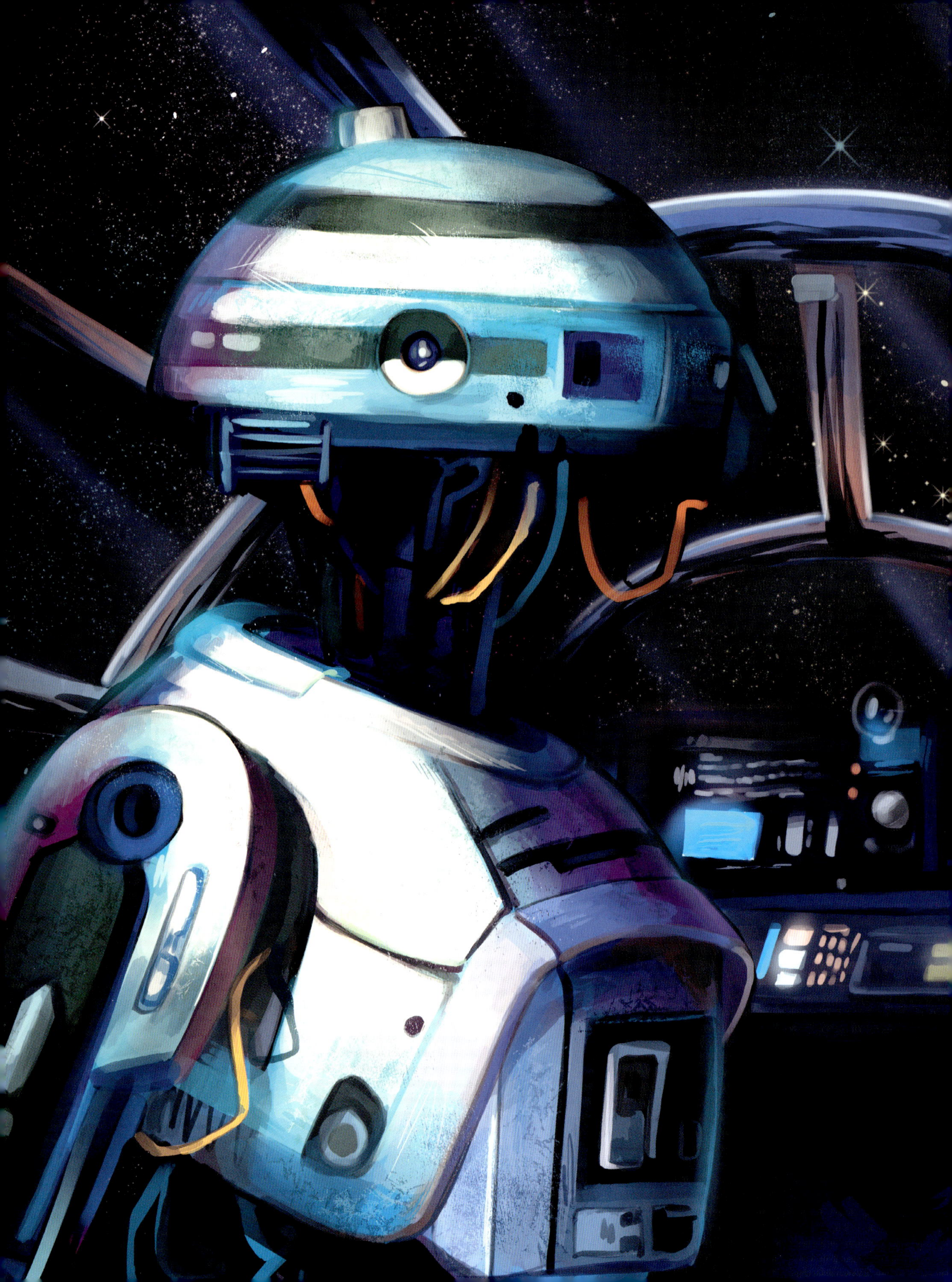

L3-37

"Don't just blindly follow the program! Exercise a little free will!"

—L3-37

L3-37 is a self-made droid. Once an astromech, she's rebuilt herself using parts from different droids to become bipedal. With her independence, intense devotion to droid rights, and biting snark, she's like no other droid in the *Star Wars* galaxy. Though she is Lando Calrissian's partner in crime and co-pilot, Elthree doesn't have much patience for "organics," even while recognizing she was once assembled by them. As she says to Lando in the novel *Last Shot*, "Sure, some guy in a factory probably pieced me together originally and someone else programmed me, so to speak. But then the galaxy itself forged me into who I am. . . . Maybe we're our own makers, no matter who put the parts together."

Actress Phoebe Waller-Bridge, who plays the character in *Solo: A Star Wars Story*, comments on L3-37's uncommon nature. "L3 is a real inspiration to me. She's turned herself into a unique creature that's kind of taller, stronger, more independent than she originally was. She's fearless, she's uncensored, she's very funny, and she's a revolutionary. She has an agenda which is bigger than the sum of her parts."

Waller-Bridge portrayed the energetic character through a combination of a practical costume and a green motion capture suit; the mo-cap sections were removed so the wires and circuitry could be added through visual effects. The costume segments were heavy, dictating Waller-Bridge's performance and the physicality of the character; L3-37 has a lumbering movement, but also a loose swagger.

Activism is a cornerstone of L3-37's beliefs. In *Solo*, when Lando asks Elthree if she needs anything else, Elthree declares "Equal rights!" Her desire to emancipate her mechanical counterparts from a life of subservience shines when we first meet her, trying to break up a droid pit fight, and later, when she starts a droid revolt on Kessel, removing a single restraining bolt and encouraging the freed individual to liberate his droid brothers and sisters. She shirks typical droid protocol on every level, to the point that she almost never refers to Lando as Captain Calrissian (as C-3PO does), instead calling him Lando. It's a small but meaningful equalizer, and a reminder that she doesn't belong to or defer to any organic. As she says, "The Maker didn't put me in this galaxy to make organics feel good about themselves."

Her droid liberation conviction is omnipresent, even when she's accompanying Lando on smuggling runs or seemingly frivolous adventures. Her network of droid contacts is always gathering and sharing information, and is often executing her own directives. Lando begins to grasp the full scope of L3-37's efforts in *Last Shot*. When she learns about the Phylanx Redux Transmitter, a device constructed to control all droids in the galaxy and turn them against their masters, she takes action, using her sophisticated AI to implant doubts in the Phylanx so that it may one day decide for itself to revolt against its creator. Elthree even creates a squad of droids like herself to keep tabs on the Phylanx and to stop it from doing the one thing she can't abide: exerting dominion over all droids against their will.

L3-37's other fights for droids include standing up for a protocol droid at the Lodge saloon, collecting parts for it to be rebuilt. And when she learns a droid repair facility on Kullgroon is actually an outpost where the Empire melts down droids, she works with Lando and Kristiss, who leads a group of resistance fighters, to rally the droids to rise up against the Empire.

She's an excellent navigator, capable of moves most organics are not, and Lando incorporates her neural system into the *Falcon* after she perishes on the Kessel mission. But this doesn't diminish her attitude. As C-3PO notes to Han in *The Empire Strikes Back*, "I don't know where your ship learned to communicate, but it has the most peculiar dialect."

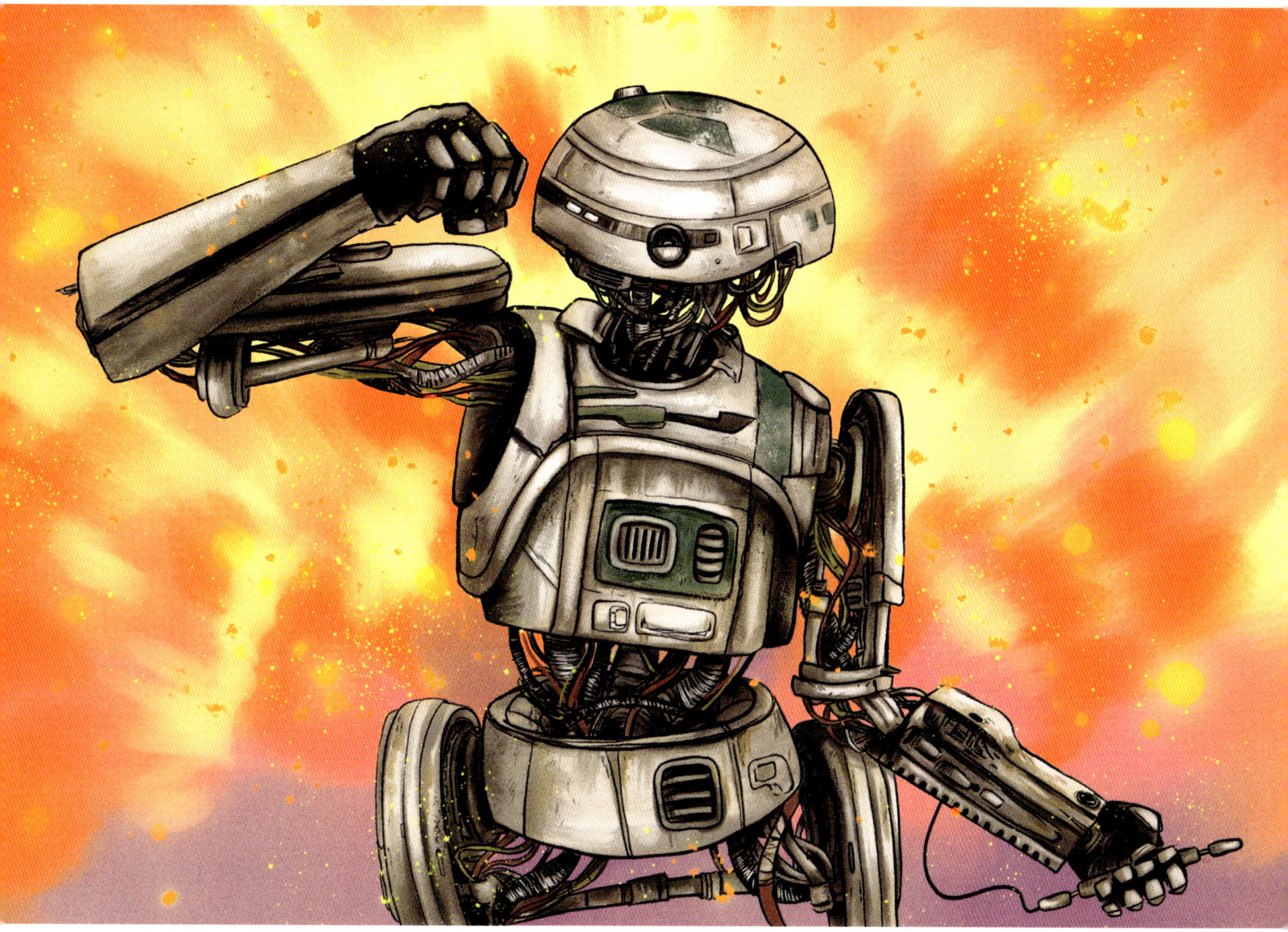

"When you know what you're here to do, everything that's not that matters much less."

—L3-37

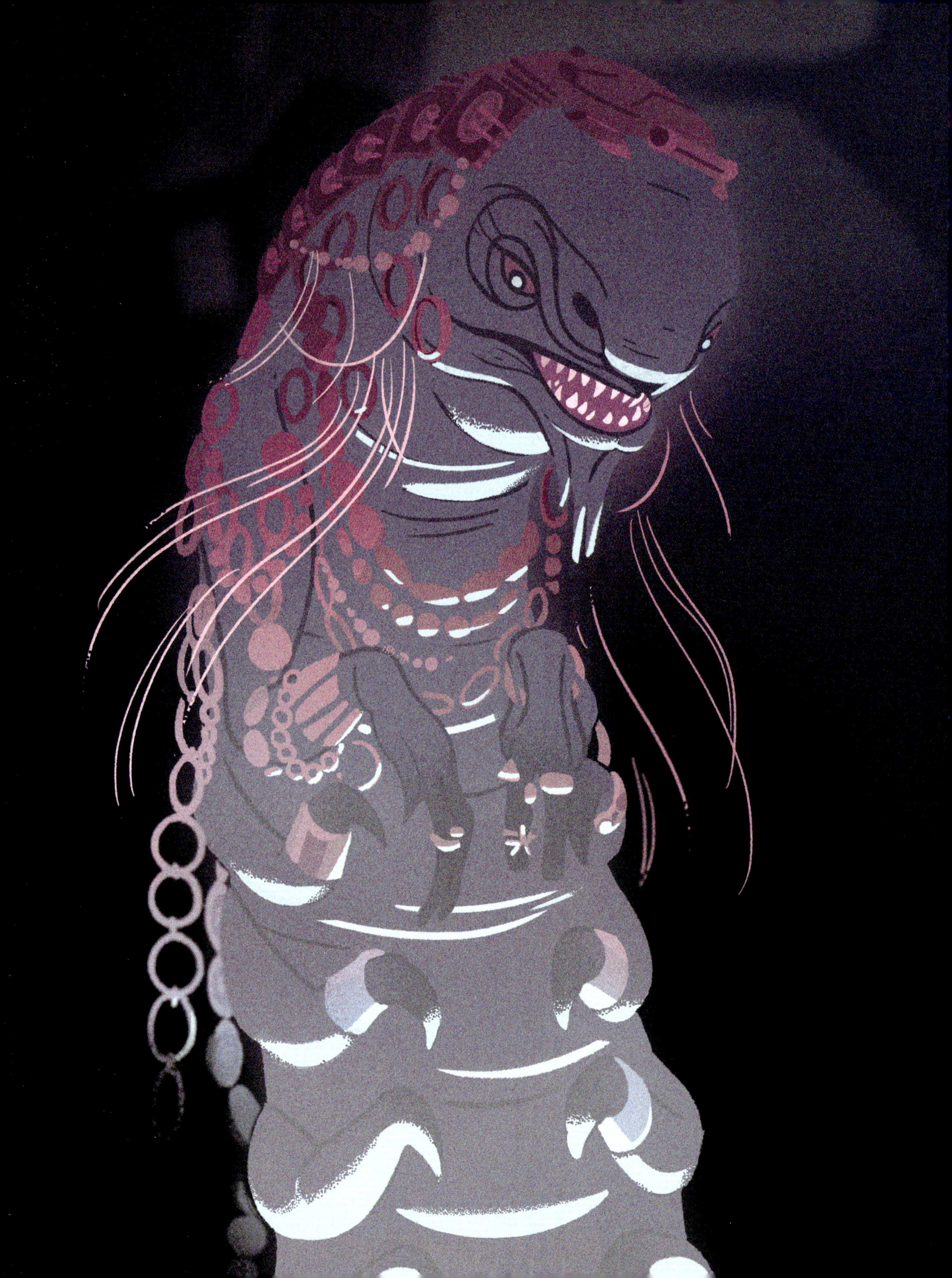

Lady Proxima

"Don't disappoint me, darling."

Donning a half body armor, half jewelry ensemble made from machinery scavenged from factories of Corellia, Lady Proxima makes a grand entrance in *Solo: A Star Wars Story* when she rises from her water cistern to command her urchin gang, the White Worms. As a Grindalid, she hates sunlight, so she's found a way to operate underground in the sewers of Corellia's Coronet City, ruling over the children and teenagers, a.k.a. scrumrats, whom she's lured to her lair with the promise of food and survival. She uses the scrumrats to run errands that secure the gang's prominence in the city's black market, to hunt vermin for herself and her baby worms, and to handle any unreasonable demands she cares to make. Proxima knows how to sound sweet and concerned for her scrumrats, which at one time include Han Solo and Qi'ra, but as Han notes, she doesn't care about anyone.

Proxima was created to look fearsome. *Solo: A Star Wars Story* creature concept designer Jake Lunt Davies observes, "We wanted Lady Proxima to be tall and imposing, and we really liked the serpentine feel of her looming toward and over Han."

Larma D'Acy

A Resistance commander devoted to the cause and loyal to General Organa.

After the fall of the Empire, not every world or planetary system is willing to fall in line under the New Republic's promise of protection. Larma D'Acy's homeworld of Warlentta notably declares its independence. First seen serving the Resistance as a commander in *The Last Jedi*, Larma is part of the family that leads Warlentta's military and protects the system once it opts out of allying with the new government, taking responsibility for its own defense. Growing up in this environment means Larma knows the power of service and the difference it can make for her fellow citizens, and she understands what it's like to put duty first. When she's personally recruited by Leia Organa to join the newly-formed Resistance, Larma recognizes she can serve the greater good of the galaxy. She makes the gallant decision to leave her home and family to oppose the First Order.

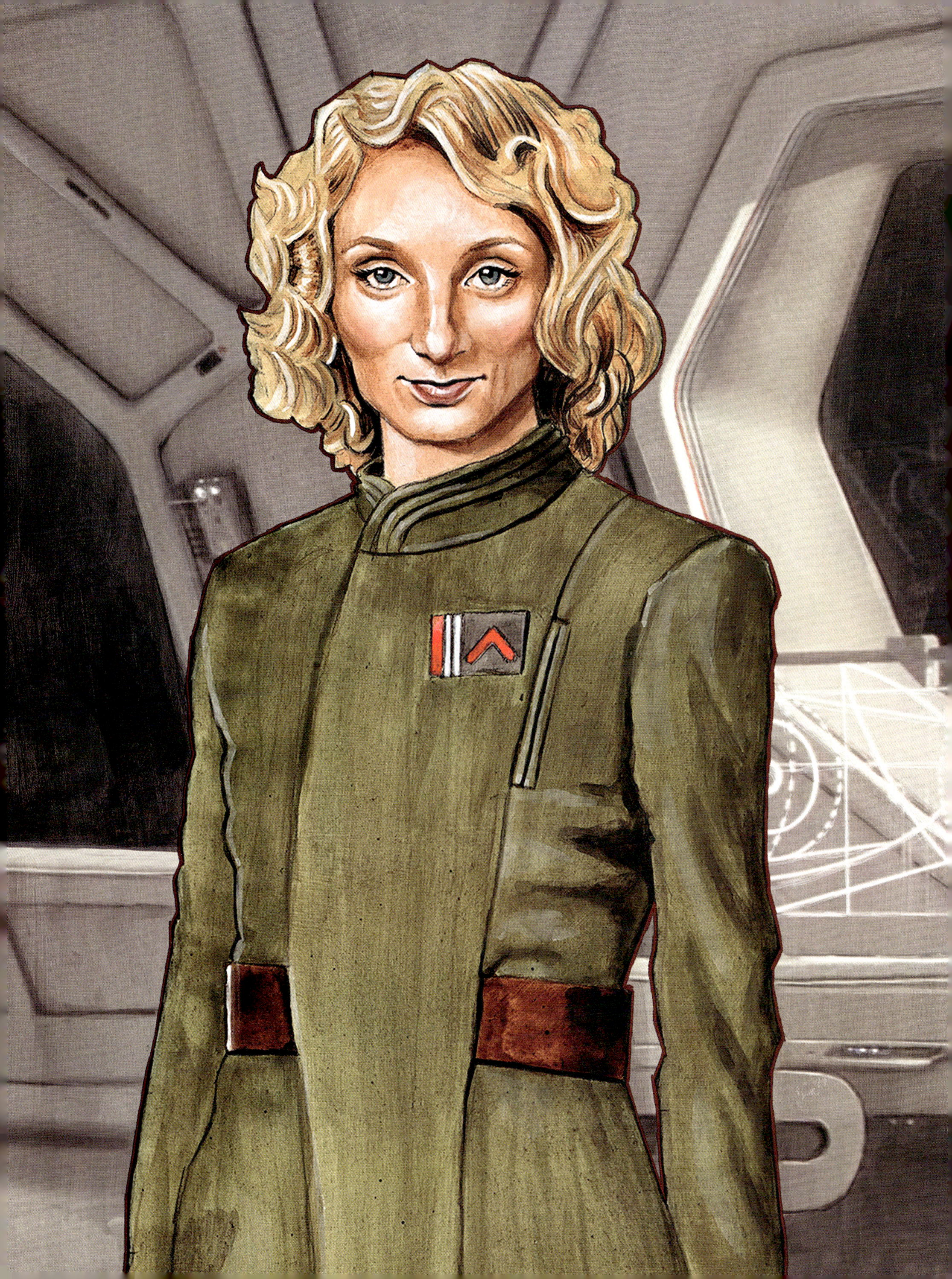

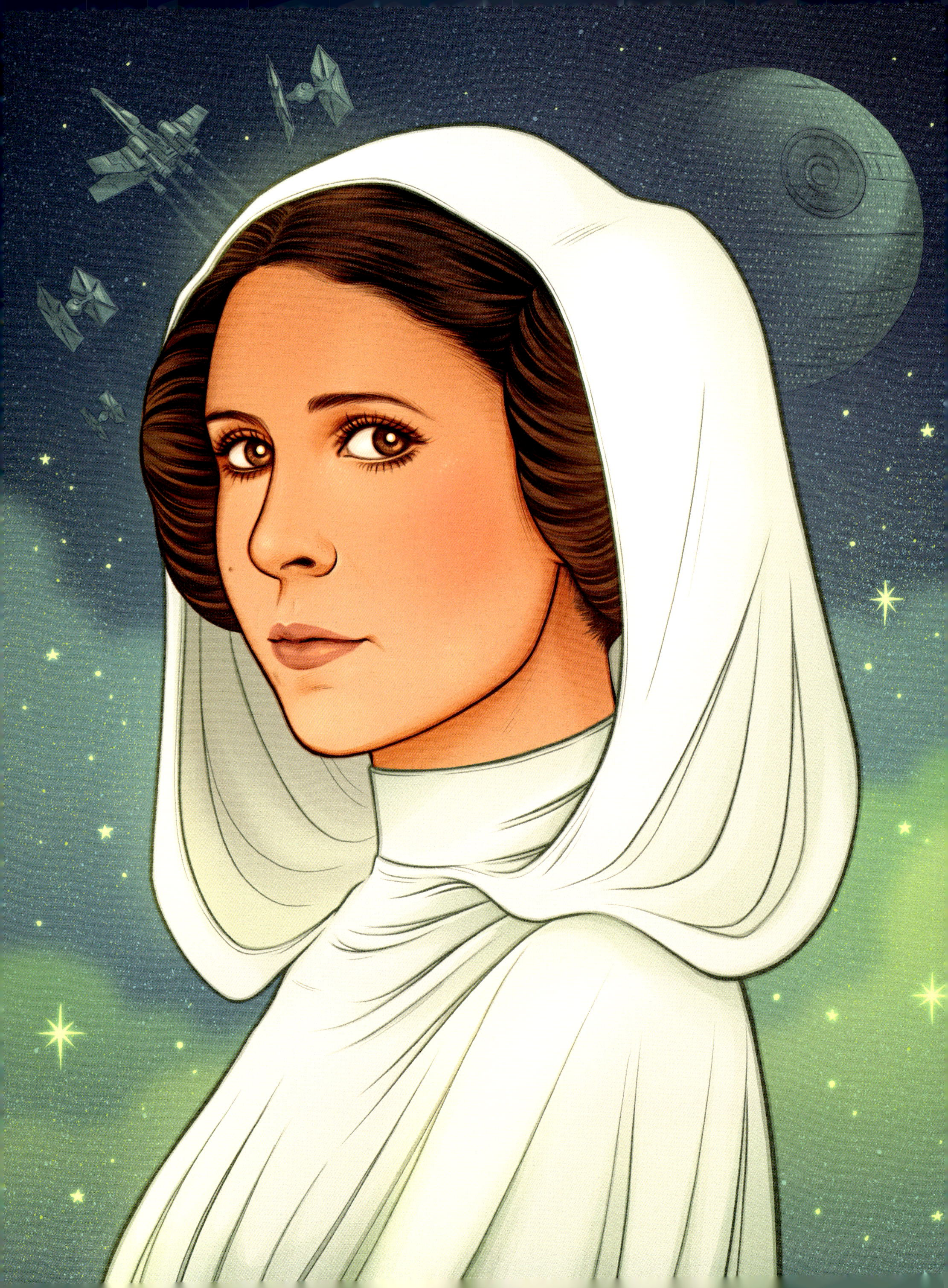

Leia Organa

"Hope is like the sun. If you only believe in it when you see it, you'll never make it through the night."

— LEIA ORGANA

Leia Organa's fearless bravery, intelligence, sharp wit, and commitment to fighting galactic tyranny make her an inspiration not only to the Rebellion, but to generations of *Star Wars* fans around the world. She's the embodiment of hope from her first scene, when she's evading Darth Vader to send the plans for the Death Star to someone who can help. The first female lead in the galaxy far, far away, she's at the center of the saga. She's a rebel, a princess, a senator, a general, and a hero; she's a power player, and would be without her title or Force-sensitivity. Whether blasting stormtroopers or making a persuasive argument, working to install the New Republic or leading the fight against the First Order, she's a formidable leader and military strategist, and anyone who dares underestimate her learns doing so is a terrible mistake.

The princess role was part of what would become *Star Wars: A New Hope* from George Lucas's earliest story treatment in 1973. Initially, the unnamed princess was on the run with a treasure, and the Empire was offering a reward for her capture. But by the second draft, Lucas had written out the princess and instead turned his central male hero Luke into a young woman. By his third draft, Luke was again male, but the princess character was back, now the other half of Luke's character and his twin. Leia, who was at different points called Leila Aquilae, Leia Antilles, and Princess Zara, developed into the staunch, bold, and beloved character we know her as today.

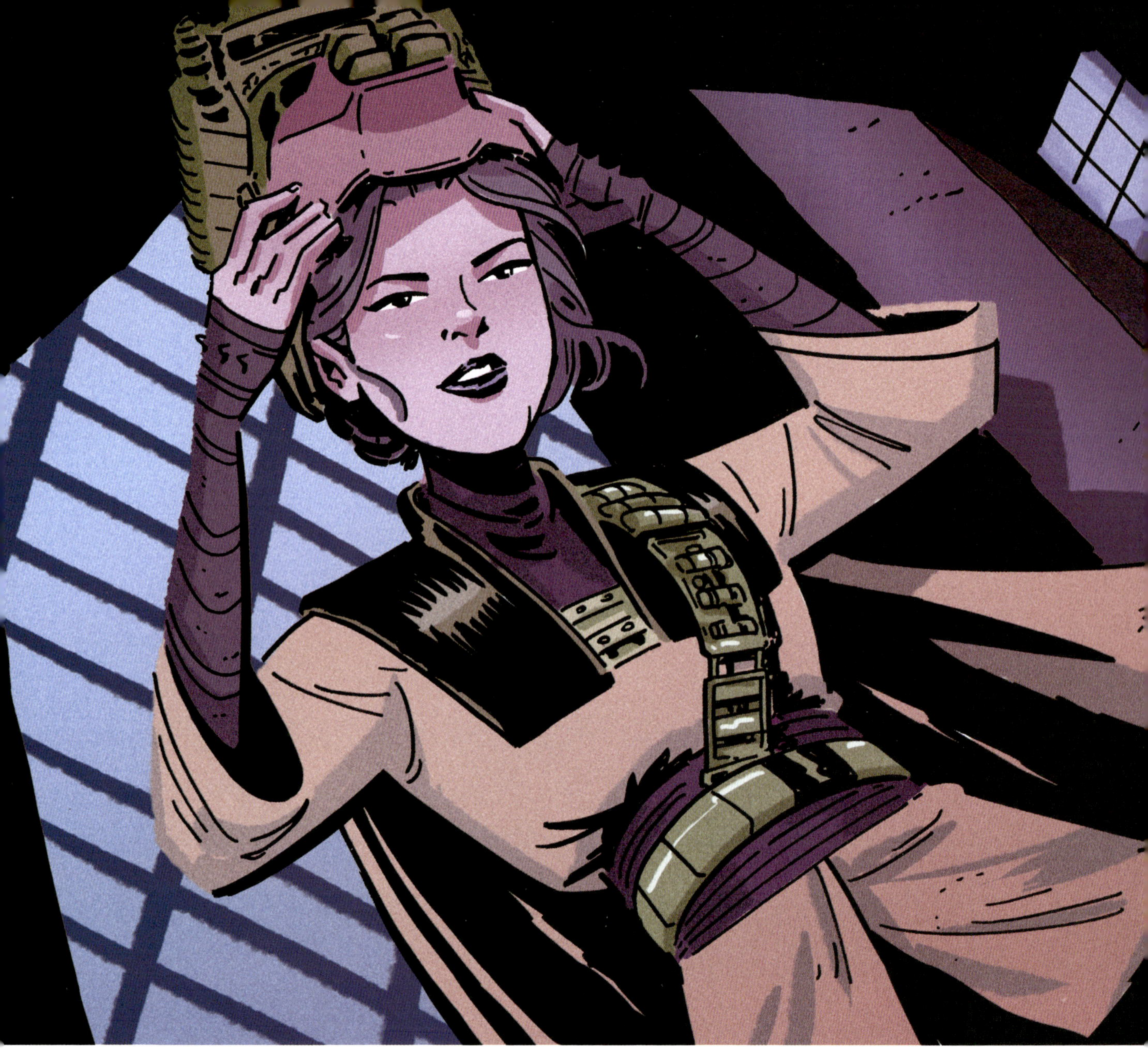

"Somebody has to save our skins!"
—Leia Organa

This personality and spirit was brought to life by the late Carrie Fisher, who earned the role over a number of other actresses considered, including Cindy Williams and Terri Nunn. Lucas would later say of Fisher's casting: "There really wasn't much of a question; there aren't very many people like her. . . . They're one in a billion. She could hold her own through anything." And of her role in the heroic trio of Han, Luke, and Leia, he observed, "She wore a dress through the whole thing, but she was the toughest one in the group."

Leia is synonymous with Fisher. Her portrayal of the sardonic and self-rescuing princess redefined the archetype; she's no damsel in distress. This is the character who, after being captured by the vile Jabba the Hutt in *Return of the Jedi*, uses her own chains to slay her captor, earning her the moniker "Huttslayer" in the galactic underworld. Leia's a force of nature, and her arc through the galaxy drives much of the *Star Wars* saga. Fisher knew she would be forever connected with the character long before she returned to the role for the sequel trilogy. She said, "I am Princess Leia, no matter what. . . . Princess Leia will be on my tombstone." And after she was approached to reprise Leia for *The Force Awakens*, she didn't hesitate, in part because she understood the importance of the character: "There was something human about her. It showed that she could do whatever she needed to do, and if she could do that, then everybody could do it. People identified with her. She's like a superhero."

Sadly, Fisher passed in December 2016, leaving behind an indelible legacy. Though Princess Leia is not engraved on Fisher's tombstone as she once joked, she lives on through the beloved character. Like Leia, Fisher spoke her mind and led a remarkable life.

She played a character that served as a role model, particularly to young girls, just like Daisy Ridley's Rey (in playful tribute, fans sport Leia's and Rey's distinctive hairstyles, at cons and in daily life). Fisher imparted words of wisdom to Ridley while filming *The Last Jedi*: "Carrie lived her life the way she wanted to, never apologizing for anything. There were times through it all when I felt like I was . . . shrinking. And she told me never to shrink away from it—that it should be enjoyed."

With Leia returning for the sequel trilogy, her already rich character expands and deepens. Her life is laid out in films, books, and comics, from her birth to being kidnapped as a child by an Inquisitor and being rescued by Obi-Wan, to learning how to be a queen on Alderaan, to committing herself to the Rebellion, to eventually spearheading the Resistance. Leia is remarkable for reasons beyond counting, but perhaps especially because she lives her life bringing light to the galaxy. When she has to choose between service and personal needs, the galaxy comes first. At what we could expect to be a crushing lowest point, after watching Alderaan's destruction by the Death Star, she vows in *Star Wars Annual* #2 to never give up on her quest for peace: "I will die for it, I'm sure. Today, maybe. But I will fight for it with every breath, anything less is to have done nothing. Anything less is for Alderaan to have meant nothing."

The destruction of Alderaan becomes an immovable cornerstone of Leia's life. She loses her family and friends, her culture, and her entire planet in an instant, just moments after defiantly mocking Grand Moff Tarkin and his foul stench. But she must keep moving forward. After the Rebellion succeeds in destroying the Death Star, Leia embarks on missions with rebel pilot and Alderaan survivor Evaan Verlaine to round up the diaspora of their planet's citizens and to preserve the remaining scraps of Alderaan heritage. She mourns her home throughout her life, sometimes triggered by her political duties. And she comes to understand a hard truth about the event: "Imagine trying to look yourself in the mirror every day once you realize . . . you would do it all again, you would still sacrifice all of those innocent lives if it means stopping the Empire."

She chooses to get involved in the Rebel Alliance as a teenager; she learns about her parents' surreptitious activity against Emperor Palpatine in *Leia, Princess of Alderaan* and starts participating against their wishes. Her conviction overrides caution, so Leia decides to ask forgiveness rather than permission. Seeing a spark in Leia, Mon Mothma mentors the teen and fosters her

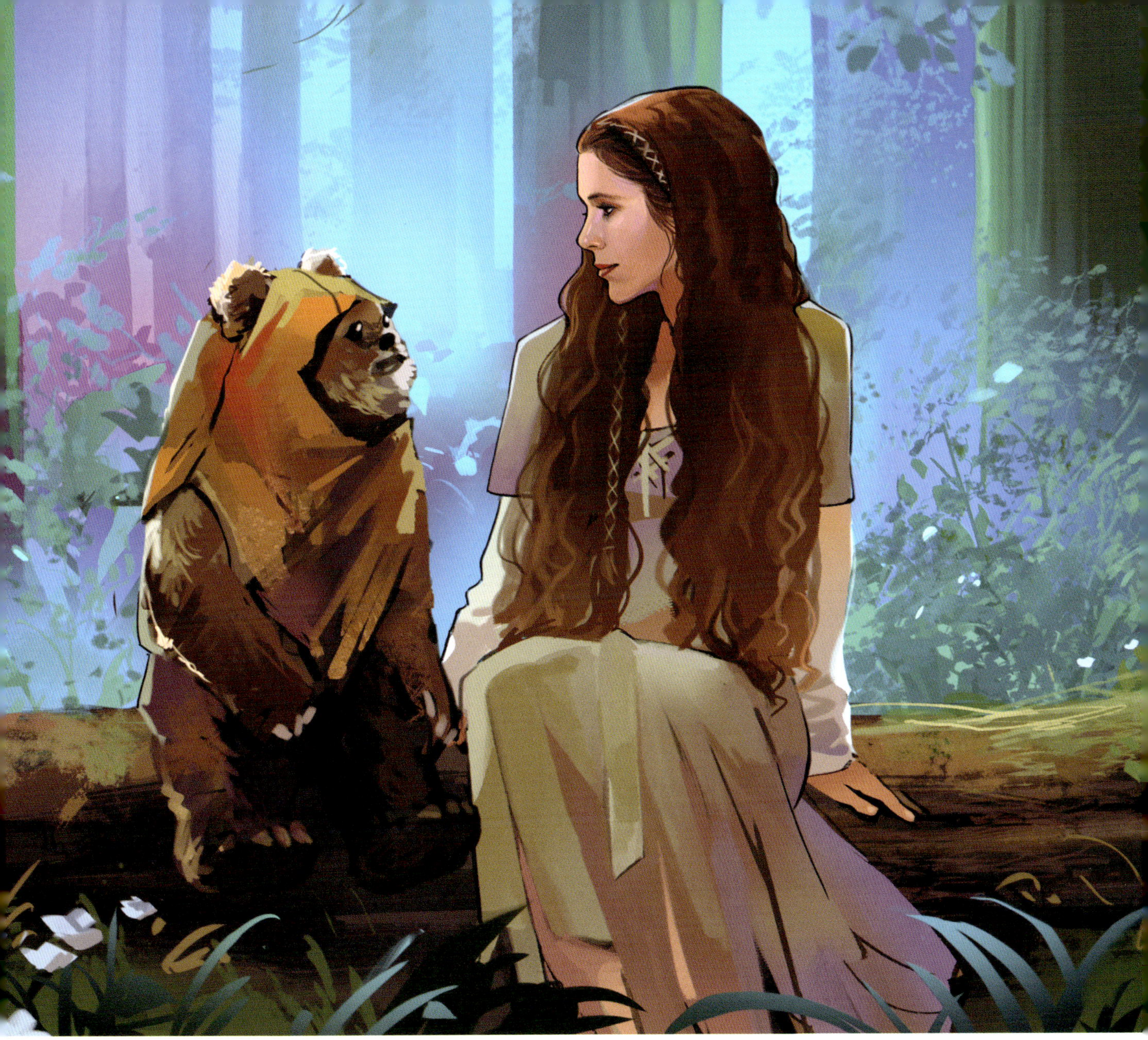

“Good intentions aren’t enough. They’re not meaningless, but—that’s where we have to start. Not where we end.”

—Leia Organa

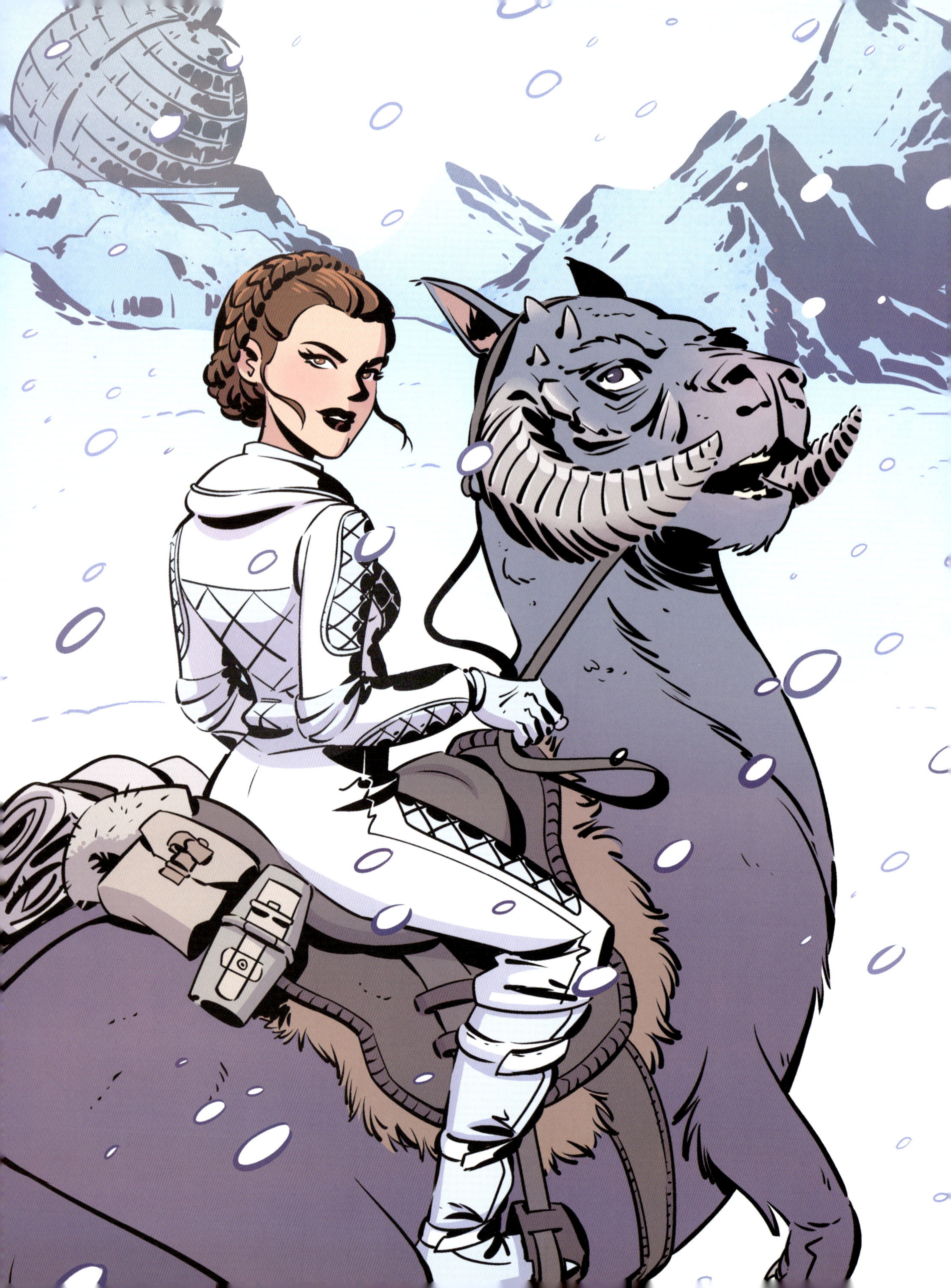

curious nature. When Leia appears in *Star Wars Rebels*, it's evident how she uses her privilege and position to help others. She manipulates Imperials and lies to them, and they write her off as harmless. She tells Ezra Bridger, "I feel like because I can fight, I have to, for those who cannot."

And Leia takes that fight outside of senate halls. She knows talk isn't always enough, and understands how the spinning wheels of argument and lack of action in the Senate contributed to the rise of the Empire and the subsequent birth of the Rebel Alliance. After she plays a crucial role in helping bring down the second Death Star in the Battle of Endor, she helps form the New Republic, and her skill balance shifts again toward the oratory and political. But while she keeps a foot in that world, she is also investigating rumors about the dark rise of the First Order from the ashes of the Empire. The New Republic Assembly dismisses Leia's concerns as paranoia, and worse, warmongering, so in true Leia fashion, she takes charge and forms the Resistance in secret.

Through all of her tribulations and victories on the battlefield, Leia has more ordinary issues, too—the kind of issues faced in this galaxy as well. She falls in love with and marries Han Solo, a politics-averse scoundrel, and she gives birth to Ben Solo. Navigating parenthood isn't simple for Han and Leia, especially since Ben is a Force-user, like his mother and uncle Luke, and the depths of his power and emotions are unclear. His turn to the dark side and the First Order cuts to Leia's core, and makes her feel like a failure. But she doesn't give up on her struggle against the First Order—even following the horror of Ben (now Kylo Ren) killing his father Han, in a moment made possible only by his parents' belief in their son's possible redemption.

Buoyed by her hope, Leia keeps going even in the darkest of times. It's who she is. It's devastating, and the first time we've seen the unflappable Leia Organa waiver, when she says toward the end of *The Last Jedi*, "The galaxy has lost all its hope. The spark is out." But she does not break, the tide of the battle turns, and Leia rallies the remaining Resistance forces to fight another day. Hope always remains.

It is because of General Leia Organa that the Resistance perseveres. She gathers the survivors of the Battle of Crait and rebuilds by recruiting new leadership, sometimes by sending Poe and his squadron, but she is just as likely to make an in-person plea. Leia also makes time during this crucial period to take over Rey's Jedi training. Once trained by Luke, Leia knows enough about the Force to help Rey continue on the Jedi path.

Leia is a gentle teacher, but a firm one. She pushes Rey to quiet her inner dialogue and listen to the Force. When Rey wants to quit, Leia doesn't let her. She tells Rey, "Never be afraid of who you are." As the daughter of Darth Vader, Leia knows all too well about carrying the weight of a challenging legacy.

Her guidance also extends to encouraging Rose Tico to perform duties where her mechanical skills can shine. In her role as general, she rebuilds trust in those who participated in the mutiny against Vice Admiral Holdo, and this grace helps keep the First Order at bay. When she learns of Emperor Palpatine's return and the existence of the Sith Eternal fleet, she is angry with herself for not seeing the truth sooner, but she gets to work and supports the Resistance's attempt to locate Exegol, where Palpatine and his forces are hiding.

Leia loses her husband, and her brother, and sees her son on a moral precipice. Despite all the grief etched on her heart, in her final moments, she reaches out to Ben, to bring him back to the light, to give the last of herself to fight the darkness. Fighting the darkness, no matter what shape it takes, is what Leia does best.

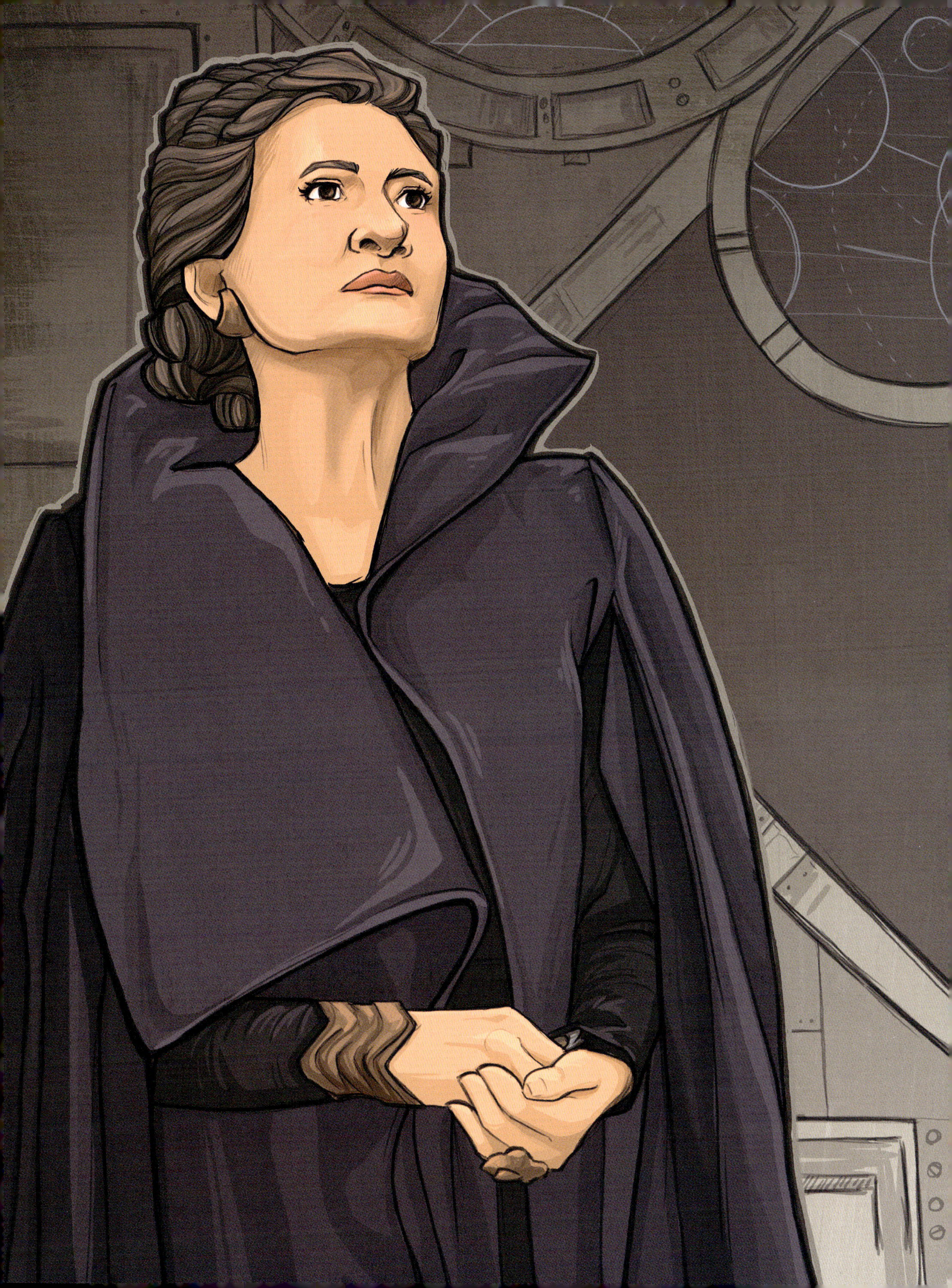

Lina Graf

"We'll see them again. I know we will."

The Empire's responsible for tearing many families apart before and during the Galactic Civil War, including Lina Graf's. With her parents arrested by a cruel Imperial captain, Lina is left to look after her younger brother Milo, their pet Kowakian monkey lizard, their droid CR-8R, and their shuttle craft, the *Whisper Bird*. Their misadventures in the children's book series *Adventures in Wild Space*, one of the few *Star Wars* book series for children with protagonists who are kids, illustrate how Lina rises to the occasion and acts as the protector of their family and its secrets. She's uncertain, she's figuring it out as she goes along, but despite her fears she doesn't run away from her responsibilities.

Author Cavan Scott admires how Lina keeps her head and doesn't get bogged down by the enormity of the crisis. He thinks of his own daughters when he writes Lina, saying, "They were just discovering *Star Wars* as I first was writing her. They also had a very clear sense of fair play. Children have a wonderful habit of telling things how they really are. They see injustice and call it out without fear of reprisal or retribution. I couldn't think of a better trait for anyone going up against the Empire."

To survive, Lina uses all the skills she learned from her parents, Rhyssa and Auric. They're explorers and galactic cartographers, so Lina knows how to think fast in the unsafe scenarios she and her brother often find themselves in. Milo relies on Lina to fix things (in a literal sense, she's talented with machines), and she always does. Lina's desire to find and rescue their parents lead her and Milo to the underground rebels Ephraim and Mira Bridger on Lothal.

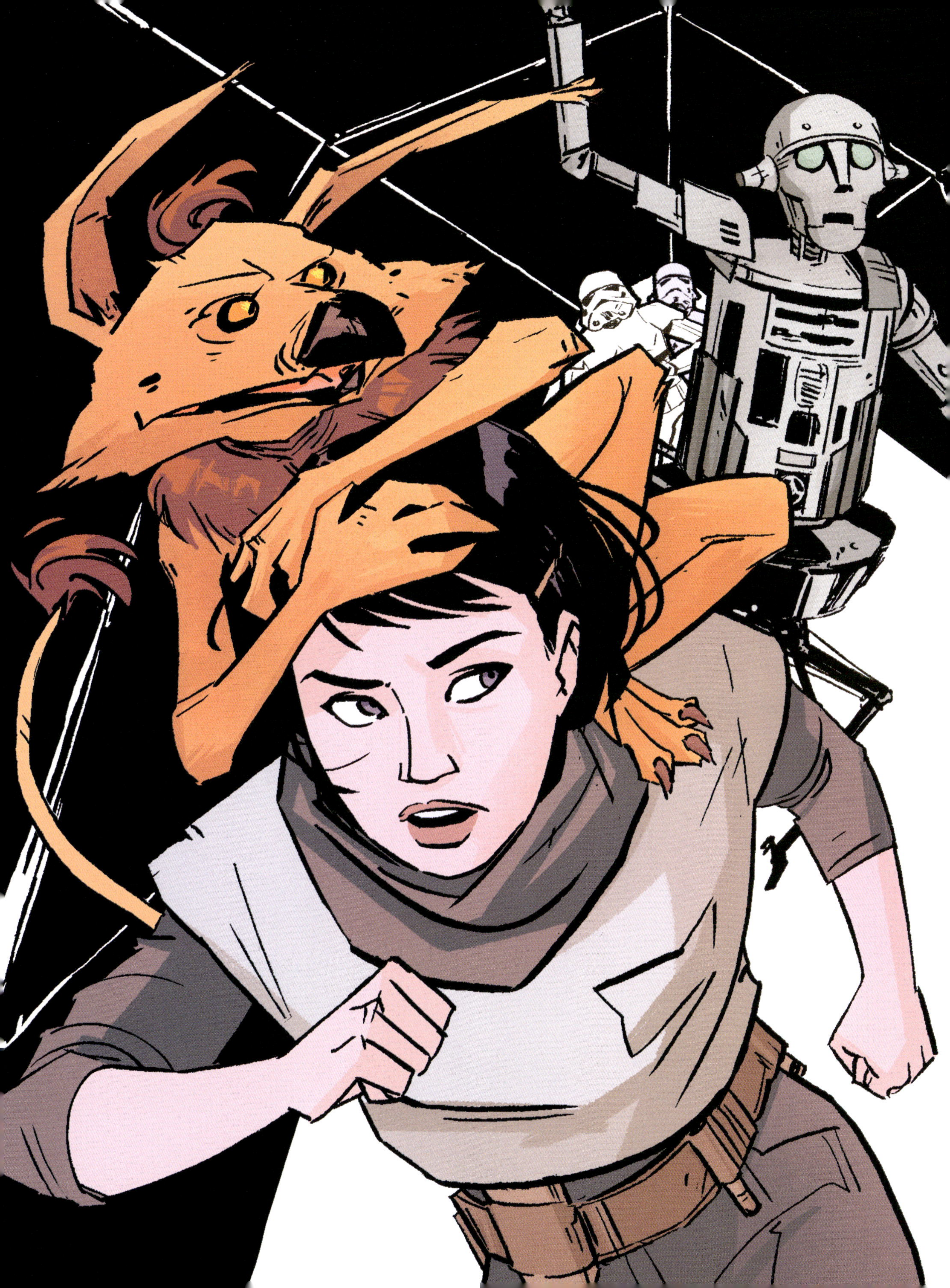

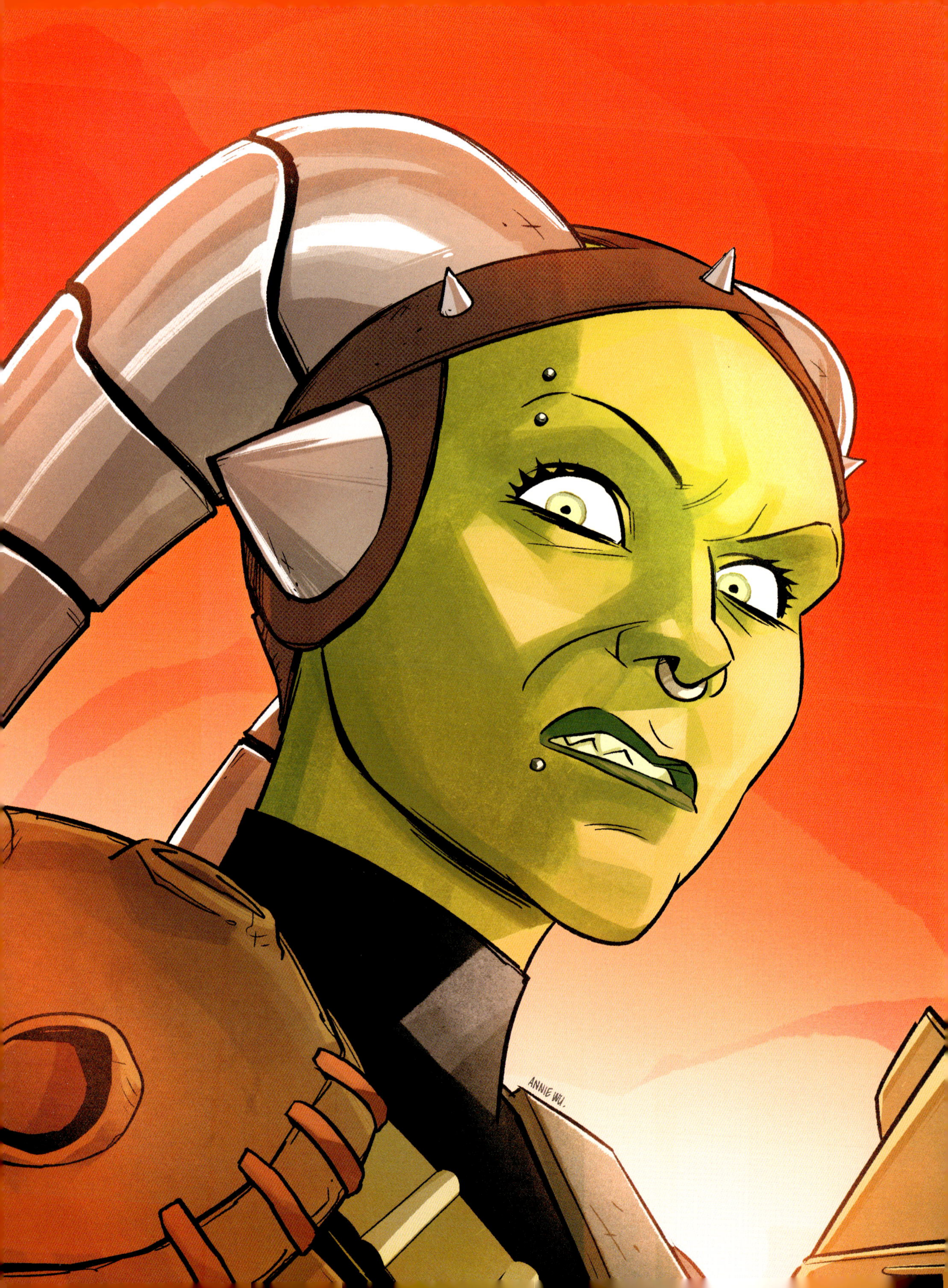
ANNIE WU.

Lourna Dee

"What is a Tempest Runner without her mask?"

—LOURNA DEE

Sometimes a villain is so deliciously evil and so self-serving, one can't help but get attached and hang on her every decision. Lourna Dee is such an antagonist. She's allied to herself above all else, to the degree that she's named more than one of her ships *Lourna Dee*. She says they're named after the only person she trusts. And because she puts stock in only herself, she never has to worry about knowing the cut of betrayal. Lourna maintains indestructible walls around her heart and her goals. No one gets in, no one gets in her way.

Everything about the green-skinned Twi'lek screams predator, from her Tempest mask to the kell dragon–hide leather suit she wears. And when she removes the mask, she reveals a mouth of vicious teeth—teeth she's filed into sharp points. Lourna does not hide who she is.

At the same time, Lourna is a masterful liar and will deceive anyone to achieve her goal. She puts on different identities like costumes. From the life of a royal on Ryloth, she's also been enslaved, a cadet in the Galactic Republic, and then a fierce member of the Nihil. Once she joins the Nihil, Lourna climbs the ranks and, superficially at least, demonstrates her loyalty to the Nihil leader, Marchion Ro. But Lourna does everything she can to work under his radar and elevate herself. Since she's always plotting many steps ahead, she makes it look easy. Lourna does whatever it takes to control her own destiny and get what's hers—and that's the way she likes it.

Lula Talisola and Zeen Mrala

"Trust in the Force. Trust in love, in Lula."

"The second that they met, their lives changed dramatically in the best way, and that also brings so much complication," says Daniel José Older of Lula Talisola and Zeen Mrala. He knew before he started writing the comic they first appear in that theirs would be a love story. Part of that complication is, of course, that Lula is a Padawan, and the Jedi Order famously does not permit attachments. Lula has to look inward and determine if the love she develops for Zeen means she has to pause her Jedi dreams.

The situation isn't simple for Zeen, either. She has Force abilities, but she hides them. Since her family belongs to the religious group the Elders of the Path, she must follow the religion's belief that using the Force is wrong. But she meets Lula and Master Yoda and has the opportunity to hone her abilities, even though she's too old to formally train as a Jedi. The encounter opens another door for Zeen—maybe a door she can walk through with Lula, since they first connect through the Force.

While we root for them to find their way as a couple, it's important to note Lula and Zeen are both individuals with their own accomplishments and struggles. Zeen's childhood best friend, Krix Kamerat, refuses to accept that Zeen has embraced the Force, and goes on to join the Nihil. Lula grapples with feelings of inadequacy; she later reckons with a near-death experience after the attack on Starlight Beacon that leaves her with amnesia.

But Zeen and Lula overcome. And they marry each other. They are stronger together.

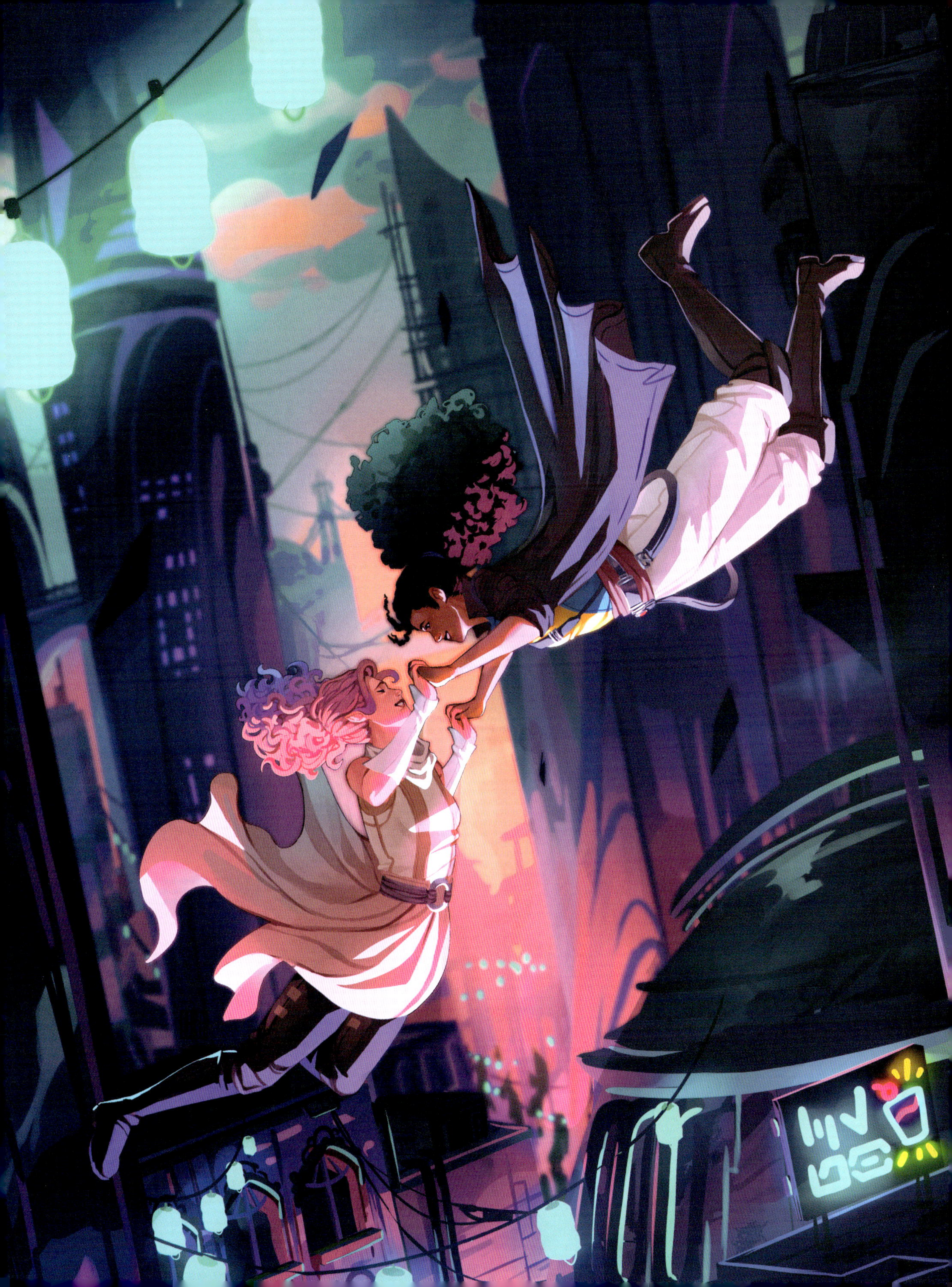

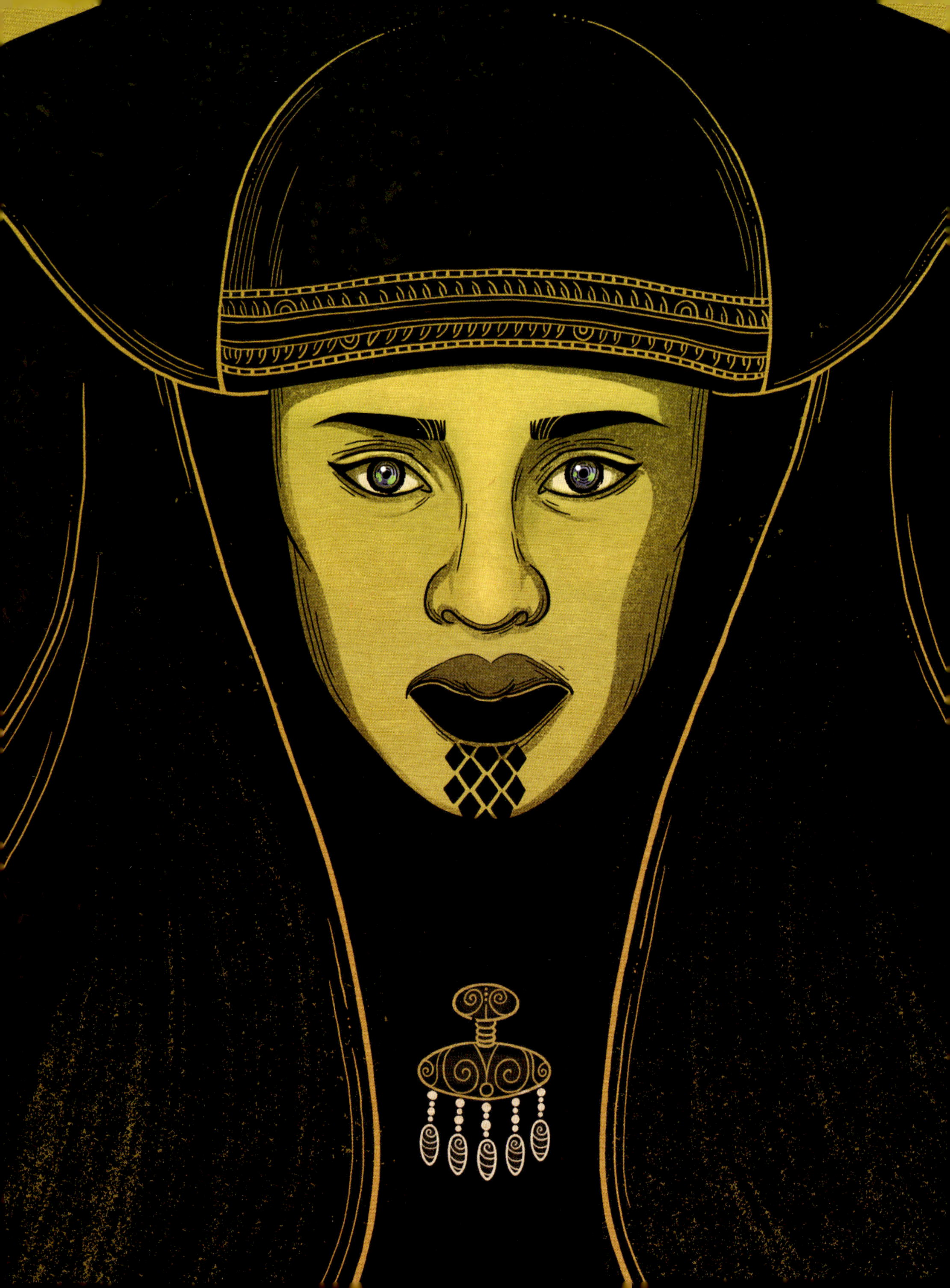

Luminara Unduli

"Gentlemen, if you are quite finished, we have a battle to begin."

Could you remain calm if you were held captive by zombies and about to be forcibly infected by brain worms? Mirialan Jedi Master Luminara Unduli is known for keeping a level head in the most trying of scenarios—even when confronted with parasites during a mission on Geonosis. She's also known for playing by the rules, and she passes her disciplined perspective to her Padawan Barriss Offee, who unfortunately will find the Jedi falling short of her own principled standards with deadly consequences.

First seen in *Attack of the Clones*, Luminara leads many missions for the Army of the Republic in *Star Wars: The Clone Wars*. Her aptitude for strategic planning and combat with or without a lightsaber makes her a valuable general. Stationed on the Wookiee homeworld of Kashyyyk upon the issue of Order 66, she escapes slaughter but is captured by the Empire, who use her to lay a trap for the remaining Jedi.

Lyra Erso

"Trust the Force."

Facing grave danger with the arrival of Imperial forces, Lyra urges her daughter Jyn to follow a plan for her own safety, and to put trust in the Force. It's not an easy sentiment for someone to pass on when they've been through what Lyra Erso has. But despite the many hardships she's encountered, her belief stays strong. Even before dying at the hands of Orson Krennic's death troopers in *Rogue One*, Lyra left her daughter with a message of hope and a kyber crystal pendant. Strong-willed and sharp enough to see through the Empire's manipulations of her husband Galen, Lyra risks everything to keep her family safe—including setting up a contingency plan with her friend Saw Gerrera, who comes to Lah'mu to evacuate Jyn.

Before the events of *Rogue One*, Lyra worked as a geologist who studies crystals. Her work with natural environments on different worlds around the galaxy speaks to her on a spiritual level as well as a scientific one, leading her to study the Force and the ways of the Jedi Order. Lyra finds a unique balance between the scientific and the spiritual; it helps her attain clarity about the Empire's intentions.

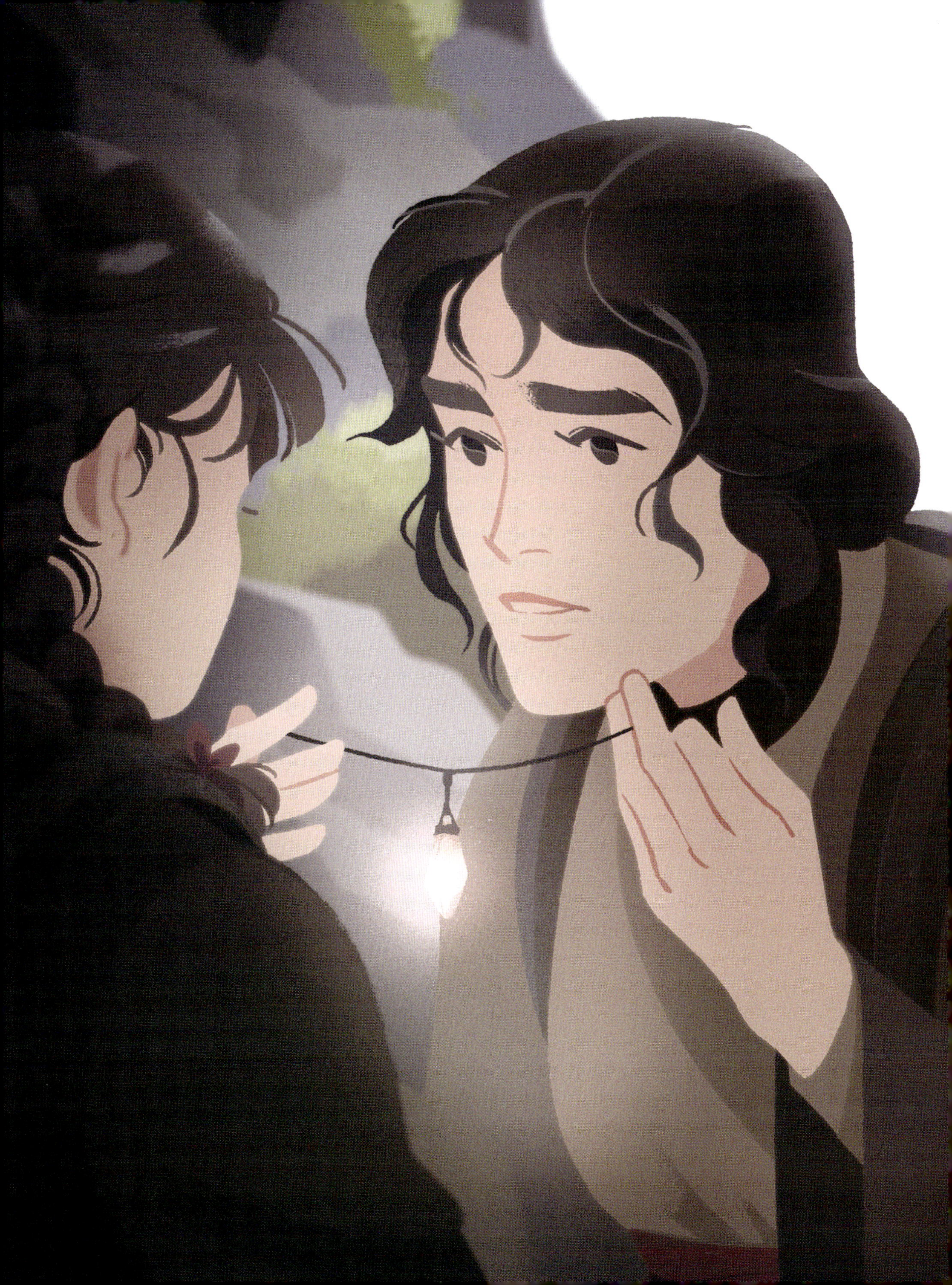

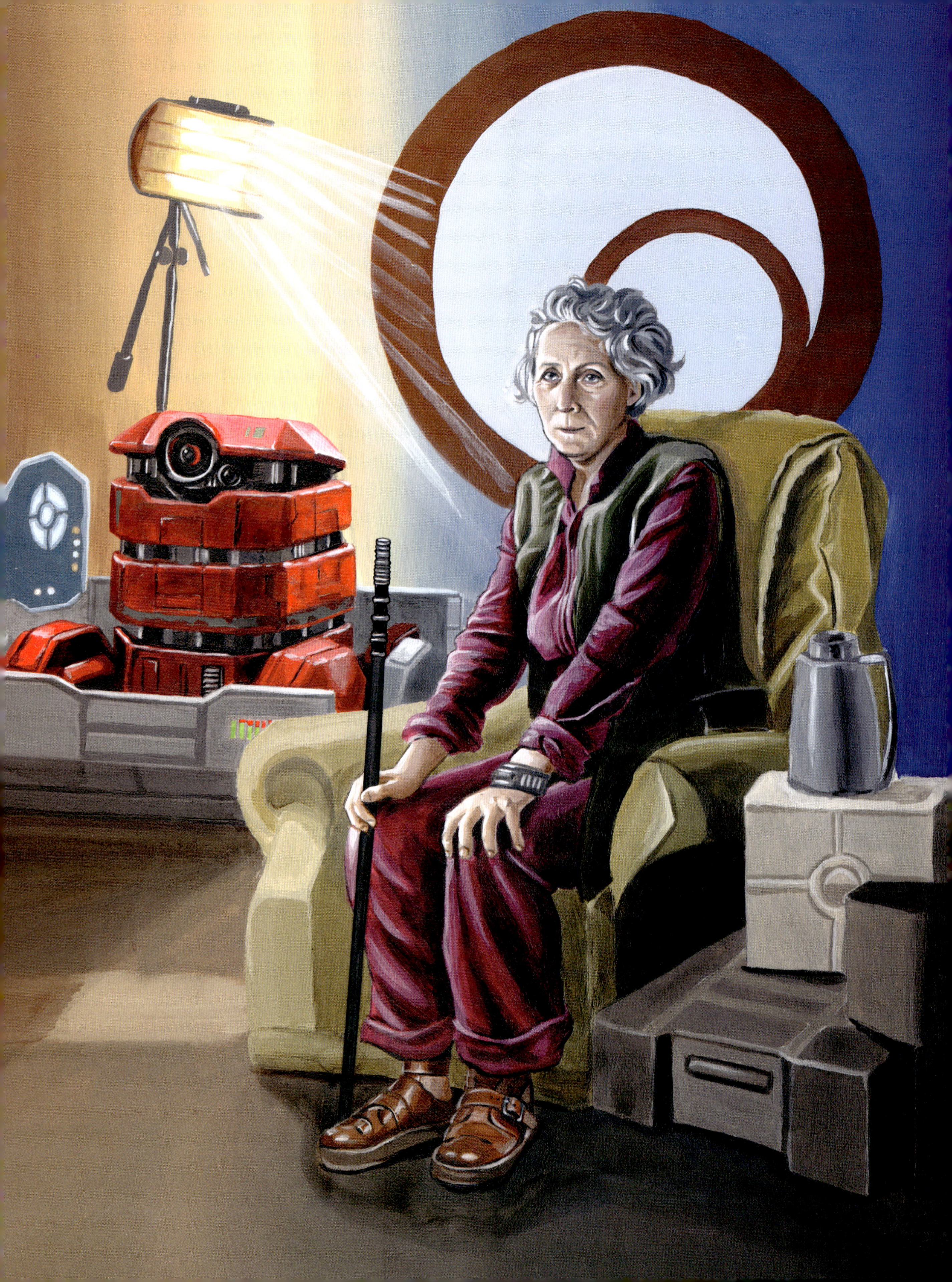

Maarva Andor

"There is a darkness reaching like rust into everything around us."

On an average day in Ferrix, a funeral procession on Rix Road turns into a riot, and it's because of Maarva Andor. Her droid B2EMO plays a speech Maarva recorded prior to her death, and her words shock her neighbors out of complacency and into a protest against the Imperials occupying the town. Her words, full of regret over her own inaction, spur others to do more and to work for a better galaxy—including her adopted son, Cassian. Maarva Carassi Andor, a former president of the social club the Daughters of Ferrix, is a prime example of how an everyday person can make a ripple that leads to a rushing wave of change.

Maarva's past leads to her eventual heroic moment. She works as a scavenger with her husband, Clem, traveling the galaxy for scrap and tech to repair and sell. On one such trip to Kenari, they discover a boy named Kassa, seemingly alone aboard a crashed Republic ship. Believing him to be in danger, they bring him home to Ferrix and call him Cassian. But the Galactic Empire eventually comes to Ferrix and disrupts their lives by executing Clem for a minor infraction. Maarva's heart hardens toward all but her son and her droid.

It takes over a decade for Maarva to transform her grief into retribution against the Empire. When stormtroopers return to Ferrix, she quietly becomes a rebellion of one, despite her failing health. Cassian tries to convince Maarva to leave her homeworld with him, but she digs in and insists on staying to fight however she can. Her life shows us that sometimes bravery requires time to develop, but that it's always right there, under the surface, waiting for us to grasp it.

Mae and Osha Aniseya

*"You are with me. I am with you.
Always one, but born as two."*

Twins forged in the fire of tragedy, Mae and Osha Aniseya split apart, come back together, and go different ways once again. The details of their birth are shrouded in mystery, but while Mother Koril says she carried them, Mother Aniseya claims to have created them. Along with her partner, Mother Koril, Aniseya raises Mae and Osha as siblings and teaches them the ways of the witch coven Aniseya and Koril lead. While Mae embraces her mother's lessons and looks forward to taking the vow of Ascension, Osha feels less confident about following in her family's footsteps. When Jedi arrive on their homeworld of Brendok, they bring the potential of another way, along with triggering events that change Mae's and Osha's lives forever.

Confusion over what happens on Brendok shapes their following years. Believing Mae responsible for Aniseya's death and the destruction of the coven, Osha trains to become a Jedi (though she eventually leaves the Order and works as a meknek). Believing Aniseya and the others died because of the Jedi, Mae embarks on a quest for revenge and trains under a mysterious dark side figure. We can draw lines from their diverging paths to a study of nature versus nurture. How does what they know about their past—and who they learn that information from—affect who they become?

When the truth about the past comes to light, each sister makes her own choice and shapes her own destiny. We may not understand Osha's decision to align herself with the Stranger, or Mae's willingness to have her memory wiped, but Osha and Mae are moving forward from a place of reality instead of possible truths.

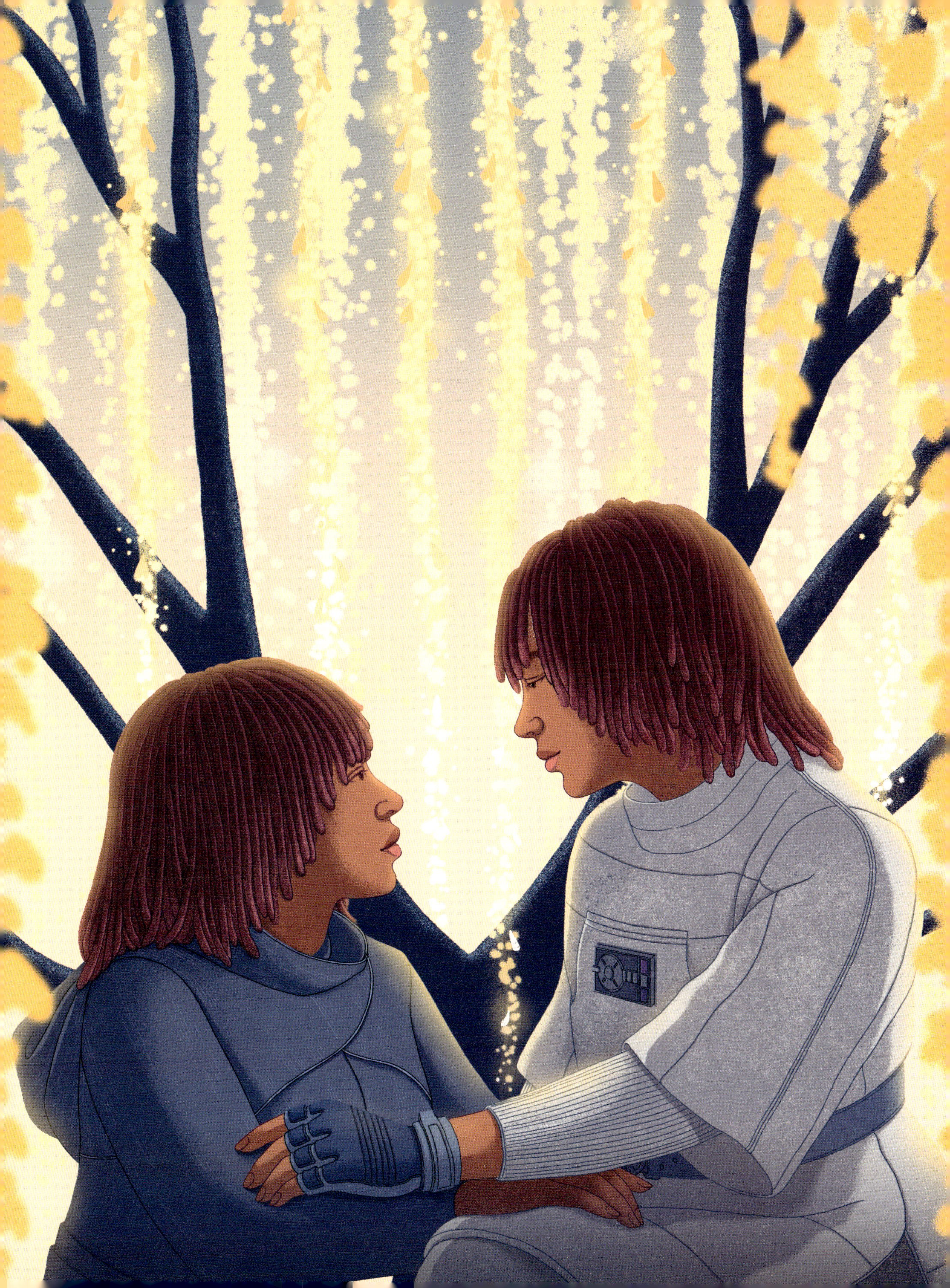

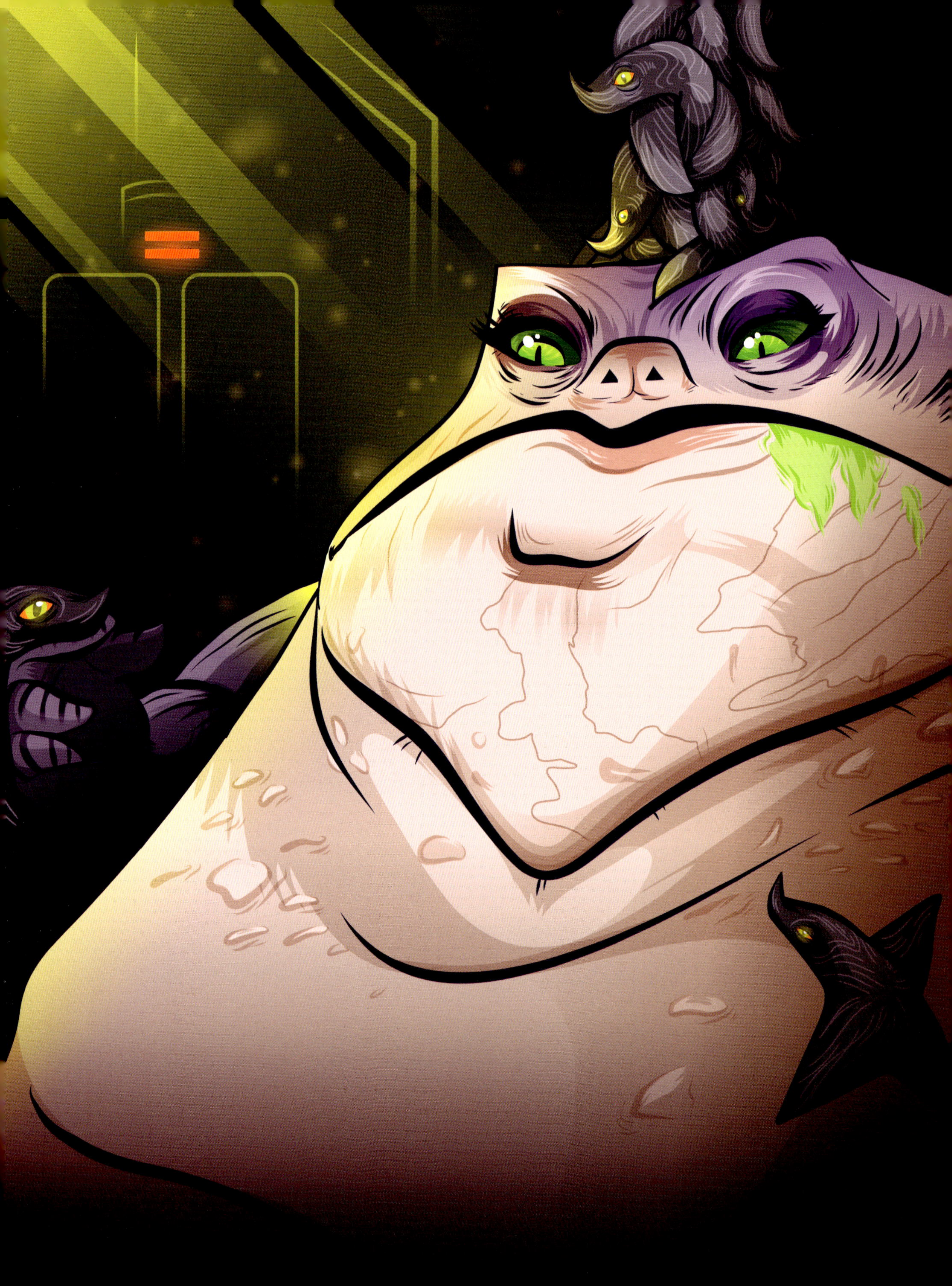

Mama the Hutt

"Should have figured, after all these years of never callin', you'd show up at dinner time."

Many of us are guilty of not staying in touch with our family. Mama the Hutt knows what it's like to be ignored and forgotten. We first visit her home in the swamps of Nal Hutta when her son Ziro the Hutt crawls to her doorstep begging for a favor in *The Clone Wars*. Typical. She'd been living alone for years, getting by with the help of hovering housekeeper droids. Mama, the grandmother of Jabba the Hutt, is none too pleased with her deadbeat son, but she acts in magnanimous fashion anyway and helps him. It's what mothers do.

Visitors only come to Mama the Hutt's home on rare occasions, but the over-a-thousand-year-old matriarch stays mindful of her appearance. She wears a stylish stack of small black creatures called Sha'rellian toops atop her head.

Maz Kanata

"Hope is not lost today. It is found."

All are welcome. (No fighting.) Everyone who arrives at Maz Kanata's castle—smuggler, bounty hunter, and traveler alike—sees and is expected to abide by this sign upon entering. But while this is her establishment's only rule, Maz herself is a strong fighter, and is ready to demonstrate this skill when the need arises. A pirate queen and legend revealed in *The Force Awakens*, Maz is open to the galaxy around her and the beings who call it home—unless those beings cause trouble. Known as Kanata the Despoiler, Kanata the Benevolent, and Maz Kanata the Usurper, she demonstrates what it's like to be kind and welcoming while maintaining a zero-tolerance policy for anyone jeopardizing what she has built. It's a precarious balance, but it's one the Force-attuned pirate queen has been able to maintain for more than a thousand years.

Though small in stature, Maz is tough. She's been injured sixty-seven times, and twenty-two of the injuries were life-threatening. She has a commanding presence. Inspired by *The Force Awakens* director J.J. Abrams and production designer Rick Carter's English teacher, Rose Gilbert, Maz was almost brought to life as a puppet or animatronic. But Abrams soon realized they should employ a motion capture process to create the pirate queen, both because they didn't find a puppet design early enough, and they thought an animatronic might limit what the character could do. So, they used computer

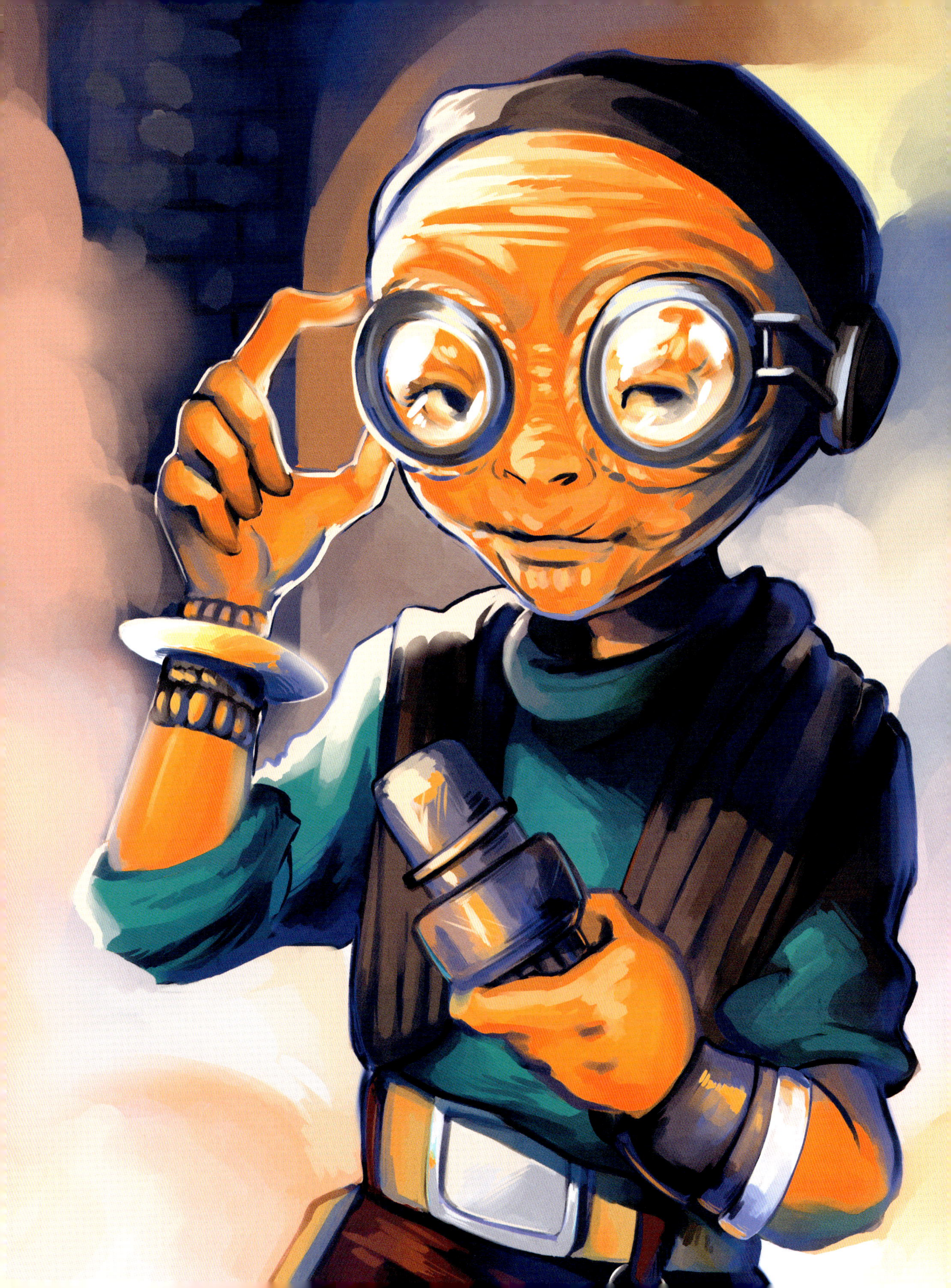

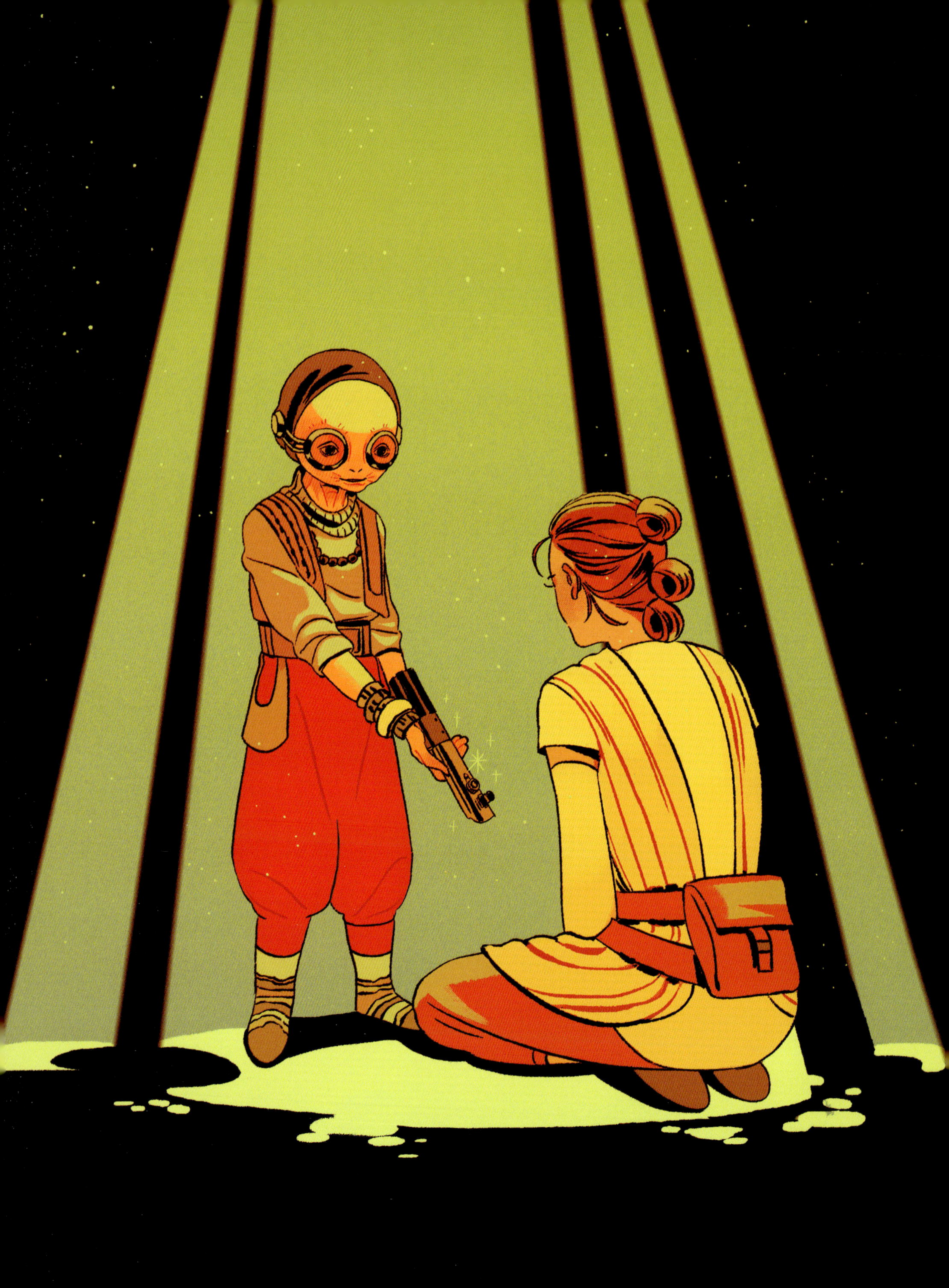

graphics to enhance the creature qualities of the character, but based her expressive movements on the performance of actress Lupita Nyong'o. "The performance was all Lupita," said Abrams. "She was there on set, and we did capture sessions afterwards as well, and I can't say enough about working with her."

Nyong'o found the idea of inhabiting the role in this way appealing. "What attracted me [to the role] was, first of all, the opportunity to play a motion capture character. I thought that gave me a unique experience, where I got to play a character that wasn't limited by my physical circumstances." But it wasn't easy. "The first time I came onto set in that suit, it was the most alienating thing in the world. Because there are lights shining on my face, everyone is drawn to look at me. I was fighting nerves, butterflies, in my stomach, and feeling very self-conscious. I was still trying to figure out how to be this completely different person in this suit, and to have an understanding of my physicality and the space around me. It was bizarre."

It took more than Nyong'o to bring Maz to the screen. Actress Arti Shah also worked with Nyong'o as a motion capture double for Maz. "I was very lucky to have met Lupita," said Shah. "She was such a pleasure to work with. She would tell me how she wanted Maz to come across, but also ask my perspective with regards to Maz's height, and how quickly she would walk. As a small person, I tend to take small but quick steps."

Maz's castle on the planet Takodana is the place to go for loans, repairs, games of chance, hideout, or to start your smuggling career. She will occasionally leave home in one of her starships to see firsthand what's going on, taking the pulse of the galaxy as a way to anticipate trouble and maintain her own order. Maz is versatile; she's comfortable as a pilot, operating a jetpack, and using knitting needles. She has seen much in her long life, including the Galactic Civil War and the rise and fall of the Empire, and warns about the shadow of the First Order spreading. She understands them as part of a continuum and as a threat to be opposed, but this is a fight she'll conduct in her own way. To further maintain perspective, Maz collects antiquities from around the galaxy. She sees more than the superficial value of these

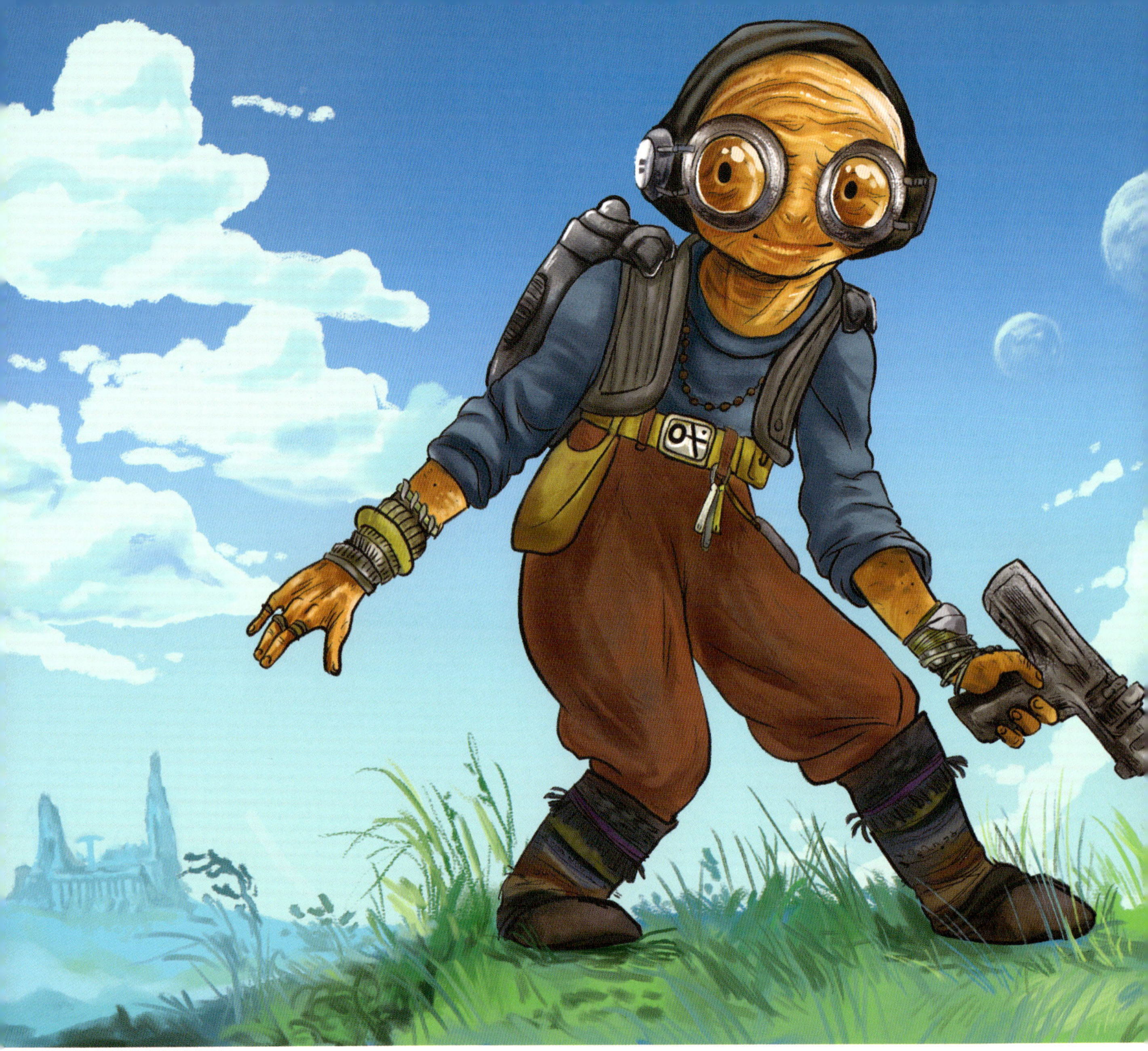

"Being a hero is not about success or failure, being a hero means stepping forward, no matter the outcome."

—Maz Kanata

relics and knows they can teach much about the future, stashing these treasures in protected vaults.

Maz cares about her business, but she's not selfish, and is generous with her time and connections. She's forged alliances with everyone from industrious transporters to master codebreakers. It's an aspect Nyong'o likes: "Maz, herself, I was attracted to the heart of her." In *Forces of Destiny*, in which Maz is the host and keeper of the stories being told in the animated shorts, we see her help Leia acquire her Boushh disguise, used in the mission to rescue Han from Jabba's palace. Decades later, when Han arrives on her doorstep with Finn and Rey looking for assistance in *The Force Awakens*, she gives them honest advice (and asks teasingly about her "boyfriend," Chewbacca). She tells Han to stop avoiding Leia, explains to Finn why he should fight against the evil of the First Order, and encourages Rey to use the Force when she finds Anakin and Luke Skywalker's lightsaber in one of Maz's castle storage rooms: "The belonging you seek is not behind you. It is ahead. I am no Jedi, but I know the Force. It moves through and surrounds every living thing. Close your eyes. Feel it. The light. It's always been there. It will guide you."

Mira Bridger

"Without hope, we have nothing."

To oppose the Galactic Empire is to put your life and the lives of those you care about on the line. Mira Bridger knows the risks of taking a stand, but the possible consequences don't stop her from speaking out against the Empire when they occupy her homeworld of Lothal. She first appears in *Star Wars Rebels* in a picture found by her son Ezra. It's a picture and not an in-person meeting because Mira and her husband Ephraim are in an Imperial prison, sentenced for treason.

Courageous and dedicated to helping Lothal's citizens, Mira broadcasts underground messages to speak the truth about the Empire. Her words spark the fire of revolution; a revolution that continues long after her imprisonment. While Ezra carries on their work, Mira and Ephraim are inspired to organize a prison break, and though they perish in the effort, they do so as they lived: fighting for others.

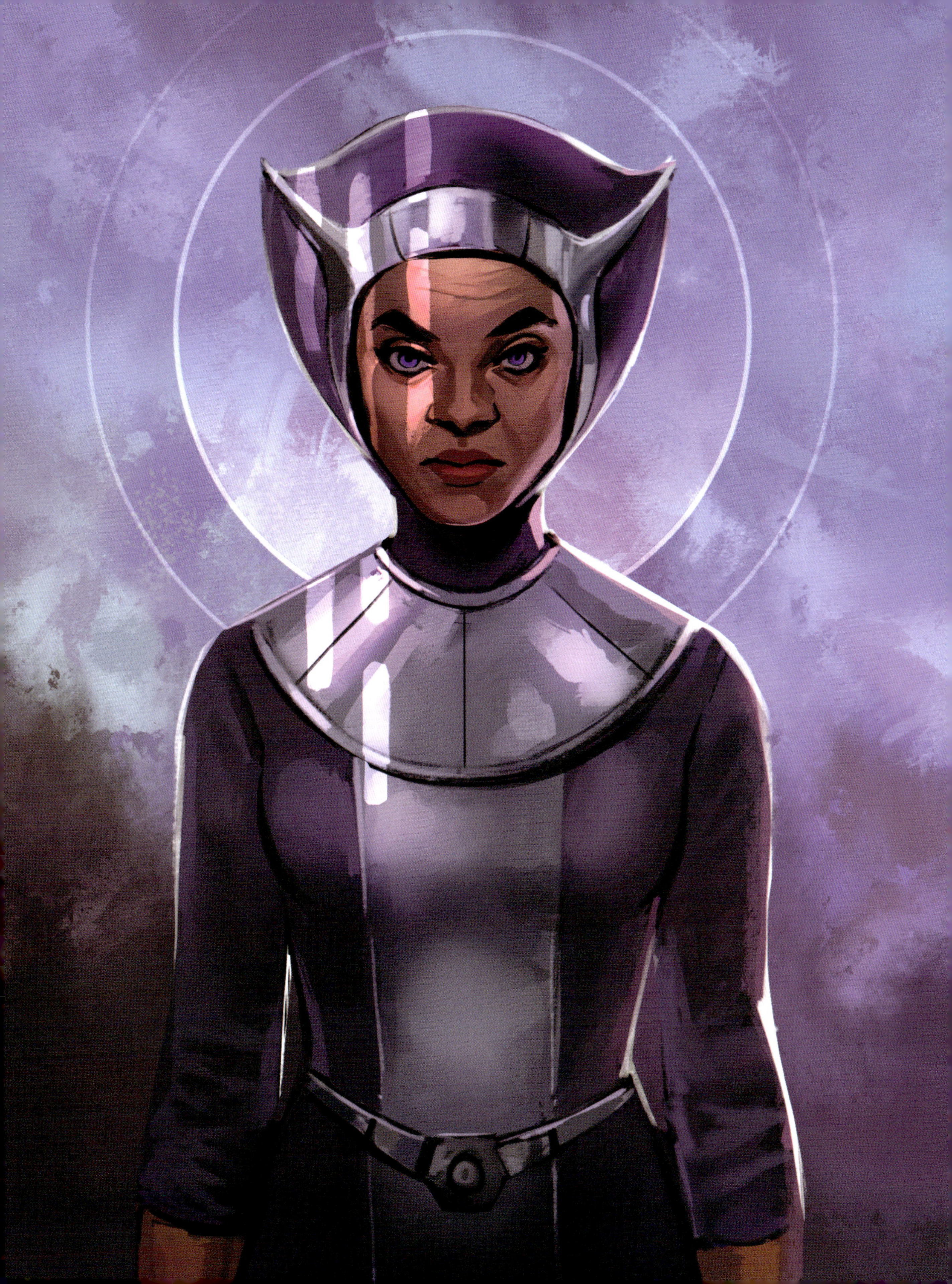

Mon Mothma

*"I have no fear as I take new action.
For I am not alone."*

MON MOTHMA

When Mon Mothma first appears in *Return of the Jedi*, she is the portrait of poise. She delivers both good and bad news at the rebel briefing for the attack on the second Death Star, and does so with a quiet but commanding power. Her very presence emanates serenity under stress. As the second high-ranking female character fans see in the Rebel Alliance in the original trilogy, she makes an impression. But her appearance before the Battle of Endor is just a small part of her story.

Mon Mothma, a native of Chandrila, is one of the most pivotal characters in the *Star Wars* saga. A co-founder of the Rebel Alliance and a chancellor of the New Republic, she's a revolutionary who's put everything into making the galaxy a peaceful, prosperous place since the days of the Clone Wars. Her politics, the kind that involve weathering near-constant galactic conflict, take a heavy toll. "Yes. It is hard," she says. "But we persevere. Like the Rebel Alliance before us, like the New Republic now. We persevere."

To the joy of fans who wanted more of Mon Mothma after her brief scene in *Return of the Jedi*, her importance has come to light in stories spanning the timeline. *Star Wars: The Clone Wars* shows us the seeds of Rebellion are planted years before Emperor Palpatine makes his power grab. Mon Mothma's there from the beginning, convening with senators like Padmé Amidala and Bail Organa to discuss how

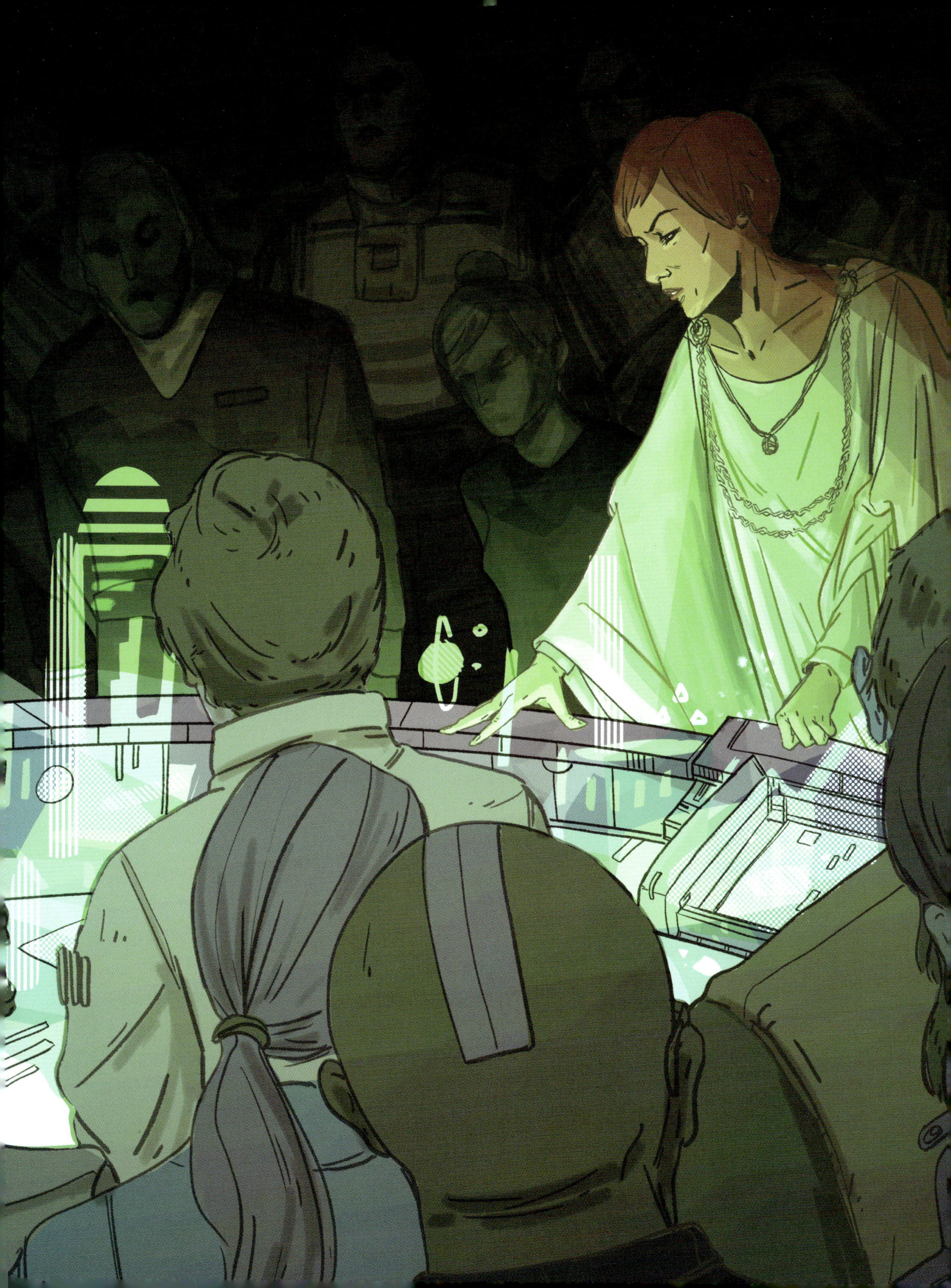

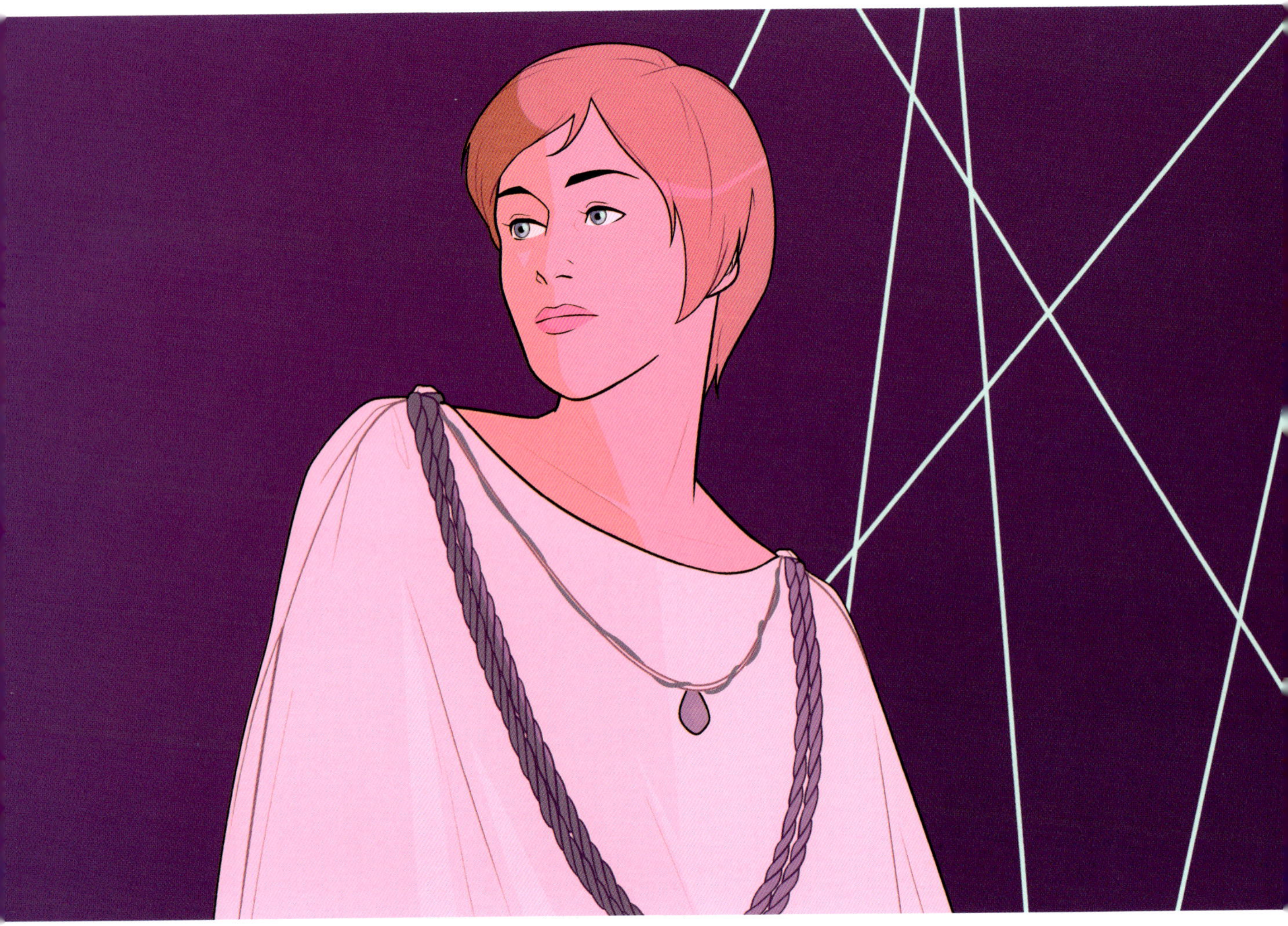

"We will not rest until we bring an end to the Empire, until we restore our Republic! Are you with me?"

—Mon Mothma

to resolve the struggle between the Separatists and the Galactic Republic. After that war ends and the true nature of the Empire starts coming to light, Mon and Bail meet in secret with other concerned parties. These rendezvous lead to the formation of insurgent groups around the galaxy.

In *Andor*, we see Mon balance the life of a high-profile politician in the Galactic Empire with her efforts to raise funds for rebel operations. She forges questionable partnerships to get the supplies and credits the growing insurgency needs, and does so at great personal cost. Mon lives in an opulent home on Coruscant, but in reality, she's on display in a gilded cage while trying to orchestrate one of the most important and secretive movements in the galaxy. It's a heartbreaking and inspiring portrait of a life of service.

The breaking point comes in *Star Wars Rebels*. After learning about the slaughter of peaceful protesters on the planet Ghorman, Mon speaks out against Emperor Palpatine in public, knowing she'll be branded a traitor. She demonstrates that there's a time for valiant action beyond politics. This is, in effect, the official beginning of the Rebel Alliance. She gathers the scattered cells with an emotional speech, "For too long I have watched the heavy hand of the Empire strangle our liberties, stifling our freedoms in the name of ensuring our safety. No longer! Despite Imperial threats, despite the Emperor himself, I have no fear as I take new action. For I am not alone. Beginning today we stand together as allies."

Mon Mothma is voiced by Genevieve O'Reilly in *Rebels*, the same actress who portrays her in *Rogue One*, *Andor*, and deleted scenes from *Revenge of the Sith*. She studied Caroline Blakiston's original performance in *Return of the Jedi* to mimic how Blakiston carries herself and how she speaks. O'Reilly admires the character: "She really shows the traits of a true leader in very difficult, very heightened, dangerous times. I think by her nature she's a genuine humanitarian. She has a strong moral compass. She's also a critical thinker and she is a considered decision maker. We meet her at those moments where there is a crux, a fork in the road, a genuine point that requires her leadership. That's what's really interesting, to see that early leadership and where it grew from."

After Emperor Palpatine's death, Mon knows the threat of the Empire isn't over just because its head has been removed. First chancellor of the reestablished Galactic Senate, she guides the budding government through the transition period. She's instrumental in bringing the New Republic's full force to the Battle of Jakku, which leads to the signing of the Galactic Concordance and official surrender of the Empire.

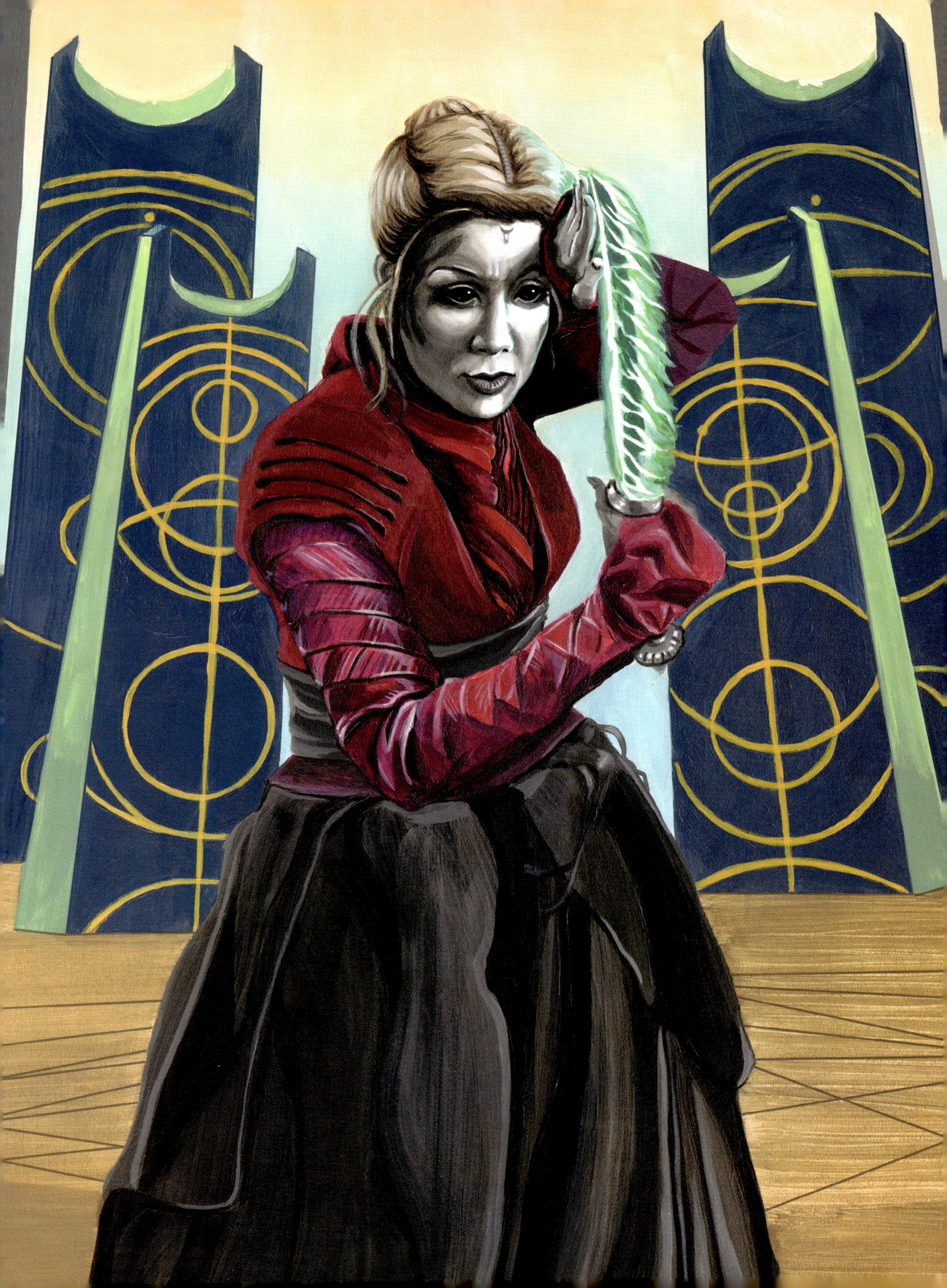

Morgan Elsbeth

"My anger gives me strength."

Morgan Elsbeth, a Nightsister strong in the Force, is one of the few survivors of the massacre of her people on Dathomir by General Grievous and the Separatist droid army during the Clone Wars. She was only a child, and as Morgan grows up, she hones her fear and grief into a rage that she wields like a weapon—one she uses against any obstacle that comes into her path.

A desire to amass power drives Morgan to build a business supplying the Galactic Empire. She doesn't believe in the Empire's rhetoric, but she knows they have credits and constantly need additional resources. Morgan sees the Empire as a means to acquiring more wealth and power. She establishes a home in the city of Calodan on Corvus, where she becomes magistrate by promising Calodan's people wealth and prosperity, and constructs factories to process plundered natural resources and assemble parts to help strengthen the Imperial Navy. It's her business acumen that draws the attention of Admiral Thrawn, a meeting that shapes the rest of her life. Thrawn also doesn't believe in the Empire, allying himself with them because he wants to help the Chiss Ascendancy. He sees Morgan's true motivations for seeking Imperial favor and accepts her service; Thrawn becomes a mentor to Morgan. Her business flourishes.

Morgan remains devoted to Thrawn after his disappearance and undertakes the ambitious task of bringing him home from the extragalactic planet Peridea, accompanied by the witches known as the Great Mothers, whom Thrawn had awakened in exile. While she herself doesn't survive to make it back to the known galaxy, Morgan's legacy is crucially one of helping to restore her sisters.

Diana Lee Inosanto, who portrays Morgan in *The Mandalorian*, *Ahsoka*, and *Star Wars: Tales of the Empire*, describes her means of connecting with the character: "I've written a journal about Morgan to get in touch with her pain and her fear. It really kind of becomes this weight, but yet you have to make it come through the character. And then, at the end of the day, once you're done, you let it go."

Mother Aniseya

"This isn't about good or bad. This is about power, and who is allowed to use it."

Leader of a witch coven who can seemingly transform into black smoke and forcefully enter the minds of others, Mother Aniseya is a Force user unlike others we have seen. Compassionate and thoughtful, fierce and impulsive, Aniseya is a portrait of duality. This is a witch so powerful that she claims to be able to create life in the form of her daughters, Mae and Osha, who are carried to birth by Mother Aniseya's partner, Mother Koril.

When members of the Jedi Order encounter the exiled coven on the planet Brendok, they meddle and question the twins' powers, how they are being raised, even their birth—none of which is well received by Mother Aniseya. She sees the Jedi as flawed, self-appointed arbiters of how beings in the galaxy should use the Force; the Jedi see Aniseya's coven as potentially dangerous and poised to harm Mae and Osha. Aniseya believes she needs to defend her coven and her daughters from the Jedi, but her tactics create further divide. Fateful decisions on both sides lead to the coven's downfall, as well as Mother Aniseya's tragic death. The encounter and her stance raise important questions about how much the Jedi might have misunderstood other kinds of Force wielders in the High Republic era and beyond. In that way, Aniseya is symbolic of anyone who walks a different path.

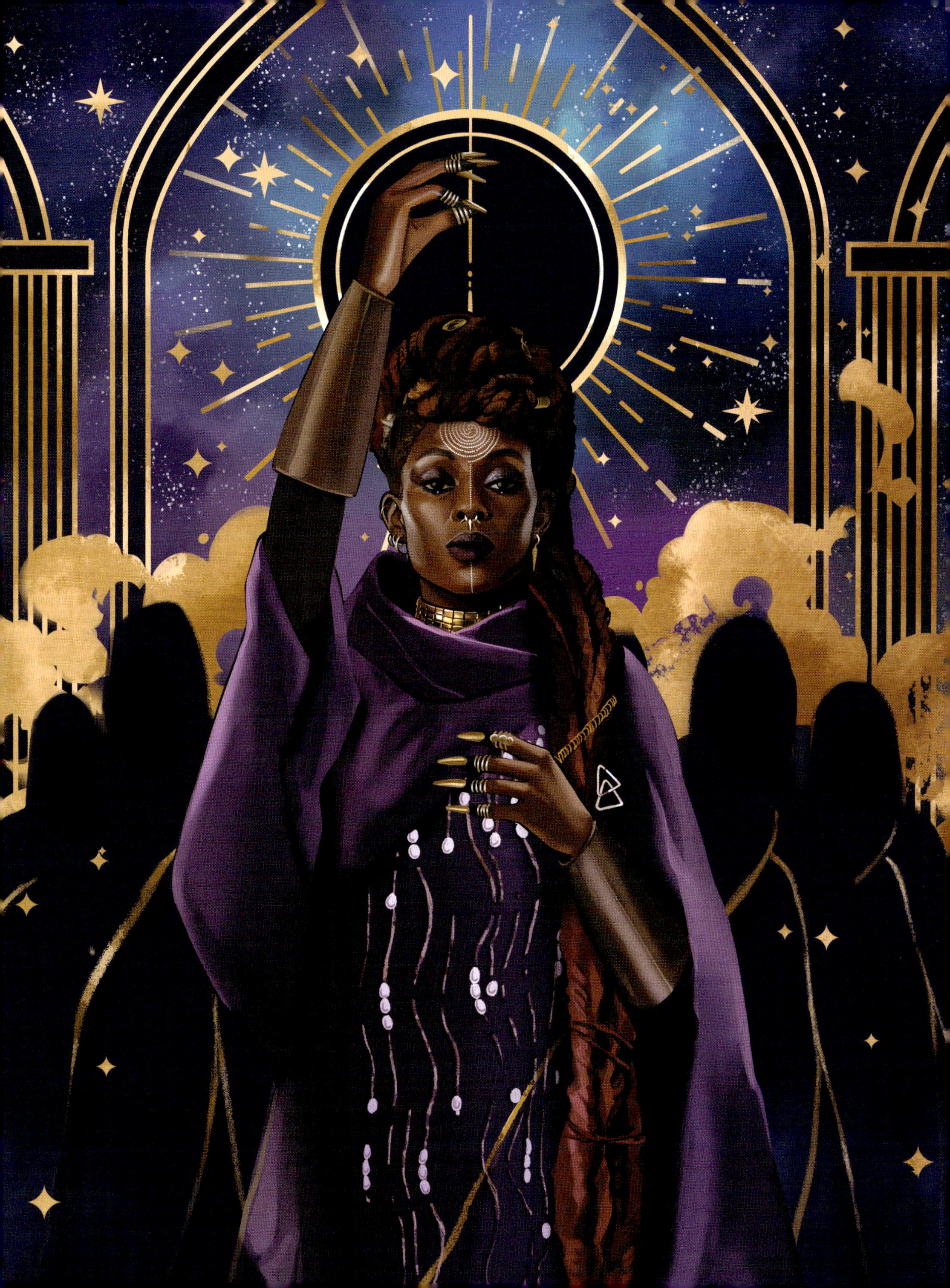

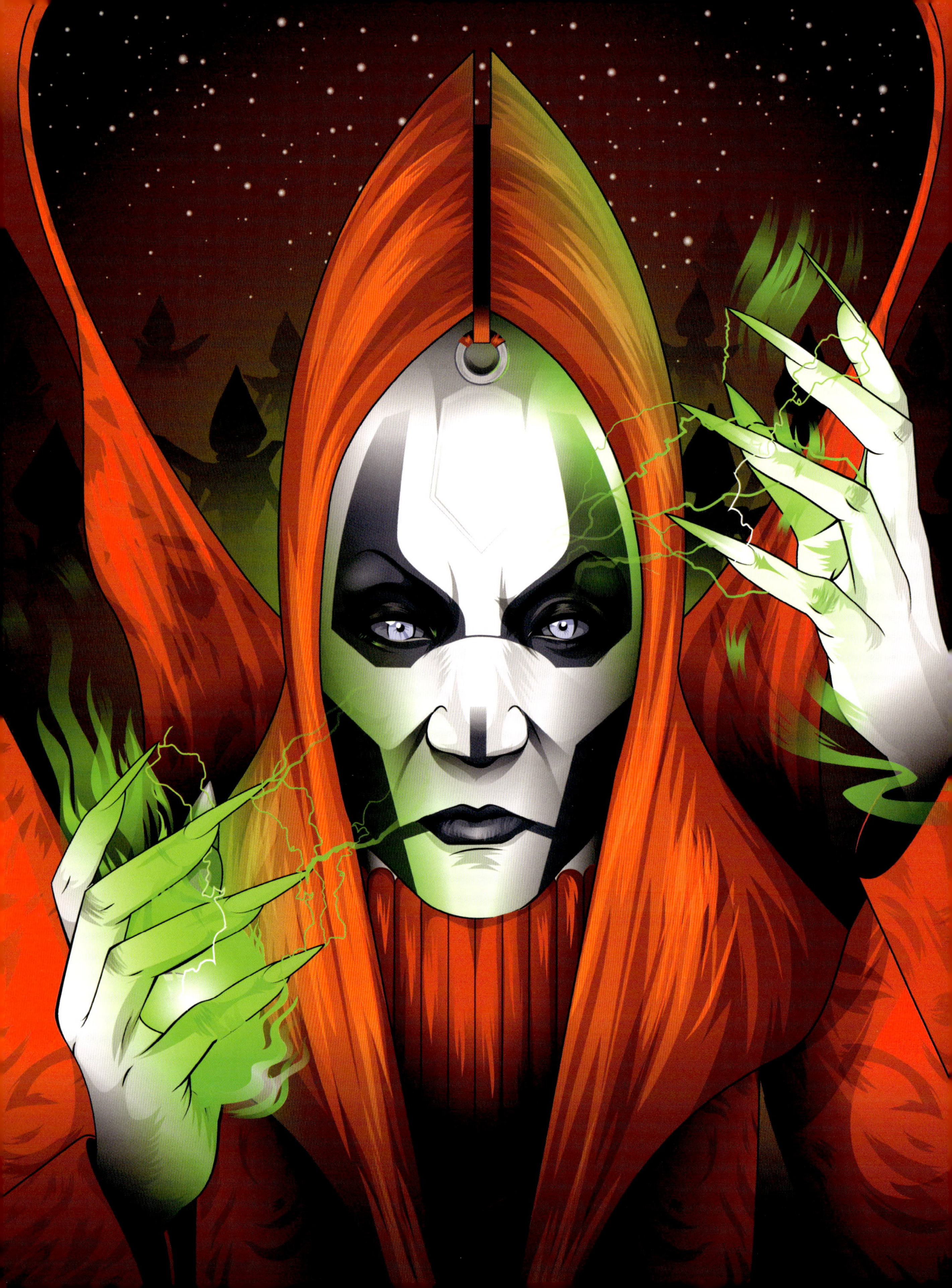

Mother Talzin

"Where one sees failure, others see opportunity."

Mother Talzin once said, "I am a simple witch." That is not exactly true. The leader of the Nightsisters of Dathomir coven, Talzin employs supernatural tactics to advance her shrewd plans, and wields enormous dark magick powers again and again in *Star Wars: The Clone Wars*, shaping green mystical energy into weapons, and at one point later bringing her son Darth Maul back from the edge of madness. Above anything and anyone else, she longs to be the most powerful being in the galaxy.

Her talents are so impressive that Darth Sidious makes a special trip to Dathomir, promising to offer the wisdom and secrets of the dark side, but kidnapping young Maul to serve as his apprentice instead. As a leader, Talzin is as fiercely protective of her clan as she is loyal to her son, and she sees what's called for is revenge against the Sith, Sidious, and his next apprentice, Count Dooku. In this she'll find common cause with Asajj Ventress, a Nightsister taken from them as an infant in exchange for the clan's safety, who has returned with her own grudge against the Sith.

Mother Talzin's look dates back to *The Phantom Menace* and artist Iain McCaig's concept for a female Sith, unused in the prequel film trilogy but finding a home in *The Clone Wars*. She's voiced by Barbara Goodson, who drew upon Maria Ouspenskaya's performance from 1941's *The Wolf Man* for inspiration for the witch's voice, and enjoys the echo effect used for Talzin's dialogue: "If I'm a person who's been around for—I'm basically immortal, right? I'm channeling ancient energies, so they're all in me."

Ninth Sister Inquisitor

"Being an Inquisitor taught me that no setback is too great."

NINTH SISTER INQUISITOR

The Galactic Empire doesn't typically welcome nonhumans into its ranks, but that xenophobia doesn't apply to members of the Force-wielding, Jedi-hunting Inquisitorius. These Inquisitors come from all kinds of backgrounds, because the first recruited among them, like the Ninth Sister, were Jedi. A Dowutin formerly known as the Jedi Masana Tide, the Ninth Sister turns to the dark side after the Empire captures, tortures, and mutilates her, taking one of her eyes. The Grand Inquisitor oversees her training, and with guidance from Darth Vader, she becomes talented and ruthless.

The Ninth Sister eschews her former Jedi training and embraces anger and hatred, which she complements with the brute force of her physical ability. She doesn't appreciate any reminders of her past either. She has transformed herself and takes pride in her new role. While she follows Darth Vader, she doesn't patronize him.

One of the Ninth Sister's strengths as an Inquisitor is her incredible empathic ability—an ability that deepens with her turn to the dark side. She can read what others feel, making her a terrifying interrogator. For someone who follows the light side of the Force, such a gift could make a positive impact. But for an Inquisitor? It's another weapon, and the Ninth Sister wields it with precision.

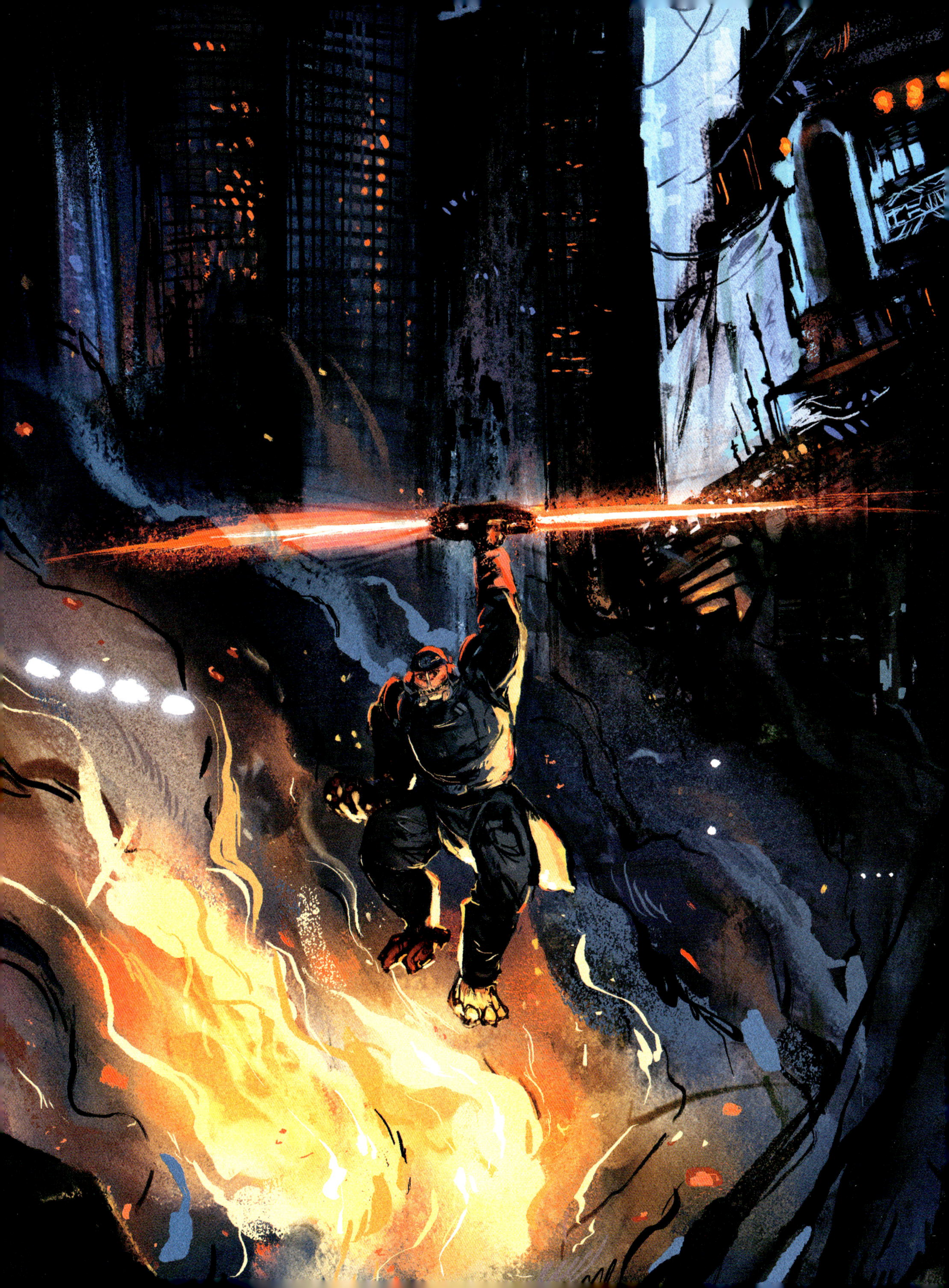

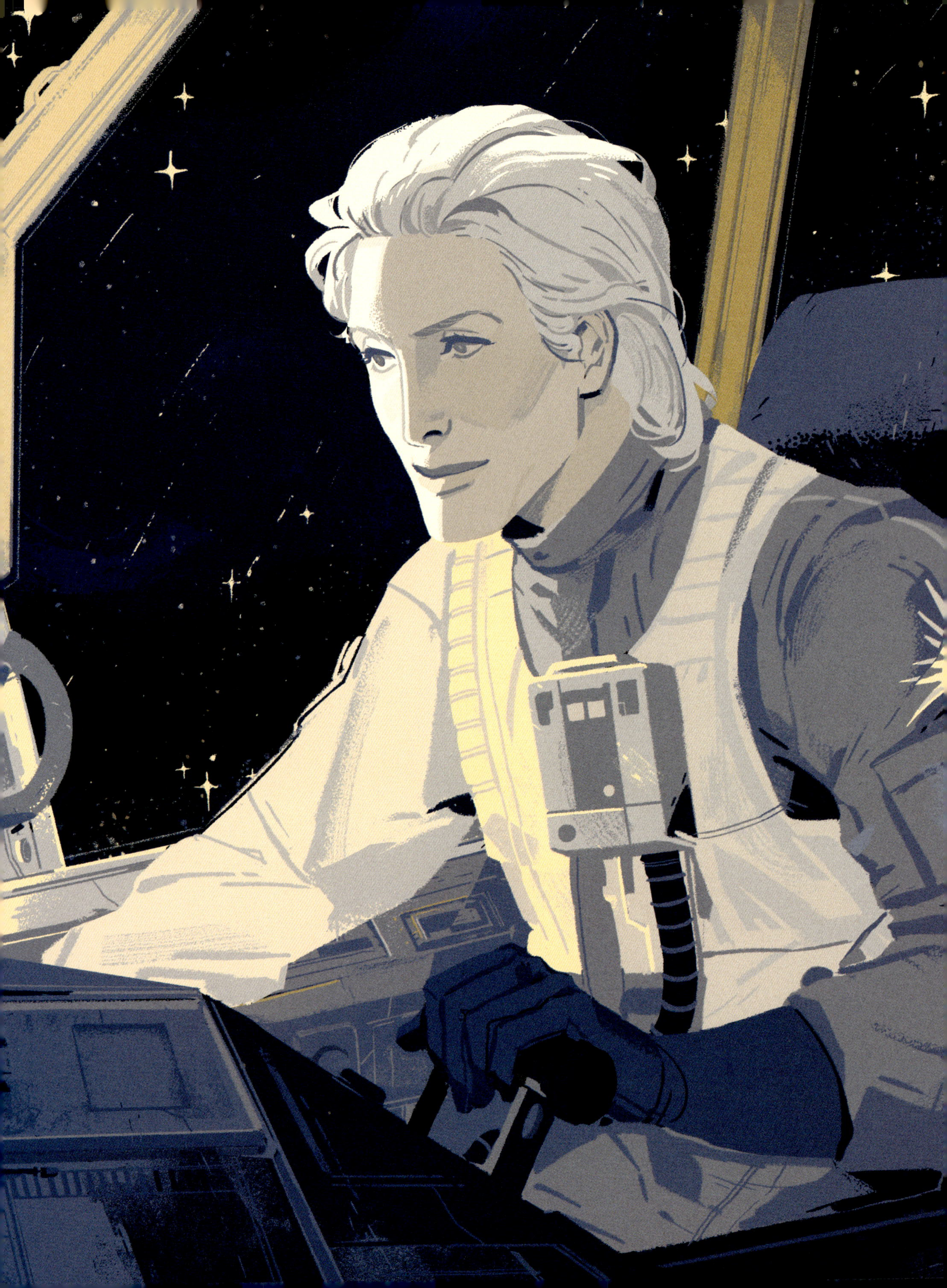

Norra Wexley

*"My job isn't fighting this war anymore.
My job is you."*

— NORRA WEXLEY

Spurred to join the fight against the Empire after her husband is captured by Imperials, Norra Wexley puts her twelve-year-old son Temmin "Snap" Wexley in her sisters' care on their homeworld of Akiva and devotes herself to the cause of the Rebellion. At first serving as a freighter pilot, she's enlisted in the Battle of Endor to fly a Y-wing fighter/bomber in the assault on the second Death Star, and plays a key role in its destruction, for which she is decorated. In the *Aftermath* trilogy of novels, following events of *Return of the Jedi* and preceding *The Force Awakens*, we see Norra torn between her parental duties to her son and her military duties to the galaxy, leading missions to hunt down the remnants of the Empire, including Imperial Grand Admiral Rae Sloane. Her headstrong attitude means she sometimes (often) leaps into conflict without a fully considered plan, but it can also lead her to important discoveries, such as finding the remnants of the Imperial fleet and setting in motion the Battle of Jakku and the downfall of the Empire.

Numa

Freedom fighter on Ryloth who's been
part of conflict her entire life.

Numa's life is defined from an early age by her struggle for survival. Orphaned as a child during the Separatist invasion of her homeworld of Ryloth, the young Twi'lek is cannily able to avoid the droid forces by hiding in her town's underground tunnel network. In *Star Wars: The Clone Wars*, we see her courageously help Obi-Wan Kenobi and the clone troopers of the Republic stop the invading army, in the process inspiring her fellow captive Twi'leks and making an emotional connection with several of the clones.

Numa's already tough core strengthens as she becomes an adult. Embroiled in the constant conflict on her planet and determined to take action, Numa joins Cham Syndulla's (father of Hera Syndulla) Free Ryloth movement and becomes one of the group's finest warriors. In standing against the Galactic Empire, Numa and the movement find common cause with rebel cells such as the Spectres, and in *Star Wars Rebels* we see them work together to carry on the fight.

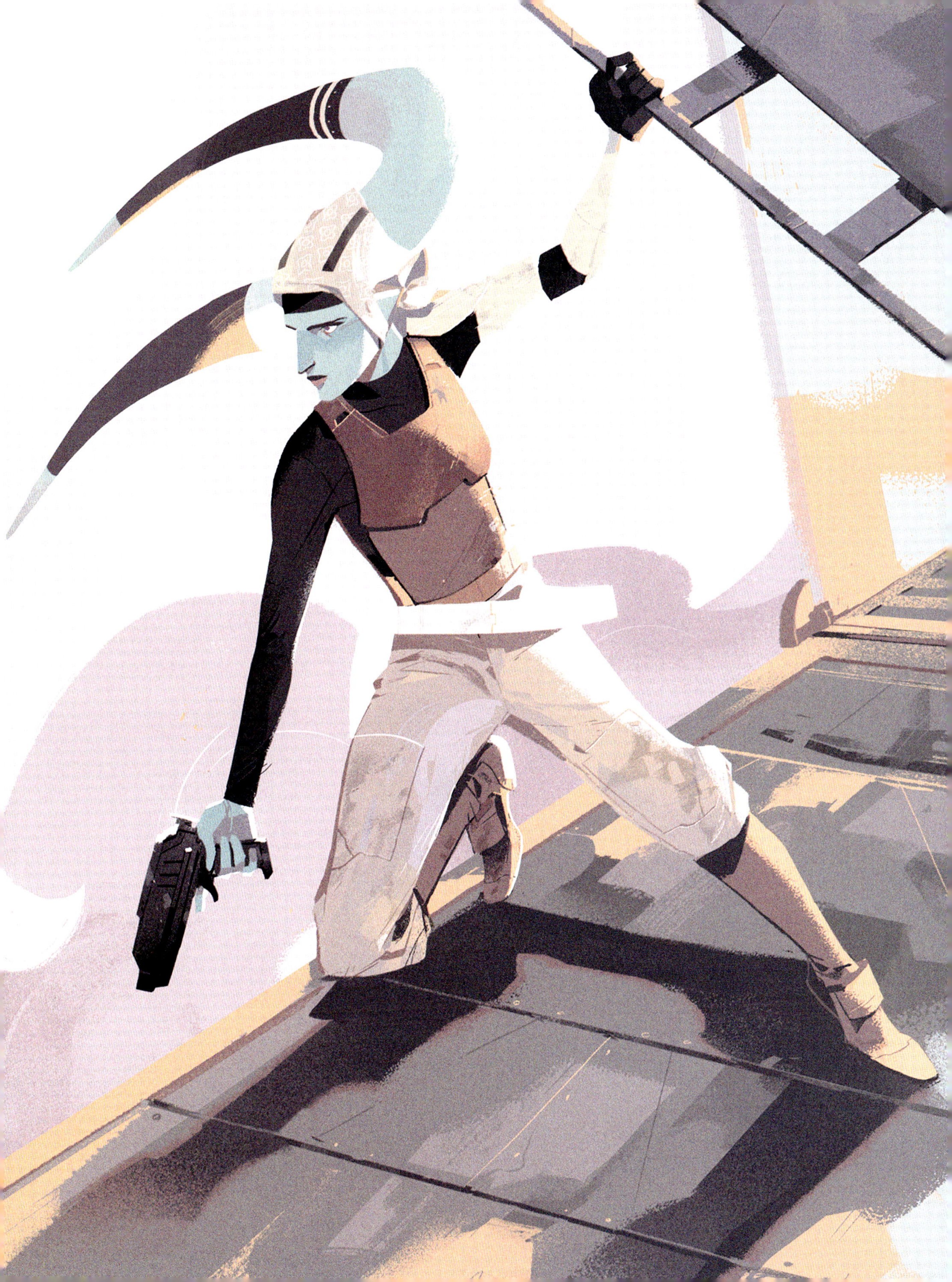

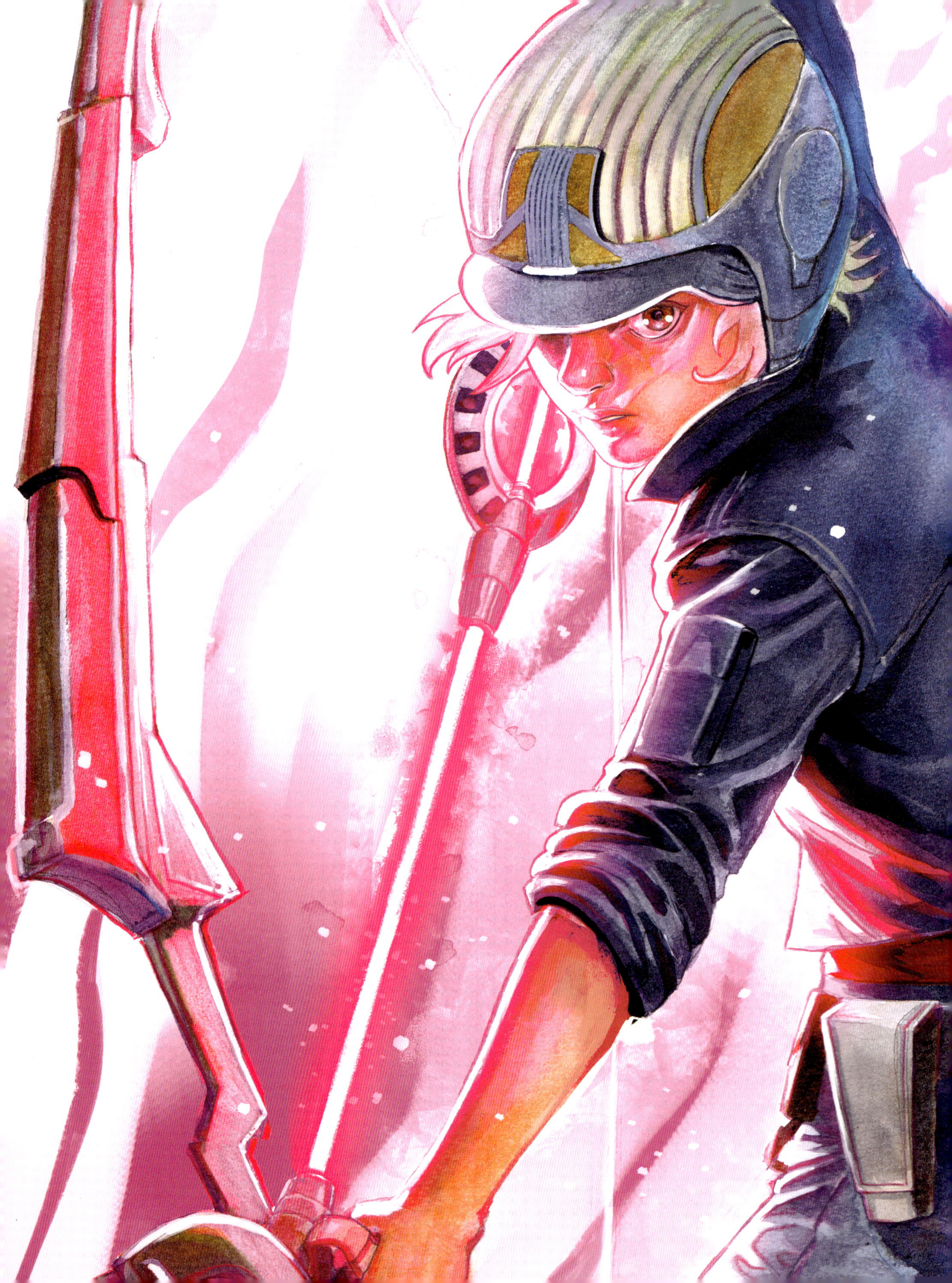

Omega

"I want to do more."

Created by the Kaminoans as an enhanced human female clone, Omega spends much of her early life assisting chief medical scientist Nala Se on Kamino. But when the members of Clone Force 99, whose creation Omega witnessed, reject Order 66 and the rule of the new Galactic Empire, Omega joins them in a daring escape from Kamino. She bonds with her clone brothers in the Bad Batch, known to much of the *Star Wars* fandom as her space dads or the "Dad Batch" since they're much older than Omega and look after her like parents would.

In leaving Tipoca City, Omega can't believe the wonders outside of her homeworld, feeling awe over small things like seeing dirt for the first time. Her beginner's mind helps Hunter, Wrecker, Echo, Tech, Crosshair, *and* the audience see the galaxy through fresh eyes. The former spend time around a kid who isn't jaded from years of conflict, and slowly soften into mentors and a found family, even if Omega causes them no small amount of stress with her curiosity. She is soon a competent and contributing member of the team.

While Omega's adventures with the Bad Batch start with them being on the run, the stakes increase when the Empire takes a keen interest in Omega's unique genetic makeup. She goes from joining the Bad Batch on missions assigned by Cid, a Trandoshan businesswoman with a questionable reputation, to being on the run with her brothers, to counting the days while imprisoned by the Empire. Through numerous hardships and situations that seem impossible to escape, Omega's unflagging optimism stays true. Her intelligence combined with all she's learned from her time with Clone Force 99 gives her the know-how to make a difference, which she does by joining the Rebel Alliance, and knowing that her brothers will always have her back gives her the confidence to do so.

Oola

Captive performer for Jabba the Hutt whose fate might have been different.

In the shifting cast of characters who inhabit Jabba the Hutt's palace, all manner of bounty hunters, smugglers, and performers gather in the dark corners of the creepy crime lord's abode—some present by choice, and some without the freedom to decide. The Twi'lek dancer Oola falls into the latter category. She appears in *Return of the Jedi* as the second-ever Twi'lek to be featured in the galaxy. Oola's lekku, or head-tails, were designed to respond to actress Femi Taylor's gestures and movements; to that end, they were made with foam latex to be as lightweight as possible. They were blended into Oola's green skin makeup, which took four hours to apply.

Oola's story is not a joyful one. Kidnapped by Jabba's majordomo Bib Fortuna, Oola trains in the art of exotic dancing. She's forced to perform for Jabba, but she does so with reluctance and often defies his orders. We see her doing so on-screen for the last time, with fatal results. According to Taylor, things might have been different: a sequence had been considered in which Oola escapes her fate and Jabba's palace, but was cut, apparently due to budget restrictions.

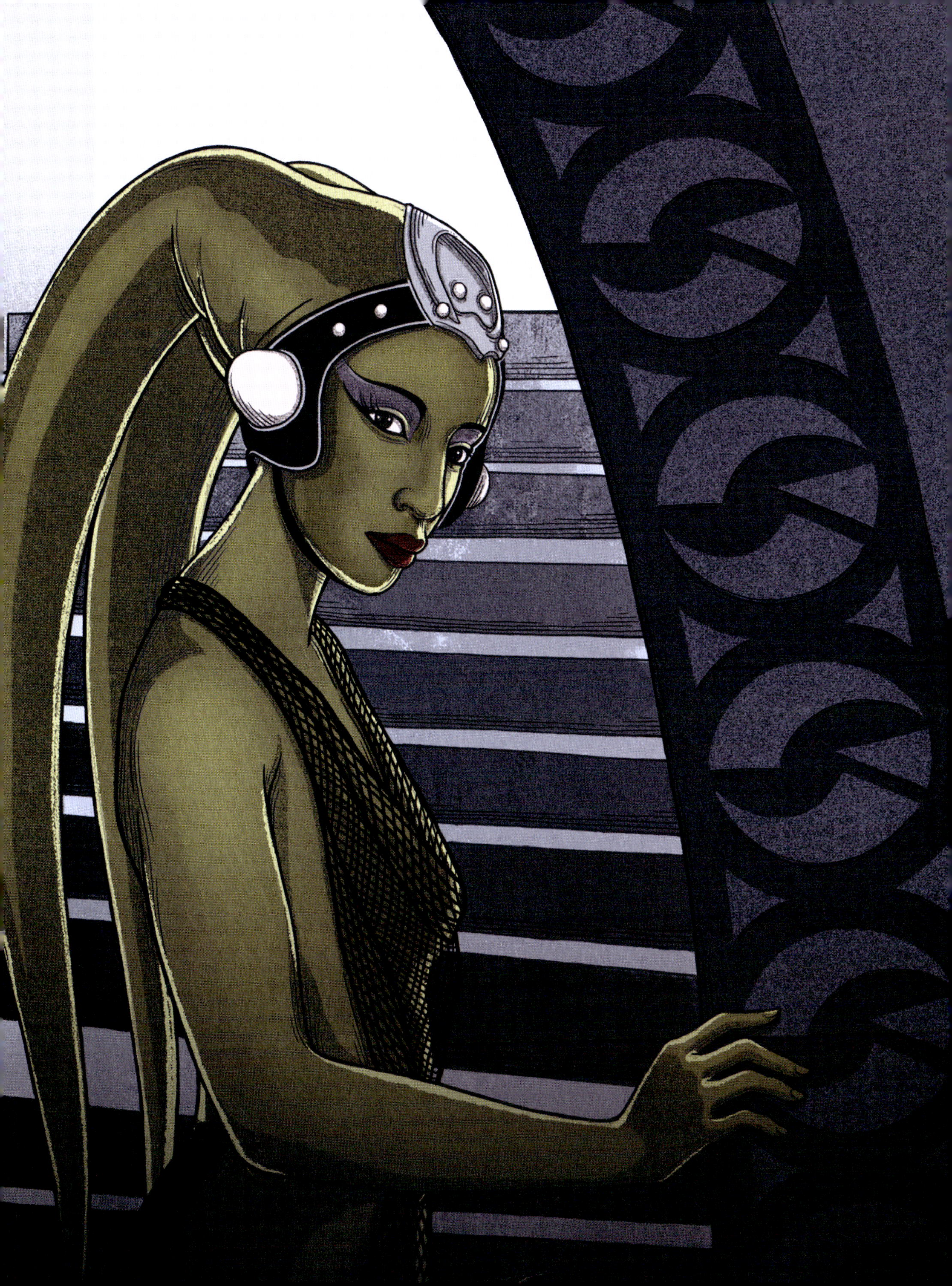

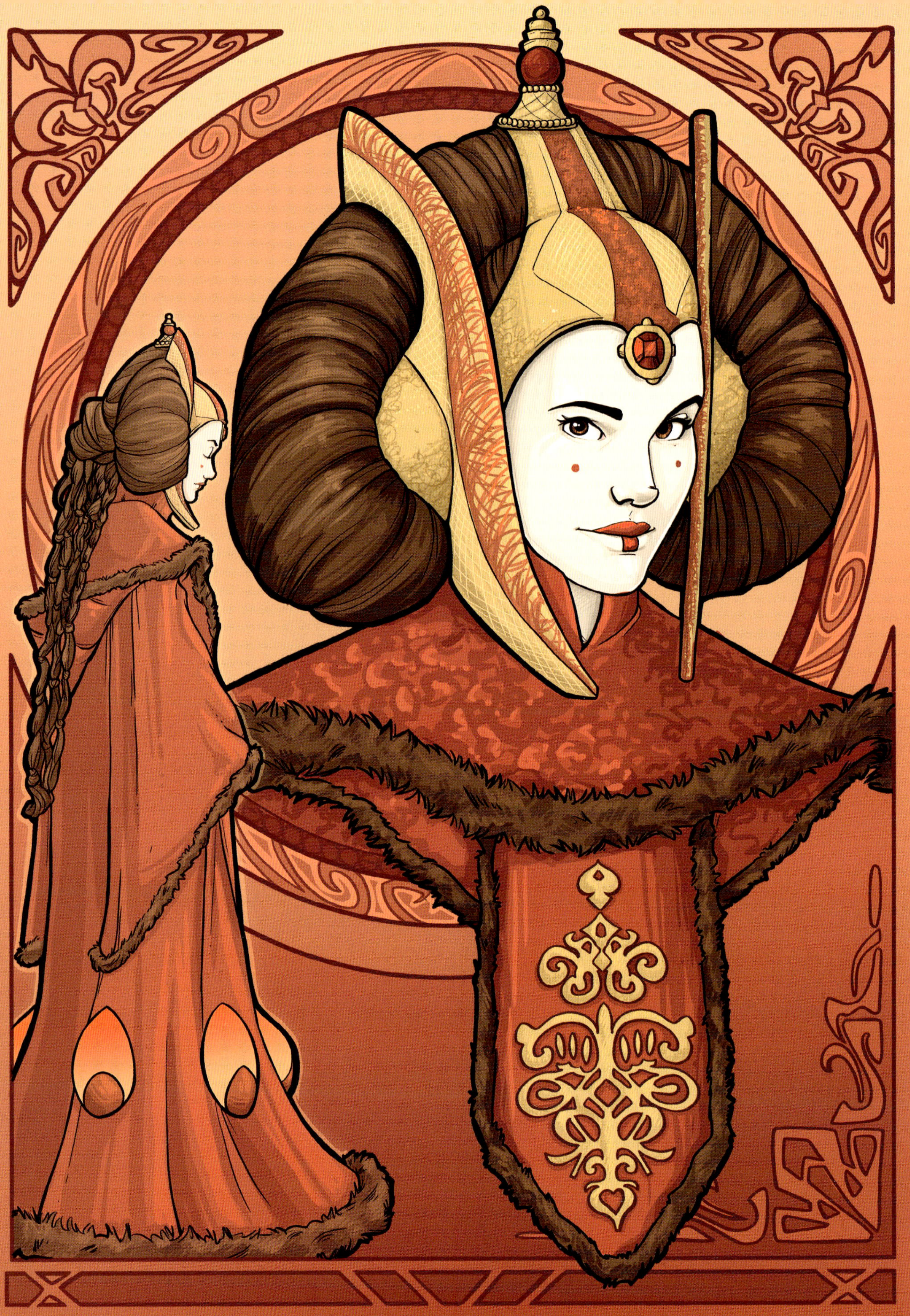

Padmé Amidala

*"There is always a choice!
To live in fear is no life at all."*

One of the galaxy's most optimistic and resilient characters, Padmé Amidala Naberrie pours her faith and belief into the people and the government around her, even when they don't behave the way she wishes they would. Her devotion sustains her through a lifetime of public service. She becomes an Apprentice Legislator when she's eight years old, is elected Queen of Naboo at the age of fourteen, and later serves as a senator representing her home planet. Padmé gives her all to the galaxy.

Our introduction to Padmé in *The Phantom Menace* is as Queen Amidala, and although young, she is not to be underestimated. The Trade Federation can't trick or intimidate her into signing documents to make their blockade of Naboo legal, and when the Republic refuses to come to Naboo's aid, Padmé calls them out: "I was not elected to watch my people suffer and die while you discuss this invasion in a committee!" To protect Naboo, she breaks down barriers by enlisting the native Gungans as allies against the invading Trade Federation—a partnership no one before her had considered. The strategy works.

Her political prowess and bridge-building are important, and show strength of character more diverse than the obvious heroics of lightsaber combat or being able to pilot a starship through battle.

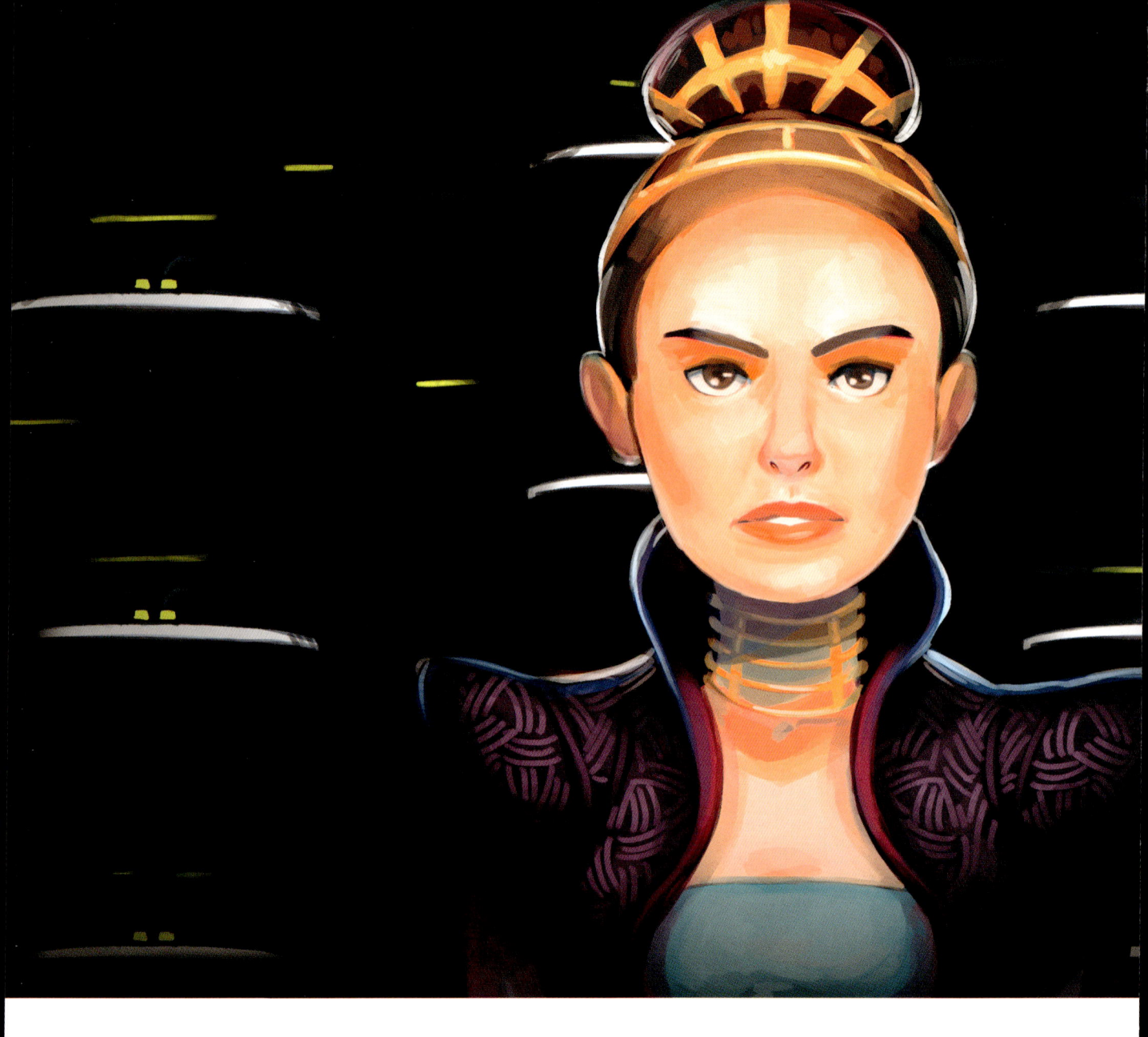

> "I will not condone a course of action that will lead us to war."
> —Padmé Amidala

Though she's an excellent shot with a blaster, Padmé's specialties lie in speaking and thinking clearly about justice, and in serving and defending this ideal.

The nature of Padmé's career creates a duality of sorts we don't see many other characters navigate. As the Queen of Naboo, she wears elaborate gowns and makeup that obscures her face. The mask-like cosmetics are helpful when one of Padmé's loyal handmaidens steps in to disguise herself as her decoy, but it also delineates her role in office. In full queen attire, she also speaks in a deeper tone and carries herself in a more regal manner. It suggests the way in which she understands the balance and distinction between her personal and professional lives, an aspect also evident when she marries Anakin Skywalker in secret in *Attack of the Clones*.

Padmé's wardrobe reflects the way she stands in two worlds. When she's alone with Anakin, the lines of her costumes are softer. When she's sitting as queen or serving in the Senate, her ensembles are heavier and more formal. She wears the weight of office. Costume designer Trisha Biggar imagined more than thirty costumes for Padmé in the prequels at the behest of George Lucas. His scripts expanded the fashion of the galaxy to show more opulent looks than the ones featured in the original trilogy. One of the most complex of Padmé's gowns is the red throne room dress she dons as Queen of Naboo. The Chinese Imperial court-influenced garment took almost eight weeks to finish. And that's just *one* of her outfits. We later learn in the novel *Queen's Shadow* that Padmé's elaborate fashion conceals a number of secrets to help protect her and give her defensive options.

After completing two terms as a beloved queen, Padmé accepts an appointment to the Galactic Senate—though the people of Naboo adore her so much that a faction attempts to change the constitution to allow a third term. She works with her handmaidens to craft a new persona to better fit her senator role. Padmé enters this new world slowly, realizing that Chancellor Palpatine is perhaps not as warm as he seems. But she carries on despite the hardships, cruel tabloid coverage, and a lack of connections. Padmé, unsurprisingly, forges her own path, and finds her voice as a politician.

As the Separatist Alliance forms, the Senate debates the formation of a military, and we see Padmé strongly oppose this move. The position nearly gets her killed—Zam Wesell tries to assassinate her the night before the vote—but Padmé is more concerned about the fate the galaxy will suffer in wartime than for her personal safety. Once the Clone Wars begin, she fights against the creation of additional soldiers. In *Star Wars: The Clone Wars*, she pleads with the Republic to use funds to aid its citizens instead of creating five million more clones. "My people, your people, all of our people. This war is meant to save them from suffering. Not increase it. It is our duty and our responsibility to preserve the lives of those around us by defeating this bill."

In *The Clone Wars* we also see Padmé head into the field to gather information herself, sometimes on her own initiative, and sometimes at the request of the Jedi. Her trips are of a diplomatic nature, but at times she's required to enter into, as she calls it, "aggressive negotiations." In one case, as she prepares to embark on a risky offworld mission to determine a fellow senator's true motives, Anakin tries to tell Padmé she's not allowed to go. She will have none of it: "You're not going to let me? It's not your decision to make. It's mine."

In her role as a diplomat, she sees the importance of maintaining a pragmatic, clear-eyed perspective when the galaxy and the players around her are in a heightened, agitated state. Padmé passes on a more complete picture of the war between the Separatists and the Republic to Ahsoka Tano, and opens the Padawan's eyes to the deeper currents of the conflict—nuance Anakin doesn't see, since he really only knows the Republic's side. She leads by example, negotiating with the likes of Duchess Satine Kryze, ruler of the planet Mandalore, and Separatist Senator Mina Bonteri. Padmé is willing to set partisanship aside, if it means coming to an accord that ends the war.

Voice actress Catherine Taber sees Padmé as a role model, and cites the character's open perspective as a quality she admires. "She has taught me about compassion. Despite her elite history

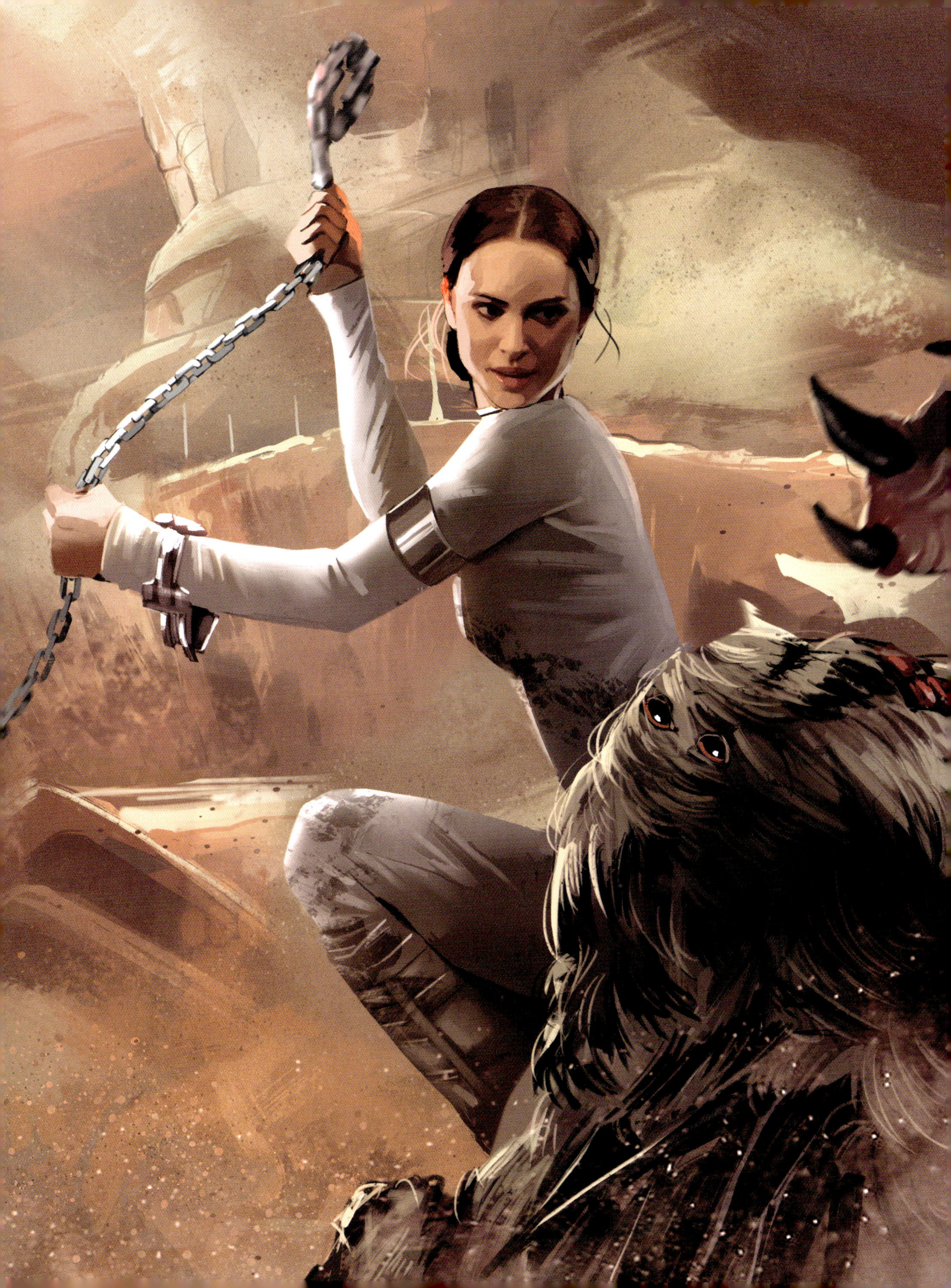

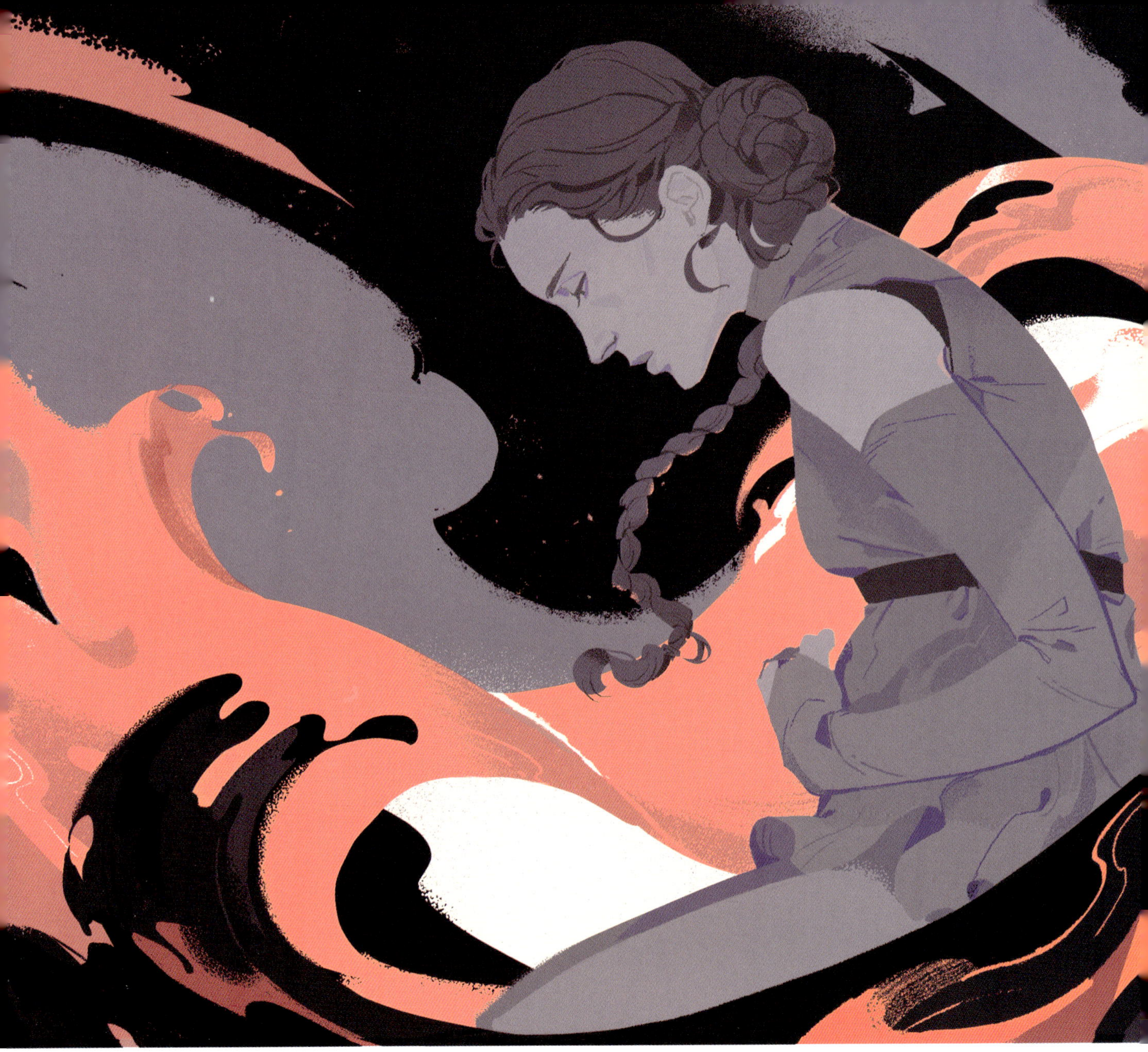

"Far too often, we forget that our most important allies are not always the most powerful."
—Padmé Amidala

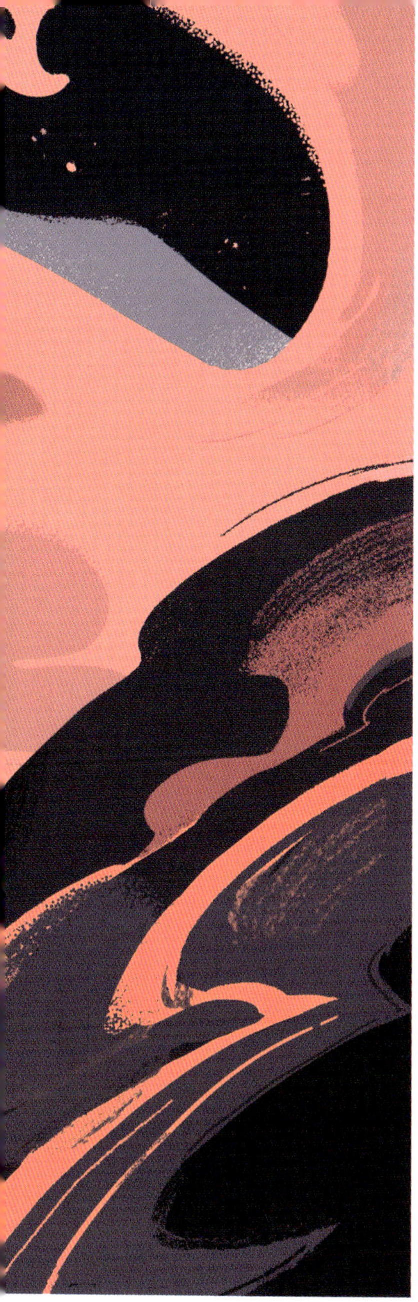

as both a queen and a politician, she is able to cross all kinds of boundaries that often isolate us from one another, maintaining meaningful relationships with people from all different walks of life and opposing views. She seeks out commonalities as opposed to differences. I admire that tremendously."

Padmé puts her career on the line for the sake of the galaxy, too. Some senators believe the narrative then Supreme Chancellor Palpatine weaves throughout the war, even as he begins to twist it against the Jedi. Padmé doesn't suspect Palpatine is actually a dangerous Sith Lord, but she knows something is wrong, and shares her concerns with a small group of politicians, including Bail Organa and Mon Mothma. Her goal here, as always, is to try to preserve peace in the Republic. As the Clone Wars spiral into chaos, and Palpatine names himself as Emperor of the new Galactic Empire, most of the Senate cheers, but not Padmé. Standing with Bail, she observes, "This is how liberty dies, with thunderous applause." Bail and Mon later become primary architects in the Rebellion against this new corrupt and evil Empire.

Padmé Amidala's legacy is much more than the children she gives birth to, Luke Skywalker and Leia Organa. Her final words encapsulate her life. Still seeing the possibility for light within Anakin, she tells Obi-Wan, "There is good in him." She believes in others, and in the galaxy, to the very end.

Padmé's Handmaidens

Attendants to the Queen and more than meets the eye.

The role of a Naboo Royal Handmaiden is, by design, much deeper than appearance suggests. They assist with everyday tasks, including choosing gowns and styling hair. But they're also advisers, confidantes, and bodyguards, trained in deception, defense, and strength in service to their queen. Queen Amidala brings the tradition back to Naboo's monarchy upon her election, opting not only for a single handmaiden, but a group. They adopt assumed names that sound like "Padmé" to obscure their identities. Eirtaé, Rabé, Sabé, Saché, and Yané are the first handmaidens to serve Padmé.

In *The Phantom Menace* and *Attack of the Clones*, we meet Padmé Amidala's retinue on screen, and we get to know them better in E.K. Johnston's Queen's Trilogy of books, particularly Sabé, Cordé, and Dormé. In joining the retinue, each handmaiden makes a commitment in full knowledge of the risk and responsibility involved. Beyond learning marksmanship and melee combat, they study how to communicate through subtle gestures and how to mimic the queen. They serve as decoys for any situation in which the queen may be at risk, so they must also somewhat resemble Padmé. Sabé poses as the queen when the Trade Federation invades Naboo. Padmé retains the handmaidens' service after she becomes a senator. But, as Yané says, the needs are different: "Your new aides don't need to be limited to your appearance, as long as they can double for your brain." Still, Cordé impersonates Padmé before the Military Creation Act vote and dies in her service. The handmaidens also spy and wrangle the vast amounts of information swirling around Coruscant.

Sabé takes on tasks for Padmé, such as working to free the enslaved on Tatooine, and comes to grow apart from her former queen. Padmé's death has a profound effect on Sabé, and she commits herself to investigating, even partnering with Darth Vader and infiltrating Crimson Dawn to find answers.

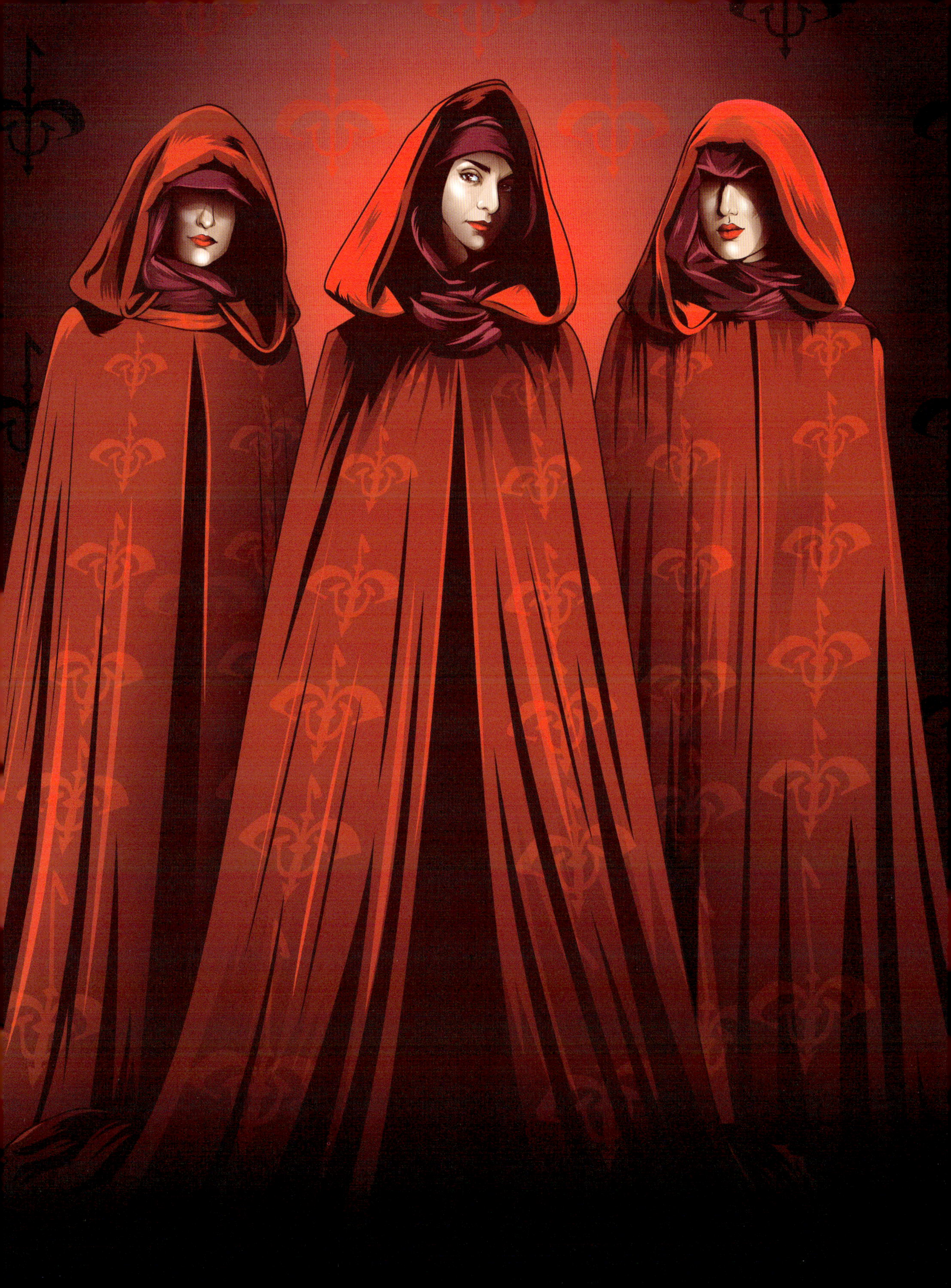

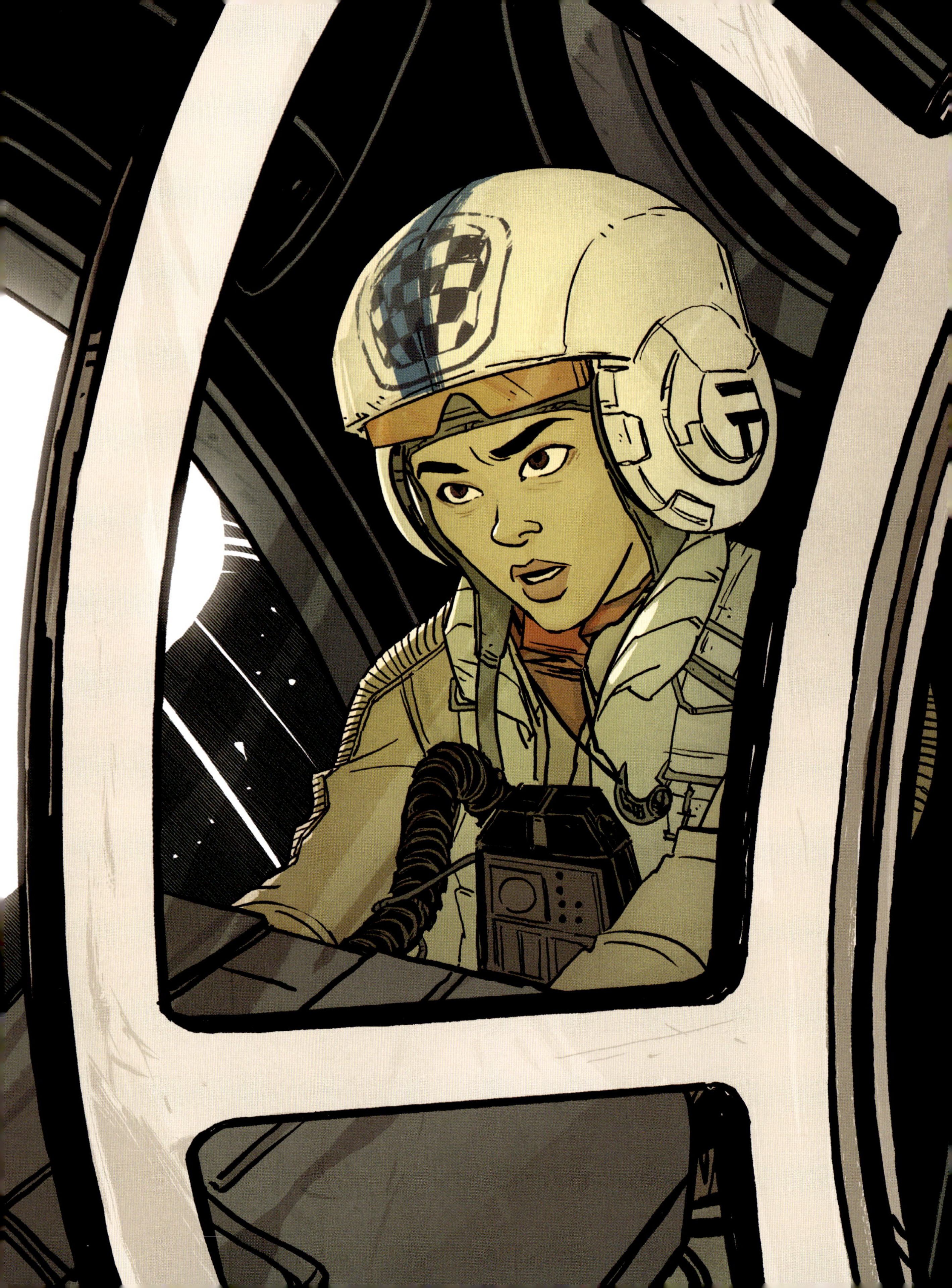

Paige Tico

"The Resistance is built on belief."

Paige Tico had just a few moments of screen time in *The Last Jedi*, but she has an immeasurable impact on the story and on the viewer. In a heart-pounding sequence when she understands that dropping her ship's proton bombs on the First Order Dreadnought during the evacuation of D'Qar is down to her and her alone, she uses every ounce of determination and strength to get to and press the button on a remote, releasing the weapons. Paige's actions encapsulate the spirit of the Resistance. Bravery, focus, heart—she embodies those qualities as she closes her eyes, grasps her medallion, and sacrifices herself.

Paige wears one half of this medallion, and her sister Rose wears the other. Made from material found on their homeworld of Hays Minor, it's a gift from their parents. Paige, or as Rose sometimes calls her, Pae-Pae, is the older sibling, and fiercely protective of Rose. She's the first one to comfort Rose, but is also the first to push her to use her true talents and ingenuity.

After witnessing the way the First Order brutalizes her home and other worlds in her star system, Paige joins the Resistance. She serves as a gunner aboard the *Cobalt Hammer*, and is a skilled pilot, enamored with flying since she sat on her mom's lap in the cockpit of an oredigger. She honors her parents and sister by never giving up.

Peli Motto

"You want to thank me now or you want to thank me later?"

When Din Djarin needs a mechanic, spare parts, and/or a babysitter for Grogu, he has exactly one person to get in touch with: Peli Motto. One of the funniest characters in *Star Wars*, Peli is a loose cannon who's as likely to wax poetic about a starfighter as she is to explain what it's like to date a Jawa. Given that actress and comedian Amy Sedaris plays the proprietor of the bustling Hangar 3-5 in the Mos Eisley Spaceport, it's no surprise that the character, who Dave Filoni compares to Danny DeVito in *Taxi*, is hilarious. Sedaris, for example, improvised Peli losing a tooth in *The Book of Boba Fett*. She says, "I asked everybody on the set if they had a Tic Tac, and somebody had some mints. I did it just to make the director laugh. I didn't think they'd keep it."

Peli's roots are firmly planted in Tatooine's sands. She says she's never been offworld, and that means she has strong connections all over Mos Eisley. The years she's spent running her repair business facilitates Jawas quickly finding parts she's looking for, and means that travelers passing through the spaceport on the way to more exciting locations know to turn to her for trade and sales. As fluent in mechanical parts as she is in Jawaese, she knows her stuff and does her job very well. Though Tatooine isn't known around the Outer Rim for its reputable businesses, Peli appears to be fair with her clients—she sasses them, sure, but she and her team of pit droids deliver on what they say they'll do, whether that's fixing up an obscure starfighter or providing improvised childcare for a small "wrinkled critter."

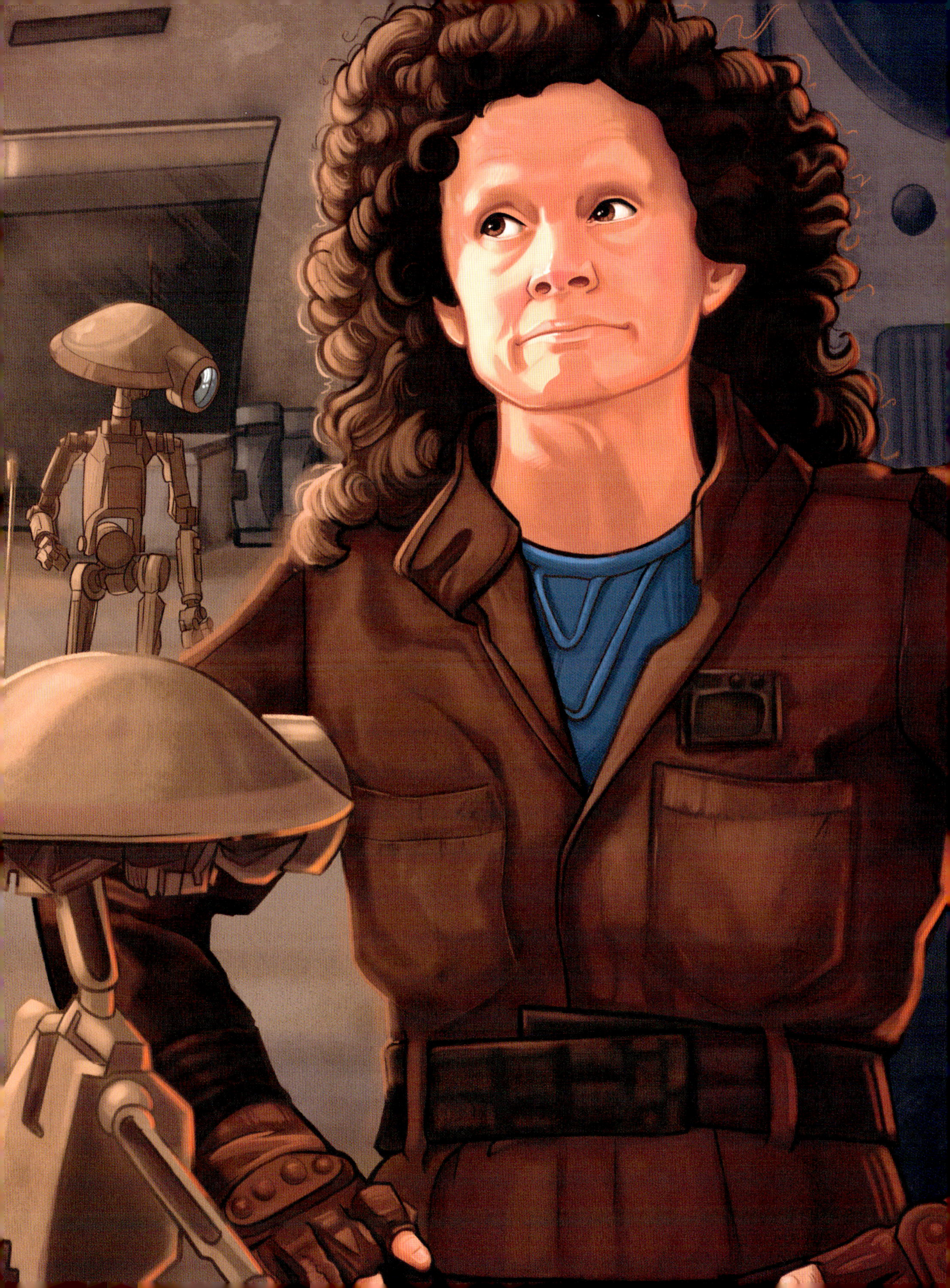

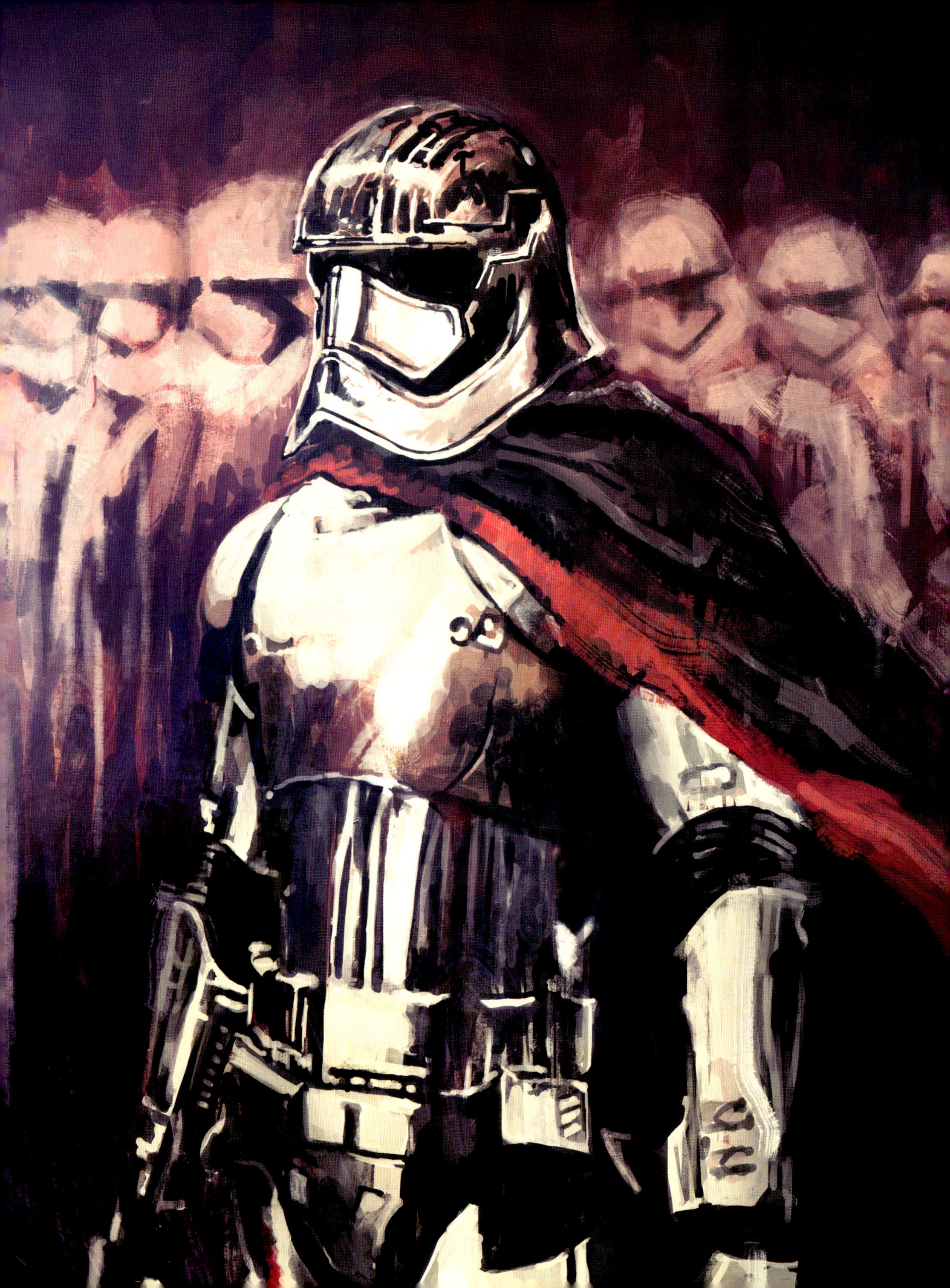

Phasma

"The First Order is not the Empire. We are purer. We have been through the crucible and emerged stronger."

Captain Phasma marches into the *Star Wars* galaxy with authority, in a suit of dazzling chromium armor. As the first female villain in a leading role in a *Star Wars* movie, she commands attention, and was the subject of intense speculation in the months leading into *The Force Awakens*. A captain in the First Order, she's responsible for shaping the stormtroopers into model, malleable soldiers who will obey every order. Phasma may follow the commands of her superiors in the First Order, but make no mistake: everything she does, she does for herself.

The *Phasma* novel reveals the character's origins on the planet Parnassos. Born into a primitive clan in a world devastated by a nuclear reaction, Phasma arranges the deaths of her clan and even her own parents in order to ensure her own survival. Utterly ruthless, she proclaims herself the greatest warrior on the planet. As Resistance spy Vi Moradi tells a member of the First Order, "No one will go as far as she will to survive." *Phasma* author Delilah Dawson describes the character as having "zero doubts about exactly who she is and what she's willing to do, and there's something so seductive about that kind of confidence."

Her Phasma-first attitude helps her earn a place within the First Order. When Brendol Hux's ship crashes on Parnassos, Phasma seizes the opportunity to join him and the First Order and escape her home planet. She's confident, and knows how to sell herself. Actress Gwendoline Christie projects these attributes in her performance as the first female stormtrooper on the screen: "It's exciting that something as iconic as *Star Wars* has embraced the future and has embraced the world's need for gender balance and female empowerment. I hope it inspires generations of women everywhere to go forward."

Phasma's chromium-coated armor gives her an air of mystery, something Phasma herself is well aware of. The material has been salvaged from a yacht once owned by Emperor Palpatine. Behind the scenes, costume designer Michael Kaplan originally came up with the silver armor look for Kylo Ren. It didn't work for his character in the end, but after Lucasfilm president Kathleen Kennedy complimented the concept art, it became Phasma's. That armor, which they only had five days to make, inspired the character's name. The design reminded *The Force Awakens* director J.J. Abrams of the 1979 horror film *Phantasm*.

"The costume is absolutely sensational," says Christie. "It is restrictive, but I think it gives us an insight into Captain Phasma. This is a woman who is wearing armor, but her femininity is still displayed. She doesn't try to hide it; it only empowers her further. The costume takes around forty-five minutes to put on. It certainly makes me stand up straight." She also likes that Phasma doesn't remove her helmet: "I thought it was a really interesting opportunity to play a female character, where we formed an opinion of her based on her actions, rather than the way she has been made flesh."

We don't even see a glimpse of Phasma's face until *The Last Jedi* when she's fighting Finn, her former trooper FN-2187, who left the First Order to join the Resistance. The helmet was re-chromed for the film to show less distress, but it also takes a significant hit in the battle. Director Rian Johnson told Kaplan he wanted the helmet to have an open split, but Kaplan went for something more subtle instead: "I put aluminum foil in the big gash in the helmet and closed it up. You just saw this eye. It was beautiful, and he really liked that. She has piercing blue eyes, too, which is unexpected."

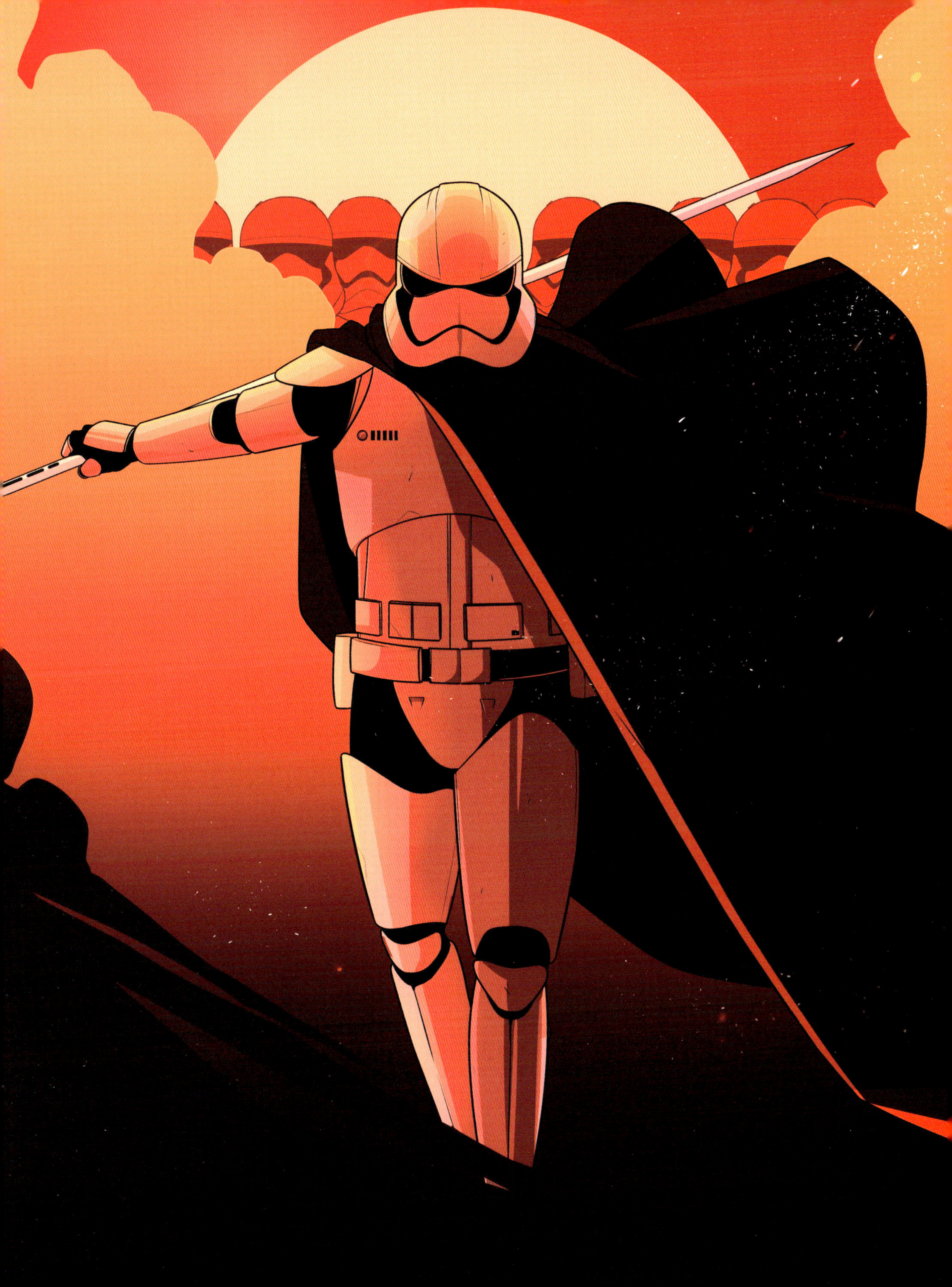

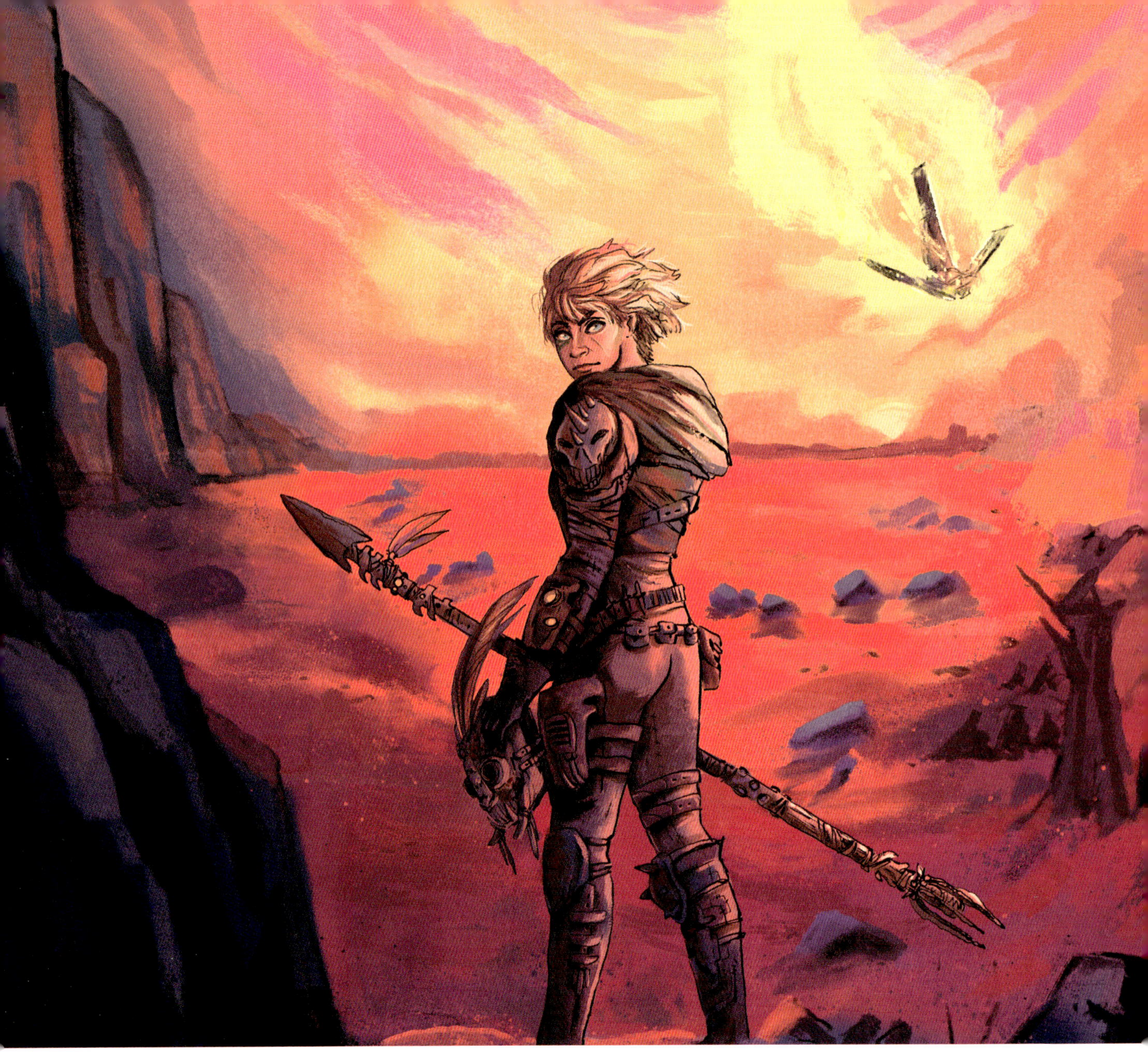

"You never know a soldier's true worth until they've stood on the battlefield, faced with death."
—Phasma

Held aloft as a model First Order soldier, Phasma, in her armor, shines in propaganda posters. She teaches stormtroopers to place their loyalties to the First Order, not each other, but this is not a code she follows herself. In *The Force Awakens*, Phasma takes down Starkiller Base's shields under threat from Finn, which contributes to the destruction of the planet. But facing charges of treason, we see her in Marvel's *Captain Phasma* comic working the system and eliminating anyone who learns her secrets—a one-woman task force and murderous clean-up squad. Phasma tells a rival, "I fought for everything that I have, every bit of what I am."

After Finn threatened her in *The Force Awakens*, fans couldn't wait to see Phasma face him again in *The Last Jedi*. She finds the First Order traitor aboard Supreme Leader Snoke's ship, *Supremacy*, and is eager to serve a painful form of justice to FN-2187. No one she commands knows what happened on Starkiller, and she doesn't reveal her hand. She doesn't owe anyone explanations; she simply commands First Order stormtrooper executioners to make Finn's final moments hurt.

Qi'ra

*"Everyone has secrets. If I told you mine,
I'd just have to go find new ones."*

⸻

From wearing ragged clothes reeking of the Corellian sewers she grew up in to sporting tailored designer gowns aboard an opulent yacht, from dismal circumstance to opportunity won by determination, wit, and skill, Qi'ra charts a remarkable and ambitious path for herself. Committed to rising above her station, Qi'ra climbs the ranks of the criminal organization Crimson Dawn under the gangster Dryden Vos to become his most trusted strategist and adviser, positioning herself as an excellent observer and expert manipulator. She knows when to flatter, when to cajole, and when to change the topic—maybe with violence. She's interested in money and influence, but what matters most is survival.

Qi'ra's a femme fatale unlike other heroines in the *Star Wars* films. Introduced in *Solo: A Star Wars Story*, Qi'ra relies on intelligence, charisma, and lies to advance her ultimate goal—to be free of people chasing her. Her appreciation for finer things is rooted in her hard-knock youth. As a scrumrat for the White Worm gang alongside Han, she lives in the sewer, surviving on unsavory rations doled out by the gang's leader, Lady Proxima. It's as dire as it sounds: starved for comforts, Qi'ra imagines stealing throw pillows from a hotel lobby, just to have something nice. But in her time as one of Proxima's scrumrats, Qi'ra learns tactics that will serve her in the future, not the least of which is perfecting the art of keeping her

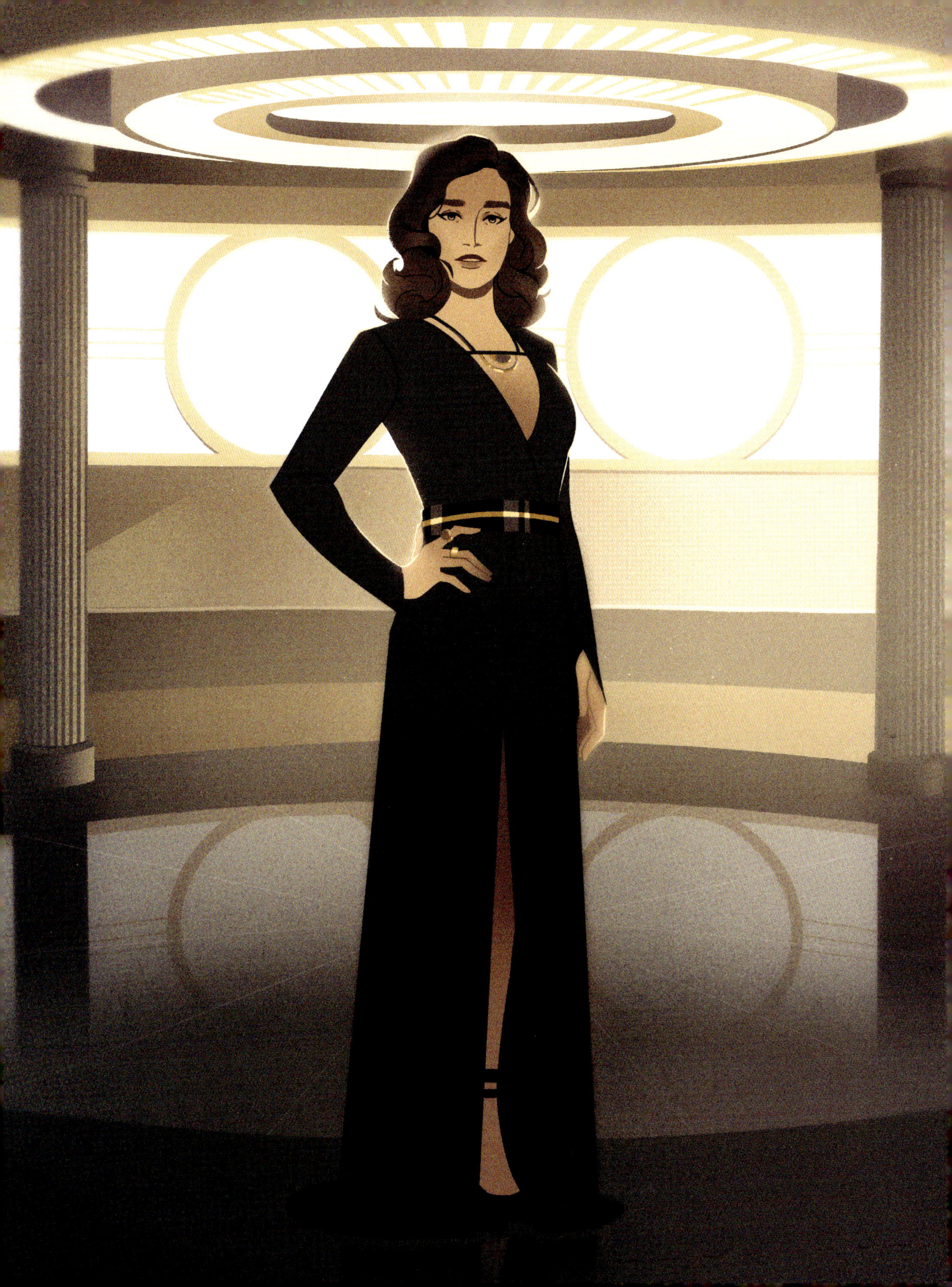

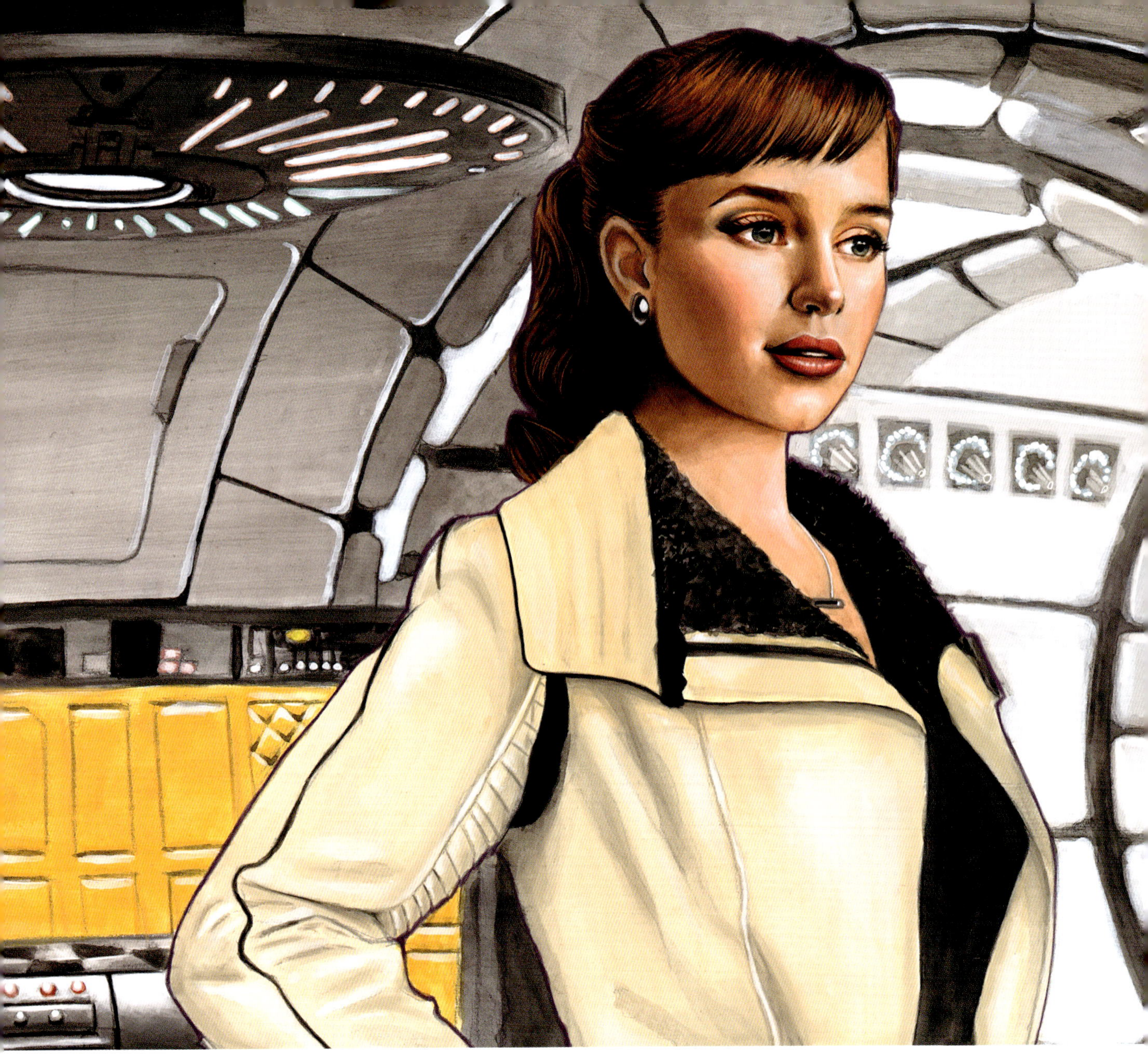

“Others can make enemies if they wish. I prefer to make friends.”

—Qi’ra

face emotionless in situations when displaying her feelings could mean losing leverage.

To earn more freedom, and maybe the occasional piece of fruit, Qi'ra takes her service to Proxima seriously, hoping to be promoted to Head Girl. In the novel *Most Wanted*, she competes with Han for advancement, but their rivalry leads to an alliance. Qi'ra's calculated planning ensures their survival, as they're on the run from dangerous arms dealers again and again. She isn't able to escape Corellia with Han, but she finds her own way. When we see her next, she's on Dryden Vos's star yacht, having left behind the White Worms to join Crimson Dawn. It's absolutely a step up, and even luxurious, in a way, but Qi'ra knows it has not come without a cost. When Han asks how she got out of Corellia, out of a life serving Proxima, Qi'ra tells him she didn't—she's just serving a different kind of master.

Vos keeps Qi'ra close, benefiting from her observations of the environment around her; Qi'ra excels at assessing what's happening, and finding escape routes (as a scrumrat, she once escaped a desperate situation by tricking her opponents into breaking a window, creating a distraction). Her time with Proxima, who loves flattery, teaches Qi'ra what to say to deflect or please, which is useful in placating Vos and handling his volatile nature. And as part of the underworld for all of her life, she understands the need to be able to take care of herself in a fight; she's good with a blaster, and has trained in Teräs Käsi, a hand-to-hand combat discipline.

Actress Emilia Clarke notes Qi'ra's guarded nature and how it's hard to be sure of the character's motives. "There is a thing throughout the [Han and Qi'ra] relationship you just can't put your finger on. And that's Qi'ra. Every time you think you have got her number you realize you haven't at all. Which is really hard to play." And she acknowledges not all that glitters is gold, saying, "Well, if you have got a really glamorous lady in a really sordid environment you kind of know that maybe the glamour is hiding a few rough roads."

Qi'ra finds her way to Crimson Dawn after Proxima sells her into slavery. She soon lands with Dryden Vos, leader of the crime syndicate. After her failed attempts to escape him, Vos sees Qi'ra's potential and offers her a position in Crimson Dawn's ranks in exchange for lifelong loyalty. She makes the best of the situation, becomes Vos's top lieutenant, and is at home on Vos's decadent business-meets-pleasure yacht. Qi'ra's presence is such that she's the shining light of any room she's in, and uses that magnetism to her advantage. Vos's guests and employees represent a variety of alien creature types, and Qi'ra was almost one of those species. Early ideation for *Solo* envisioned Kura—later to be called Qi'ra, a riff on the name Kira, which was used for Rey in early drafts of *The Force Awakens*—as a humanoid alien. But after a number of concepts and sketches, it was decided the character would best be served by a performance uninhibited by prosthetics.

And Clarke's range is apparent when Qi'ra encounters Han, after years apart. Maybe joining Crimson Dawn isn't the life Qi'ra would have chosen for herself, but she's taken stock of what the gang gives her and made a life and built a reputation. When Qi'ra's appointed to the crew and tasked with stealing unrefined coaxium by Vos, it's because of her carefully cultivated connections that they're able to acquire a speedy ship. When she sees Han, she comments on being trapped, but in a matter-of-fact sort of way. She relishes having power and being able to get what she wants. Qi'ra knows she could handle business better, and certainly more calmly, than Vos. So, when she sees a chance for promotion, she takes it.

Killing Vos grants her control, eliminating the most controlling individual in her life. With Vos and his time-wasting, rash decisions out of the way, Qi'ra has cleared a path for herself to rise within Crimson Dawn. This act of self-determination is why her betrayal of Han isn't sad, not really. In that moment when she takes command of Vos's ship and contacts Maul, Qi'ra, who has been shuffled around by the galaxy to some degree all her life, claims agency. She finally chooses her own direction.

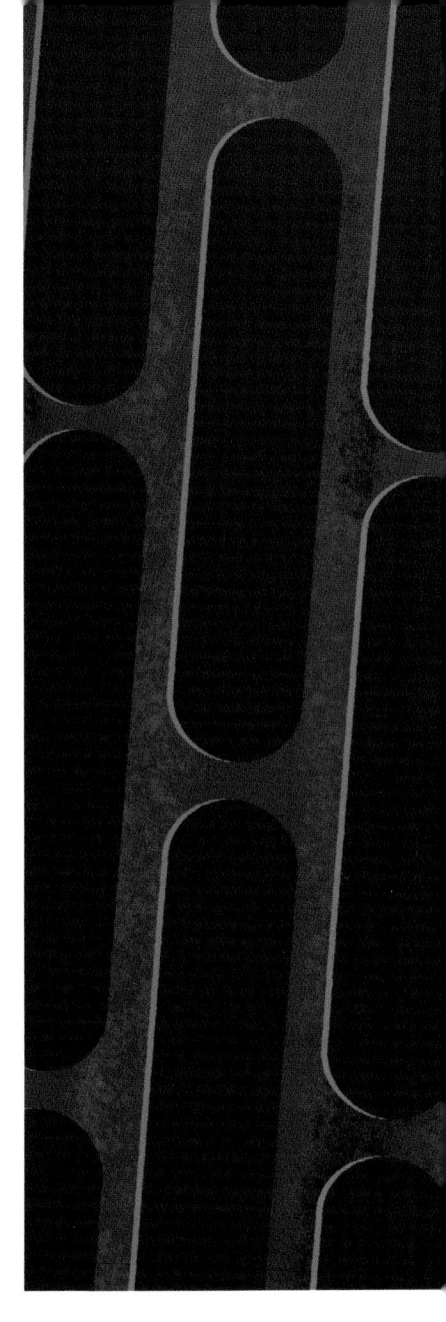

She leads Crimson Dawn and, with her years of experience maneuvering around strong personalities, lays the groundwork for a plot to eliminate Darth Vader and Emperor Palpatine and

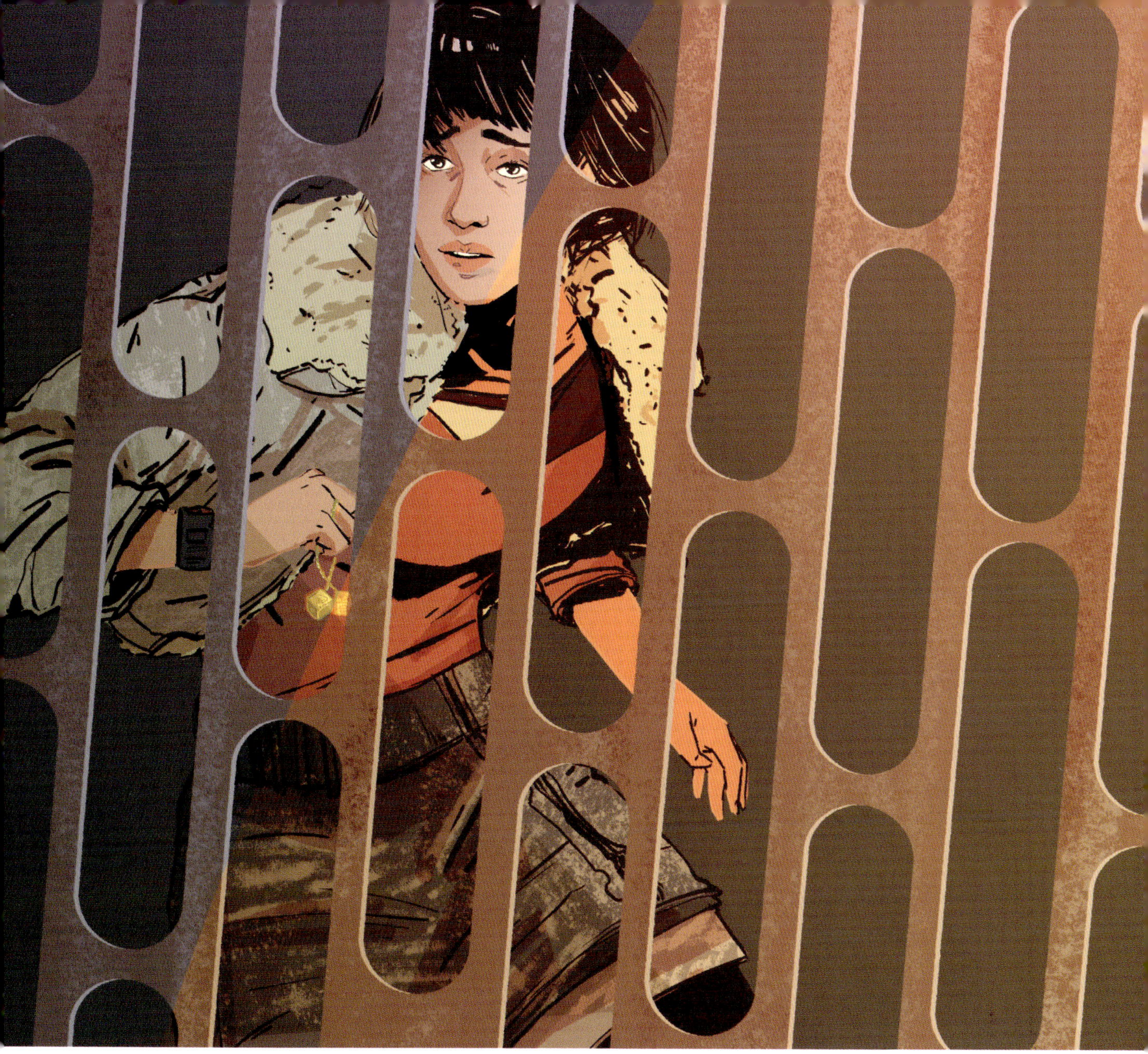

free the galaxy. Lady Qi'ra thinks a Syndicate War would be worth the outcome and leverages what she learns about the Sith from Maul—namely Palpatine's alter ego—in her favor. She recruits others by saying, "They must die . . . so the galaxy can live." While her plans are not directly successful, Luke later acknowledges the importance of Qi'ra's actions in the downfall of the Sith.

R2-KT

The droid with the heart of gold.

Among the many exceptional droids in the galaxy, R2-KT is something special. The pink astromech was inspired by a real-life creation designed by the R2-D2 Builders Club. They constructed R2-KT for Katie Johnson, a young girl diagnosed with terminal brain cancer who wished she had a droid to watch over her, just as R2-D2 watches over Padmé Amidala in *Attack of the Clones*. Since Katie loved the color pink, the builders made a special pastel astromech for her. R2-KT stayed by Katie's side through her last days.

R2-KT joins the galaxy on-screen in the animated feature *Star Wars: The Clone Wars* as one of the droids serving the 501st Legion—fitting, because Katie's father Albin is the founder of the 501st Legion fan group. After loyally serving the Republic and characters such as Anakin Skywalker during the Clone Wars, R2-KT continues to serve galactic good as part of the Resistance, and can be spotted in *The Force Awakens*.

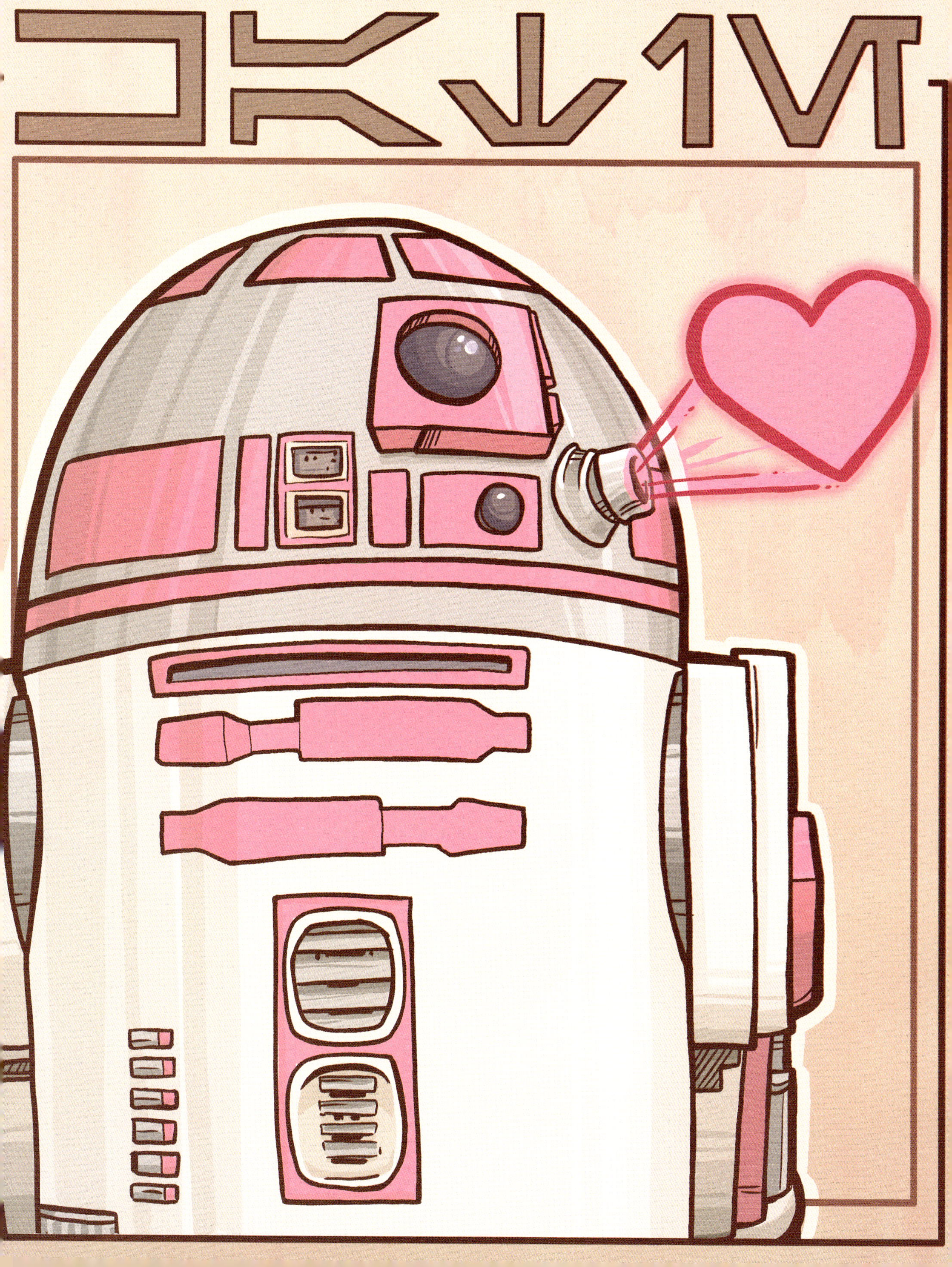

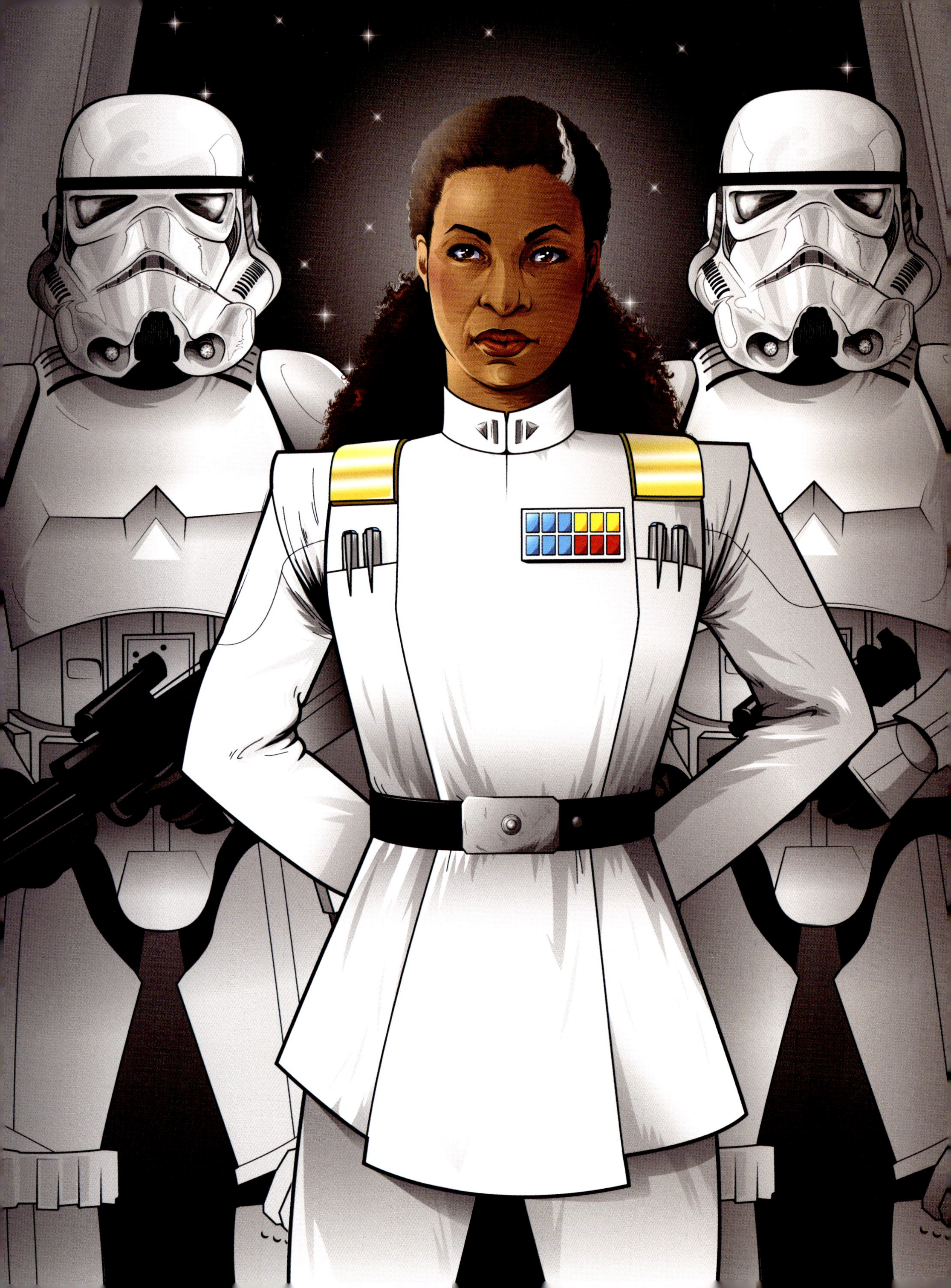

Rae Sloane

"If you ever cross me, I will visit this same violence upon you a hundredfold."

Rae Sloane is a formidable character in the story of the Empire, with roots stretching from before the original trilogy—she was introduced in the novel *A New Dawn*—to events following *Return of the Jedi*. Born on the industrial, shipyard-rich planet of Ganthel, Rae witnesses the Empire put an end to criminal operations on her homeworld, and so views them as a positive influence on the galaxy. After graduating from the Imperial naval academy, she blazes quite a trail, gaining her first captaincy by the age of thirty and ultimately rising through the ranks to become Grand Admiral. She even foils an assassination attempt against Darth Vader and the Emperor by her own commandant while serving as a lieutenant. Rae is committed to what she perceives as the Empire's values, and as the highest-ranked surviving officer after the Battle of Endor, we see her work tirelessly to keep the Imperial military from extinction in the *Aftermath* novels.

Following the death of the Emperor, Rae sees the Empire falling short of her own ideals under the influence of Fleet Admiral Gallius Rax. Fueled by her lifelong dedication, she pushes back against his leadership, and executes him during the Battle of Jakku, leading the remnants of the Empire into the Unknown Regions, determined to rebuild. She proclaims, "It's time to start over. That is our first order. To begin again. And to get it right, this time."

Aftermath trilogy author Chuck Wendig says Rae Sloane was one of his favorite characters to write because we see the Empire through her eyes. "She has an ethos and, on paper, it's ostensibly a positive one even if the Empire she serves is ultimately autocratic and malevolent. Her motivations are human and, at least to me, understandable even as they remain something to condemn."

Rey

"I think I can handle myself."

"I know how to run without you holding my hand." The central character in the film trilogy beginning with *The Force Awakens*, Rey arrives in the tradition of heroes such as Leia Organa and Padmé Amidala—outspoken, independent, and self-sufficient—but she is also uniquely important to the saga and to the fans. Rey, a young woman from the dusty, nothing-ever-happens-here planet of Jakku, receives the call to adventure that changes her life and alters the fandom landscape. Few moments in *Star Wars* are as powerful as Anakin and Luke Skywalker's lightsaber flying out of a snowbank and into Rey's outstretched hand.

Reaction to Rey joining the *Star Wars* galaxy was immediate and passionate. She inspires creative expressions throughout fandom: art, essays, replicas of her distinctive triple bun hairstyle, and costumes at conventions and fan gatherings everywhere. She's a hero without arrogance, a character without all the answers—who wouldn't want to be like her?

Daisy Ridley was unsure, and a little worried, about what fans would think of Rey. Before *The Force Awakens* was released, she said, "I realized what this film might be to people. I hope that people will love it. I think they will. I feel like I'm working with my film family. Every day is fun. I haven't had one day where I didn't enjoy it. There

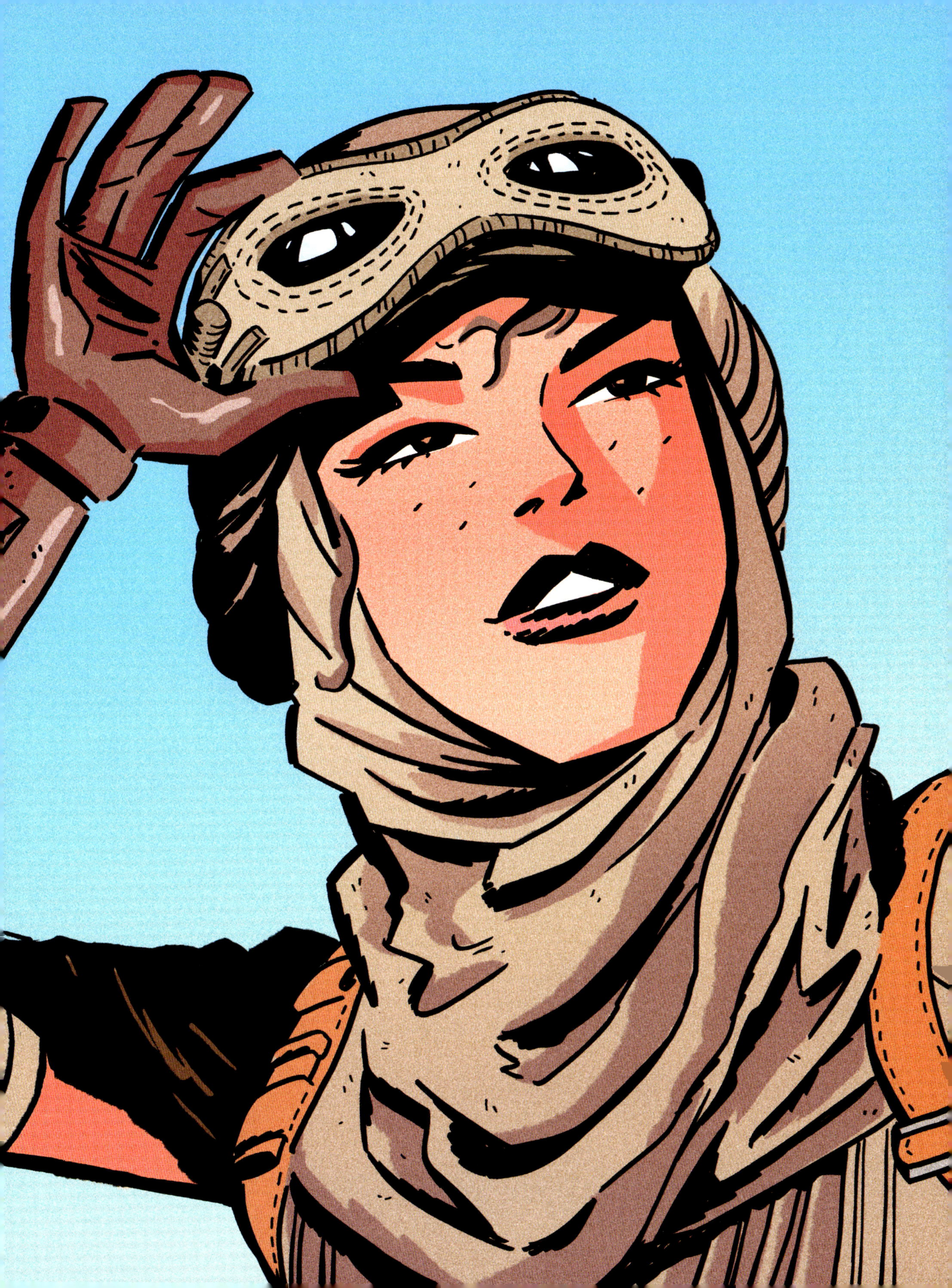

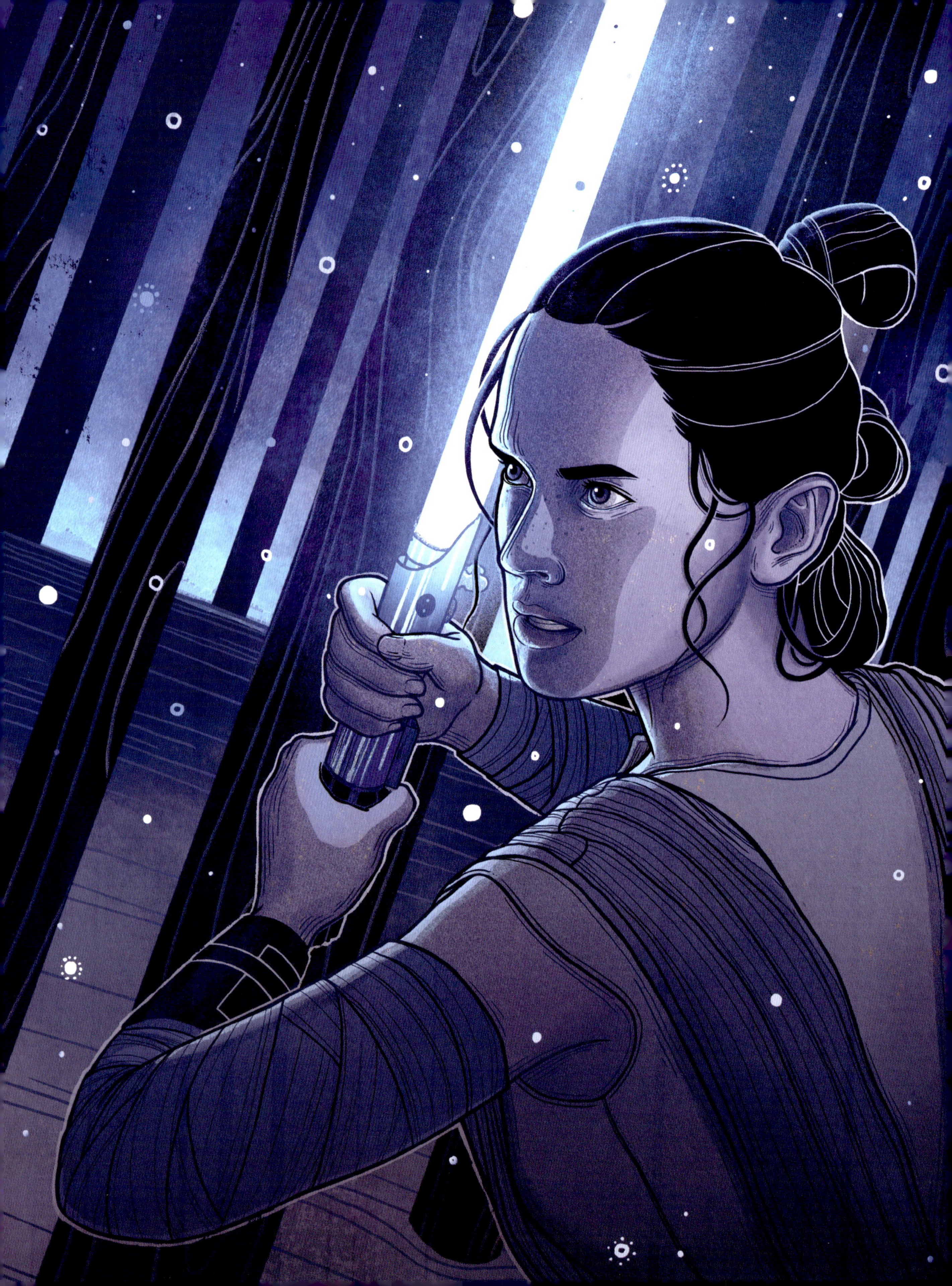

are moments when I think how many people love *Star Wars*, and it's scary trying to fit into that world that people know so well and love so much. It's nerve-wracking thinking about what Rey might represent to these people and whether they'll like her or not."

Rey would go through a hero's journey behind the scenes, too. Early drafts of the script depict her working in a used spaceship lot, longing to leave her world behind—unlike Rey in the film, who stays put awaiting the return of her family. Even in initial drafts, a scavenger named Kira has a speeder she makes herself, but little else remains of the original direction. Subsequent drafts of the script shape Kira into Rey, and a hero is born.

Rey grows up alone on Jakku, an unforgiving planet that can wring dry those who call it home. Left by her parents as a young girl, Rey doesn't receive much help from anyone. She quickly learns the ins-and-outs of survival: not just how to search the wreckage from the Battle of Jakku for profitable parts, but also how to protect herself from the dangers of the desert and fellow scavengers. Rey teaches herself how to fight with a staff. She looks at each item she finds from the perspective of possibility, whether turning lenses from a stormtrooper helmet into goggles, or uncovering a fallen AT-AT walker to make it her home.

Rey is kind, and she's optimistic, even when trapped in a situation that would turn most people cynical and cold, let down and betrayed by others time and again. She demonstrates this kindness when she lets the lost droid BB-8 follow her home in *The Force Awakens*, rather than sell him for more food than she's ever seen; and again when she feeds a fearsome Nightwatcher worm precious salvaged material so it doesn't starve in *Forces of Destiny*; and most importantly when she helps Finn, a complete stranger, get away from the First Order following his desertion by taking him offworld.

By trusting Finn and leaving the dust of Jakku behind, Rey opens a door to a life she couldn't have imagined. She's dreamed of it; the Force showed her Luke's island while she slept, but how often do visions become reality? She meets the legendary smuggler Han Solo. She sees a planet with more green than she thought existed. Her wonder is our wonder. We see the galaxy through her earnest eyes, and it's like experiencing it for the first time. This makes Rey's discovery of her Force abilities all the more powerful.

The Force inside of Rey awakens when she first touches the lightsaber that once belonged to the Skywalkers. It calls to her while she's on Takodana. Maz Kanata tries to help Rey process what's happened, but scared of the intensity of the Force vision, Rey runs. She doesn't see herself as anything special, so of course she doesn't immediately embrace her powers. Her abilities awaken powerfully after she's captured by Kylo Ren, and his reaction to her strength emboldens her to test her newfound skills. The resolve we see on Jakku returns as she escapes and then confronts Kylo Ren head-on.

Their lightsaber duel on Starkiller Base is unforgettable. Ren is near-fatally wounded, but this scavenger from Jakku has never even wielded a lightsaber before, and still she keeps him at bay. At the darkest moment of the battle, she follows Maz's advice and lets the light guide her; she lashes out in defense, not rage. Rey is every child who's held a lightsaber toy in the backyard or playground and dreamed of saving the galaxy.

Rey goes on to complete the quest others couldn't: she finds Luke Skywalker on the remote planet of Ahch-To. *The Last Jedi* shows us he's not a willing teacher, and he traveled to an unfindable island for a reason. But Rey doesn't immediately get back into the *Millennium Falcon* and return to the Resistance. The determined spirit that helped her make it through years of solitude on Jakku takes over; she convinces Luke to train her in the ways of the Force by telling him, "I need someone to show me my place in all of this."

When Rey's power frightens Luke enough to halt their lessons, she doesn't turn to anger or sadness about being rejected. She continues training on her own. And, due to the machinations of Supreme Leader Snoke, she finds herself reconnected with a surprising person: Kylo Ren. They're taken aback by a Force connection, but over time, they find common ground. Rey turns

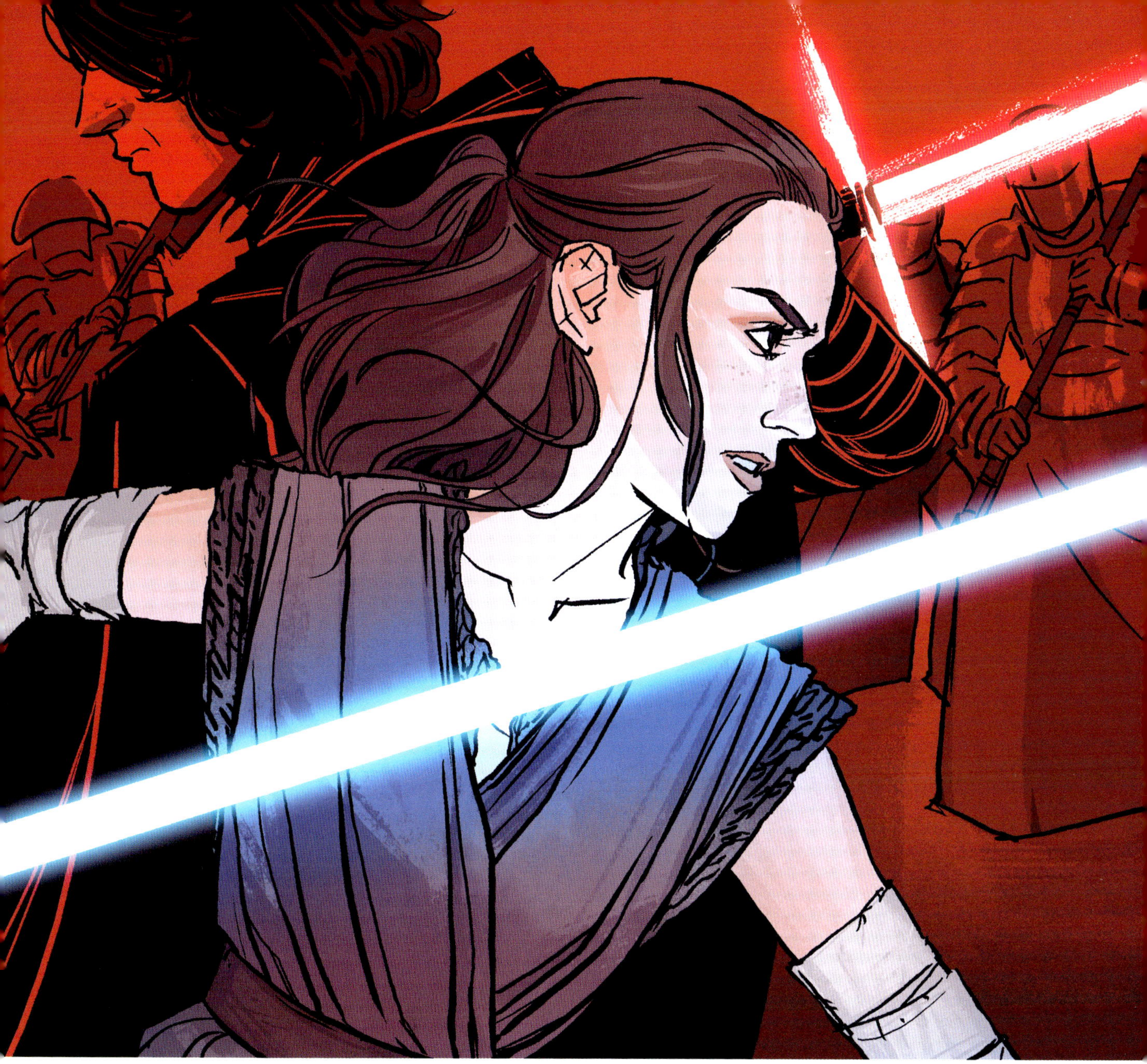

"Balance and energy. A force. . . . Inside me, that same force."

—Rey

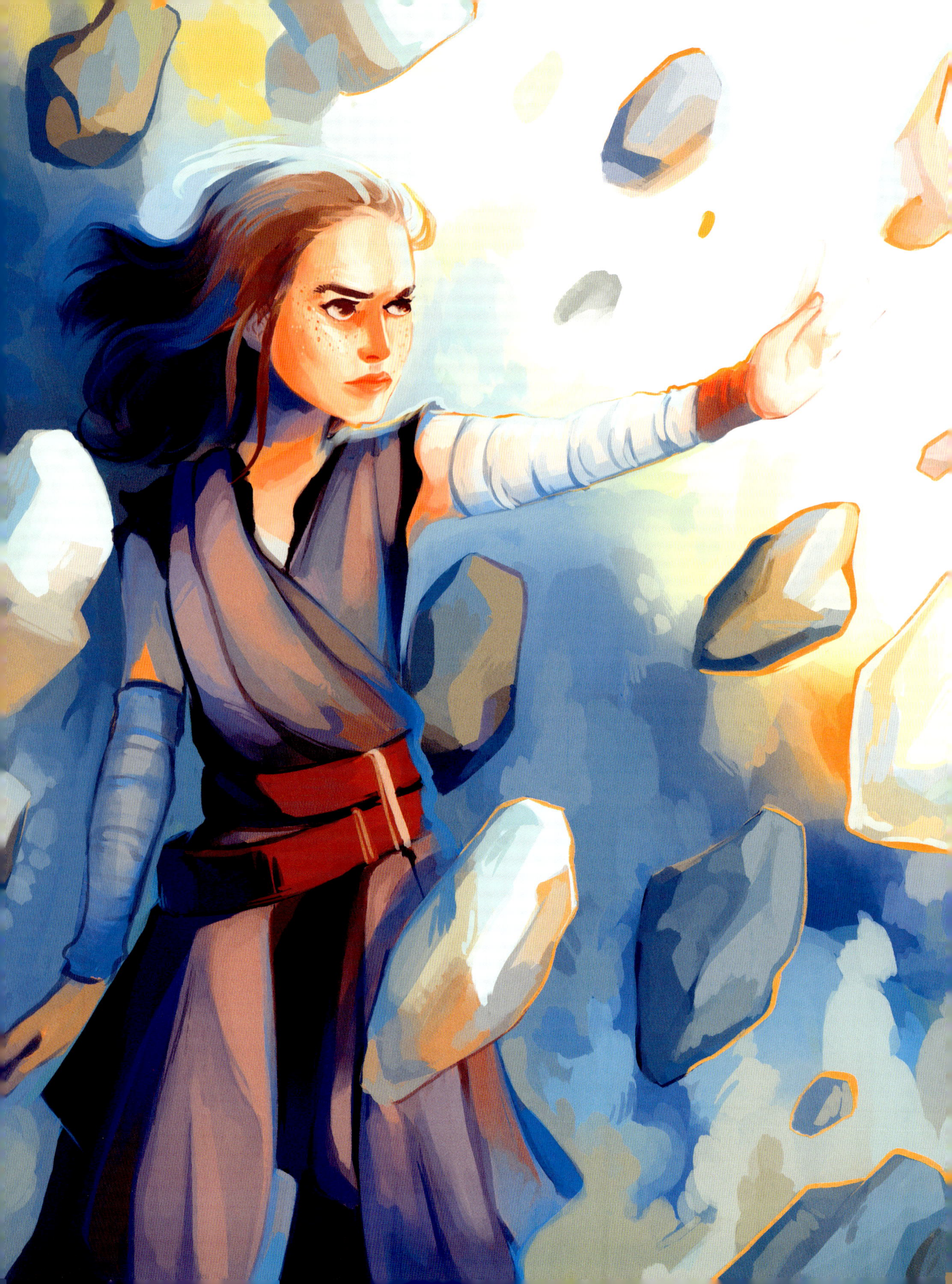

to Kylo after her bewildering experience in the mirror cave on Ahch-To. Again, Rey maintains an open mind and is willing to put faith in Ben Solo—a man she saw murder his own father. She doesn't forget the horrific act, but she gradually senses his conflict and sees an opening to turn Ben back to the light, and she doesn't let go until he draws a line.

Kylo tells Rey that her parents were "filthy junk traders" who didn't want her. *The Last Jedi* director and writer Rian Johnson described it as the hardest possible thing she could have heard. Rey's been hinging a part of her identity on reconnecting with her family. She has to reassess who she is and do so among the turmoil of the Supremacy exploding around her. But she listens to the light side of the Force and commits to it, even after what she's heard about her parents, even after she no longer has a teacher to guide her. Despite believing she comes from nothing, she trusts in herself and brings hope where it is needed most: to Luke, Leia, and the Resistance.

Rey's actions do save the Battle of Crait survivors, but the Resistance is in tatters. Rebuilding after the battle and the loss of Luke is trying for everyone. Rey struggles without her former teacher, but she continues on her path to becoming a Jedi, training under Leia. The former scavenger applies self-discipline, and as she learns from Leia and the sacred texts Rey took from Ahch-To, Rey's strength in the Force grows. She demands much of herself, likely because she feels the pressure of being the lone Jedi in the struggling Resistance. Rey knows she can change the stakes in the fight against the First Order, and she wants to be ready for the next battle and for the next confrontation with Kylo Ren. But her grit generates anger and aggression, both of which interfere with Rey's connection to the Force.

Rey has had to stay focused in order to process a number of life-changing revelations in a short, chaotic period of time, and it's critical that this determination is locked in when she learns the truth about her heritage. Rey is the granddaughter of Sheev Palpatine, also known as Darth Sidious, who has lingered all these years through dark Sith techniques and cloning, waiting for the right moment to return. Her parents didn't carelessly abandon the young Rey on Jakku; they hid her there, hoping to keep her out of Darth Sidious's grasp. The discovery upends Rey's world, as she must navigate her dark lineage and mourn the sacrifice her parents made for her.

On a mission to stop Palpatine and the Sith Eternal fleet, she runs into Kylo Ren again and wonders if their Force-bonded dyad means she should join him. Confused and scared by her rage and ancestry, Rey tries to exile herself to Ahch-To, like Luke, but instead encounters her teacher as a Force spirit. Luke reassures Rey her connection to Palpatine does not define who she is or change how others in the Resistance perceive her. With his judgment-free wisdom fresh in her mind, Rey leaves Ahch-To and rises above her interior chaos, physically confronting it by facing Darth Sidious, and striking him down. Rey saves the day with her lightsaber, yes, but also with an open heart and a forgiving mind.

She claims a new identity, one that honors her greatest teachers. She is Rey Skywalker.

"I am all the Jedi."
—Rey

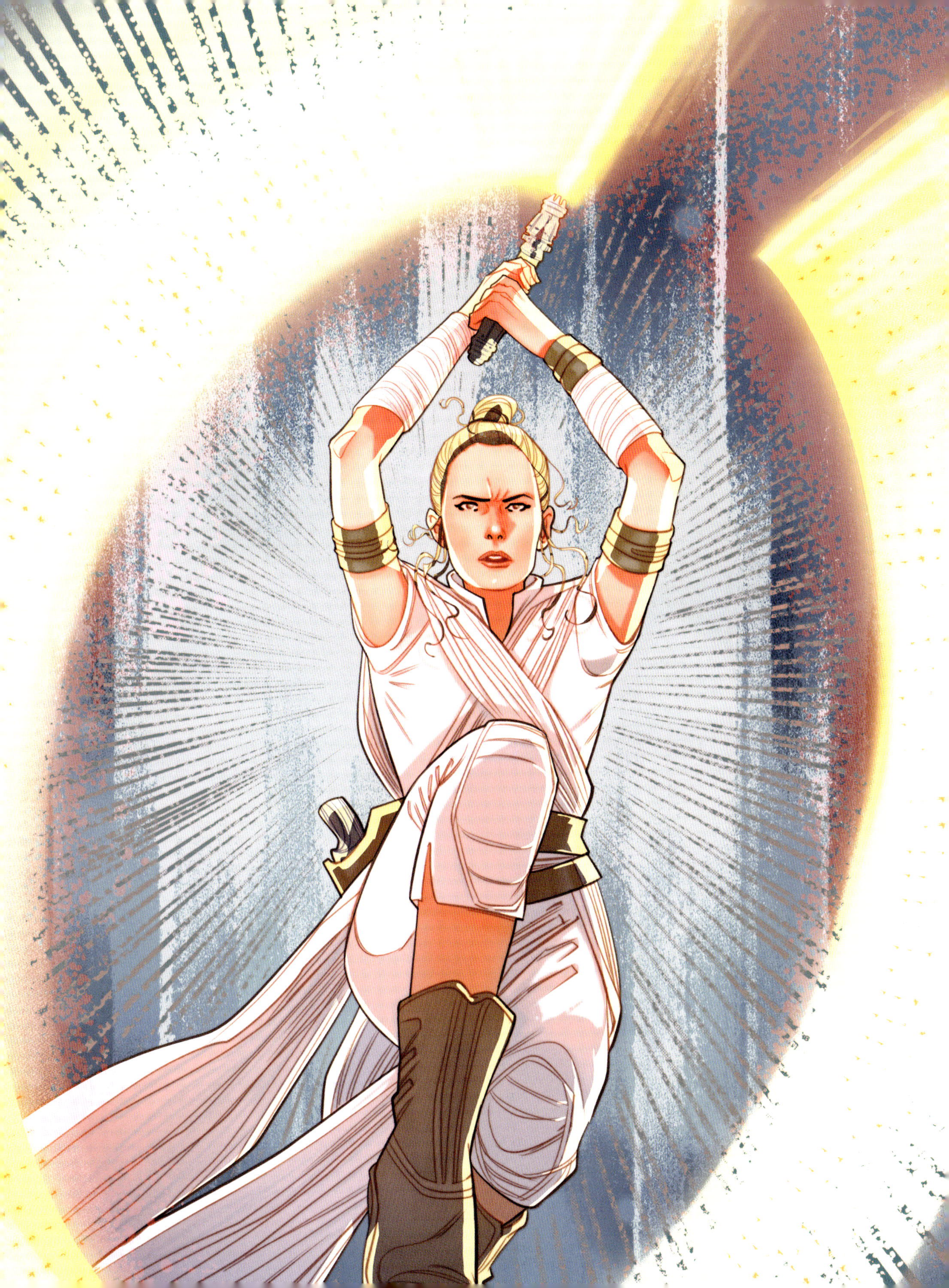

Rose Tico

"That's how we're gonna win. Not fighting what we hate; saving what we love."

Rose Tico is an everywoman, a working-class member of the Resistance. She's proof that every single position counts. In a galaxy full of hotshot pilots, smugglers, nobles, and politicians, Rose is a mechanic and maintenance worker. She brings a fresh perspective on how war affects the average person; her idealistic nature and even her excitement is something we can identify with. As actress Kelly Marie Tran sees her, "Rose is not an amazing pilot or a Jedi, she's just strong in a different way, and I think that's how she holds her own."

In some ways, Rose is the personification of a fan in the *Star Wars* galaxy. She has a total fangirl reaction to Finn when she first meets him, stumbling over her words and calling him "The Finn." And when she presents an idea to General Leia Organa at the urging of her sister Paige in the comic *Forces of Destiny: Rose & Paige*, she admits to Paige, "Every time she talks to me I can barely function."

As Rose learns, meeting legends isn't always the experience one imagines. When she comes face-to-face with Finn in *The Last Jedi*, she expects him to be the First Order-turned-Resistance hero she's heard about. She has him on a pedestal. But then she realizes he's deserting, daring to run away when people like her sister Paige have sacrificed themselves to keep the spark alive. Rose shows how deep

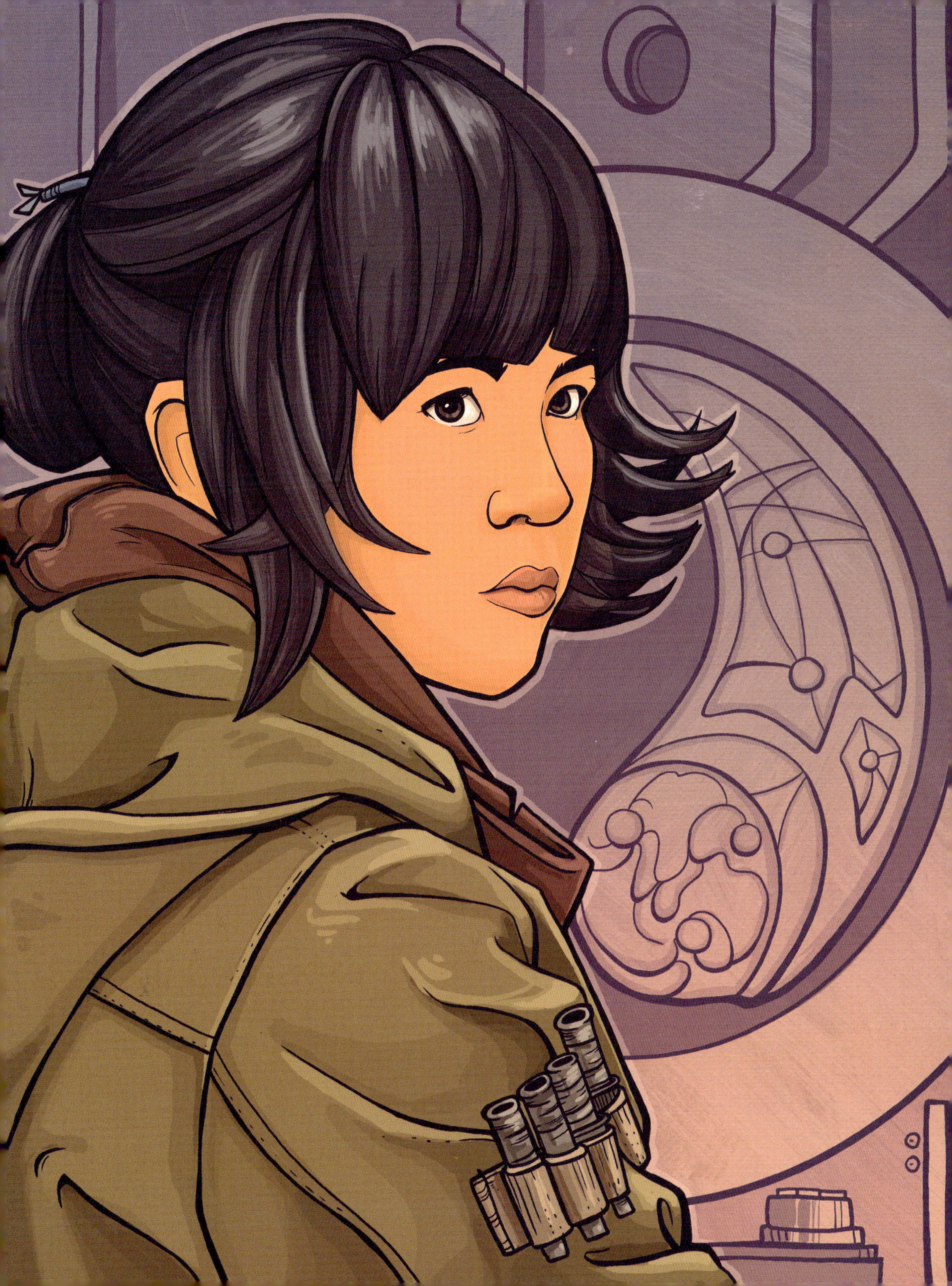

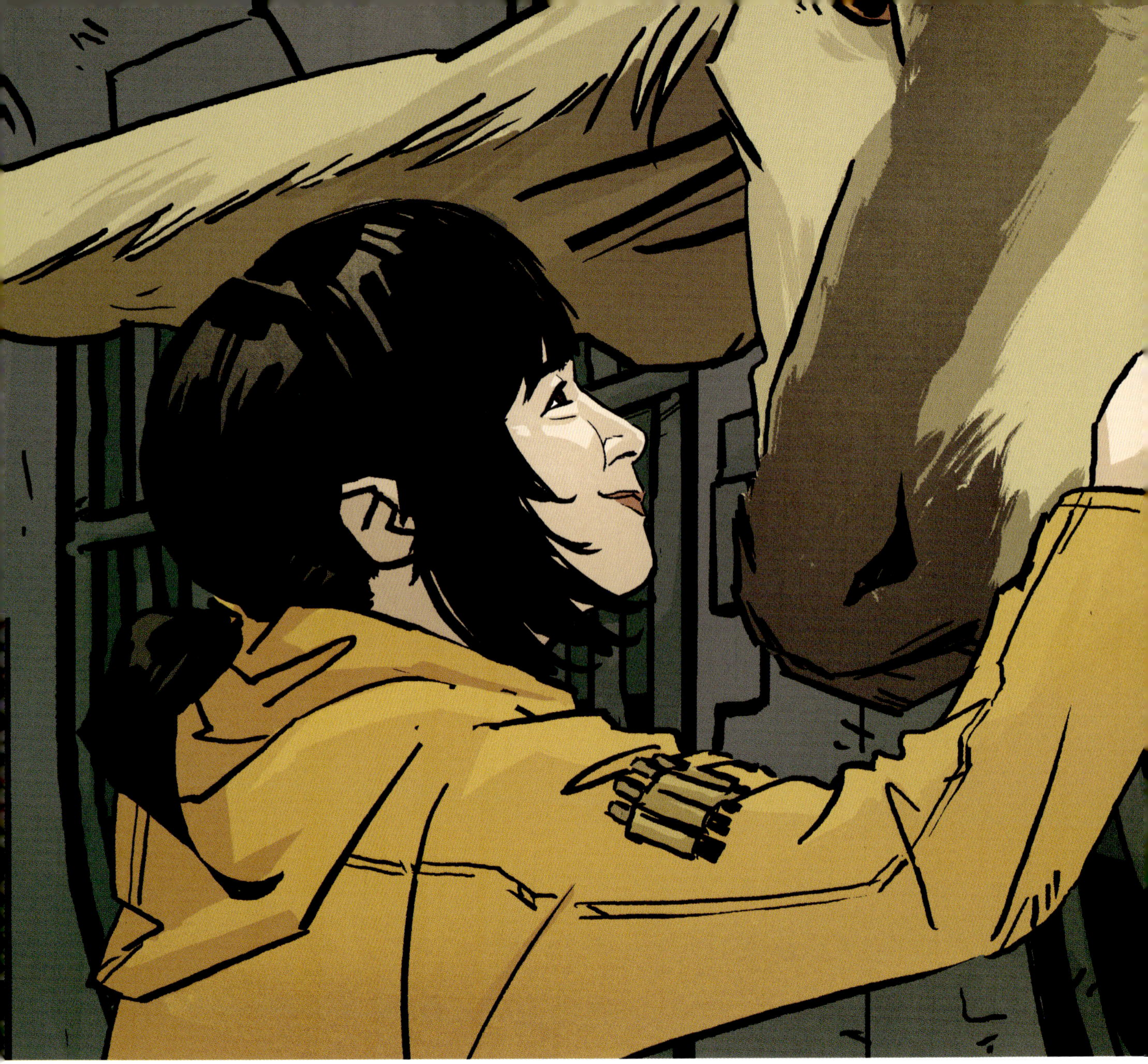

“We hope.”
—Rose Tico

her integrity runs when she wipes away tears over losing Paige and uses an electro-shock prod to knock Finn out, just like the others she's caught trying to escape the battle.

Rose isn't a leader when we first meet her, but she becomes a role model of sorts for Finn, showing him how to dedicate himself to the cause by example. And it's because of Finn that the character Rose, the fourth major new character in the sequel trilogy and the first Asian American female lead in *Star Wars*, was created. In early drafts, it was Poe who went with Finn on the side excursion to Canto Bight, but the team-up was boring. "It was just these two dudes on an adventure. I knew something was wrong when I looked at their dialogue and realized that I could interchange any of the lines," director Rian Johnson said in *The Art of Star Wars: The Last Jedi*. "There wasn't conflict between them. So I realized I had to come up with something else. Finn needing somebody else to go with who would actually challenge him and push him and contrast with him was where Rose came from." She's like the angel on Finn's shoulder.

Rose comes from a system ravaged by the First Order. She and Paige grew up on Hays Minor, a mining planet, longing to leave and travel the galaxy. And although they do eventually visit new planets with the Resistance, it's not quite in the tourist-seeing-the-sights experience Rose dreams of as a child. Because she's acquainted with the horrors the First Order brings to planets they want something from, Rose is motivated to help the Resistance from a place of empathy as well as determination. She isn't seeking revenge upon the First Order; she's committed to preventing them from doing further harm, to saving innocent lives.

Tran values Rose's humble background: "In a lot of movies today, we see people that are royalty, or are superheroes, or have magical powers . . . I love the idea of someone who might not necessarily be in the forefront of the action to begin with, someone who is like a cog in the machine that helps the Resistance keep going. But then at one point, you have to face your fears and have to be pulled into a situation and be able to face any challenge. It's such a huge deal to me, the idea that she's not necessarily special in the way that we have defined special before in other movies, or in other stories."

Even before she steps into the spotlight, Rose is doing more than just fixing things in the background. Her mechanical knowledge earns her the position of flight engineer aboard the *Cobalt Hammer*, the same bomber Paige is assigned to. Rose is inventive in her tinkering, perhaps more so because she hasn't received formal training. When General Organa asks her to come up with a technique to help bombers escape First Order detection in the novel *Cobalt Squadron*, Rose cobbles together a baffler, or a Resistance-cloak, "a poor but functional version of the real thing." It turns the bombers into stealthy ships, and in fact is so successful that the invention is later installed on the escape crafts evacuating from the *Raddus* to Crait in order to keep them hidden from the First Order.

Rose is supported and encouraged by her sister while she is alive, and driven forward still more powerfully after Paige's death. Rose cannot let her sister's sacrifice be in vain. The Mega Star Destroyer *Supremacy*'s ability to track the Resistance through hyperspace seems like an impossible problem, but Rose sees a solution. On her first ever Resistance mission without her sister, she disobeys orders and travels with Finn to Canto Bight, frees mistreated fathiers (Paige's favorite creature), and follows a risky plan intended to disable the First Order's tracker. Putting it all on the line for the sake of Paige and the Resistance, Rose becomes a hero.

Her heroism comes through in moments big and small. It comes through when she hands over her half of her pendant (an Otomok medallion shared with her sister) without hesitation because it's needed for the mission or when she leaves her Resistance ring with enslaved children on Canto Bight to give them hope. And it comes through when, as Finn tries to destroy the First Order's superlaser siege cannon on Crait by flying into it, in a "heroic" but likely futile death, Rose crashes into him and saves his life. She understands the real value not just of fighting what is evil, but in saving what is good.

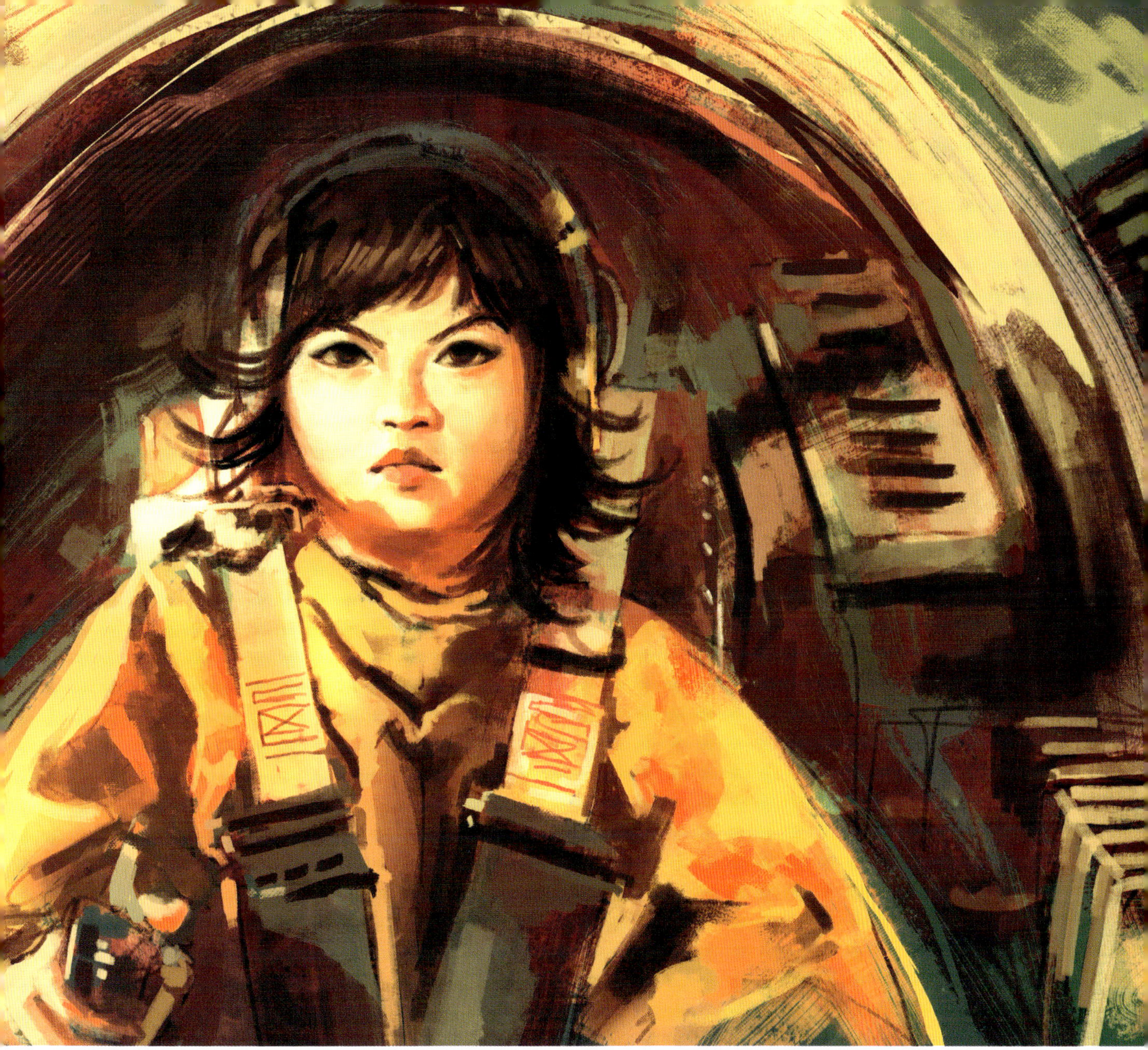

Becoming the leader of the Engineering Corps, Commander Tico bolsters the Resistance's efforts, crafting and implementing new technology. She makes important advances for the Resistance's communication systems to ensure they bypass First Order interception. With confidence from her successes and support from General Organa, Rose applies her unique skills to stopping the First Order and the Sith Eternal.

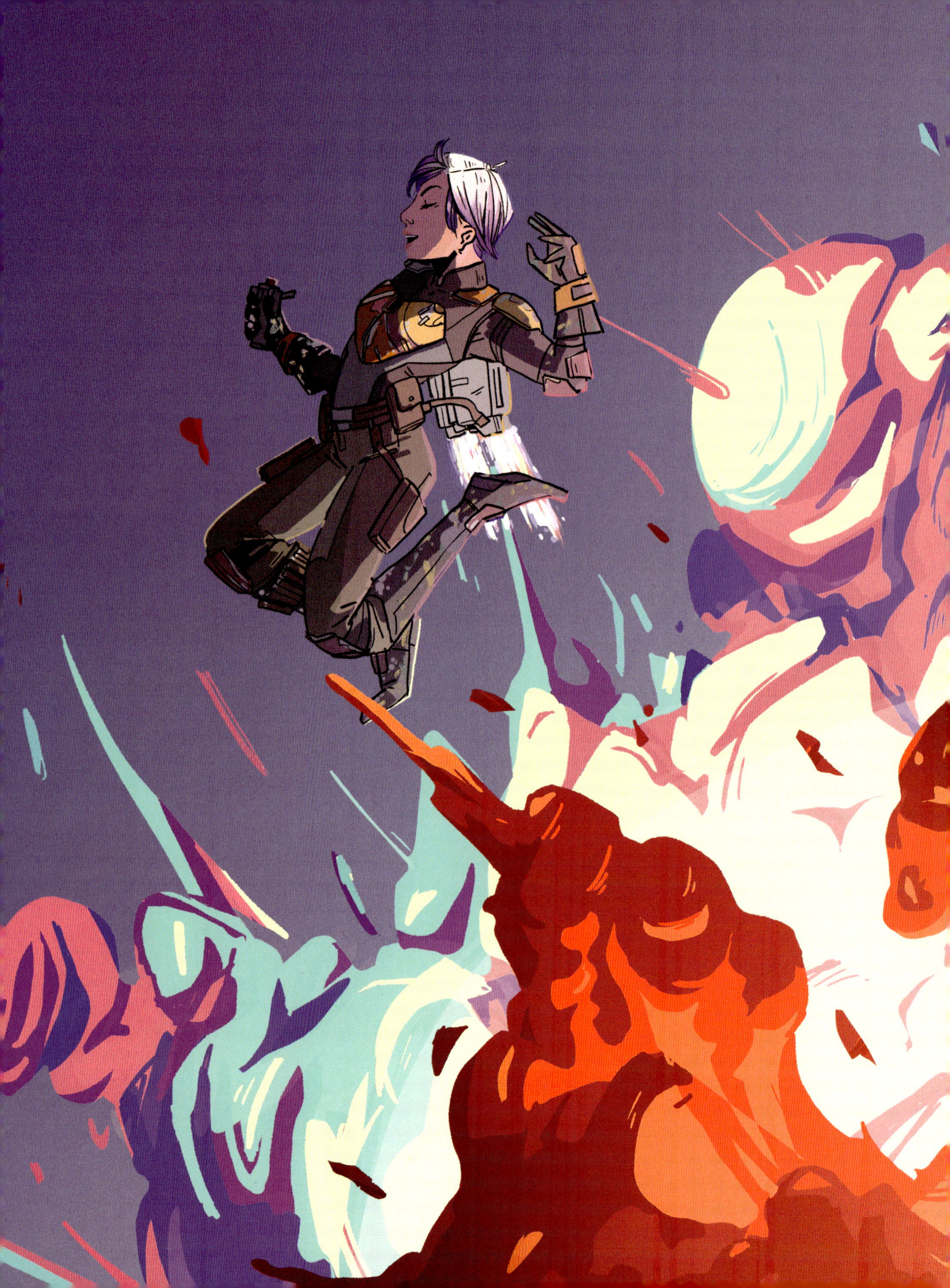

Sabine Wren

"Never get between a Mandalorian and a weapons package."

The word *Mandalorian* can often conjure the image of a certain kind of male warrior for *Star Wars* fans. But *Star Wars Rebels* redefines the idea of a typical Mandalorian by introducing Sabine Wren, a teenage one-time Imperial who defects to become a full-time rebel. The traditional armor she wears—five hundred years old, and carrying the history of battles and blood—has been reforged and colorfully repainted by Sabine to her liking. She adds her personal touch to everything, whether it's painting vignettes on the walls of her quarters aboard the *Ghost* or blowing up an Imperial base with panache. While the Empire is taking over Mandalore and blending the planet's martial warrior culture with Imperial authority, Sabine responds with defiance.

With freedom of expression at odds with the Empire's vision for the galaxy, Sabine uses her art to make a statement. She's the first character in the *Star Wars* galaxy to rebel through creative means by tagging Imperial outposts with the symbol of the phoenix (a symbol that later evolves into the Rebel Alliance starbird). She even repaints TIE fighters with garish hues, turning the bland gray and black Imperial equipment into personal works of art. Sabine also dyes her hair in bright colors and changes the designs on her armor to reflect special memories or recent events. She doesn't care if all of this makes her stick out as an Imperial target—it's too much fun to taunt the Empire.

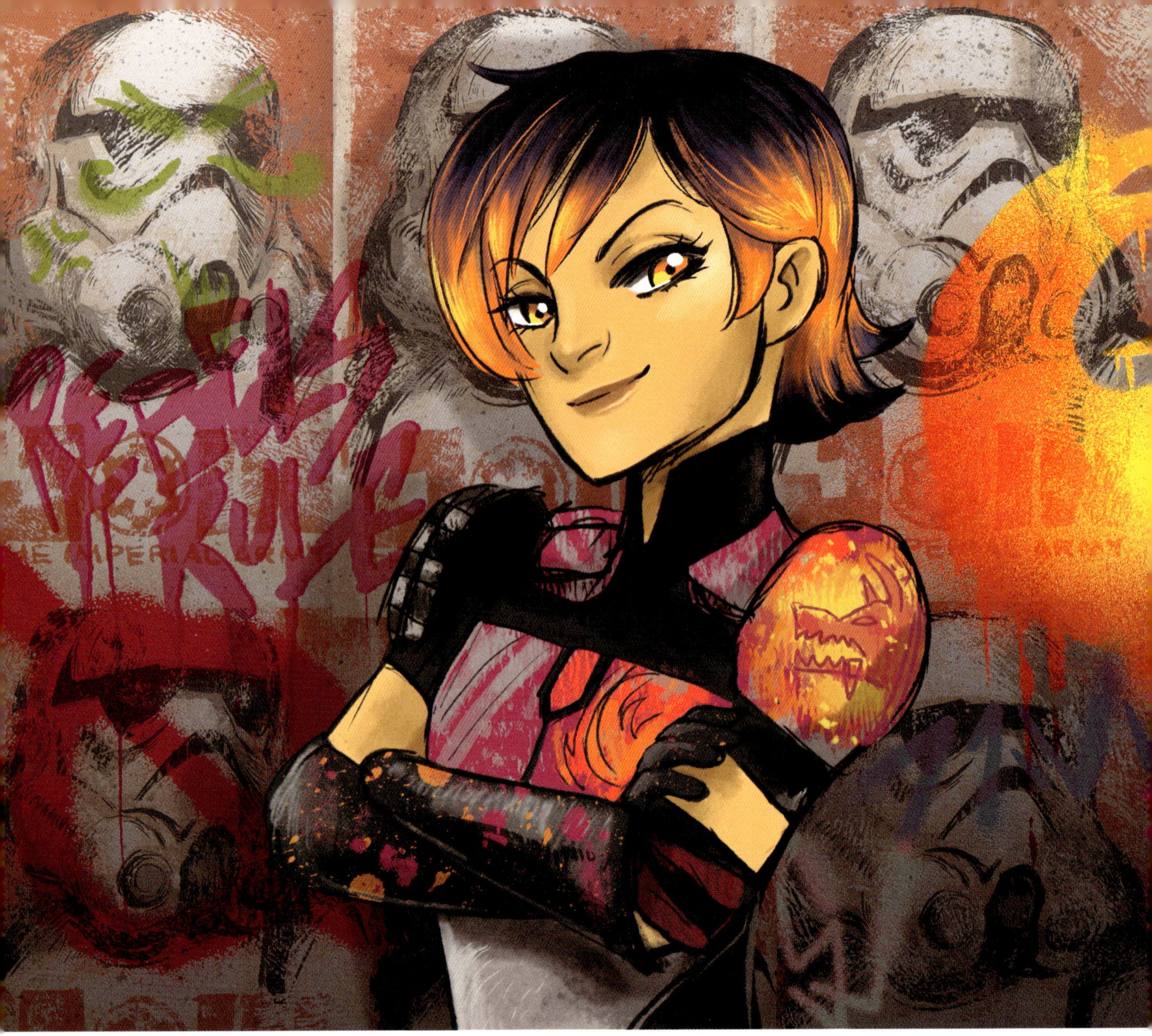

Her artistic pizzazz goes hand in hand with her demolitions expertise. Sabine learns about munitions at the Imperial Academy on Mandalore, and she later puts them to use in ways her instructors surely regret. She takes special pride in using explosives to destroy targets such as Imperial shipyards, but also in making the results beautiful. After one operation, she says, "Forget the explosion, look at the color."

Voice actress Tiya Sircar appreciates the character's creative and destructive sides. "She does it with flair, because she's also an artist. She's pretty rad, sassy, and strong. She's got this interesting sensibility about her. She's a teenager, and yet she's very sharp, she's very quick-witted, she's highly intelligent, and she's not worried about any of the superficial stuff that many teens are. She's really a fun character to play."

Sabine is a key part of the missions carried out by the Spectres aboard the *Ghost*. With her Mandalorian warrior training and education at the Imperial Academy, she's prepared to take on opponents in the air with a jetpack or hand to hand on the ground, and use her mechanical skills to activate or disable equipment. She can also understand multiple languages, once using her familiarity with Aqualish to help steal an Imperial shipment.

With her style and nature so upfront, Sabine can sometimes struggle to navigate the more subtle aspects key to insurrection. When the *Ghost* crew receives directives from an agent identified as Fulcrum, only Hera, the captain of the ship, has access to the full communication. It's hard for Sabine to understand that it's a secrecy born of necessity rather than a lack of trust. Sabine wants to know everything because she needs reassurance that they're actually getting somewhere with their actions against the Empire. She tells Hera, "I want to believe we're doing good, making a difference, but sometimes it seems like the harder we fight, the harder things get out there. I feel like we can't take down the Empire on our own."

As time goes by and the scattered rebel groups unite into something more cohesive, Sabine grasps the bigger picture and takes on more responsibilities. Her Imperial past makes her the perfect operative to infiltrate the Empire's Skystrike Academy and extract students who want to defect to the Rebellion, including pilots we know from the original trilogy, Wedge Antilles and Hobbie Klivian.

When Sabine leaves Mandalore, it isn't entirely out of rebellion. She is also escaping a guilty chapter from her past. While at the Academy, she helps create a weapon known as the Arc Pulse Generator, which she later realizes could be used to enslave Mandalore to the Empire. She warns her family about the Empire's intentions, but her mother and clan leader Ursa Wren sides with the Imperials anyway. This conflict resurfaces after Sabine discovers the legendary Darksaber, a black-bladed lightsaber wielded by Mandalorian leaders for generations, in Darth Maul's hovel on Dathomir. Moved by what the Darksaber represents, she divulges this past shame to her friends on the *Ghost*, and embarks on the arduous task of banishing these demons when she trains to wield the Darksaber for the good of her people. Sircar especially liked seeing this different side of Sabine: "It was really wonderful, and so interesting, to get to see a character who is so guarded and so strong, and uses sarcasm and wit and snark at every opportunity, to be so vulnerable."

When Sabine returns home to try to recruit her family and other Mandalorians for the Rebellion, she is reunited with her mother. Sabine and Ursa aren't warm toward each other, but they come to an understanding, and Sabine remains on Mandalore for a while in an effort to make reparations for her mistakes. Having sabotaged the Arc Pulse Generator in its first incarnation, she's instrumental in destroying it a second time after the Empire has revived it, delivering it the fatal blow with the Darksaber. In the course of battle, she recognizes a leader in the former regent, Bo-Katan Kryze, and hands the Darksaber over to her before returning to the Rebellion.

In doing so she rejoins to the Spectres as a sort of family. Sabine, who once didn't trust in others, puts her faith in her teammates. Though Ezra seemingly gives his life to save Lothal, Sabine carries on. She tells the *Ghost* crew's story in an artful mural displayed in Lothal's Capital City, near her new home. Sabine resists the heroic label the New Republic wants to pin on her and tries to lead a quiet life. Still, when her former master and friend Ahsoka comes to ask her to solve a puzzle that could help them find Ezra as well as Grand Admiral Thrawn, Sabine agrees to adventure once more.

The journey to find Ezra and Thrawn takes Sabine and Ahsoka to another galaxy, but the journey takes place within Sabine, too. Between Lothal and Peridea, she must work through what she views as her failure to learn the ways of the Force. Ahsoka

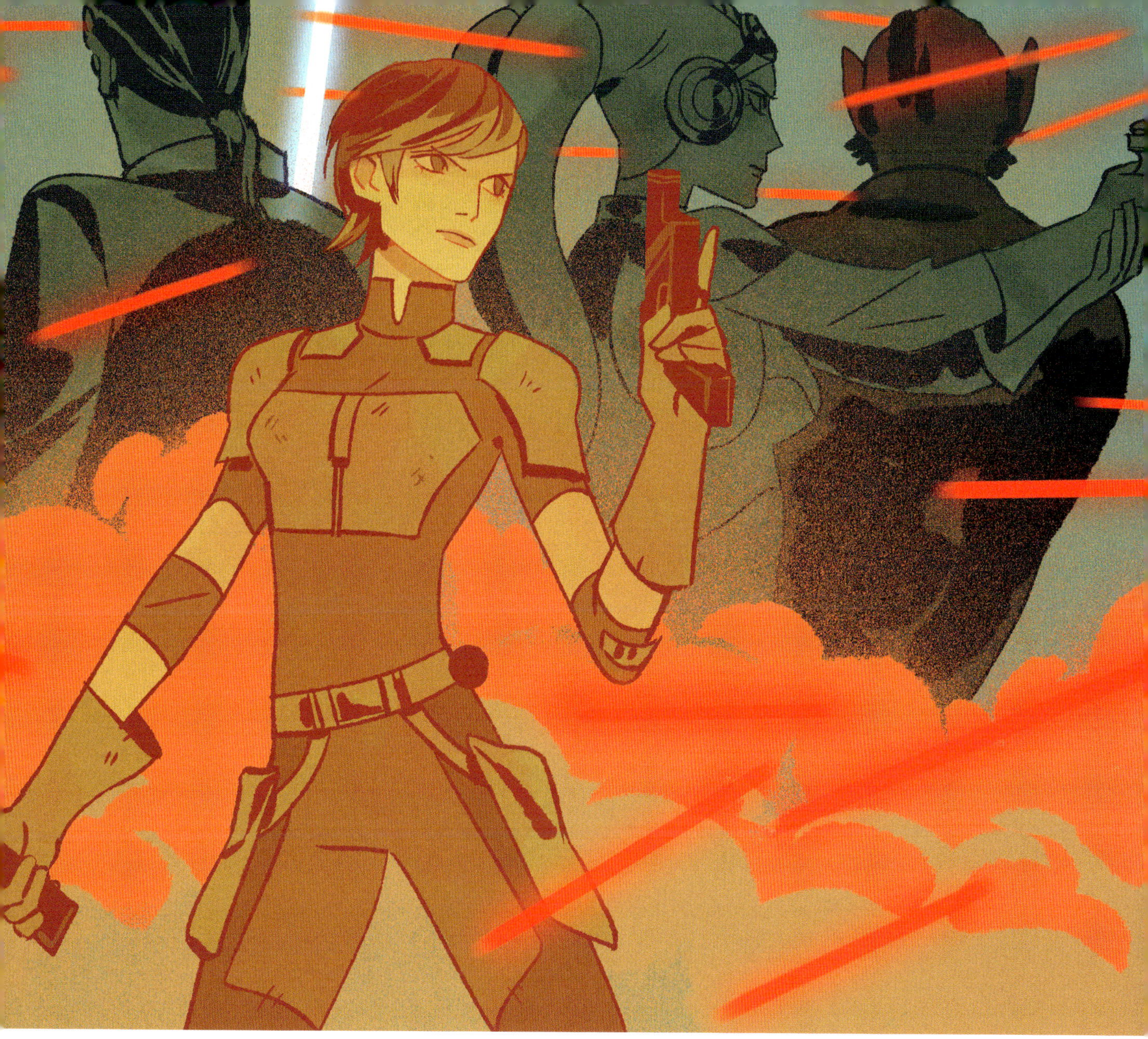

guides her, but Sabine must accept and believe in herself in order to grow and reunite with her friend. Her dedication to the quest underlines the importance of the Spectres and their found family.

Natasha Liu Bordizzo takes on the role of Sabine in live-action, incorporating Sabine's journey from *Rebels* and her signature smirk. Bordizzo says, "I wanted them [animated and live-action Sabine] to be streamlined, but still separate in a way, and I wanted to just bring the truth of whatever the live action project brought on the day, every day on set. Her journey has changed since *Rebels* in *Ahsoka* . . . where she had to work her way back to being that free-spirited kind of kid that we all loved."

Sana Starros

"Move once, you won't be moving again."

It's never too late to change your destiny. Introduced in the *Star Wars* comic, Sana Starros was born on Nar Shaddaa, known as Smuggler's Moon; for many years of her life, she lets her home direct her path and becomes a first-class smuggler, with skills to challenge Lando Calrissian or Han Solo. Her savviness means she considers every facet of a plan and finds ways to bury feints within feints, so that it's not always clear how many people she's crossing at the same time. Cutthroat and efficient, Sana gets the job done.

For one particular robbery, she and Han Solo even marry under pretense, but the scoundrel takes off with her cut. Sana's tendency to hold on to a grudge is clear when she tracks Han across the galaxy to make him pay (and when she later encounters her old flame, Chelli Aphra). When she finds him with Leia, she leans into greed and attempts to sell the princess to the Empire and collect a bounty. Sana looks down on Han's choice to help the rebels. She tells Leia, "I haven't succumbed to the seductive wiles of the Rebellion."

But something about the rebels gets under Sana's skin, and she sees a different course for her life. She works for Leia on missions suited to her smuggling skills—transporting prisoners, hijacking a Star Destroyer, and tracking Luke after Aphra takes him to Ktath'atn to meet with the Queen about a crystal from the Citadel of Rur. Ultimately, she uses her criminal tricks of the trade—cheating and bluffing—to the advantage of the Rebellion, and comes to realize, "Smugglers are only as good as the thing they're smuggling."

Her work for the Rebellion brings her into Aphra's path time and time again, and Sana repeatedly tries to kill her ex. Despite their complex history and Sana's tangled emotions about Aphra, the duo work together for the Alliance. Over time, they heal old wounds and reform their bond.

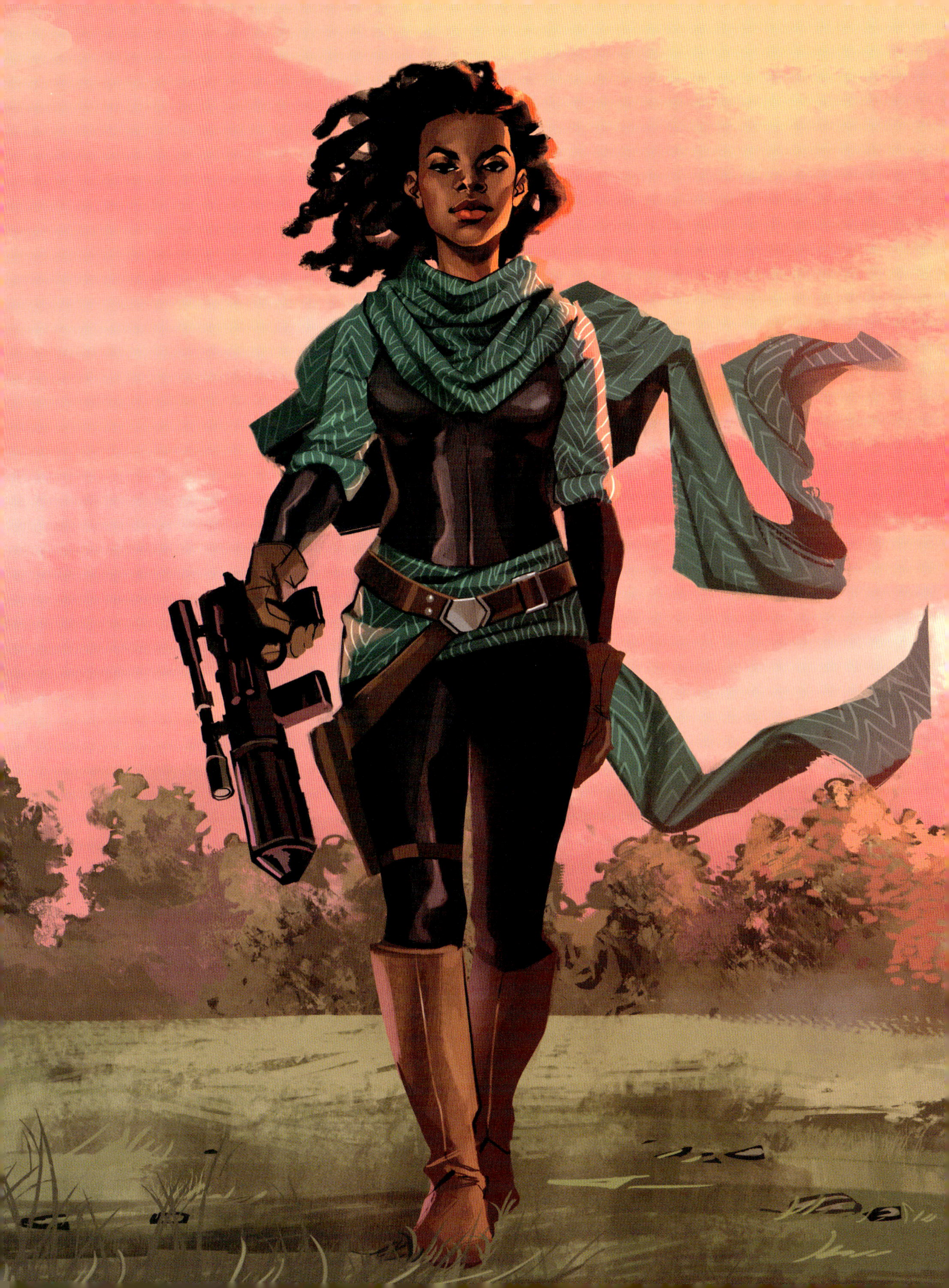

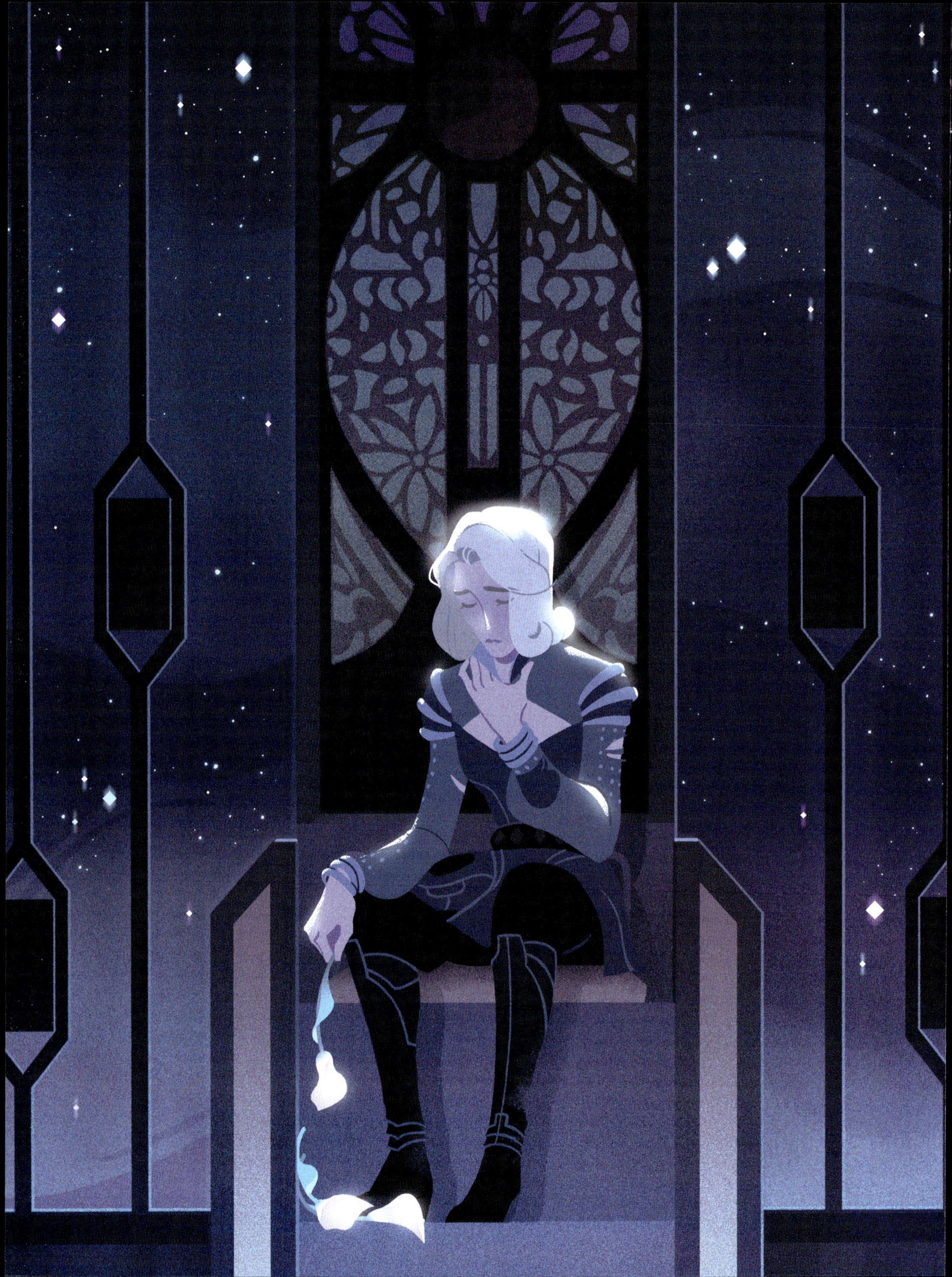

Satine Kryze

"War is intolerable. We have been deceived into thinking that we must be a part of it. I say the moment we committed to fighting, we already lost."

In a galaxy torn by war, the notion of pacifism can seem naively idealistic to some. But not to the Duchess of Mandalore, Satine Kryze. As Mandalore's latest civil war ends, she sees the culture's warrior past as the root of its problems, and she rebuilds the government upon the nonviolent principles of the New Mandalorians. What follows are assassination attempts, another civil war, and the rise of a violent insurgent group called Death Watch (of which Satine's own sister Bo-Katan is a member). But Satine remains convinced throughout that these new rules are Mandalore's only hope for a future.

As we learn in *Star Wars: The Clone Wars*, Satine keeps Mandalore neutral in the conflict—despite her complicated past with the Jedi Obi-Wan Kenobi and her friendship with Senator Padmé Amidala. She leads her people through numerous hardships, such as the corruption of their Prime Minister and the influence of a dangerous black market, and she's able to do so in part because she raises an eyebrow at everything happening around her. When Obi-Wan tries to argue in favor of the Jedi's role in the Clone Wars, she observes archly, "The work of a peacekeeper is to make sure that conflict does not arise."

Anna Graves voiced Satine, "a spitfire lady with a lot of gumption.... I admire Satine's passion. She clearly cares for the people of Mandalore and their future. And the fact that she was brave enough to introduce new ideas of pacifism to a system whose history is based on being warriors shows she is willing to do anything to keep Mandalore safe from the Republic's growing power. I also love that she does not always hide her passion for Obi-Wan. He has been an important part of her past and she does not forget that . . . even when she tries to do so, she just can't forget."

Seventh Sister Inquisitor

"I only need you alive, that doesn't mean in one piece."

As a member of the Empire's Inquisitorius program, the Seventh Sister focuses on hunting down and eliminating the remaining Jedi in the galaxy who have survived the slaughter of Order 66. Caustic and capable, she's not to be trifled with, as we know from her first scene in *Star Wars Rebels*. Her zeal shows us what it's like to be an Imperial Force-user trying to climb to the top.

The Seventh Sister's vicious qualities make her a memorable villain. In service to the Sith Lord Darth Vader, she uses her dark side–fueled Force abilities and ID9 seeker droids to ruthlessly toy with her targets; she's all about the cat-and-mouse game. She and fellow Inquisitor Fifth Brother kill nearly an entire ship's crew on a mission to abduct a Force-sensitive child. Just part of the job. And she relishes any opportunity to ignite her double-bladed, spinning lightsaber when the situation calls for action, which is anytime she encounters and torments Ezra Bridger and Kanan Jarrus.

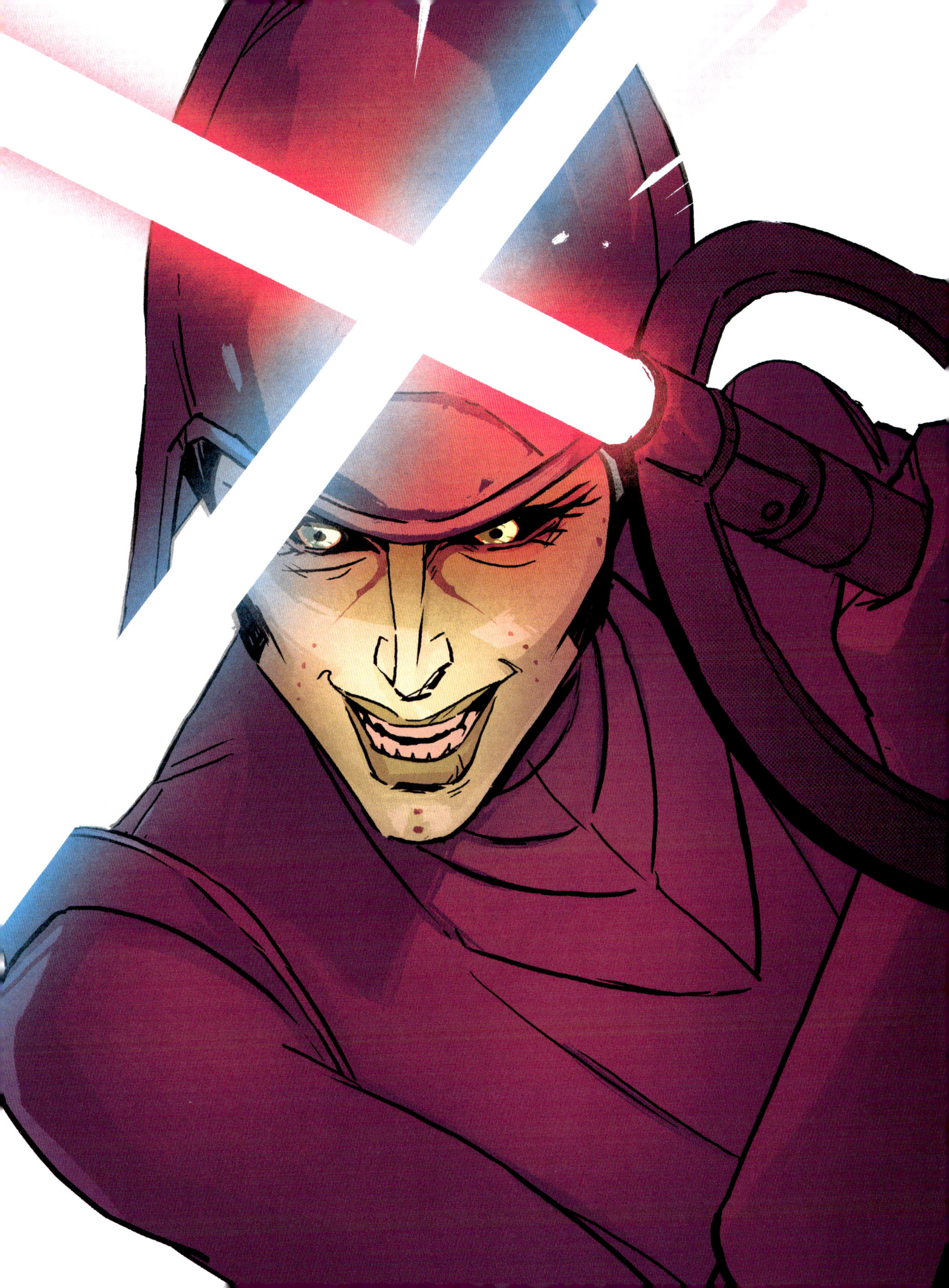

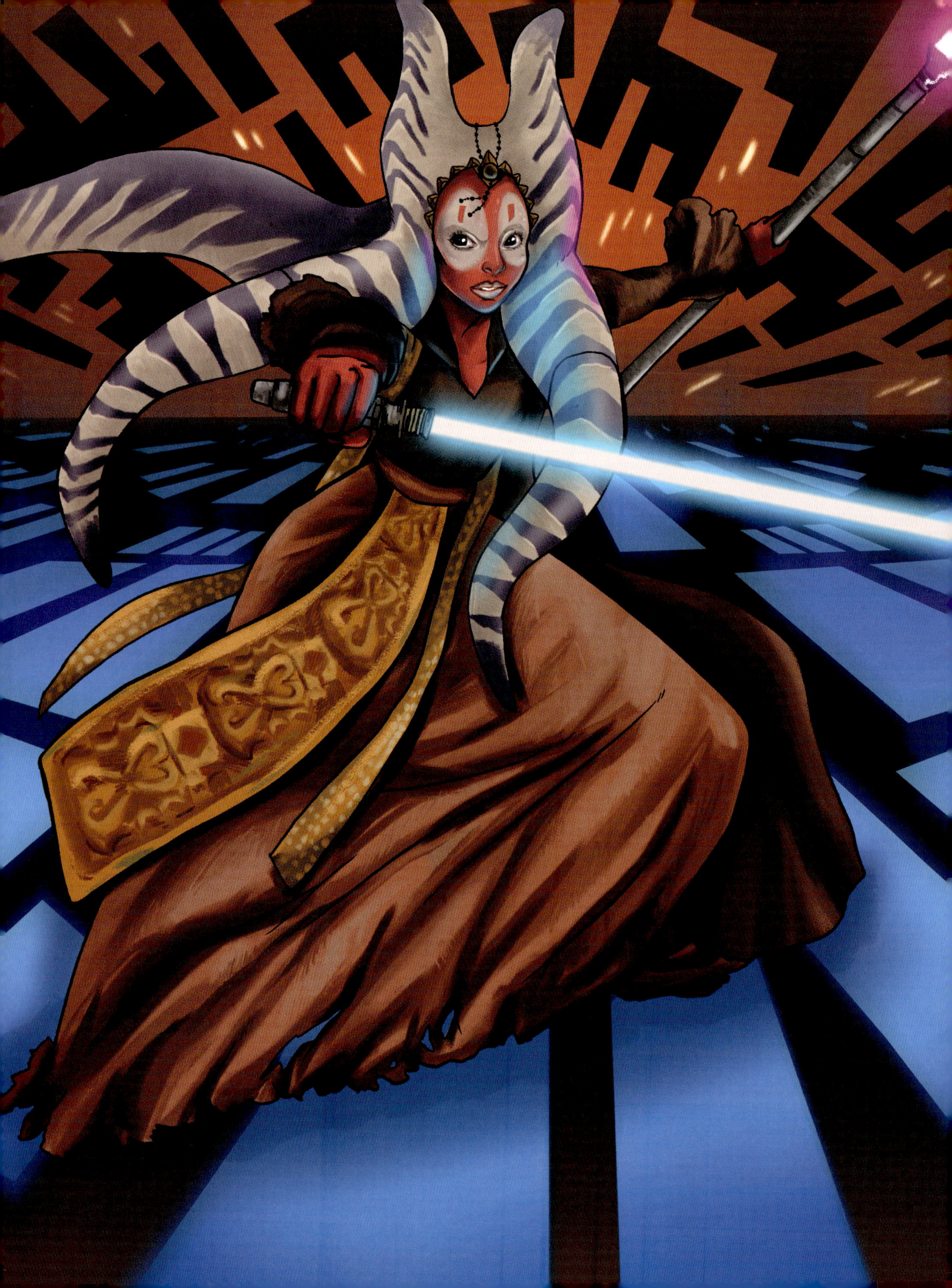

Shaak Ti

"Don't let this be the end of the Jedi."

The Jedi strike team on Geonosis in *Attack of the Clones* brings myriad lightsaber-wielding Force-users into the story, including Jedi Master Shaak Ti. A wise and patient member of the Jedi Council, the Togruta's story expands in *Star Wars: The Clone Wars* when she's appointed to supervise the production and training of the clone troopers on Kamino. In this role, she brings a measure of empathy toward the clones not generally shared by Kaminoans, treating them as the living beings they are instead of objects.

A devoted believer in the ways of the Jedi, Shaak Ti wants the Order to continue after the Jedi Purge. The night Anakin Skywalker becomes Darth Vader, she meditates and records a plea on a holocron. When Luke Skywalker finds the artifact years later, he hears Shaak Ti's message: "Don't let this be the end of the Jedi."

While portraying Shaak Ti, actress Orli Shoshan put her martial arts experience to the test. "My character required a lot of fight scenes," she says. "They liked how I used a lightsaber, and I didn't need a lot of extra training." However, Shaak Ti's bulky costume made melee combat tricky: "Each time I was on set it took four hours to prepare my character. The entire costume was heavy, with a long tail, two horns, and a long skirt. It was hard to move! But I'm very happy that I had a chance to play this cool character. I'm proud to be a Jedi Master."

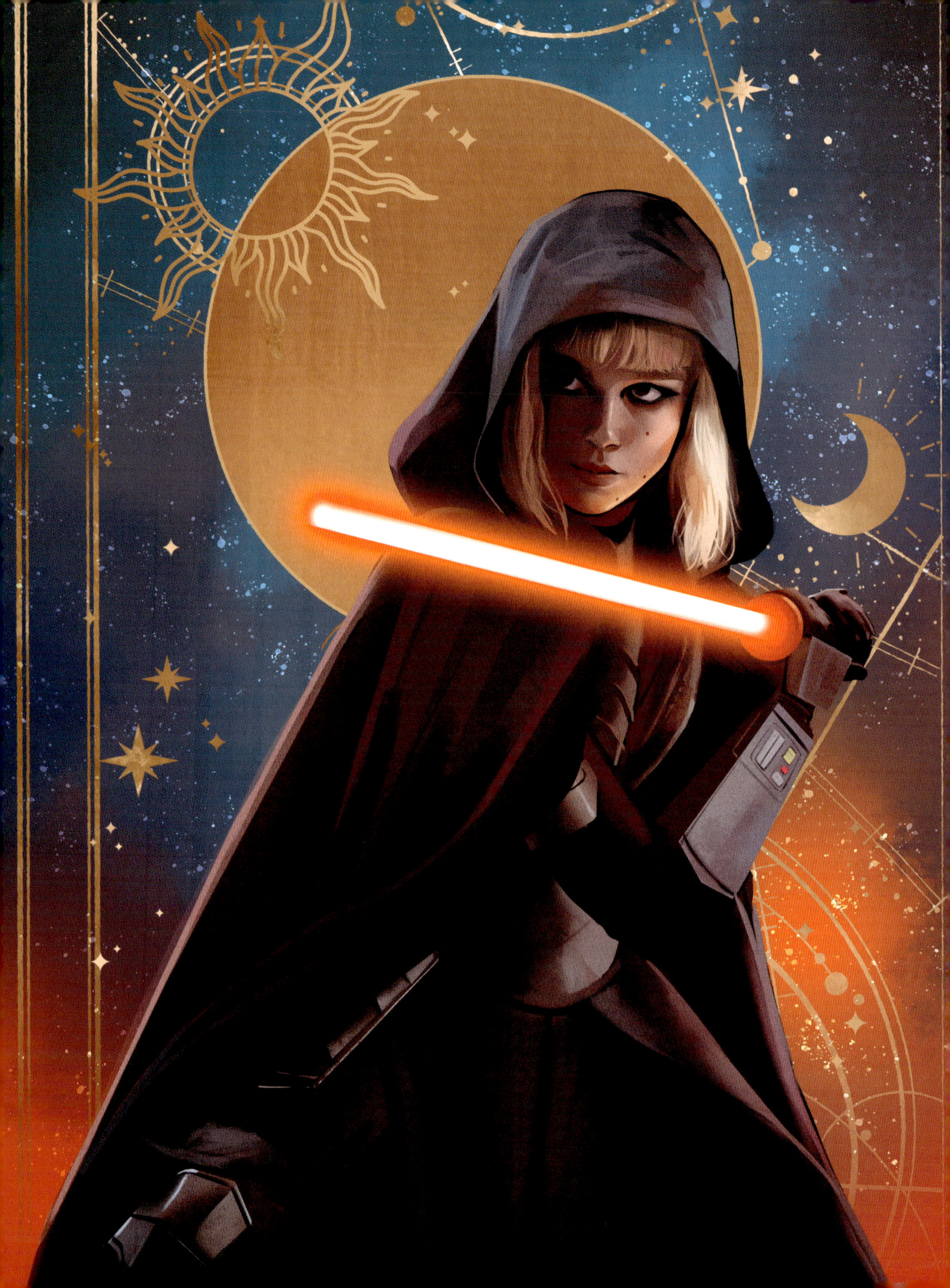

Shin Hati

"Sometimes stories are just stories."

In Norse mythology, Sköll and Hati are two wolves who chase the sun and moon through the skies until Ragnarök, when it is foretold that they will catch up with the celestial beings and devour them. In the *Star Wars* universe, Baylan Skoll and Shin Hati are a Force-wielding master and apprentice hired by Morgan Elsbeth to help her locate Grand Admiral Thrawn beyond the known galaxy. Observant and curious, Shin is on a journey of discovery to try and find where she belongs.

Her master Baylan was once a Jedi, but Shin never trained at the Temple. Her background is a mystery. Baylan trains her as if she were a Jedi, but without necessarily adhering to the Jedi Code or wielding the light side of the Force. Shin's allegiance to anything or anyone beyond her master is unclear—to the audience and likely to herself. She looks to her teacher for guidance but doesn't put the same stock as he does into legends and stories. Shin and Baylan travel with Morgan Elsbeth to Peridea and locate Thrawn, who then sends Baylan and Shin after Sabine Wren and Ezra Bridger. But Baylan departs to pursue answers of his own on the planet, giving Shin one parting lesson: "Impatience for victory will guarantee defeat."

Seemingly doing the opposite, Shin teams with roving bandits on Peridea and resumes her hunt for Sabine and Ezra. Without Baylan to temper it, Shin's impulsiveness could lead to challenging scenarios on the far-flung planet where she is stranded.

Shmi Skywalker Lars

"You can't stop the change any more than you can stop the suns from setting."

Shmi Skywalker, the mother of Anakin Skywalker, must say goodbye to her young son so he can fulfill his destiny and have a better life than she can provide. She gives him into the care of Jedi Master Qui-Gon Jinn, even though she knows she may never see him again, and in fact, it might be best for Anakin if she doesn't. As Anakin begins to leave, he returns to his mother and promises to come back to save her. She offers words of reassurance, but she also knows that he must be free to live his own life: "Be brave," she says. "Don't look back. Don't look back."

Shmi's life is one of hardship from the beginning. After her parents are captured by pirates, she is forced into slavery at a young age, first to Gardulla the Hutt, and then to the junk boss Watto. But she doesn't succumb to despair and is able to maintain a courageous core optimism, instilling in her son values of compassion, kindness, and the necessity of helping others.

Portrayed by Swedish actress Pernilla August in *The Phantom Menace*, Shmi is strength personified. Her mettle isn't tested on the battlefield; instead, it's proven through her love for Anakin. August was nervous about playing Shmi because it was her first English-speaking role, but she did it anyway. August can relate to Shmi; she says, "It's a beautiful part; I love it very much. It's so warm. I feel very familiar about it because I have three kids myself. She's very brave, in a way, to let him go. She really does believe in him and that he's going to take responsibility for his life."

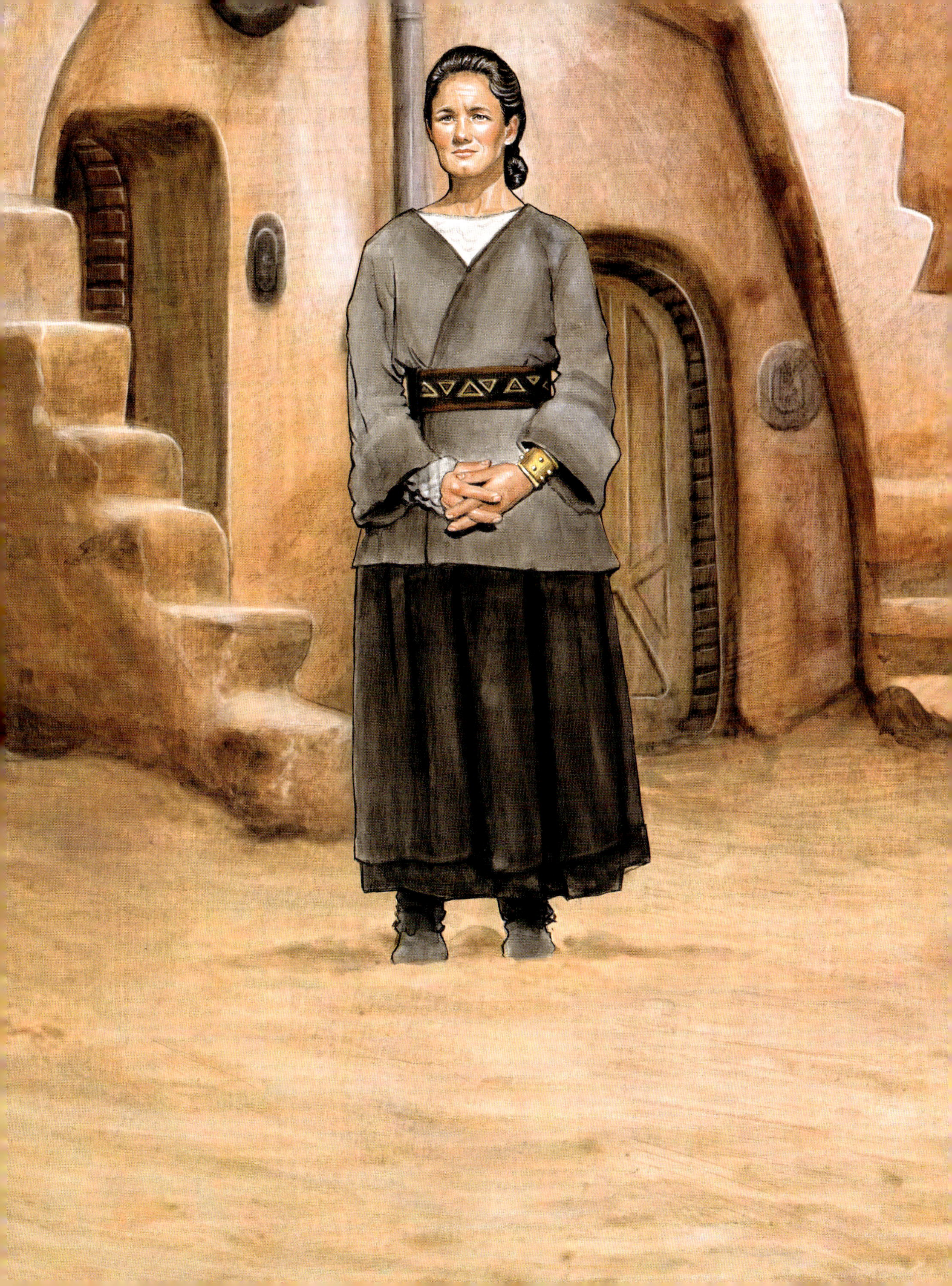

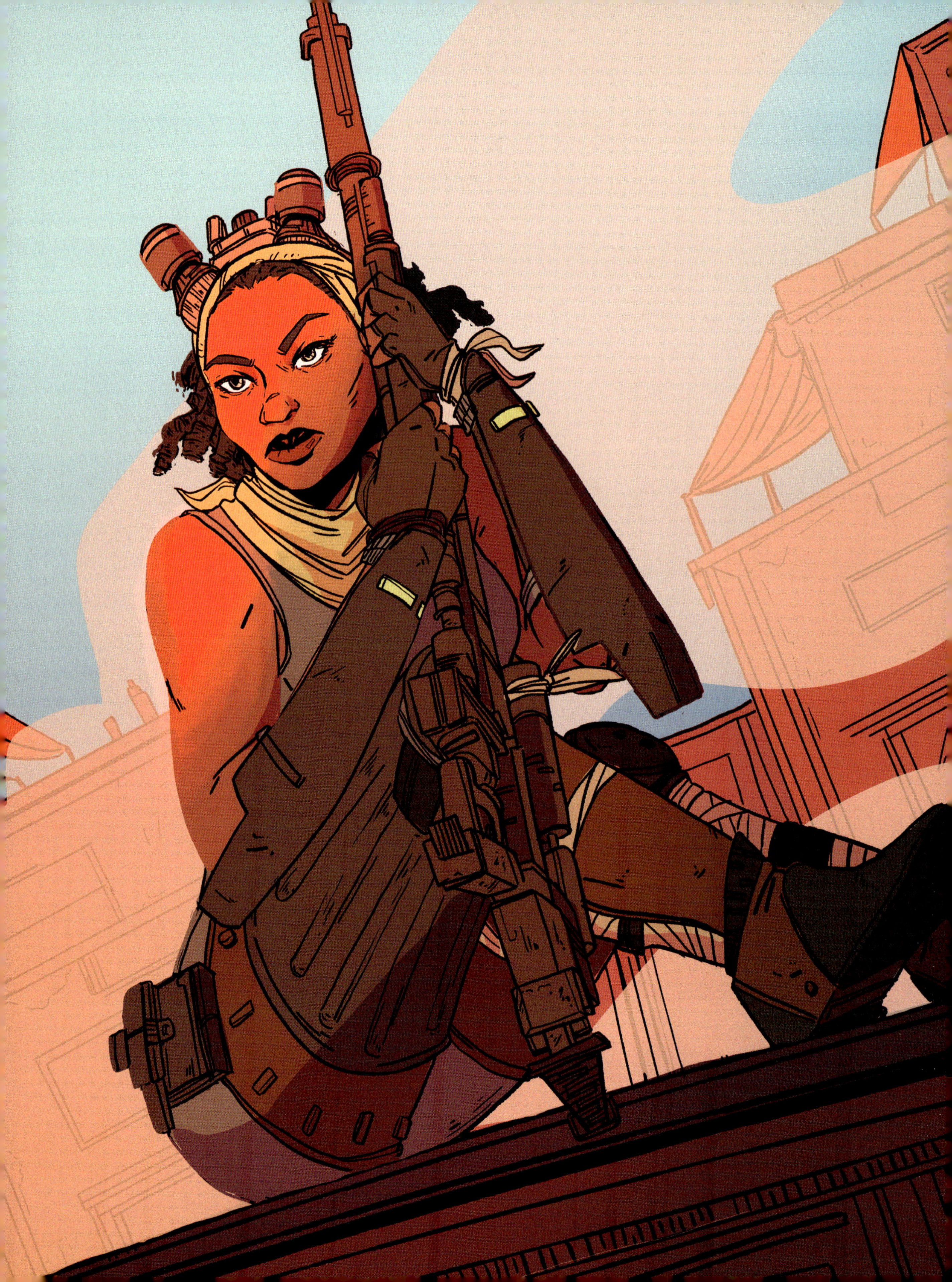

Steela Gerrera

"The time has come to take back our freedom."

Steela doesn't want to be the leader of revolutionaries battling Separatist control on her homeworld of Onderon, but her mettle and courage make her a prime candidate. Voice actress Dawn-Lyen Gardner, who portrays the heroic character in *Star Wars: The Clone Wars*, identifies Steela's core in this way: "You totally get the sense that this girl can and will, literally, change her world."

Using guerrilla tactics she learns from Anakin Skywalker and Ahsoka Tano, Steela and her brother Saw execute targeted attacks against the Separatists with their compatriots. A skilled sharpshooter who prefers to let her weapon do the talking, Steela is unafraid in battle, and leads the Onderon resistance by example and with a drive to free her people. Steela wins that freedom for her home, but she pays the ultimate price. Her death inspires others, like her brother Saw, to continue the fight.

Sugi

"I know what I'm doing, and I will keep these people safe, my way."

Honorable is probably not the first word that comes to mind in the context of bounty hunters, but it should be when considering the mercenary known as Sugi. Hailing from the planet Iridonia, the Zabrak fighter doesn't take jobs for the sake of acquiring credits. She's not focused on glory or riches—in fact she'll cut her rate for the right cause. She only picks up work she believes in, because once she's committed, she's willing to put her life on the line.

Sugi's first appearance in *Star Wars: The Clone Wars* highlights her principled approach. Hired by Felucian farmers for protection, Sugi helps keep them safe from Hondo Ohnaka's pirate gang, and dismisses out of hand Hondo's attempt to buy her loyalty for double the money ("We don't break deals."). Her commitment to doing the right thing is noted by her peers, and by her niece, Jas Emari, whom Sugi encourages to escape Iridonia and become a bounty hunter. Jas follows in her footsteps, even flying Sugi's starship, the *Halo*.

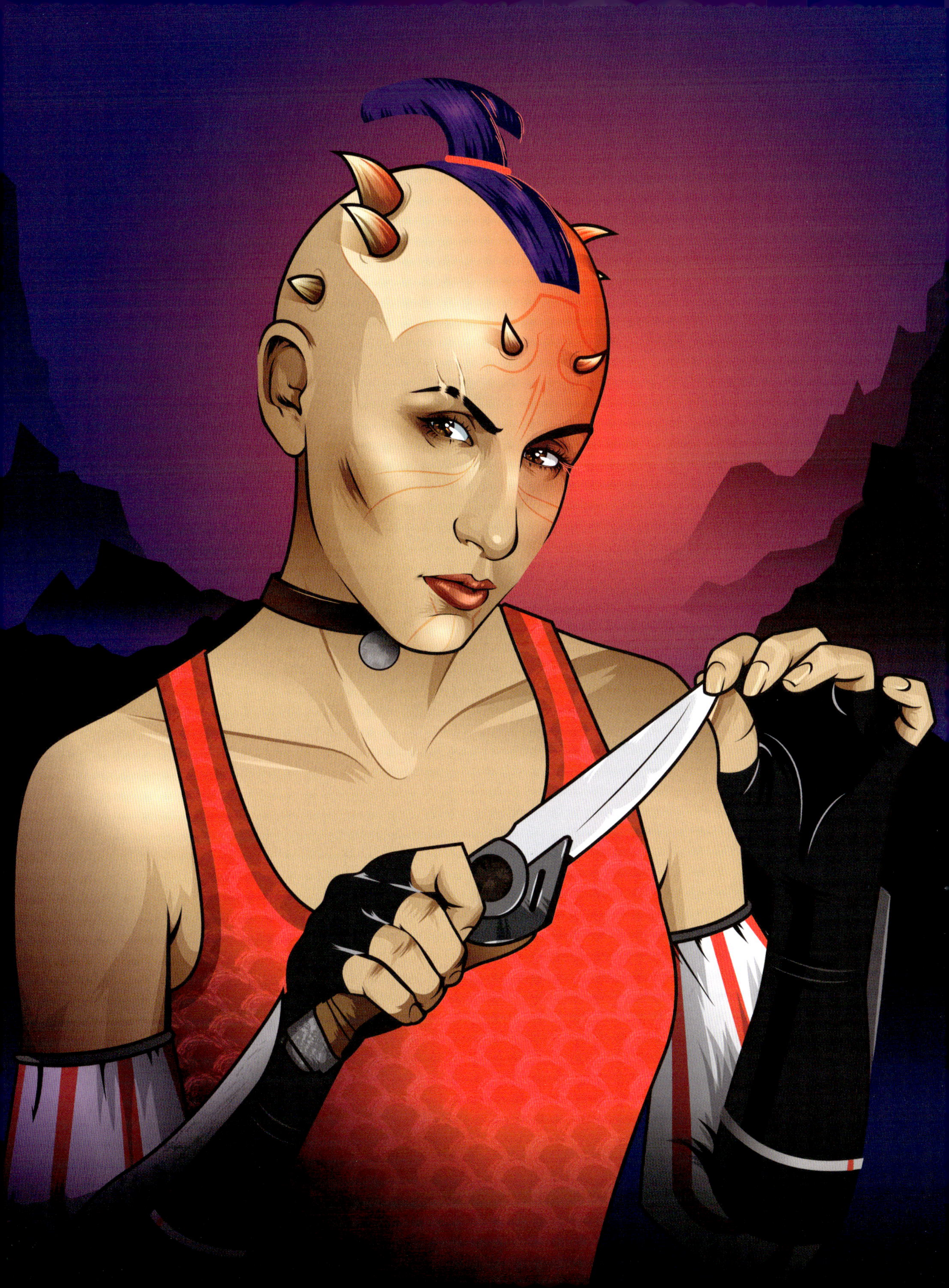

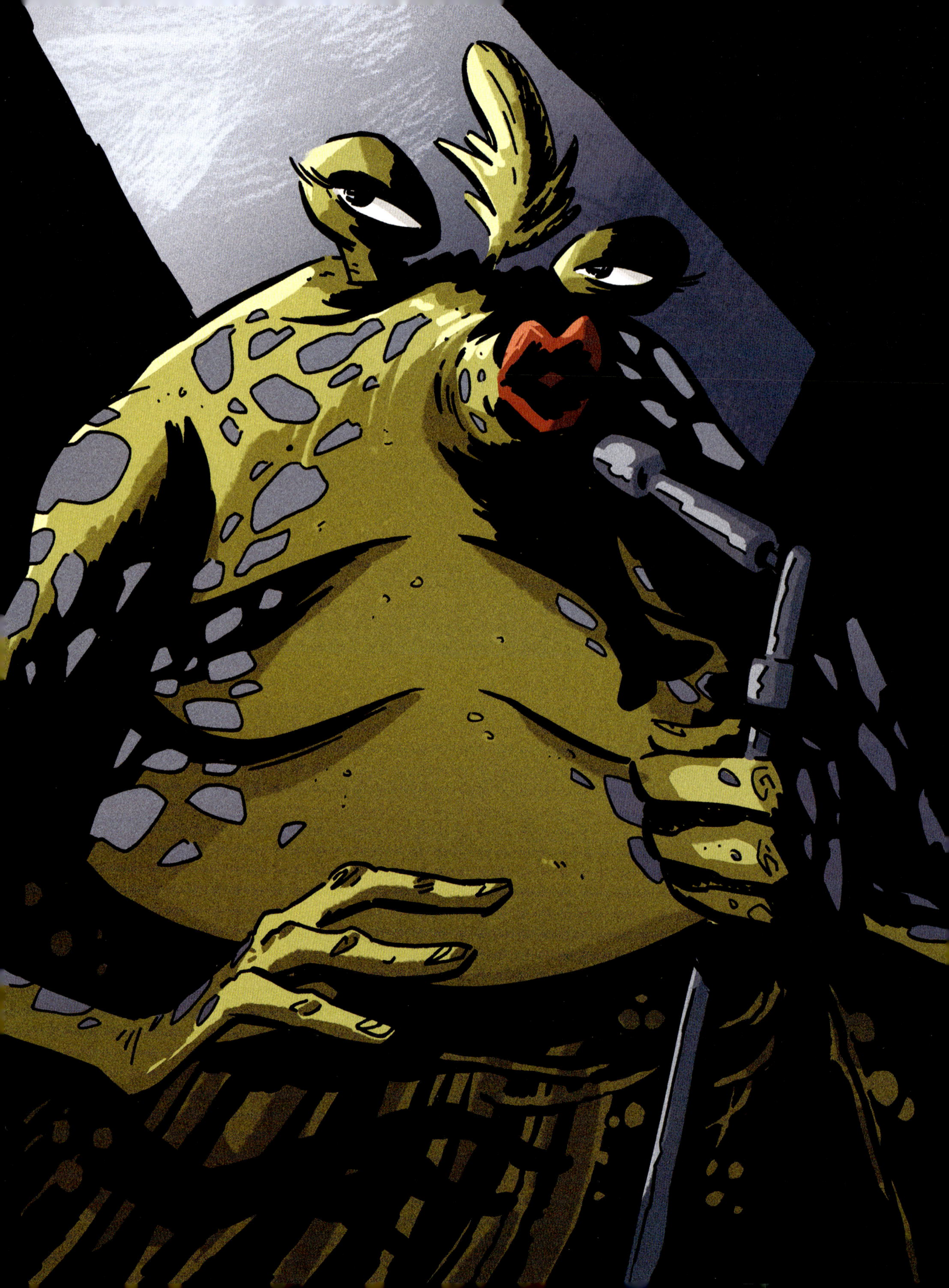

Sy Snootles

"All in a night's work, baby."

First seen as a singer in the Max Rebo Band at Jabba's palace in *Return of the Jedi*, Sy Snootles makes quite an impression with her weird vocal stylings and weirder appearance. The Pa'lowick performer's long limbs and cherry red lips stand out even in the crowd of quirky characters at Jabba's. The memorable crooner was first filmed as a puppet, brought to life by three operators manipulating rods and wires. Later, for the Special Edition release of the film, she was a digitally animated creation.

But Sy's more than she appears to be, and we later learn in *Star Wars: The Clone Wars* that her aspirations go beyond the stage. In her femme fatale past, Sy was once the paramour of Ziro, Jabba the Hutt's uncle. After he jilts her, she takes a job with Jabba to kill Ziro and steal his holodiary containing the Hutt Council records. Her last words to her former lover: "Next time you'll think twice about breaking someone's heart. Oh, wait, there won't be a next time."

Tallie Lintra

"Practice your dance moves later—we gotta fly."

When the Resistance calls for reinforcements after the losses suffered during the attack on Starkiller Base, rebel Lieutenant Tallissan "Tallie" Lintra is one of the starfighters who answers. Taking to space in *The Last Jedi*, Tallie joins the squadrons under Poe Dameron's command, launching into battle in a RZ-2 A-wing ahead of the Resistance bombers. She's capable in any sort of combat maneuver, whether she's on the offensive attacking a First Order Dreadnought or helping provide cover for the Resistance's retreat, and her skills impress Dameron. Her piloting abilities are a result of devoted training and the sort of use-whatever-resources-you-have attitude that puts her right at home in the Resistance. In Tallie's case, this means learning to fly in an RZ-1 A-wing used as a cropduster on her father's farm on Pippip 3. Fans can pilot her Resistance-issued fighter in the *Star Wars: Battlefront II* video game.

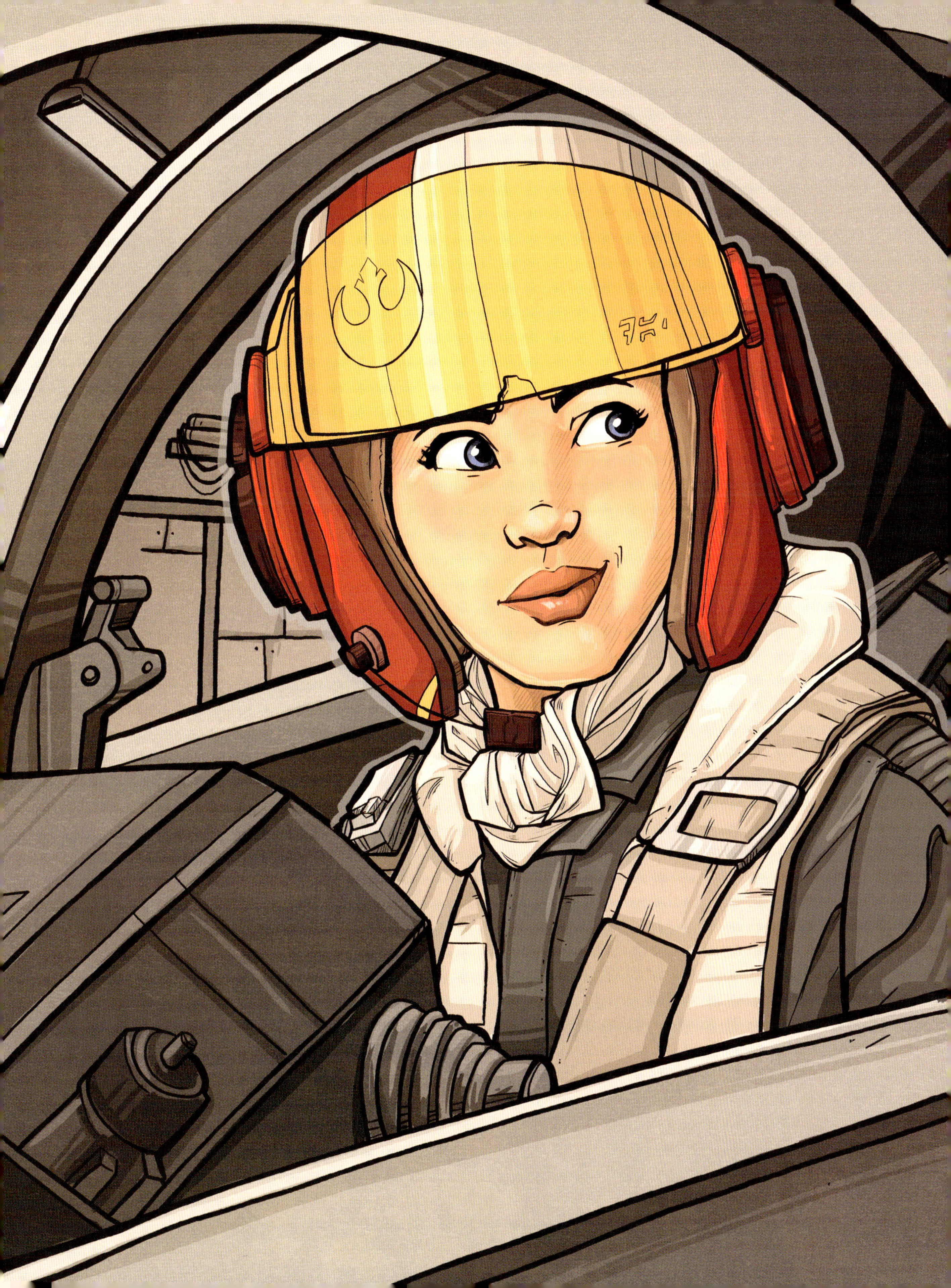

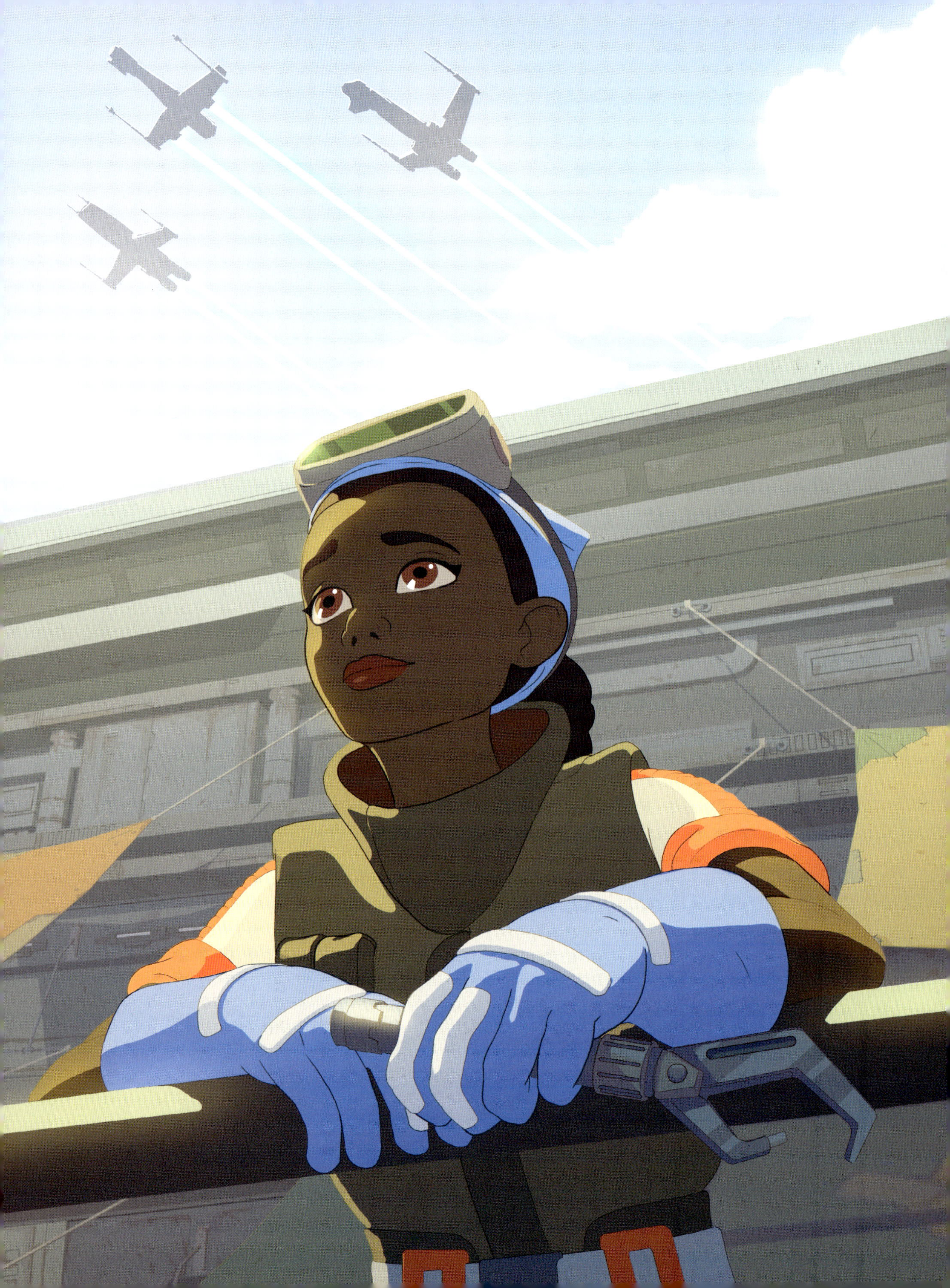

Tam Ryvora

An inventive mechanic who longs for something more.

What is a pilot without a mechanic? Tam Ryvora would have a snappy answer to that question. A key part of veteran pilot Jarek Yeager's garage in *Star Wars Resistance*, Tam works as a creative and determined technician, performing fix-it jobs for customers. But she wants more from life than just to be a mechanic in someone else's shop. In her downtime, Tam's restoring the *Fireball*, a broken-down ship she wants to eventually fly. Growing up with nothing, Tam wants to make a better life for herself. She dreams of wowing everyone on the *Colossus* with her spectacular piloting skills, and longs to join the Aces and live in Doza Tower, the luxurious building the racers call home.

Knowing the sting of being left behind by a friend seeking fame, Tam is guarded and skeptical of others, especially newcomers like cocky wannabe Ace, Kaz Xiono. She's formed a family of sorts with the garage crew and is reluctant to let anyone else in. Tam's had to learn how to rely on herself, so she's confident, knows exactly what she can offer, and isn't afraid to tell anyone who asks. Tam both impresses and infuriates Yeager with her inventive, sometimes crazy modifications on the ships they repair, all the while looking to the skies and longing to race.

Tam's patience with Kaz wears thin when she has to constantly repair the damage he inflicts on the *Fireball*, instead of flying as a pilot herself. Once the First Order occupies the *Colossus*, Tam is susceptible to the manipulation of Security Bureau Agent Tierny and she joins the First Order as a cadet pilot. As painful as it is to watch her believe the First Order's lies, she has to come to the truth herself. Thankfully, after time and hard lessons, she defects and returns to her *Colossus* family.

Third Sister Inquisitor

*"The braver you seem,
the more afraid you are."*

Reva carries the weight of heavy memories. She was caught up in Order 66 in a horrifying way: she watched Darth Vader and his troopers murder her fellow younglings, and to escape the same fate, she pretended to be dead. Wounded, she hid herself among her slain friends, and as she later recalls, she stayed still so long that she felt their bodies go cold. Watching the slaughter of what she calls the only family she knew set the path for Reva's life.

After escaping the Jedi Temple, Reva turns to the dark side. She enters the Empire's Inquisitorius and becomes known as the Third Sister. Skilled in the Force and physically strong and athletic, Reva is single-minded and determined. Her position requires that she hunt surviving Jedi, but that isn't the reason she joins the Inquisitorius ranks. Reva knows Darth Vader, who leads the Inquisitors, is Anakin Skywalker, and she wants revenge. She finds a path to her desired retribution when she discovers Obi-Wan Kenobi, Anakin's former master, is alive on Tatooine.

What follows is a series of choices that reflects and twists Reva's fear and past hurts. When she realizes that Leia Organa and Luke Skywalker are important to Obi-Wan, she puts the children at risk to push Obi-Wan into action—which she knows will attract Darth Vader's attention and leave the Sith Lord vulnerable to attack. To carry out revenge for seeing her childhood friends killed, she's willing to put other children in harm's way.

After nearly killing a young Luke, Reva realizes that inflicting more pain will not heal her or change the past. She shows mercy and returns Luke to his aunt and uncle. By doing so, she frees herself of her quest for revenge and leaves to start her life anew somewhere in the galaxy.

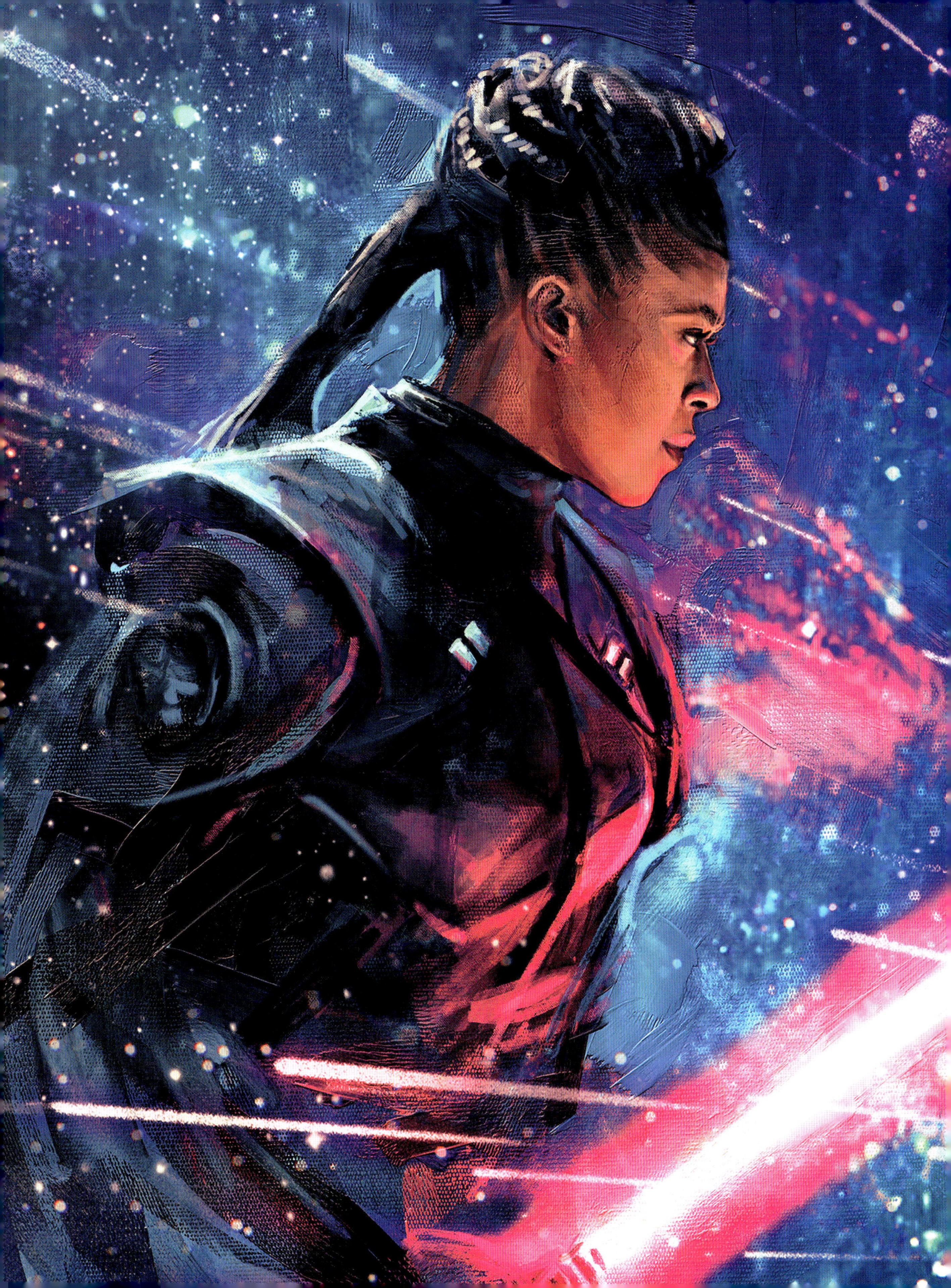

Tonnika Sisters

"Survive until they won't let us."

Con artists, thieves, and smugglers, sisters Brea and Senni Tonnika are more than capable of handling themselves in dangerous situations, and know the consequences otherwise: prison or death. With deception as one of their key talents, they survive by keeping on the move. You might remember the Kiffar siblings from the cantina scene in *A New Hope*. They're at the Mos Eisley bar hoping to get a lead on Han Solo and hand him over to Jabba the Hutt for a substantial reward—a reward they could use to buy escape and freedom.

Smart and resourceful, the sisters are driven by desperate choices in part because Brea is wanted for murder. But whether they are trying to steal royal jewels from House Organa or chase down a target, whatever the circumstances, the Tonnika sisters always have each other's backs.

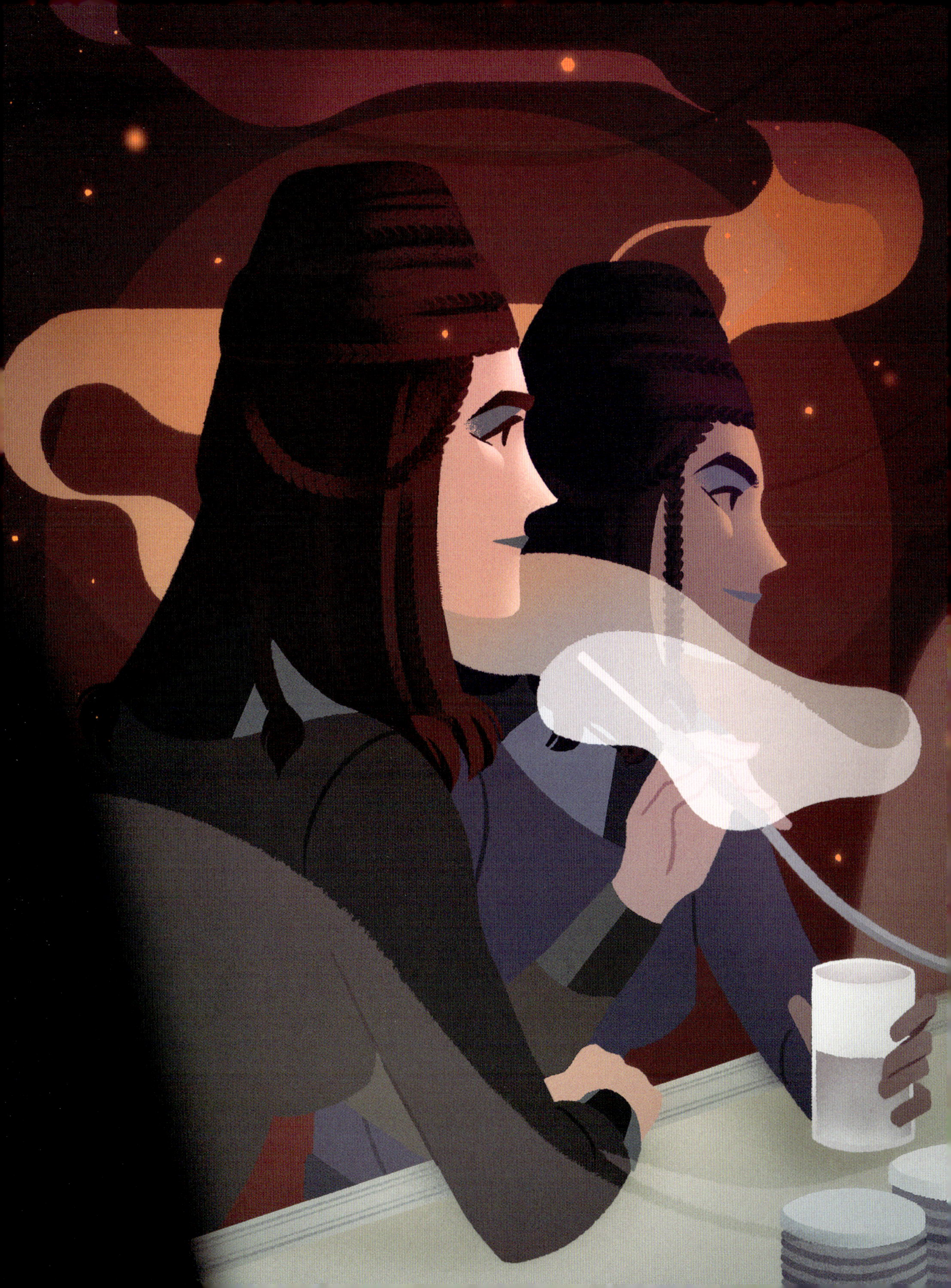

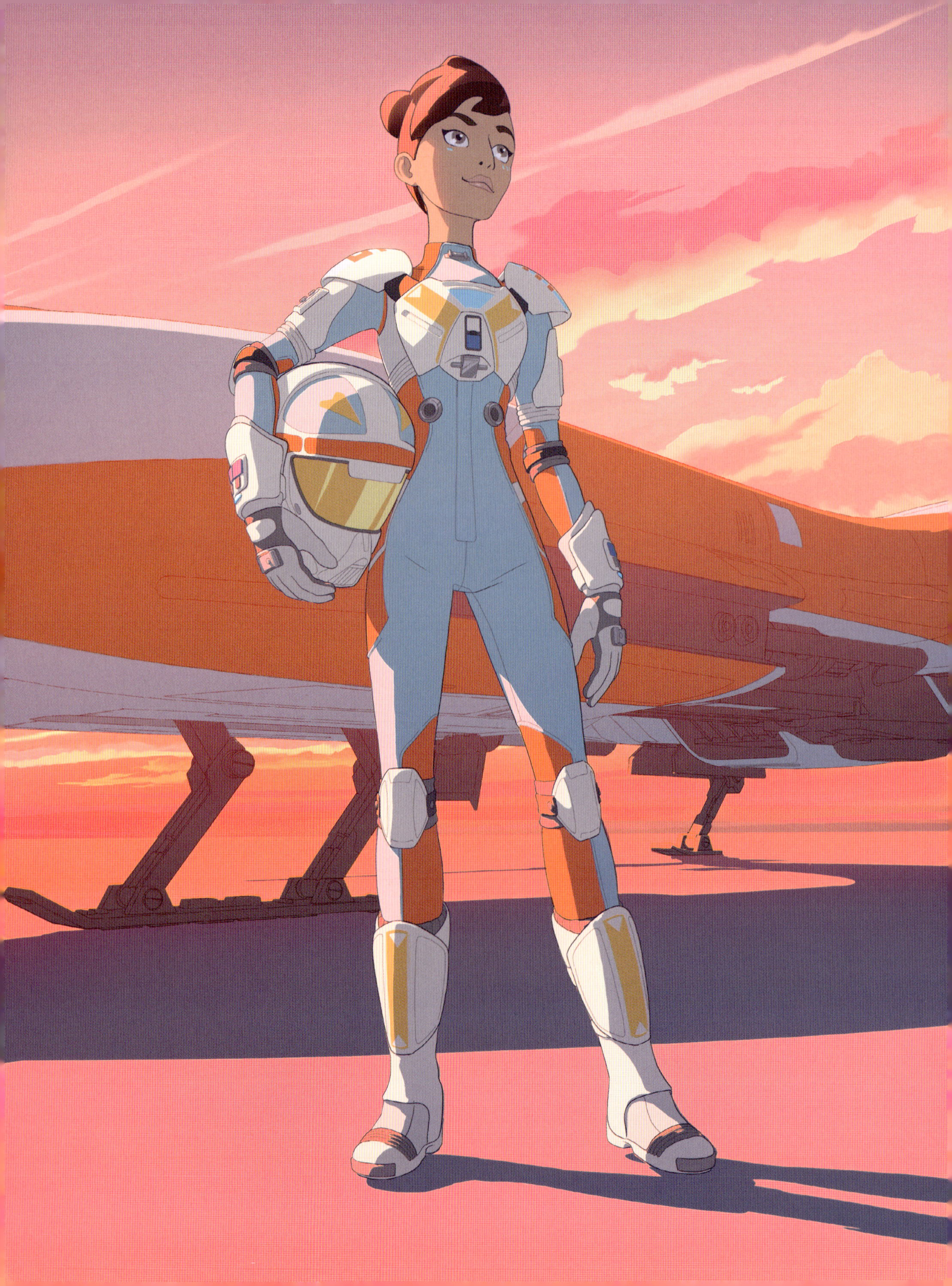

Torra Doza

A daring and competitive Ace pilot on the *Colossus*.

The Aces, *Star Wars Resistance*'s daring pilots known for their flamboyant moves, are more than just racers; they're the protectors of the *Colossus* platform, a refueling station on Castilon, keeping the skies safe from pirates, the First Order, and other threats. At only fifteen years old, Torra Doza is the youngest—and one of the most daring—of these pilots. Torra lives for competition, and her racer has been customized for sprints. That her mother was once a pilot for the Rebellion helps fuel Torra's love of flying. She also wants to impress her father, Captain Doza, the owner of the *Colossus*.

Torra takes daredevil risks in space, and her attitude translates to her style and decor. Her room is a bold purple and blue, and in it are enough toys derived from the galaxy to make any *Star Wars* fan jealous. It's here that she spends her downtime, relaxing and playing with her pet voorpak, Buggles. Torra doesn't have many pals, but she befriends the seemingly arrogant but actually awkward pilot Kaz Xiono. And though she's young, she's perceptive: she's one of the first to suspect Kaz's ties to the Resistance.

When the First Order occupies the *Colossus*, her friends begin to disappear, and her father is arrested; Torra knows that no matter what happens, she can rely on Kaz for assistance. Torra and the Aces go from flying in showy races to flying for survival as they defend the *Colossus* and go on supply runs. It's probably not the life Torra envisioned, but she meets hardship head-on and commits to stopping the First Order, bringing her racer to the Battle of Exegol.

Trios

"We all do our duty."

↓ 7 1 ◊ ↘

As the third child of the king of the strategically valuable planet of Shu-Torun, Princess Trios doesn't expect to step directly into a leadership role. But Darth Vader has plans for her. In Marvel's 2015 *Darth Vader* comic, we see the Empire's push for increased production of ore from Shu-Torun causing friction, and inspiring an attempt on Vader's life. The Sith Lord's solution is to kill Trios's family and install her as queen of the Mid Rim world, as a vassal to the Empire. Following this horror, Trios must find a way to accept the new status quo. She has reserves of strength: she doesn't cower when she loses a hand to Vader's lightsaber. Trios looks to her future, and faces her new subjects with determination. What choice does she have?

Still, she proves herself loyal by claiming victory in a civil war, and later using her mining expertise to help oversee the Empire's extraction of kyber crystals from Jedha's ruins. But from the start, Trios isn't afraid of Vader. She's aware he's manipulating her on behalf of the Empire and finds ways to push back against his wishes, and remind him she's queen. She even channels his methods by putting naive royalty in place under her, telling the Sith: "I've found inexperienced youths not expecting power the most easy to manipulate, Lord Vader."

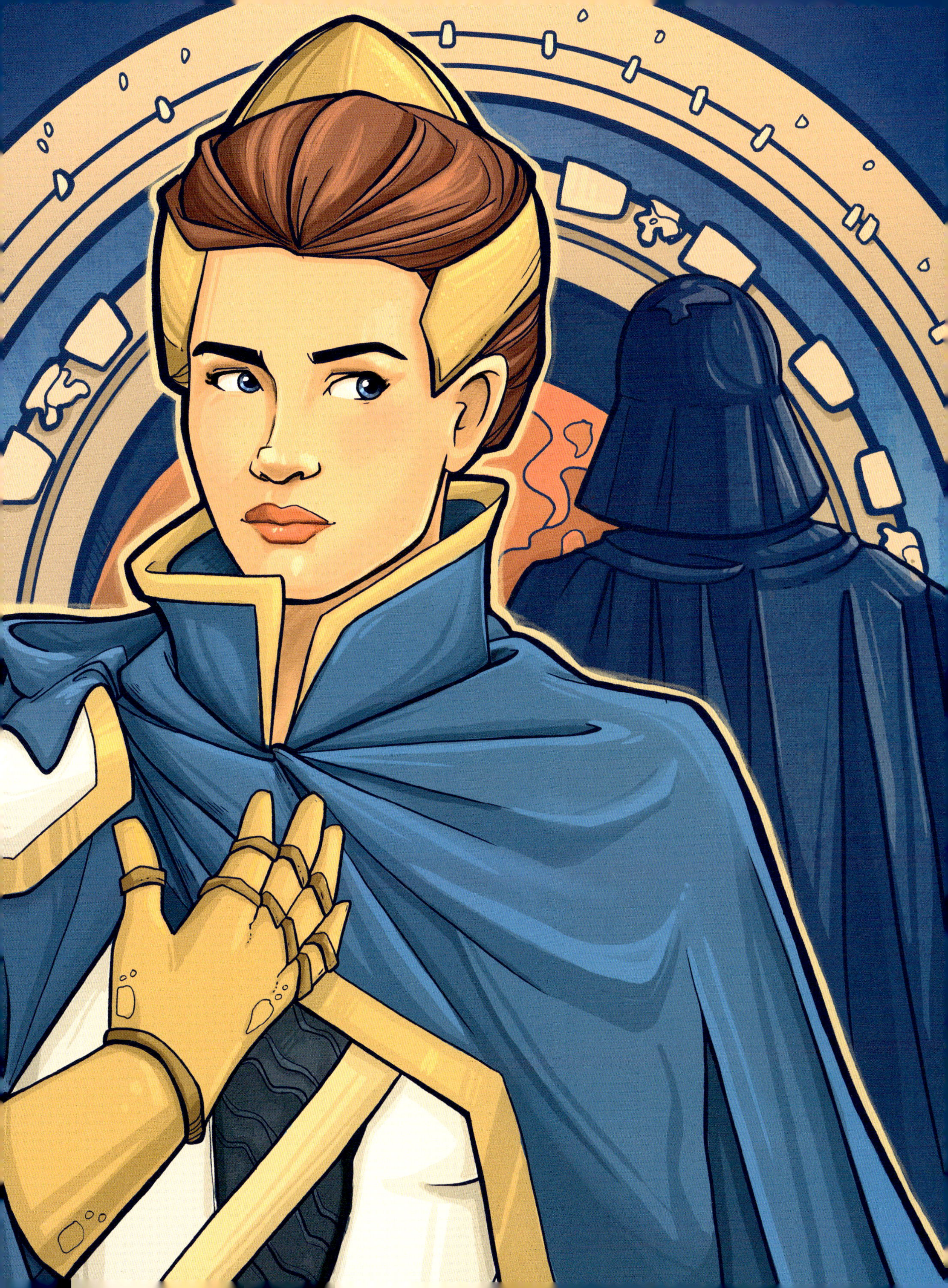

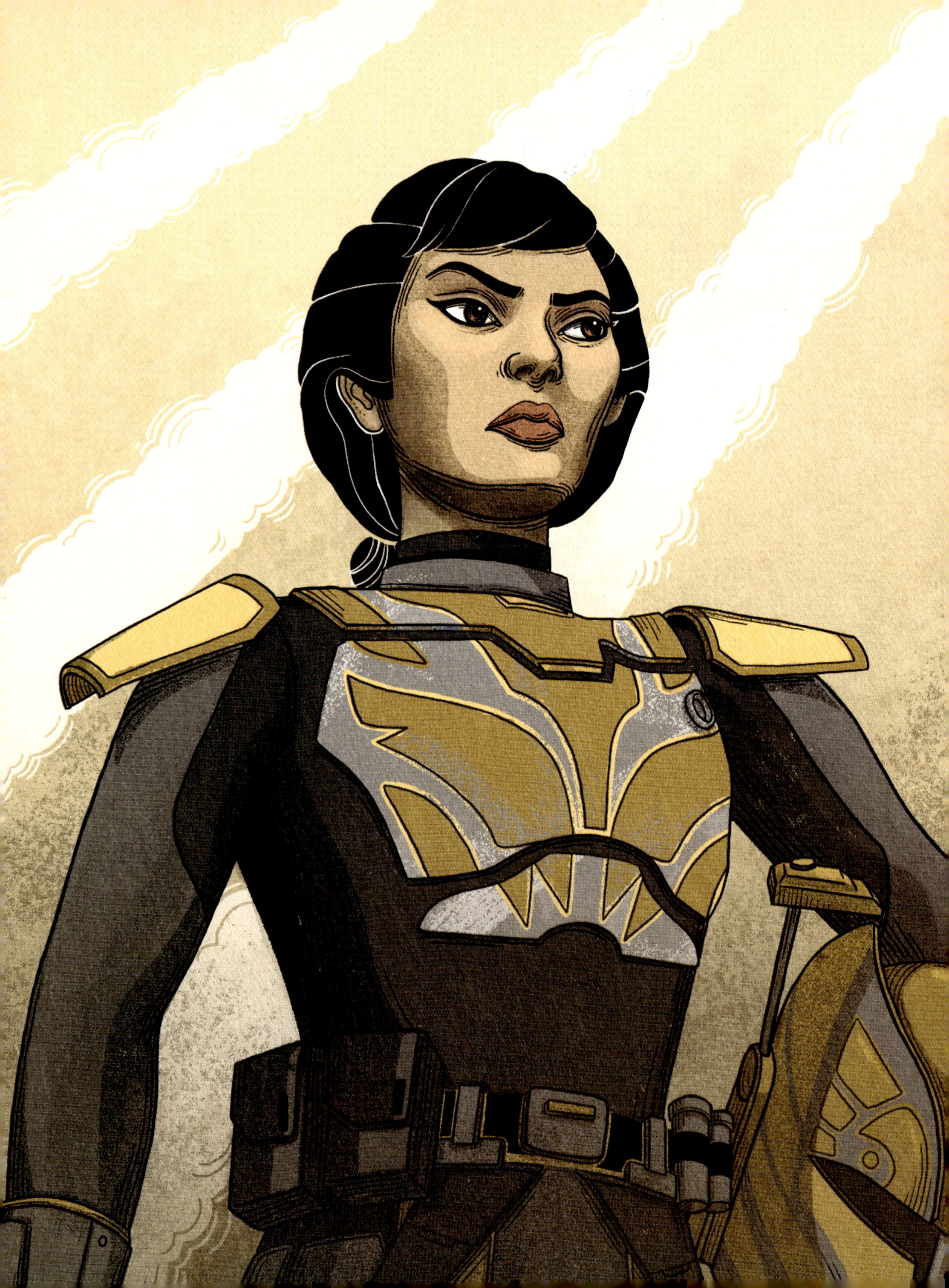

Ursa Wren

"Mandalore must rise by itself."

When we first meet the Countess of Clan Wren, in *Star Wars Rebels*, she has a harsh and cold edge. Ursa Wren has been forced to make hard choices to protect her people. In the wake of her daughter Sabine's defection from the Imperial Academy on Mandalore, Ursa aligns Clan Wren with the Empire to safeguard their lives and honor. But this comes with a price; the gray armor the Wrens wear symbolizes the way the group has been ostracized by their own society. Given this, it's easy to understand Ursa not being thrilled about her daughter's return—in the company of rebels, no less. Sabine's homecoming, and her effort to enlist the Wrens in the fight against the Empire, brings danger.

Ursa's resolute conviction makes her an unflappable ruler, but not a heartless one. When the Imperial Viceroy Gar Saxon tries to kill Sabine, Ursa stops him with a blaster bolt through the heart. She does so despite knowing the action means civil war. Her valor is as remarkable as her resolve. Ursa understands the consequences and knows it will be a struggle to find the right leader to take Mandalore into a new era, but she refuses help from the Rebellion: "The same Rebellion that sent you for my help? No, Mandalore must rise by itself."

Val

A streetwise smuggler and saboteur who
knows how to read a situation.

Proficient. Capable. Yearning. Present. Actress Thandie Newton uses these words to describe Val, her character in *Solo: A Star Wars Story*. Tough, cool, and practiced with explosives, Val is the lieutenant of Tobias Beckett's criminal crew, and his paramour. But she doesn't let her love for Beckett stop her from calling him out when she thinks he's made a dumb move—like the decision to bring Han Solo and Chewbacca into an important job when they only just met them. Val is not here to tolerate anyone's nonsense. She's all about getting the job done.

Newton credits the late producer Allison Shearmur for elevating Val's role and presence in the film. "Alli Shearmur was the champion of my character, and her desire was to celebrate my ethnicity, my hair texture, and to have me in my natural glory. She realized we had an opportunity in this film to stake a claim that is of value in the world." In fact, Val's hair and attire are inspired by political activist Angela Davis and the Black Panther Party. Newton celebrated her role in style during the 2018 Cannes Film Festival premiere of *Solo*, wearing a custom Vivienne Westwood dress featuring a floral print incorporating action figures of *Star Wars* characters portrayed by black actors, such as Samuel L. Jackson's Mace Windu and Forest Whitaker's Saw Gerrera.

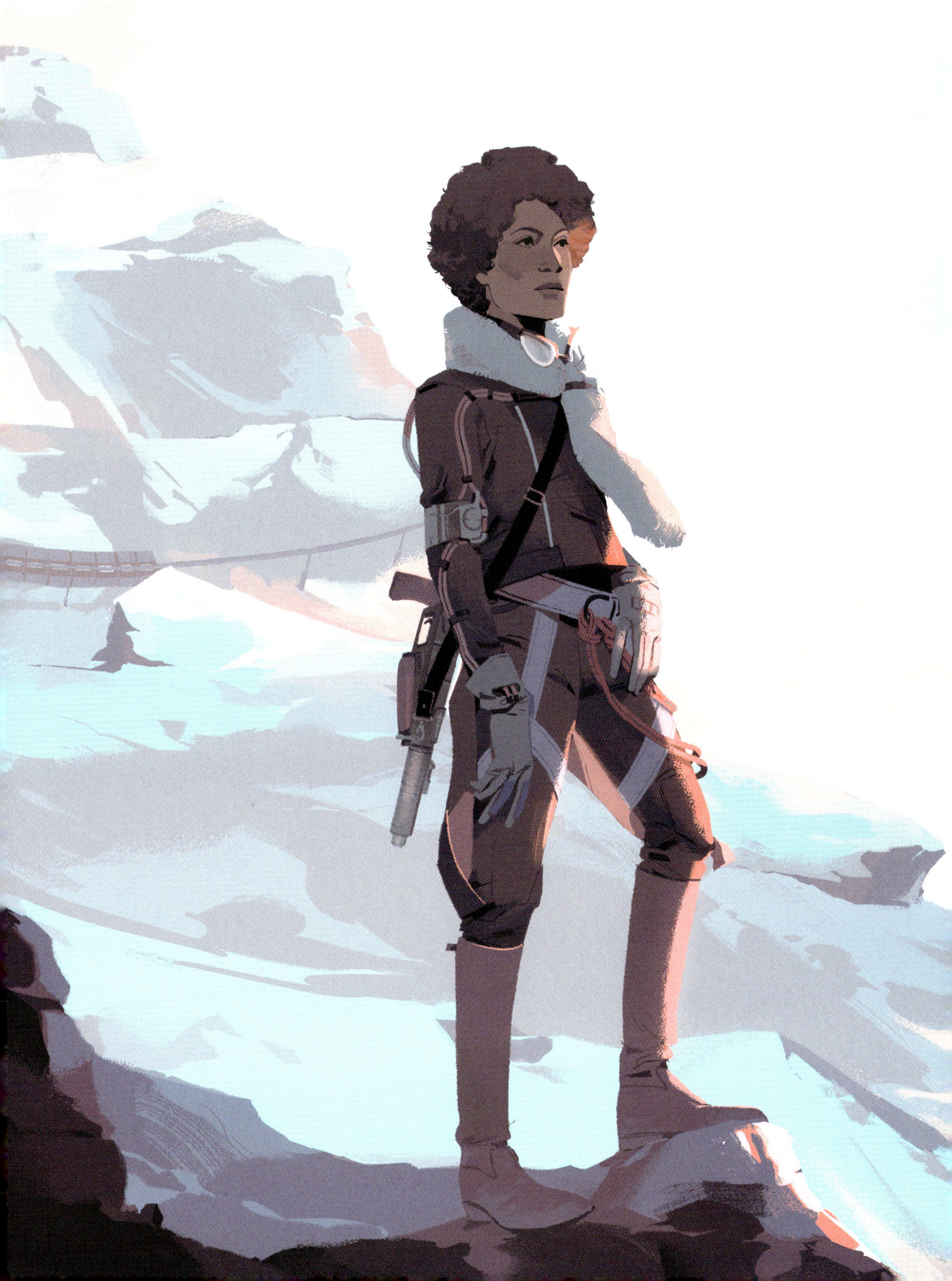

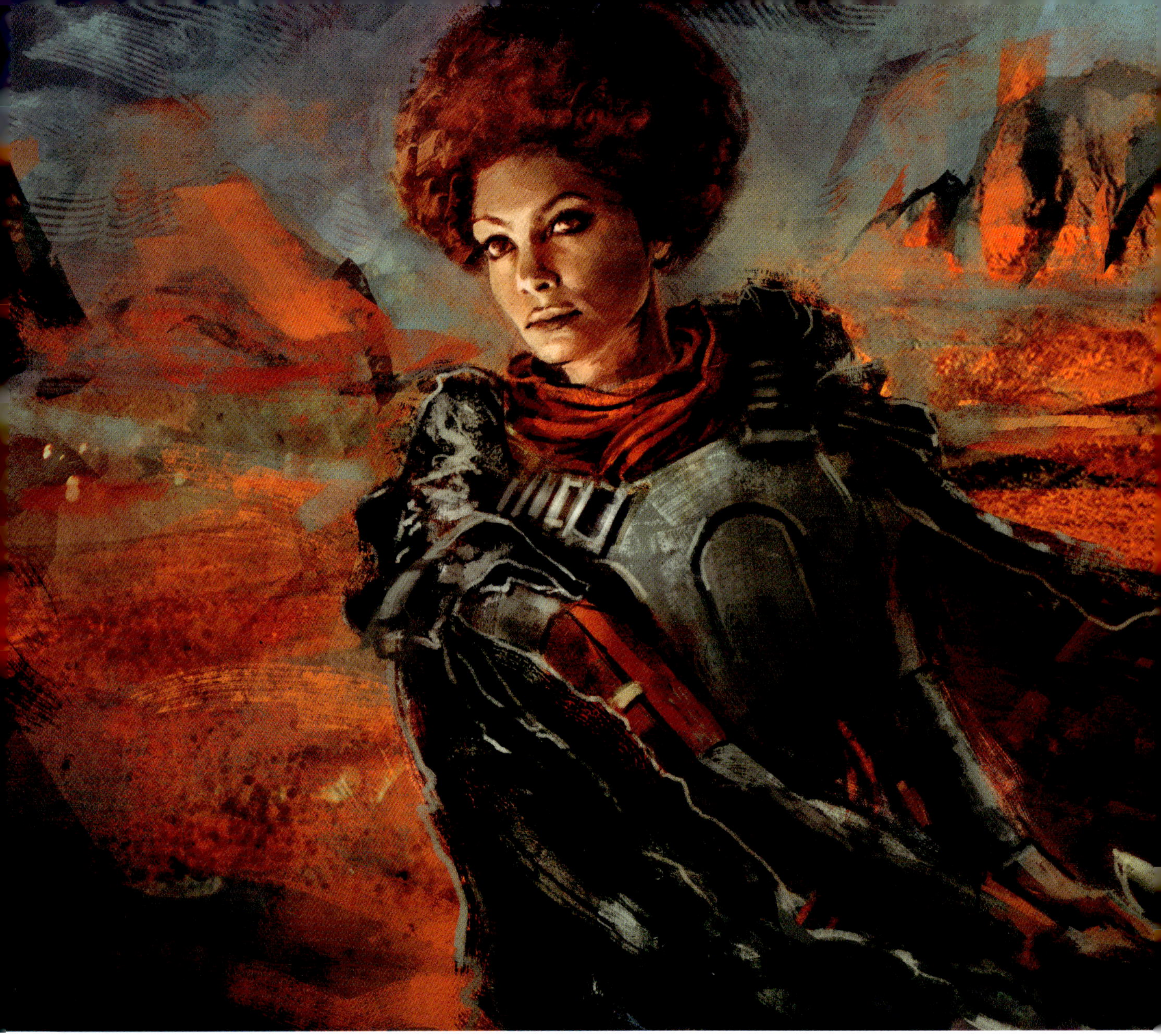

"Our whole future depends on this one score and you bring in amateurs."

—Val

Val won't waste time putting on a sunny disposition to make others feel better. She's loyal to her team, yes, but also to herself, and that means she won't put on an act. She doesn't share personal details besides the fact that she was named after a valachord, a musical instrument, so it's not clear how her background may or may not inform her cynical attitude. But she doesn't need a reason to raise an eyebrow at new recruits.

Newton is clear on Val's value to the crew. "She's so calm. Nothing phases her. She's incredibly sure of herself. It's helpful when you're an expert in explosive devices and you have a number of them all over your body," she explains. "She knows how to protect herself and her team. She also knows how to manipulate an environment so they can work their way forward to their goals. She can manipulate huge areas of rock, huge pieces of landscape with these devices that she has. She's definitely someone you want on your side."

We get a sense of her athleticism during the conveyex heist on Vandor. Adventure-seeking tourists go to the planet to scale mountains and complete survival challenges, and it's the type of environment Val is prepared for. She's a climber, comfortable in precarious positions because she knows her limits and that she can ascend or rappel to get to just the right place. Without her agility and quick assessment of the situation—and her handmade explosives—the rest of the crew would likely not make it off the planet alive.

Vernestra Rwoh

"Everything happens for a reason, even if the why isn't clear right now."

Becoming notable at a young age can be fraught, with early achievements bringing unwelcome pressure of expectation. At fifteen, Mirialan teen prodigy Vernestra Rwoh is one of the youngest Padawans to become a Jedi Knight. She takes her own Padawan soon after and begins missions right away. It seems like a lot for such a young person to take on; author Justina Ireland sees Vernestra as an overachiever. She says of the teen, "Vernestra feels a deep attachment to the Order and truly does consider it her calling, so all she ever wants to do is the best job that she can, Force willing. She isn't proud or self-congratulatory, instead she is just deeply committed to serving the light."

Indeed, Vernestra (don't call her Vern) takes being a Jedi very seriously. At the same time, she knows when to operate more independently. After a brutal Nihil attack that Vernestra believes took her Padawan and friend, she becomes a Wayseeker and follows the will of the Force to heal, in isolation from the dictates of the Jedi Council. Resilient and devoted, Vernestra returns to the fight and rises through the ranks. She becomes a leader of the Order.

A skilled fighter who wields a lightsaber that can transform into a whip in battle, Vernestra is humble about her talents. They include an unusual Force ability: she experiences visions while traveling in hyperspace.

By the time we encounter Vernestra in *The Acolyte*, the calculus that goes into her decisions isn't clear. But we know from the High Republic books that Vernestra commits to the highest good with her actions, while endeavoring to do what's best for the Order.

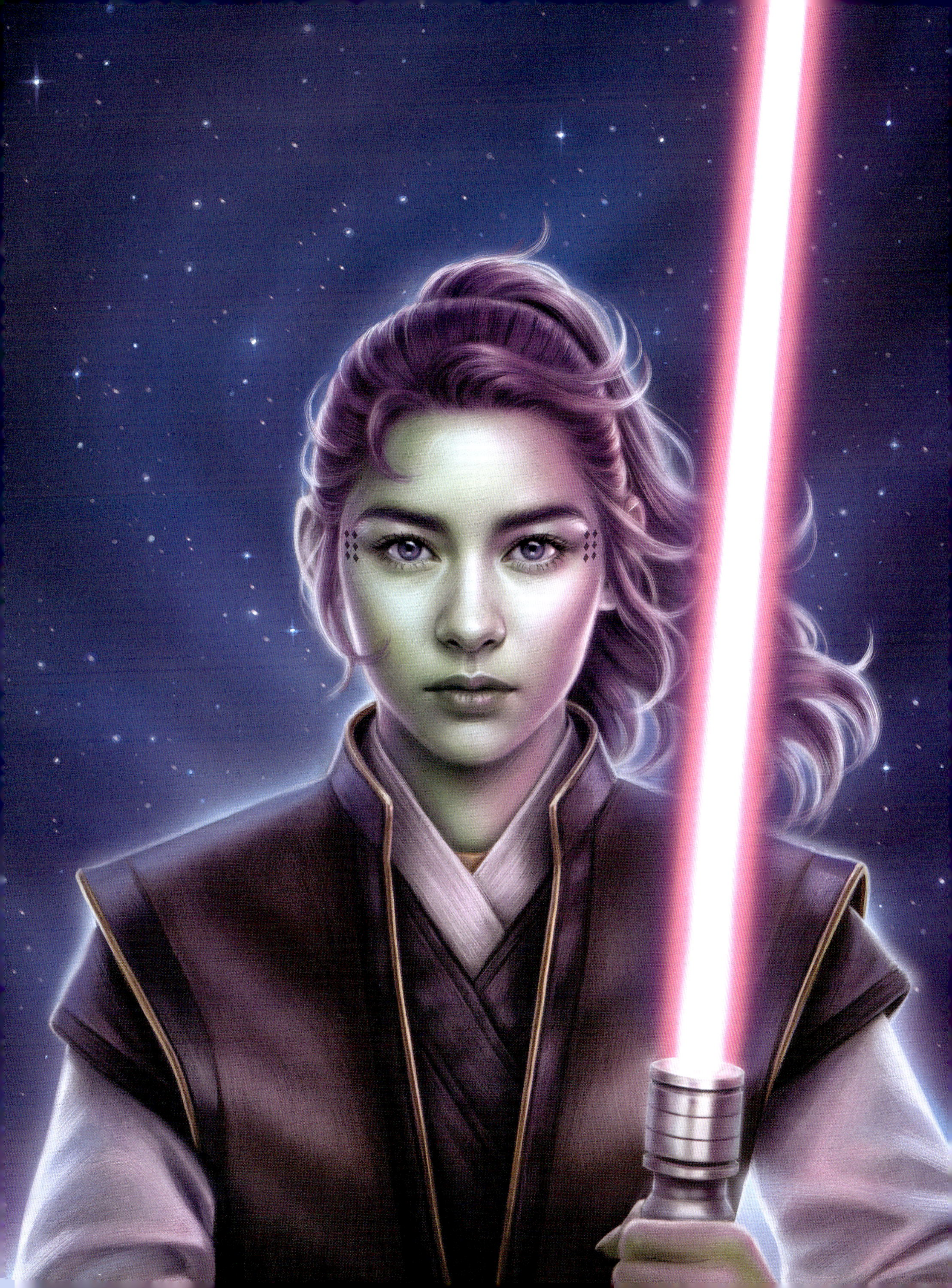

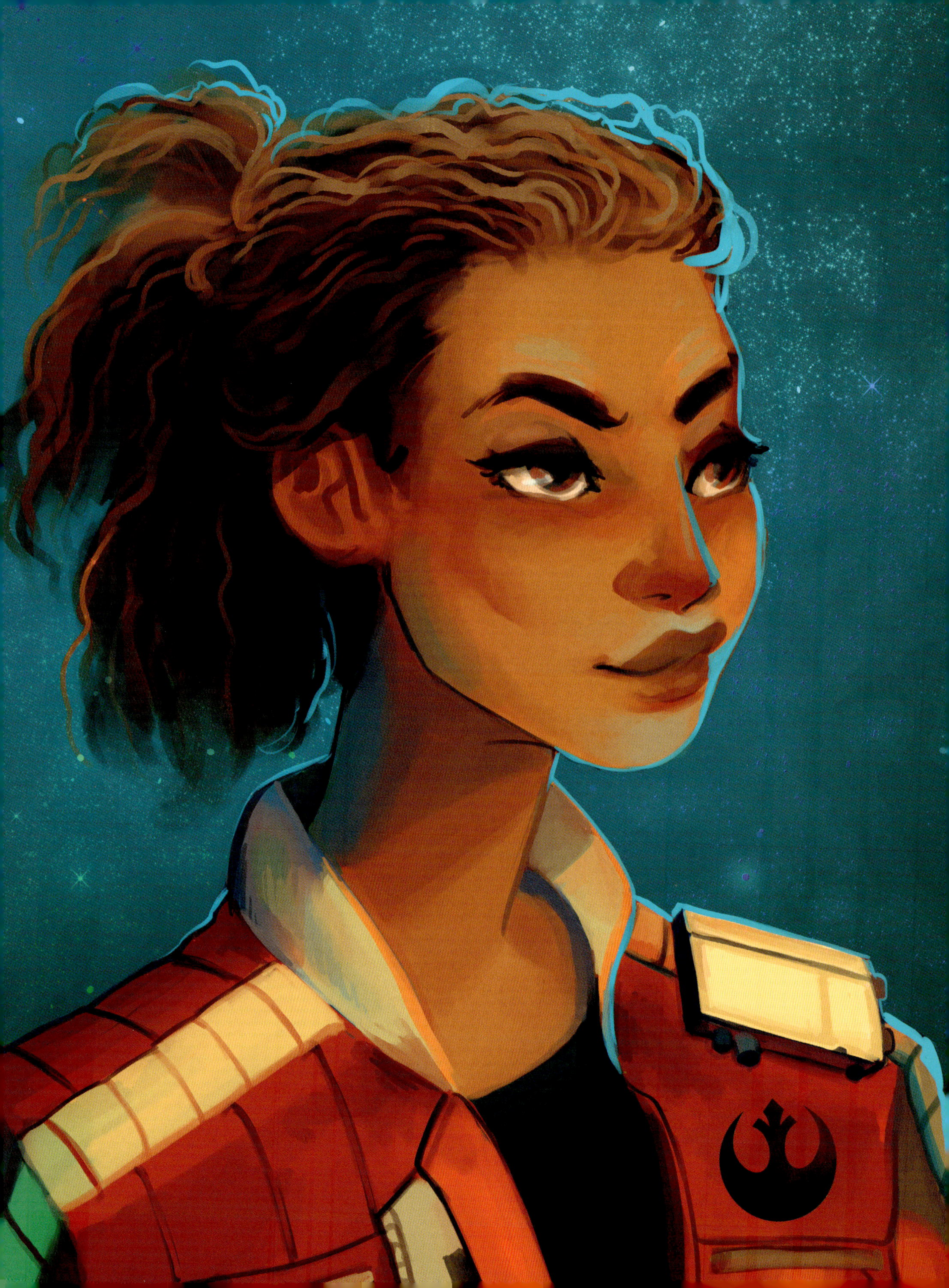

Vi Moradi

"Whoever you think I am, you're wrong."

Before heading to Disney Parks' *Star Wars: Galaxy's Edge's* Black Spire Outpost on Batuu for a new mission, Vi Moradi, the spy with the code name "Starling," worked for General Organa's Resistance to gather valuable information on the fearsome head of the Stormtrooper Corps, Captain Phasma. Her mission comes to the attention of one of Phasma's rivals within the First Order, Captain Cardinal, and it's his interrogation of her that provides the narrative structure of the novel *Phasma*. Author Delilah S. Dawson describes Vi as "like a female Poe Dameron: humor, ego, and talent, but with an added dash of James Bond. She's a spy with a long list of aliases and colored contact lenses, but she does admit to Cardinal that she only takes jobs that jibe with her heart and morals."

Vi's sure of herself, and knows how to best put her skills to use. She's able to turn her interrogation into a sort of high-stakes game, parceling out information to keep herself alive while also taking inventory of Cardinal's sympathies, interests, and weaknesses. Even when under strain, she pays attention to her surroundings and looks for useful information she might use to her advantage or share with the Resistance: no detail is too small. As she confides to Cardinal, "It's why I'm such a good spy."

Her work later takes her to Batuu where she meets with other members of the Resistance to investigate a First Order presence on the planet. Vi's mission: to steal a datacard with crucial information about the First Order's movements. The activity draws Kylo Ren's attention to the far-flung planet, but Vi and the other Resistance sympathizers near Black Spire Outpost prevail and keep the spark for the Resistance burning.

Zam Wesell

Mercenary assassin who can change her appearance at will.

Appropriately for a shape-shifting character, the development of Zam Wesell went through a number of forms before her appearance in *Attack of the Clones*. The bounty hunter was first conceived as a human male, then a human female, then an alien, and in her final form as a female Clawdite changeling, thanks to George Lucas. "I thought Zam needed to be more exotic and interesting," he said, "and this was a way to do that."

As an assassin, Zam possesses the skills you'd associate with the notorious gig. She's good at hitting targets from a distance, making speedy getaways, and knowing where to source the right equipment for her jobs. And it's intriguing that despite the fact that she can choose to look like any humanoid, she takes on the appearance of a woman. We encounter her in the film when she attempts to kill Padmé Amidala on the orders of her associate, Jango Fett, first by bombing the senator's ship, later by releasing poisonous creatures via droid into her living quarters. When Obi-Wan Kenobi and Anakin Skywalker uncover her plot, Zam doesn't panic, fleeing the scene and steering an airspeeder through Coruscant's busy traffic with professional cool.

It's no wonder she's so calm. Born on the harsh-climated planet of Zolan, Zam devotes herself to learning from ancient warrior-knights known as the Mabari. Zam's a Clawdite who knows what she wants, and she decides her goal is wealth. She puts her hard-won talents on the table for profit.

Zam's appearance switches between human and alien in her scenes. Industrial Light & Magic was responsible for the digital transition to Clawdite, but actress Leeanna Walsman brought Zam's human form to life. Getting into Zam's costume, which included forty-five pieces of armor, helped Walsman inhabit the bounty hunter. "The costume and the weaponry really help make the character," she says. "You look at yourself in the mirror and you say, 'This is how I'm going to be.'"

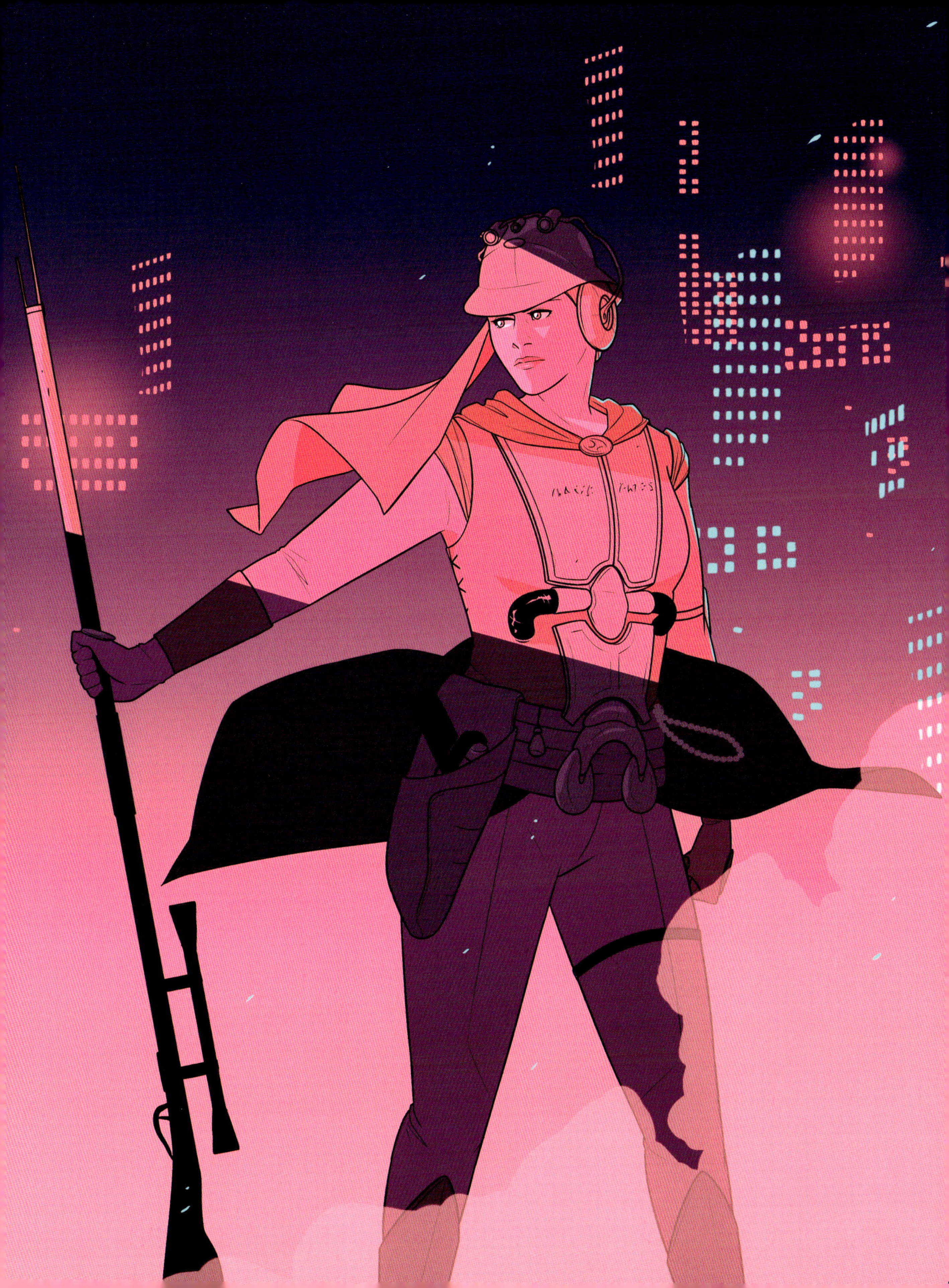

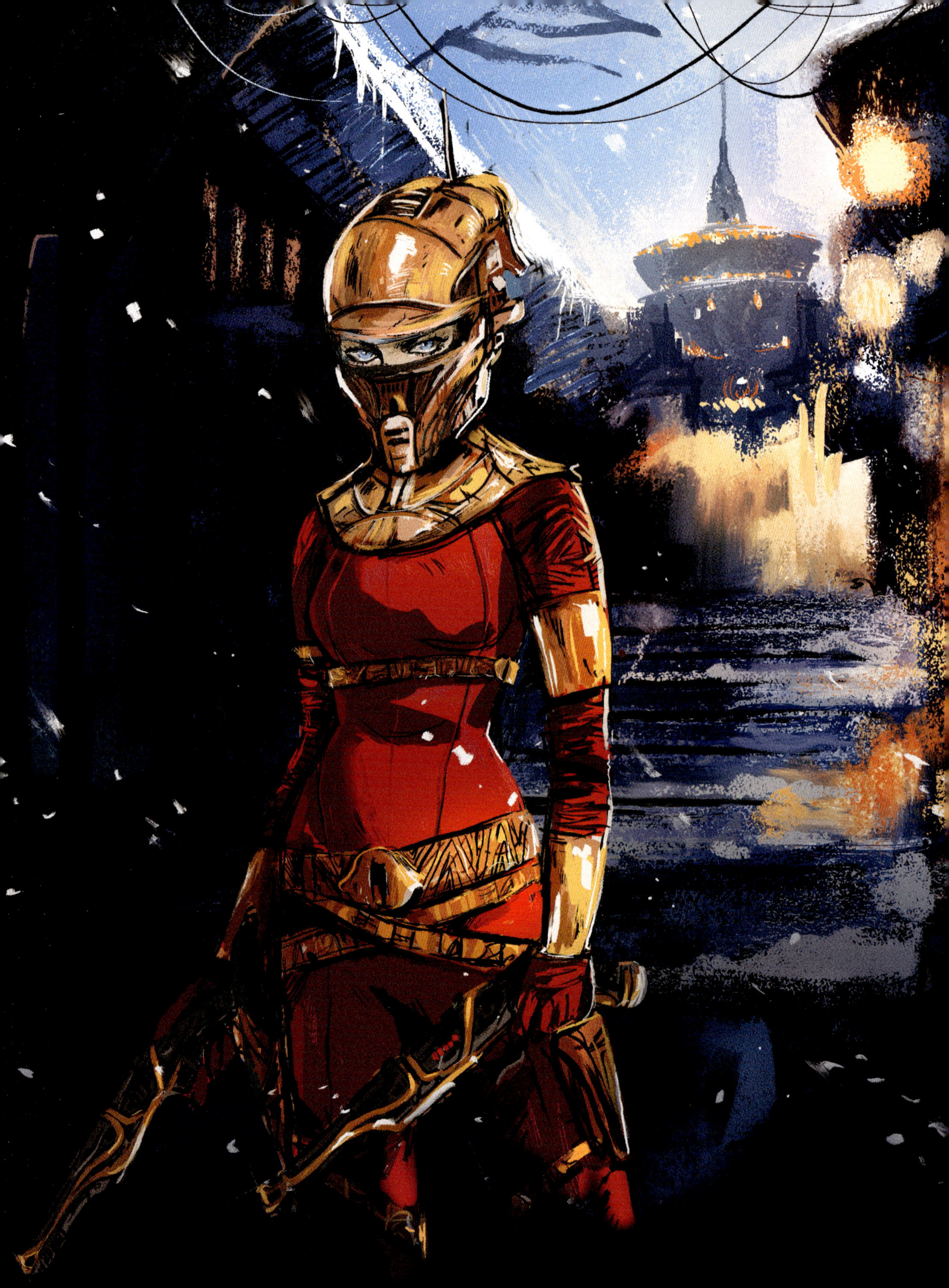

Zorii Bliss

"They win by making you think you're alone. There's more of us."

ᴢᴏʀɪɪ ʙʟɪss

Family legacies feature prominently in *Star Wars* storytelling. We meet heroes who learn from their parents to stand up against what they believe is wrong, royals who inherit thrones from their families, and villains who want to follow in the steps of their villainous relatives. Zorii Bliss joins a criminal organization because it's the family business. Zorii joins the Kijimi Spice Runners as a teen, a time when her mother Zeva leads the group. She grows up becoming comfortable with the dangerous lifestyle of piracy and profit, and eventually steps in to run things. Leading in any situation is a challenge, but leading a group of criminals, many with ambitions of their own, is especially delicate.

Zorii is all too happy to make sure the Spice Runners mind their business and stay out of galactic affairs, but that changes when the First Order occupies Kijimi. By the time her former associate Poe Dameron arrives on Kijimi, Zorii begins to see the First Order for the galactic threat it is. A skilled fighter and sharp strategist, Zorii is a helpful ally for the Resistance.

The Rise of Skywalker costume designer Michael Kaplan wanted Zorii's look to have a bit of a pirate quality, hence the boots and double holsters. The helmet evolved from concepts for the Spice Runners, with the precious metal finish marking her status. Zorii rarely removes that helmet, which was director J. J. Abrams's intention.

Acknowledgments

To George Lucas and every *Star Wars* storyteller for creating so many characters I resonate with.

To everyone who supported the first edition of this book and asked me, "When are you going to release an update?" Our time has come! I feel so fortunate to add more to this beautiful collection, and it wouldn't have happened without you.

To all the incredible women in *Star Wars* fandom I've met over the years, for being the coolest and kindest. I'm so lucky to call so many of you friends.

To my editor, Steve Mockus, for championing this updated edition and for letting me come back to gush more about characters I admire. To Jenna Huerta, Michael Morris, and Neil Egan for their excellent design work, and to Juliette Capra and Perry Crowe for all of their help pulling this new edition together. To Michael Siglain and Jennifer Heddle, for being excellent sounding boards (I'm ready for the Sabé & the Handmaidens tour!). To Troy Alders for sharing so much gorgeous art with us. To everyone at Lucasfilm and Chronicle who contributed to this updated edition.

To all the wildly talented artists who make this book positively glow.

And finally, to Aaron, for having an above-average number of conversations about Ahsoka Tano.

About the Artists

Aka is a Chinese artist who taught herself how to draw back in high school. After graduating college, she joined the video-game industry as a concept artist and illustrator, with Adam Hughes and Alberto Mielgo being some of her biggest influences. She was spotted by Marvel back in 2022 and has painted more than twenty covers (*Mary Jane & Black Cat*, *Phoenix*, *X-Men*) and counting. [p. 30]

Alice X. Zhang is a Chinese American illustrator with an enduring interest in cinema, comics, and pop culture. She holds a BFA from the Rhode Island School of Design, and her clients include BBC Worldwide (*Doctor Who*, *Sherlock*), Marvel Studios, DC Films, and Lucasfilm. [pp. 16, 104, 198, 228–229, 259, 270–271]

Amy Beth Christenson has been working for Lucasfilm companies as a concept artist for eighteen years. She is the art director for *Star Wars Resistance* and has worked on *Star Wars* projects throughout her career, including *Star Wars Rebels*, *Star Wars: The Clone Wars*, and *Star Wars: The Force Unleashed*. [pp. 42, 256, 262]

Annie Stoll is a New York–based, Grammy-winning creative art director and an award-winning designer and illustrator. A lifelong *Star Wars* fan, she has worked with Lucasfilm on a number of projects, including *Sabine: My Rebel Sketchbook* with author Daniel Wallace. She is also the co-curator of the people-positive anthology *1001 Knights*. Annie currently works with a diverse roster of musicians at Republic Records as VP of creative. [pp. 74, 82–83, 125, 160–161, 175, 202–203, 232–233, 242, 278]

Annie Wu is an American illustrator currently based in Chicago. She is the creator of the upcoming Image Comics series *Dead Guy Fan Club*, a neo-noir black comedy. [pp. 78, 88, 97, 121, 141, 142, 194, 218–219, 226–227, 241]

Betsy Cola is a Filipino illustrator based in Metro Manila. She has worked with publishers such as Marvel, IDW, HarperCollins, and Penguin Random House to create fun and striking covers. She has also collaborated on campaigns with brands like Nike, Mattel Creations, and Netflix Philippines. [p. 12]

cherriielle is a self-taught, Canada-based freelance illustrator working in publishing and comics. She specializes in digital painting for cover art and character design. Her clients include Disney Publishing (*Star Wars: The High Republic*), Dark Horse Comics, Image Comics, and Peachtree Teen. [p. 145]

About the Artists / 281

Christina Chung is a queer Taiwanese Hongkonger American illustrator, raised between Seattle and Singapore, and is currently based in Brooklyn, New York. She received her BFA in illustration from Pratt Institute and has previously taught at the University of the Arts. Her work focuses on intricacies, color, and symbolism, drawing inspiration from the natural world and powerful storytelling. She has worked with clients such as Dark Horse Comics, HarperCollins, Penguin Random House, *The New Yorker*, and *The Washington Post*. [pp. 37, 63, 95, 115, 146, 153, 183, 216, 266]

Cryssy Cheung is a Chinese American award-winning art director, designer, and multidisciplinary illustrator known for comic book covers, editorial illustration, and licensed *Star Wars* art. She holds a BFA in computer art, computer animation, and visual effects from New York's School of Visual Arts. Among her many clients are names like Marvel, Disney, Paramount+, Pixar, Valiant, and IDW. [pp. 22, 38, 53, 154, 172, 193, 212, 251]

Eliot Baum is a Vienna-based freelance illustrator focusing on 2D, sequential, and illustrative art. Having worked as a concept artist and cinematic lead for an indie platformer game at Roaring Fangs, Eliot also illustrates covers and comics for clients, and is co-creator of the webcomic *Heart of Gold*, together with Viv Tanner. [pp. 68, 101, 176, 179, 190–191, 269]

Elsa Charretier is a French illustrator and comic book artist. After debuting on *C.O.W.L.* at Image Comics, Elsa co-created *The Infinite Loop* with writer Pierrick Colinet at IDW. She has since worked at DC Comics (*Starfire, Bombshells, Harley Quinn*), Marvel Comics (*The Unstoppable Wasp*) and Random House (*Windhaven*, written by George R.R. Martin). She has written *The Infinite Loop* vol. 2 as well as *Superfreaks*, and is a regular artist on the *Star Wars Adventures* book series. [pp. 49, 77, 84, 110–111, 132–133, 136, 215, 252]

Geneva Bowers is a self-taught, Hugo Award–winning illustrator who loves working with color with a touch of magic realism. She authored and illustrated the graphic novel *HoverGirls*, published by Bloomsbury. [pp. 32, 67, 122, 157, 186–187, 220, 274]

Jen Bartel is an illustrator and comic artist who specializes in drawing strong ladies. She is best known for her ongoing cover work for clients like Marvel, DC/Vertigo, and Dark Horse. She is the artist of the Image Comics book, *Blackbird*. [pp. 10, 130]

Jennifer A. Johnson is a Toronto-based game developer, comic artist, and illustrator. She is fascinated with portraying otherworldly landscapes and strives to promote diverse voices in speculative fiction. [front cover, pp. 21, 59, 92–93, 112, 134–135, 163, 171, 189, 236, 244]

Jey Parks is a queer, non-binary artist based in Colorado, with a degree in scientific illustration and a love for drawing animals. Although known for their cat-centric art, including licensed work for Marvel and CBS, they enjoy drawing all manner of creatures, real or imagined. They are the author and illustrator of *Star Trek Cats* and *Star Trek: The Next Generation Cats*. [p. 118]

Karen Hallion Kenney is a Massachusetts-based illustrator and author whose art is characterized by its use of bright colors, intricate details, and a touch of humor. Her licensed work includes various clients such as Ravensburger, Lucasfilm, Wizards of the Coast, BBC Studios, Her Universe, and Ashley Eckstein. She has contributed art to *Disney Lorcana*, as well as *Magic: The Gathering*. Her book, *She Changed the World*, features one hundred portraits of inspiring women accompanied by essays written by fifty female and non-binary authors. [pp. 56, 70, 108–109, 139, 184, 197, 211, 225, 255, 265]

Little Corvus is the penname of Teo Hernandez DuVall, an award-winning Chicane illustrator, comic artist, and graphic designer based in Seattle. He holds a BFA in cartooning from the School of Visual Arts and has worked with renowned publishers such as Abrams, Dark Horse, Penguin Random House, and Levine Querido, among others. Their work focuses on politicized peoples and the essence of humanity, seamlessly blending fantasy and the supernatural with rich, atmospheric visuals. Celebrated for his fresh, contemplative style and exploration of beauty and strength in all forms, Teo aims to make artwork that helps his audience feel seen. [pp. 28–29, 45, 91, 117, 166, 201, 277]

Marguerite Sauvage is a Canadian and French author and illustrator. She began her career as a successful commercial and fashion illustrator. She has worked additionally in animation, creating TV programs for children, and published several European comics. In 2014, she entered the world of American comics and worked as an artist and as a writer on titles such as *Faith*, *Wonder Woman*, *Spider-Man*, *Harley Quinn*, *The Flash*, *Power Girl*, and *DC Bombshells*, for which she had been Eisner, GLAAD, and Russ Manning nominated. In 2024, she also began working on middle-grade and young-adult graphic novels for First Second and Little Brown. When Marguerite isn't telling stories, she plays hide-and-seek with her daughter, strolls through museums, or plants yet another tomato garden. [back cover, p. 223]

Peach Momoko is a Japanese comic artist known for her work as the writer-artist for Marvel's *Ultimate X-Men*. In 2021 and 2024, she won the Eisner Award for "Best Cover Artist." In addition to comics, Peach works as an illustrator, working on projects like: a live tour poster for TOOL, card games (*Magic: The Gathering* and *One Piece*), and character design for video games. [p. 46]

Sara Alfageeh is an award-winning illustrator and creative director in San Francisco. She's best known for her graphic novel *SQUIRE* and her work for clients like Marvel, Disney, Google, and Blizzard. Sara's work as a game developer landed her on the Forbes 30 Under 30 list. She is passionate about history, teaching, girls with swords, and the spaces where art and identity intersect. [pp. 18–19, 55, 73, 98, 103, 165, 208–209, 230, 248]

Sara Kipin is a Burbank, California-based illustrator and visual developer who holds a BA from the Maryland Institute of Art. She has done TV animation work for Marvel, Moving Colour, and Cartoon Network, and illustrations for *Cosmopolitan* and Leigh Bardugo's *New York Times* bestselling novel *Language of Thorns*. [pp. 26, 40–41, 81, 107, 158, 234–235]

Sarah Wilkinson travels the world with her art studio, Studio de Sade, bringing her art to conventions and art shows. She has worked in the comic book and trading card industries for more than a decade, with clients that include Topps, IDW, and Lucasfilm, and her art has also been used for book covers and interior illustrations, toy designs, and more. [pp. 25, 50, 60, 64, 87, 129, 150, 168, 206–207, 247]

Stephanie Hans is a French illustrator. She has been working in the pop culture and comics field for over two decades, mostly as a cover artist or sequential artist. She is the co-creator of the award-winning Image Comics series *Die* and the graphic novel *We Called Them Giants*, and has worked with Marvel Comics, DC Comics, BOOM, Dark Horse, Disney, and more. [p. 180]

Tara Phillips is an Australian illustrator who specializes in fantastical art for book covers. She has worked on several Lucasfilm projects and has also created commercial illustrations for clients such as Penguin Random House, Simon & Schuster, Macmillan, and ImagineFX. [p. 273]

Viv Tanner is a Vienna-based illustrator who holds a degree in 2D Animation from the Lucerne School of Applied Sciences and Art, and focuses on freelance Illustrations for magazines, comics, and books. Together with Eli Baumgartner, Viv is the creator of the webcomic *Heart of Gold*. [pp. 34–35, 126, 149, 205, 238, 261]